CRITICISM OF RELIGION

Historical Materialism Book Series

More than ten years after the collapse of the Berlin Wall and the disappearance of Marxism as a (supposed) state ideology, a need for a serious and long-term Marxist book publishing program has risen. Subjected to the whims of fashion, most contemporary publishers have abandoned any of the systematic production of Marxist theoretical work that they may have indulged in during the 1970s and early 1980s. The Historical Materialism book series addresses this great gap with original monographs, translated texts and reprints of "classics."

Editorial board: Paul Blackledge, Leeds; Sebastian Budgen, London; Jim Kincaid, Leeds; Stathis Kouvelakis, Paris; Marcel van der Linden, Amsterdam; China Miéville, London; Paul Reynolds, Lancashire.

Haymarket Books is proud to be working with Brill Academic Publishers (http://www.brill.nl) and the journal *Historical Materialism* to republish the Historical Materialism book series in paperback editions. Current series titles include:

Alasdair MacIntyre's Engagement with Marxism: Selected Writings 1953–1974
Edited by Paul Blackledge and Neil Davidson

Althusser: The Detour of Theory, Gregory Elliott

Between Equal Rights: A Marxist Theory of International Law, China Miéville

The Capitalist Cycle, Pavel V. Maksakovsky,
Translated with introduction and commentary by Richard B. Day

The Clash of Globalisations: Neo-Liberalism, the Third Way, and Anti-globalisation, Ray Kiely

Critical Companion to Contemporary Marxism, Edited by Jacques Bidet and Stathis Kouvelakis

Criticism of Heaven: On Marxism and Theology, Roland Boer

Criticism of Religion: On Marxism and Theology II, Roland Boer

Exploring Marx's Capital: Philosophical, Economic, and Political Dimensions, Jacques Bidet

Following Marx: Method, Critique, and Crisis, Michael Lebowitz

The German Revolution: 1917–1923, Pierre Broué

Globalisation: A Systematic Marxian Account, Tony Smith

The Gramscian Moment: Philosopy, Hegemony and Marxism, Peter D. Thomas

Impersonal Power: History and Theory of the Bourgeois State,
Heide Gerstenberger, translated by David Fernbach

Lenin Rediscovered: What Is to Be Done? In Context, Lars T. Lih

Making History: Agency, Structure, and Change in Social Theory, Alex Callinicos

Marxism and Ecological Economics: Toward a Red and Green Political Economy, Paul Burkett

A Marxist Philosophy of Language, Jean-Jacques Lecercle and Gregory Elliott

Politics and Philosophy: Niccolo Machiavelli and Louis Althuser's Aleatory Materialism,
Mikko Lahtinen, translated by Gareth Griffiths and Kristina Kölhi

Theory as History: Essays on Modes of Production and Exploitation, Jarius Banaji

The Theory of Revolution in the Young Marx, Michael Löwy

Utopia Ltd.: Ideologies of Social Dreaming in England 1870–1900, Matthew Beaumont

Western Marxism and the Soviet Union: A Survey of Critical Theories and Debates Since 1917,
Marcel van der Linden

Witnesses to Permanent Revolution: The Documentary Record,
Edited by Richard B. Day and Daniel Gaido

CRITICISM OF RELIGION

ON MARXISM AND THEOLOGY II

ROLAND BOER

Haymarket Books
Chicago, Illinois

First published in 2009 by Brill Academic Publishers, The Netherlands
© 2009 Koninklijke Brill NV, Leiden, The Netherlands

Published in paperback in 2011 by
Haymarket Books
P.O. Box 180165
Chicago, IL 60618
773-583-7884
www.haymarketbooks.org

ISBN: 978-1-60846-122-6

Distributed to the trade in the US through Consortium Book Sales and Distribution (www.cbsd.com) and internationally through Ingram Publisher Services International (www.ingramcontent.com).

This book was published with the generous support of Lannan Foundation and Wallace Action Fund.

Special discounts are available for bulk purchases by organizations and institutions. Please call 773-583-7884 or email info@haymarketbooks.org for more information.

Cover image of a set design for *The Firebird* painted by Natalia Goncharova, 1926.

Printed in the United States.

Entered into digital printing June 2021.

Contents

Preface	ix
Introduction	xiii
Chapter One The Paradoxes of Lucien Goldmann	1
The dialectic of grace	4
The Elect and the Damned	6
Wagering it all	10
In the world and yet not	13
Theory: the tight fit of homology	20
Homology	21
Dialectics?	23
Is Pascal among the Marxists?	25
By way of conclusion: Marxism as a secular and anti-secular project	29
Chapter Two The Stumbling Block of Fredric Jameson	31
Supersession versus a dialectic of ideology and utopia	33
Sidestepping religion	35
Magic and fantasy	37
Feuerbach versus Marx	39
The politics of fantasy	45
Apocalyptic	49
By way of conclusion: towards a dialectic of religion	53
Chapter Three The Christian Communism of Rosa Luxemburg	59
Tactics	61
A Reformer's zeal	64
Betraying the spirit	69

    A little church history 72
    Anti-clericalism 76
  Christian communism 80
    Consumption versus production 86
    Completing Christian communism 87
  Freedom of conscience 88

Chapter Four   The Enticements of Karl Kautsky 91
  Text, history, context 93
    The slipperiness of sacred texts 94
    The Bible as a cultural product 97
  Reconstructing economic history 99
    Differentiation and slaves 99
    Slaves and other modes of production 104
    The sacred economy: prolegomena to a reconstruction 107
    Transitions 109
  Christian communism 113
  Conclusion 118

Chapter Five   The Forgetfulness of Julia Kristeva 121
  Flushing out Marx 123
  Monocausality, or, the taboo of the mother 130
  Paul the Apostle, both ways 136
    Other-than-human love 141
    Crucifying the pathologies 145
    Collectives 148
  Conclusion 152

Chapter Six   The Fables of Alain Badiou 155
  Banishing the One 156
  Theology and the Event 161
    A generic procedure of religion? 163
    Pascal's miracle 165
    Kierkegaard's encounter 173
    Paul's fable 174
  Conclusion: necessary fables 178

Chapter Seven   The Conundrums of Giorgio Agamben 181
  The search for Paul 183
  Christology, or the problem of Jesus Messiah 185
  Faith, law and grace as placeholder of the void 193
  Pre-law, or trying to make sense of Paul 197
  Conclusion: relativising theology 203

Chapter Eight   The Self-Exorcism of Georg Lukács 205
  A world abandoned by God 207
  Leap-frogging Christianity 211
  Autobiographical exorcism 215
  Conclusion 220

Chapter Nine   The Bible and The Beekeeper's Manual 223
  An apparent absence? 226
  Warm Marxism 230
    Autobiography 230
    Welshness 236
    The working class 237
  Conclusion: the vanishing mediator of the Baptist chapel ... 239

Conclusion 243

References 253

Index of Biblical References 267

General Index 270

Preface

When I finished *Criticism of Heaven* after too many years, I hardly imagined there would be another book that would follow a similar path. Yet, the more I read and wrote and thought, the more I came across Marxists who have written on religion. Before I knew it, another volume came together and, as it did, the comment from Marx's *Contribution to the Critique of Hegel's Philosophy of Law* played with me once again. Marx writes:

> Thus the criticism of heaven turns into the criticism of earth, the *criticism of religion* into the *criticism of law* and the *criticism of theology* into the *criticism of politics*.[1]

So the idea of a *Criticism of Religion* took shape, one that would join *Criticism of Heaven*. Together they form the first two volumes of a five-volume series called *Criticism of Heaven and Earth*. For all the desire for a criticism of earth, law and politics, Marxists have a knack of devoting a good deal of attention to matters of heaven, religion and theology. I must admit that I am one of them. However, as this book attests, I am by no means alone.

A word on texts and translations: whereas most of the material I have used came from those conglomerations of glue, old rags, trees and recycled paper known as books, I have also made use of the wonderful resource at <www.marxists.org>. There you will find most of the older Marxist classics online, especially those for which the copyright has now lapsed. In the chapters on Rosa Luxemburg and Karl Kautsky, I used this resource extensively, for it provides access to most of their texts, especially in English translation. In most cases, typographic errors in the original publications have been corrected.

---

[1] Marx 1975a, p. 176.

However, the problem then becomes one of how to provide a reference for a citation. I decided to copy these texts into one continuous document and then give the page numbers as they appeared on my computer screen. Although this approach gives a reasonably accurate sense of where those situations may be found, the fact that the texts are available online makes it much easier to search for the quotation should anyone wish to read further.

As for the translations, I have checked all the English translations against their original versions, occasionally offering a modified translation of my own. Since most of these works are easily available in English, I cite the English first and then the German or French version. The exception to this practice is Agamben, for I do not read Italian. As I know from biblical criticism, translation is a tricky business affected by all manner of factors that range from personal temperament through pressures to finish (since it is usually paid as piece work) to the methodological fashions of translation. However, for the texts I use in this book, the translations are reasonably good, especially those of Kautsky and Lukács. One or two are less competent. With the translation of Lucien Goldmann's *Le Dieu caché* by Philip Thody, we find that the drive for sense at the expense of form is carried to an extreme, cutting sentences, thoroughly rearranging the syntax, paragraph breaks and even rearranging the sentences within paragraphs. I assume this was for clarity, or perhaps frustration at Goldmann's verbosity or some such reason, but it has made me even more wary than usual. The translation of Rosa Luxemburg's *Socialism and the Churches* by Juan Punto also calls for a comment: it is a translation of the French edition from 1937, which was published by the French Socialist Party. The English text is therefore at two removes from the German, and, during this transition, the English and German have at times drifted a good distance from one another. Needless to say, I have checked the German text closely and often made modifications to the translation.

Apart from the characters who populate these pages, a number of others have played a role in this book, whether they know it or not. Through discussions, responses to papers, suggestions after reading a slab here or there, or even a passing comment that clicked only much later, I owe much to Andrew Milner, Peter Hallward, Bruno Bosteels, Alain Badiou, Fred Jameson, Ken Surin, Ken-Pa Chin, Philip Chia, David Roberts, Erin Runions, Peter Thomas, Alison Caddick, Sebastian Budgen and Ibrahim Abraham. However, by far the greatest contribution came from Matthew Chrulew, a research assistant who tirelessly read through the manuscript, chased down references, made numerous suggestions and corrected my style more often than I care to remember. Of course, Christina Petterson heard more about this book than she probably wanted to as I launched into yet another discussion of the latest section I had written. To all these people, a profound thanks.

A few chapters have appeared in earlier, barer and somewhat different forms. This is the case with the chapters on Agamben (*Sino-Christian Studies*, 3 in 2007), Badiou (*Angelaki*, 11.2 in 2006) and Williams (*Arena Journal*, 22 in 2004). In each case, I have developed the arguments well beyond these earlier appearances.

The Hill, New South Wales
December 2007

Introduction

This book is both a commentary and an engagement. It is a critical commentary on what some leading Marxist critics have written about religion, especially Christianity in some form or other. It is also an engagement with their work, showing where it falls short, but, above all, seeking out what might be drawn from their work for the continuation and reassessment of the Marxist project itself. In other words, I explicitly seek to develop a position of my own in the midst of my close interaction with their work. I have long since ceased to be surprised at how often and how extensively these Marxists reflect upon and write about religion. More often than not, I assume that they have done so and invariably track down the texts in question. Often, they turn out to be the more neglected or forgotten elements of their work, a volume quietly shelved in the obscure section of a second-hand bookshop, or perhaps a section or chapter in a larger work that is passed over in silence. Yet they are there, and often far more extensive than most have imagined.

In *Criticism of Heaven*, the first volume in what is now a five-volume series, I imagined a gathering of the sundry Marxists who had become my conversation partners and friends through the very intimate process of thinking about their writing and their thoughts. Out in the midday sun, rather than the dark and dank early hours of the morning, they gathered to talk with me about their work. On chairs, stools and even on the grass they sat on a grassy knoll overlooking the string of coal ships waiting their turn to load up in the harbour where I live. Joining that initial gathering of eight (Ernst Bloch, Walter Benjamin, Louis Althusser, Henri Lefebvre, Antonio Gramsci, Terry Eagleton, Slavoj Žižek and Theodor Adorno) there now come another nine Marxists of various shades who are the concern of this book, *Criticism of Religion*.

One by one they turn up, by whatever means possible – train, ship, bus, or even aeroplane. And the prerequisite for joining the group is that they must bring with them the various tomes, essays and pamphlets in which they have discussed and criticised religion. The shuffling bulk of Lucien Goldmann slowly climbs the long path up the hill. Puffing on a cigarette, Goldmann regales the others with yet another long story. Eventually he pulls his book on Jansenism, *The Hidden God*, from his coat pocket and places it on the fold-up table with drinks. After some time, Fredric Jameson ambles up the hill, decked out in his favourite writing cardigan. Nodding his greetings to many of those present whom he knows rather well, Jameson digs out of large bag *Archaeologies of the Future*, his consummate assessment of utopian literature and science fiction. He is not quite sure why he has brought it, but I have insisted. Energetic as ever, Rosa Luxemburg is next. Like Engels, she loves a long walk and her well-worn boots have covered a good deal of territory to get here. From her small rucksack, she proffers a pamphlet and an essay, *Socialism and the Churches* and 'An Anti-Clerical Policy of Socialism'. Karl Kautsky follows soon afterwards, turning up in a comfortable taxi. Horrified to hear how far Rosa and Lucien and Fred have walked, Kautsky politely and urbanely greets everyone and then draws from a fine leather briefcase his *Foundations of Christianity*, his book on Thomas More and multi-volume *Forerunners of Socialism*. Both Rosa and Karl's works are blends of Marxist reconstructions of early Israel and the early Church, biblical interpretation, brief histories of the Christian Church and efforts to find longer currents of socialist thought and action before Marx and Engels. A moment later, Julia Kristeva arrives, to the surprise of many. It is not just that she has ridden a bicycle up the long hill, but many wonder what she is doing there in the first place. She ties her hair in a loose ponytail, catches her breath and reaches into the basket on the front of her bicycle. From there she produces a pile of essays on biblical and theological subjects that she stacks on the grass before her, along with an early essay on Marx, 'Semiotics: A Critical Science and/or a Critique of Science'. A towering Alain Badiou turns up next, his thick white hair as tousled as ever. Joking about the gathering of saints, he slips not merely the slender *Saint Paul: The Foundation of Universalism* from his battered satchel, but also his dense and polemical *Being and Event* and the more recent *Logiques des Mondes*. Fred offers him a glass of wine, but he refuses, commenting that he must seem a strange Frenchman, for he does not drink wine. Following Badiou is Giorgio Agamben, balding and intense. He has come by ship through the Suez Canal and across the Indian Ocean, since he hates flying. Next to Alain's book on Paul he places his response, *The Time That Remains: A Commentary on the Letter to the Romans*. The last two turn up together – a Hungarian and a Welshman. They have taken their time walking up from the train, although a pillar of smoke announces their arrival. Fat cigar in hand and pursing his lips, Georg Lukács is not so impressed at being there, since he feels that he has long since excised any last trace of romanticism, idealism or religion from his work. Yet, after various persuasions, I managed to get him there and to bring *The Theory of the Novel*, *The Young Hegel* and *History and Class Consciousness* – the last book in particular raising a cheer from the crowd. Lastly, a gentle and friendly Raymond Williams pulls a massive pipe out of his mouth, greets the others and pretends not to have anything with him on religion. Again, under pressure from me and the rest of the crowd, he peers into his leather satchel and manages to locate a sundry collection of works, especially the interviews in *Politics and Letters*, as well as his influential *Culture and Society*, *The Long Revolution* and a few of his lesser-known novels.[2]

These, then, are the texts on which I will set my critical commentary to work. Some are easier, at least to begin with, for they have written substantial pieces on religion and theology. This is particularly the case with Luxemburg, Kautsky, Kristeva, Badiou, Agamben and Goldmann. With the rest – Jameson, Lukács and Williams – the initial task is a little more difficult, for I need to track more scattered interactions with religion. This task becomes all the more intriguing when these last three critics also profess a distinct lack of interest in matters of religion. All the same, they are interested and they do engage. Indeed, I find more often than not that what they say ends up being full of promising angles on religion.

One might be forgiven for thinking that Marxists – to borrow a comment from Raymond Williams – are somewhat tone-deaf when it comes to matters

---

[2] Why not Régis Debray? Surely he should be part of our ever-increasing group? Not a few in the crowd feel the same way. After all, he has written all sorts of works on religion and Marxism, like *God: An Itinerary* and *The Critique of Political Reason*. The problem is that the book on God is not very original: it traces the development of belief in a monotheistic God (mainly Judaism and Christianity) in line with major developments in writing, from the alphabet through to the internet. And I hesitate over someone who writes things like '"Ologies" are explained by "urgies." An "ideology" is a sociurgy gone cold.... Our theoretical task relates to the "urgy"...' (Debray 1983, p. 169). Or, 'If you want to know what something consists of, ask yourself what it resists. Organize a biscuit. A sweater. A cigarette. A bout of hypochondria. A commando' (Debray 1983, p. 267).

of religion and theology. Are there not, after all, more important matters to consider in the analysis of texts, or economics, or historical epochs, or even the works of other Marxists than religion? The fact that I have been able to gather nine Marxists in this volume and eight more in my earlier *Criticism of Heaven* should put the lie to that assumption. So also should the fact that Engels had more than a passing interest in religion. I merely need mention his *The Peasant War in Germany* (1850) and *On the History of Early Christianity* (1894–5), but there is also the early religious commitment to Calvinist Christianity, a commitment he gave up with some difficulty. That he was more than competent in reading New-Testament Greek is less well-known than it should be, as is his continued interest in biblical scholarship.[3] It is, quite simply, a long and rich tradition, one that Marxism needs to tackle in a robust fashion.

A synopsis of a work is always useful, not least because it enables the reader to map the work as a whole, decide where to dip in or how to read the whole thing in the first place. This book falls rather naturally into three groups: dialectics; biblical engagements; and the passing moment of religion. To begin with, Lucien Goldmann and Fredric Jameson occupy the opening chapters on dialectics. Goldmann may be more interested in the interaction of the Elect and the Reprobate within Jansenism and Pascal, while Jameson's concern is with the possibilities of utopia, but they both engage in some sustained dialectical thinking. The second group all engage with the Bible in some way. Rosa Luxemburg and Karl Kautsky made some of the first forays, after Engels, into reconstructing the histories of early Israel and/or the early Christian Church from a Marxist perspective. Luxemburg is concerned with early Christian communism and its dissolution in the later history of the Church. Kautsky tracks similar ground, although he extends his discussion to include early Israel and the figure of Jesus. Both projects are initial and very incomplete forays, so they entice me to critique, build on and take their reconstructions further. Julia Kristeva also belongs to this group, although her readings are not so much historical reconstructions as efforts to identify what makes a range of biblical texts tick. One feature of Kristeva's work is that she has a distinct liking for Paul's (I dispense with the quaint 'St.') letters in the New Testa-

---

[3] Volume three of this series, called *Criticism of Earth*, deals with Marx and Engels. See Boer in press-a.

ment. So also does Alain Badiou, at least in part. He also draws upon Pascal and Kierkegaard in the relentless task of outlining his theory of the event. The last figure in this biblical section is Giorgio Agamben, whose book on Paul is a direct response to Badiou. Yet Agamben also marks a transition to the final section, which is concerned with what I call the passing moment of theology. This theme strengthens with the two I have gathered in the final section, Georg Lukács and Raymond Williams. Both of them sought to excise religion from their thought, but, in the process, they reveal an important strategy. The effect is to show that theology is not the ultimate source of some central Marxist and indeed political concepts; rather, it is but a moment in the longer history of these concepts. In other words, they indicate ways in which the claims of theology may be relativised.

The book begins with Lucien Goldmann. My concern is his *Le Dieu caché*, a study of Jansenism, Pascal and Racine which first appeared in 1959. What intrigues me about this book is the deep insight into Pascal and Jansenism, particularly in terms of what I call the dialectic of grace. For Goldmann, that dialectic shows up in two contradictions, namely the tensions between the Elect and the Reprobate and between refusing the world and yet living within it. In the first contradiction, Goldmann argues that the opposition of the Elect and the Damned is not one that operates between two distinct groups, but, rather, one that creates a tension within each group and individual. As for the second contradiction, the profound tension comes from the fact that both sides of the contradiction are true, for we live in the world and are yet not part of it. The celebrated argument of the wager is then a way of dealing with these paradoxes. Rather than being caught up in the theological niceties of these contradictions, what I see are their ramifications for political thought and action. While I am not taken with Goldmann's method of homology or 'genetic structuralism' (it is too mechanical and crude) I do engage with Goldmann's efforts to link Pascal with Marx, with one significant difference: I seek the link at an entirely different level to Goldmann, namely in the tension of Marxism as both a secular and an anti-secular project. I will pick up this crucial feature in my conclusion.

In Chapter Two, I turn to Fredric Jameson, whose engagements with religion have been more extensive than one might at first think, especially in the zone of utopian thought. Although my focus is Jameson's most extensive work on the subject, *Archaeologies of the Future*, I actually begin with some of his earlier reflections on the dialectic of ideology and utopia, which then becomes a useful way to assess Jameson's thoughts in the utopia book. I move on to track the way Jameson continually skirts the long and deep role of religion in relation to utopian thought and practice, seeking to sidestep the question of religion time and again. In the end, he does face up to religion in the context of his discussion of the tensions between fantasy and science-fiction literature. Here, he makes a dialectical move, drawn from Ludwig Feuerbach, that turns the regressive concern with magic in fantasy into its most utopian feature. While I am critical of such an argument, not least because it is a regressive move back to Feuerbach that does not help fantasy all that much, I also want to push Jameson further. So I seek out other dialectical possibilities in his various hints concerning religion and utopia, especially in relation to apocalyptic, the valorisation of medieval theology as a form of thinking, and his 'transcoding' Thomas More's Reformed and ascetic proclivities as revolutionary in their time.

With the third chapter on Rosa Luxemburg, I turn to those who engage with the Bible. In this chapter, I focus on two neglected works written more than a century ago, *Socialism and the Churches* and 'An Anti-Clerical Policy of Socialism'. Here, I find some of the more surprising elements of Marxist thought on religion. Two stand out: Luxemburg's positive appropriation of Christian communism as an earlier phase of what later became Marxist communism; her argument that communism today should follow a policy of freedom of conscience, including the matter of religious belief. In order to dig out these two moments, I pass through a number of steps. To begin with, I am interested in her call for a politics of alliance between the socialist and the Catholic workers, since socialist and Catholic are so often embodied in the one person. As always, Luxemburg's texts have an immediate political relevance, and, in the case of these texts, it was the need to provide some ready education regarding the positions of Marxism for the large number of new recruits to her party. Further, there is in Luxemburg a zeal that comes close to the Protestant Reformers. This zeal shows up in her scathing criticisms of the venality of the Catholic Church, the argument that the Church has betrayed the communist spirit of early Christianity, and her historical narrative that seeks to show how the Church became, from its beginnings as a communist movement, part of the ruling class. Then I come to Luxemburg's enthusiastic valorisation of Christian communism, where she points out that socialism is closer to early Christianity than the Church, that socialism will complete what was begun then, and that what was a limited communism of consumption must be transformed and completed by a communism of production. Although she understands early Christian communism as a historical given, I argue that it remains a powerful and motivating story since it has become a political myth. Finally, there is her startling argument that socialism is not opposed to religious belief and practice, since they are matters of freedom of conscience. By avoiding the potential (liberal) traps of such a position, it seems to me that this argument is worth reconsidering for socialism today.

The fourth chapter picks up Karl Kautsky's search for the origins and sustained strength of that 'colossal phenomenon' called Christianity. In that quest, Kautsky delves back to produce a far more extensive study than Luxemburg, seeking nothing less than a comprehensive Marxist reconstruction of the social and economic context in which the Bible arose. His *Foundations of Christianity* is, in other words, a reconstruction of the history of ancient Israel, the ancient Near East and the early Church. For all its flaws, the great value of the book is that it begins what is still an unfinished project. For me, the enticement is to take that project further. In doing so, I focus not on the errors in his reconstruction, but, rather, the questions that are still important now. So, I begin with the problem of using ancient texts like the Bible for the sake of historical reconstruction, an issue that remains a basic problem in biblical scholarship. Given that these texts are highly unreliable as sources of historical information, then how do we use them? Second, I engage critically with Kautsky's reconstruction, especially the following issues: the function and validity of the narrative of differentiation which moves from a simple undifferentiated state to one that is complex and differentiated; his argument for a slave mode of production in both the ancient Near East and the Hellenistic world; the need for a new reconstruction in Kautsky's spirit; the perennial question of transitions between modes of production, especially in order to understand the economic and social turmoil to which the New Testament and early Christianity respond. Third, I pick up an argument he shares with his sometime comrade, Rosa Luxemburg: if early Christianity was a communist movement, then what sort of communism was it? At this point, I develop further the argument that early Christian communism was and remains a powerful political myth: it probably never existed, but that only enhances its mythical status. Indeed, it turns out that Kautsky's discussion of early

Christian communism is part of a larger programme to recover a longer tradition of communist thought and action that predates Marx and Engels.

Julia Kristeva, the focus of the fifth chapter, needs an extra word of introduction. She has kept Marxism at arm's length, so I begin by identifying moments in her thought where she resorts to Marxist arguments, as well as drawing attention to a dense early essay called 'Semiotics: A Critical Science and/or a Critique of Science'. Here, she identifies some inescapable discoveries by Marx, above all the immanent method, without which our work founders. So, in this chapter, I propose to recover this hidden Marx from within Kristeva's dominant psychoanalysis. Having done so, I turn to some of her better readings of biblical texts to see what a Marxist Kristeva might make of them. The structure of the chapter is as follows. I begin by tracking the strategies by which Kristeva conceals Marx, arguing that she can never quite rid herself of him. From there I focus on two of her better readings of biblical texts, namely the taboos in Leviticus 11–14 and her interpretation of Paul in the New Testament. As for the Leviticus texts on taboos, I argue that, while her identification of the taboo of the mother is a real insight, it stops far too short. What it needs is to be placed within the wider workings of what I call the sacred economy. As far as her interpretation of Paul is concerned, once again I bring a much more Marxist angle. Thus, her argument that Paul provides a mechanism for dealing with most of the psychological pathologies – by means of a mythical narrative of death and resurrection and by means of an unstable collective, the 'church' – must be understood within the context of a brutal transition from a sacred economy to the ancient mode of production of the Hellenistic world. Further, in order to bring out the distinctly political nature of the old Pauline slogans, I bring her into conversation with the current interest in Paul by Badiou, Agamben and others. In sum, while the psychoanalytic Kristeva can offer some genuine insights into these biblical texts, a more Marxist Kristeva is able to offer a more comprehensive assessment of what is of value in her interpretation regarding both the Levitical taboos in the Hebrew Bible and Paul in the New Testament. Thus, Kristeva's (often frustrating) shortcomings incite me to look further, to seek out Marx and then to see how her incomplete readings of biblical texts might be enhanced.

From Kristeva I move to Alain Badiou, who shares with her an interest in matters biblical, especially the letters of Paul. In this sixth chapter, I explore Badiou's simultaneous banishment of theology and its ghostly presence in his thought, as well as the play between truth and fable in the work of Alain Badiou. As is well-known by now, a crucial feature of Badiou's philosophy is the truth-event: an inexplicable and unexpected break in the 'Order of Being' that completely re-orients those who experience it. For Badiou, this event sets in train a series of truth procedures that must be identified and acted upon in order to be a truth. Although the four modalities of the truth-event are love, politics, art and science, there is also the half-presence of what may be called a theological mode of the procedures of truth. For all his efforts to banish theology as an instance of the 'one', theology turns up again and again, especially in his meditations on Pascal, Kierkegaard and Paul. In each case the central event – the basis of the claim to a truth – is the resurrection of Jesus. Yet, as Badiou points out in his discussion of Paul, this event is a fabrication and the truth associated with it is a 'fable'. The problem is that both fable and truth exhibit the exemplary features of the procedures of truth. This chapter takes such an anomaly in Badiou's thought to argue not that it destabilises his system of thought, but that what Badiou calls truth cannot avoid the fabulous. Indeed, any event also deals in what I call the necessary fable.

Giorgio Agamben, the subject of the seventh chapter, has offered an arresting interpretation of the messianic – as the 'time that is left' – in Paul's Epistles in the New Testament, one that is deeply indebted to Walter Benjamin. However, I am not so enamoured with Agamben's argument, for it contains profound problems. To begin with, he relies on the pseudo-Pauline epistles in an effort to outline Paul's thought on messianism, a move that creates some problems if one is seeking to uncover the 'authentic' thought of Paul. Second, his discussion of messianism entails an inevitable slide into Christology, which brings with it a thicket of difficulties surrounding saviour figures and the logic of Christology itself. Further, he sets up the prime opposition in Paul between faith and law, which is both a response to Badiou's emphasis on grace and a spectacular sidelining of Paul's concern with grace. I argue that despite himself, Agamben actually wants a theory of grace in order to overcome the trap of the law. However, the centre of Agamben's argument is that he identifies the category of 'pre-law' as crucial to understanding Paul, an undifferentiated moment in which all of Paul's oppositions can be seen side by side. In order to find this pre-law, Agamben reconstructs a hypothetical history of law that relies on both the shaky ground of etymology and a version of the narrative of differentiation. Yet, despite the problems with such a reconstruction, I do pick up one idea from the form of Agamben's argument, and that is his effort to relativise the absolute claims of theology. His effort to find a pre-law may be flawed, but the athletic act of leaping back over theology provides an instance of this relativising attempt.

From this point, Agamben opens up the last group, Lukács and Williams, who both enact such a relativising move in their own ways. So, in Chapter Eight, my concern is Georg Lukács, for he is one of the best examples of an effort to exorcise every last trace of romanticist, idealist or religious categories from thought. My question is whether Lukács's premise is not mistaken: instead of assuming that religious ways of thinking comprise the source that must be overcome, I argue that they may better be understood as one moment or mode of much richer and deeper traditions of thought and action. The chapter begins by contrasting Lukács's *The Theory of the Novel* with *The Young Hegel*. What we find here is that, in the second work, he attacks a position he held in the first. Thus, in the *Theory of the Novel*, he argues that the way to overcome a world 'abandoned by God' (the context of the rise of the novel) is to search for a revival of the lost and integrated classical world, such as he finds in Dostoevsky. In his later *The Young Hegel*, he attacks Hegel for a very similar argument: the alienating 'positivity' of Christianity must be overcome by means of the recovered republican freedom of ancient Greece and Rome. However, it seems to me that, in attempting to excise the content of his older argument, he has missed something in the form – the awareness of a longer tradition that includes a religious moment within it. The second part of the chapter engages with some of Lukács's many autobiographical sketches, for here too we find a more intimate effort at exorcising the spirits of theology from his thought and life. Again I ask whether this is the best strategy, especially in light of a certain nostalgia in the later preface of *History and Class Consciousness* for his 'messianic utopianism'. In bringing the critical and autobiographical efforts at self-exorcism together, I close by asking what it might mean to see religion and theology as passing moments in the longer trajectories of thought and action. What is needed, then, is a way of dealing with such moments without banishing them.

Finally, I turn to Raymond Williams, who in *Politics and Letters* comments that the only books in his parents' house in the small town of Pandy in Wales were the Bible and the *Beekeeper's Manual*. This chapter focuses on the rather neglected Bible and its associated religion. In contrast to the general perception (fostered at times by his own comments) that Raymond Williams showed little interest in religion, this chapter begins by tracing the references to religion in some of his major texts, such as *Culture and Society* and *The Long Revolution*. These references mostly seek to historicise religion as an initial moment in areas such as drama, education, and literacy. More striking, however, is the far greater presence of religion in his novels, where the tension between the Baptist chapel and established Church of England appears quite often. Indeed, it turns out that the values Williams was keen to espouse, such as neighbourliness, community, humanity, working-class solidarity, trust, faith, and even socialism were values that centred on the chapel, which is as much a religious as a social and political focus of the Welsh towns in his novels. However, when he espouses these values in what may be called his 'warm Marxism' he refers to his autobiography, the innate tendencies associated with Welshness and the working class. In other words, the fourth source of these values, the chapel, disappears. I suggest that chapel functions like a vanishing mediator, enabling Williams to espouse such values and then, when its task is done, it is ushered off the scene. Religion, it seems, has a greater presence in Williams's work than might appear at first sight. However, there is one final question that Williams's work raises: is religion, or more specifically Christianity, the undeniable source of the values and institutions that are so important to Williams, a source he seeks to historicise and leave behind, or is their religious content but a passing phase in a much longer history? At this point, I pick up the argument at the close of my chapters on Agamben and Lukács concerning the passing moment of religion and suggest that it applies just as much to Williams.

The conclusion brings together and rearranges the various elements I have drawn from each of these critics, namely: the enticements for Marxist reconstructions of the economic and social conditions of religions such as Christianity, particularly those that endure and remain global forces; the necessary fables or myths of religion that continue to have political valence, such as Christian communism, the narrative that responds to psychological pathologies, and the very nature of apocalyptic scenarii; revolutionary possibilities, particularly where some elements of religion may be relativised as the passing moment of longer and deeper revolutionary themes, and where religion itself may be 'transcoded' as a revolutionary impulse (in terms of the time that remains, unstable collectives, monasticism, Reformation etc.); finally, dialectics, especially the tension between living in the world and yet not, which I recast as a way to understand Marxism as both a secular and anti-secular project.

Chapter One
The Paradoxes of Lucien Goldmann

> We should never forget that, for Pascal, man is on every level a paradoxical being, a union of opposites, and that to seek God is to find him, but to find him is still to seek after him.[1]

Lucien Goldmann's *Le Dieu caché* is as much ignored these days as it was discussed when it first came out in 1959.[2] An allusion to Port-Royal, the *noblesse de robe* and Blaise Pascal is all that seems to be needed to evoke a whole argument by Goldmann concerning Jansenism and its historical context in the struggle over royal absolutism in seventeenth-century France, an argument whose problems are now all too apparent. There is more than enough to criticise in Goldmann, so I prefer to focus on what is still valuable, namely, the insight into the heart of Pascal's thought in terms of the dialectic of grace and the political consequences that flow from it. This dialectic shows up most brightly in two closely related contradictions: that between the two great poles of the Elect and the Reprobate, and that between refusing the world and yet living within it. In the first contradiction, we find ourselves in the impossible intermediate state of being in between the Elect and the Damned; in the second, the profound tension comes from the fact

---
[1] Goldmann 1964a, p. 295; 1959, p. 327; translation modified.
[2] However, see the useful effort to rehabilitate Goldmann by Cohen 1994.

that both sides of the contradiction are true, for we live in the world and are yet not part of it.

These are the gems of Goldmann's book. I seek not merely to chip those bright stones from his text, but also to see what ramifications they have for political thought and action. Before I proceed, however, a few preliminary comments. Written in that curious in-between space of the 1950s as Europe was recovering from the Second World War, *The Hidden God* is one of the few book-length engagements with theology by a Marxist. However, unlike Theodor Adorno and Ernst Bloch,[3] who have also written books on theological matters, this book is really Goldmann's *summa*. Along with Jansenism, French history at the time of the rise of absolute monarchy, Pascal and Racine, he also has a good deal to say about Marx, Engels, Lukács, Kant, Descartes, Augustine and so on. The problem is that it goes on far too long. Not only is the Racine section tacked onto the end, but one can go on for page after page through a rather droll and repetitive text until a spark flies and insight suddenly bursts into flame. Needless to say, I focus mostly on those sparks, the brightest two of which are the contradictions to which I direct most of my attention.

Pascal really is Goldmann's hero and the text is strewn with appreciation of Pascal as 'the first exemplary realisation of *the modern man [l'homme moderne]*'.[4] Yet, for all these supposed achievements, why is the Marxist Goldmann so interested in one who was an arch-conservative, defending the fixed ordering of society on the basis of privilege and the rights of the king? This question comes to a head when Goldmann notes but plays down Pascal's consistent criticisms of social injustice.[5] He notes that Pascal points to the impossibility of any human law achieving full justice, to the perpetual abuse of power and wealth in sinful human society.[6] Goldmann even recognises that these

---

[3] Adorno 1989; 2003a, Volume 2; Bloch 1972; 1985, Volume 14.

[4] Goldmann 1964a, p. 171; 1959, p. 192, translation modified. Goldmann cannot help himself. Pascal becomes a precursor, if not the first philosopher of dialectical thought and tragedy (Goldmann 1964a, p. 55; 1959, p. 65), the creator of a new moral attitude (Goldmann 1964a, p. 171; 1959, p. 192), a biologist before his time (Goldmann 1964a, p. 227; 1959, pp. 254–5), the great precursor of modern aesthetics (Goldmann 1964a, p. 270; 1959, p. 302), and the first man to bring the questions of risk with its possibilities of failure or success into philosophical thought (Goldmann 1964a, p. 302; 1959, p. 337). In short, it is Pascal who opens a new chapter in philosophy (Goldmann 1964a, p. 234; 1959, p. 263). Needless to say, I find these hero-worshipping sections a little over the top.

[5] Goldmann 1964a, pp. 272–82; 1959, pp. 304–14.

[6] Pascal 1950, pp. 112–24.

criticisms are radical and anarchic. And yet he is nonplussed, missing the point that intelligent conservatives are often the best to heed, for they see the problems all too well, raising all the right questions. As Fredric Jameson has commented more than once, intelligent conservatives repay careful attention. One might not like their answers, but the questions are usually spot on. This, I suspect, is the reason Goldmann likes Pascal so much: as a very intelligent conservative he asks all the right questions.

In what follows, my main concern is *The Hidden God*, drawing in other texts where needed.[7] I begin with the central issue of the dialectic of grace, especially the questions of living in between the two states of the Elect and the Damned, the mediation of the wager and then the tension between withdrawing from the world and yet living within it. While my agenda in the discussion of the dialectic of grace is to draw out the political implications of Goldmann's text, for the remainder I find Goldmann wanting. One of the strange and frustrating things about Goldmann's book is that his insights rely upon a problematic method. The main features of that method are homology or 'genetic structuralism' (the contradictions of Jansenism are a direct reflection of the political tensions between the legal officers and the absolute monarchy), a banal dialectic of the part and the whole, and a theory of world vision that is nothing more than the idea of a cultural dominant for a specific economic base. Rather than repeating the criticisms that have been made of this rather vulgar Marxism (although I am quite fond of a good bout of Marxist vulgarity), the more important question is how Goldmann is able to generate his insights with such a method. Is there something to be said for it, or is it more like scaffolding that one removes once the building is complete? My suspicion is that the secret lies with Goldmann's curious dependence on Lukács, especially the pre-Marxist *Soul and Form*.[8] While Goldmann claims that he draws his genetic structuralism from Lukács, it seems to me that this is really a sleight of hand: while it appears that he develops his method from Lukács, what he really does is use specific texts from Lukács to illuminate his interpretation of Pascal and Jansenism. The difference between method

---

[7] At least I am most interested in the discussion of Pascal and Jansenism in *The Hidden God*, rather than the strange section on Racine tacked onto the end of the book. In contrast to this section, the small book on Racine (Goldmann 1981) is much better, but then it repeats many of the points made in *The Hidden God*.
[8] Lukács 1974, 1971a.

and content is important: the content of the quotes from Lukács are far more useful than the method he apparently draws from Lukács. The problem is that the method – homology – hardly does justice to the sophisticated and complex dialectic that Lukács employs. Given the value of Goldmann's take on the dialectic of grace in Pascal and Jansenism, and given the inadequacy of his method, I propose a more useful method for understanding the economic and social context of Jansenism. Finally, I take up Goldmann's efforts to link Pascal with Marx, with one significant difference: I seek the link at an entirely different level to Goldmann, namely in the tension of Marxism as both a secular and an anti-secular project.

The dialectic of grace

The issue is grace, especially the 'high' view of grace championed by the Jansenists. Since grace is so central, it led the Jansenists to the doctrinal position of Predestination. They took their cue from Paul's texts in the New Testament, especially Romans 8:29, where we find the path that leads from foreknowledge, through predestination to glorification:

> For those whom he foreknew (προέγνω) he also predestined (προώρισεν) to be conformed to the image of his Son, in order that he might be the firstborn among many brethren. And those whom he predestined he also called; and those whom he called he also justified; and those whom he justified he also glorified.

But how did terms such as foreknowing [*proginōskō*] and predestining [*proorizō*] find themselves in the same boat as grace? The short answer is that the predestination of some to salvation and others to damnation is the exercise of God's inscrutable but perfectly just will. The long answer is that a number of key assumptions underlie the idea that grace manifests itself in the predestination of some to salvation. The first is the utter unknowability of God, and that applies also to his exercise of grace, which is equally inscrutable.[9] The second is the utter sinfulness and depravity of human beings (one of my favourite doctrines): we can do no good work on our own, and so we must

---

[9] Pascal 1950, pp. 99–100.

rely entirely on God for any such good work.[10] The third is the irresistibility or inamissibility of grace. The argument goes something as follows: we can do nothing good on our own, let alone anything that gets us a millimetre closer to salvation. Thus, the only way to salvation, or indeed to do anything good, is through God's grace.[11] However, if God offers to give us a hand, if he offers us grace, how do we receive it? Well, we can hardly say 'yes thank you' or 'no thanks', since that would put us utterly depraved creatures in the unacceptable position of controlling whether God can get through to us or not. So grace comes to us whether we want it or not: it is completely undeserved, unexpected and irresistible. However, not all are saved, for some are damned. Being saved or damned has nothing to do with us, for we can neither accept nor reject grace – it all lies in God's nimble and inscrutable hands. Thus, the decision whereby some are saved and others are damned is God's alone. To put it slightly differently: given that we are all fallen and sinful creatures, the default position is that we are all damned. The fact that God actually has decided in his grace to save some of us is a cause for wonder and thanks.

This longer answer appeared in the posthumously published manifesto of Jansenism, the *Augustinus* of Cornelius Otto Jansenius (1640). As the title suggests, it was a reappropriation of Augustine's work, asserting the absolute priority of grace and a predestination in which some are elected to salvation and the rest condemned to damnation irrespective of their own acts or volition. Indeed, it was Augustine who first articulated predestination before Calvin took it up with his admirable rigour. For Augustine, the inaccessibility of the reasons for God's choice between the elect and the damned did not make that choice any less just, for God's justice is perfect. Augustine put in a little contradiction of his own, namely that although God does not override free will, grace does not depend on human acceptance but on the infallible and eternal decree of God.

The problem for the Roman Catholics in the seventeenth century – for it was a movement within Roman Catholicism – was that Jansenism came far too close to the positions of Luther and especially Calvin. There were differences, of course, and they fascinate me, but Jansenism came at a time when the Counter-Reformation was well under way. And one of its ideological

---

[10] Pascal 1950, pp. 37–78, 99–100.
[11] Pascal 1950, pp. 272–3.

centre-pieces was the work of Luis de Molina (1535–1600), especially his *Concordia liberi arbitrii cum gratiae donis* of 1588. Over against the Reformers, Molina gave as much room as possible to human works and obedience to the divine commandments. Basically, Molina argued that freely chosen human co-operation with the gift of grace was the ultimate cause of the efficacy of grace. This effectiveness, which boils down to the ability of human beings genuinely to obey God, comes not from grace itself, but from the human decision to obey. Thus, in opposition to the Calvinist and Jansenist position on the total depravity of human beings, who can do no good on their own, Molinism (as it came to be known) gives human beings as much involvement as possible in ensuring their own salvation. Molinism just escapes espousing self-earned salvation by arguing that the free act of human beings to co-operate with God is itself foreknown by God. In short, we can get to the line, but we need a helping hand to get over it. Jansenism was anathema to such a position, and watered down the stark opposition to the Reformers that Molinism represented. It is hardly a surprise, then, that the Jansenists were harassed, hounded and condemned.

If we grant the argument for predestination, then a number of contradictions arise. Of these, Goldmann identifies two that were central for the Jansenists, especially Pascal. The first is the age-old problem: how do we know who is of the elect and who not? Or, to put it slightly differently, if God's grace is available to all, then why are only some chosen? The second contradiction arises from the utter sinfulness and depravity of the world: do we attempt to make our troubled peace with the world, or do we reject it and withdraw?

The Elect and the Damned

In a few enthralling pages,[12] Goldmann goes to the heart of the tension between the Elect and the Damned. This opposition, he argues, is not so much a great divide between two groups of people, between the sheep and the goats, between those who are saved and those who are not. On the contrary, it is a division that we bear within ourselves:

> From the point of view of God there are the Elect who cannot be damned and the Reprobate who cannot be saved. On the other hand, from the point

---

[12] Goldmann 1964a, pp. 290–5; 1959, pp. 322–7.

of view of man, who ignores every divine decree, the categories of 'Elect' and 'Reprobate' are in each individual case merely permanent *possibilities*. He thinks of himself as an intermediate being who brings them together, but who has not yet chosen and who can never make a definitive choice in *this* life.[13]

As one who has always been intrigued, and even at times affirmed the idea of predestination, primarily on a political and economic level, this is an extraordinarily intriguing argument. But what are the implications of asserting that the unbearable tension between the Elect and the Damned lies within? To begin with, it means that one is caught in between the two extremes: 'one does not show his greatness by being at one extreme, but by touching both extremes at once and by filling in the whole space between them'.[14] Further, the one who must fashion a life between the permanent possibilities of the Elect and the Reprobate is an 'intermediate being [*être intermédiaire*]. What this does, in effect, is introduce a third category between the Elect and the Damned, a third category that then breaks the hold of the binary opposition. And this is precisely what Pascal does, according to Goldmann: he introduces a tripartite division into human existence. Along with the Elect and the Damned, there are also the Called who do not persevere in their calling. The trick with the third category is that it assumes the perspective of human beings. God may have two categories, but what God is up to is well beyond human knowledge since His ways are inscrutable. So we are left with what we know as human beings (the Bible notwithstanding).

Once we take such a perspective, once we assume that all human beings are in fact intermediate beings, then the only possible approach to others is to assume that all people are of the Elect. The reason: since we cannot know God's mind and thereby whether anyone is or is not of the Elect, and since we should not pretend to act like God, we must assume that all have been chosen under pain of making the wrong call. If some do not seem to be of the Elect

---

[13] Goldmann 1964a, p. 293; 1959, pp. 325–6, translation modified. See also: 'The two extreme categories of the Elect and the Reprobate are, in this respect, the two permanent possibilities between which man must choose. They express, on the plane of the individual the two possibilities represented by the wager, in so far as to fear to wager that Nothing exists is to fear damnation, and to wager that God exists is to hope for salvation' (Goldmann 1964a, pp. 294–5; 1959, p. 327).

[14] Pascal 1961, p. 113; 1950, p. 127; translation modified.

through the way they live and act that must mean that they have been called but have given up seeking. In short, Pascal's position means that we must act as though there were no distinction between people.

This is a real insight by Goldmann, it seems to me, one that goes far beyond an exposition of Pascal's thought. On a more personal level, I have often quipped that I have never met anyone who believes in predestination and yet claims to be one of the Damned. After reading Goldmann, I became aware that my quip has a grain of truth in it. For Goldmann's discussion of Pascal brings to the surface certain aspects of the theology of grace all too carefully concealed in the cobwebbed back rooms of Calvinism. For one who imbibed the paradoxes of Calvinism as part of daily life – from Bible readings uttered by a stern but inconsistent father after every evening meal to the ban on studying, working or buying anything on a Sunday – the questions with which I still deal in the capillaries of my existence turn around the question of grace.[15] For this reason, Goldmann's argument fascinates me. What he manages to do is bring out what might be called the universal or democratic nature of the high view of grace.

Extreme, stark, rationalist and brutal – these are the epithets one more often finds attached to Calvinism and Jansenism. Certainly not democratic. Yet, as Goldmann traces out the dialectical logic of Pascal's argument, this is where we end up. The bottom line is that we should assume that everyone is of the Elect and treat them accordingly. The trick lies with attributing to God all of the less desirable features: God is not such a good dialectician, nor indeed is He much of a democrat. Omniscience, it would seem, has its down side too. As far as the dialectic is concerned, God may have already decided who is of the Elect and who of the Damned without too much fuss, but then the dialectic is really the domain of mere mortals like Pascal. It is not that we forever oscillate between salvation and damnation, between heaven and hell, for that would be a frozen dialectic. Rather, by introducing the third term of the intermediate being, Pascal effectively sublates the opposition. It can then conveniently be shunted off to the side (it is only for God to know) and the real issue is allowed to come to the fore, namely that we should act as though everyone is of the Elect.

---

[15] See further Boer in press-b.

As for democracy, the issue now concerns the universal, or more specifically the tension between the particular and the universal. In Pascal's case, it becomes a tension between the universality of grace and the particularity of salvation. Again the solution of this old conundrum lies in distinguishing between divine and human perspectives. Thus, what from God's perspective seems to be the particularity of grace (only the Elect will be saved) is, from the human perspective – the only one we in fact know – universal (act as though all are of the Elect and treat them accordingly).

The result is the same: an inherent democratic push within Pascal's thought, although I must admit to disliking the word 'democracy' in light of its tired and battered use in our era. All the same, I would like to think such a democratic logic unveiled by Goldmann may provide one of the reasons for the unexpected tolerance of Calvinism in the home of my parents, The Netherlands. To all appearances, one would have assumed that Calvinism, with its stark doctrine of predestination, would have been among the least tolerant of all forms of Christianity. Yet, in practice, it was not so, for The Netherlands provided safe haven for all manner of religious refugees – Jews, Mennonites and other disparate arms of Radical Reformation, and, of course, the Jansenists when they fled the final persecution in eighteenth-century France. Yet it turns out to be Pascal (in Goldmann's reading) and not Calvin who provides the theoretical reason as to why the Calvinists in The Netherlands may have been so tolerant: the need to treat all as of the Elect.

One more political implication emerges from Goldmann's treatment, namely a distinct political allegory. The strange thing is that it is not the political implication Goldmann himself draws out. He is (far) too keen on the role of faith and the wager within Marxism (on these see more below), but, for some perverse reason, is not interested in the Elect and the Damned. Yet, that is precisely where I would like to locate such an allegory. All too quickly, I can lump people in political versions of the Elect and the Damned: depending on one's political persuasions it may be the bourgeoisie and the proletariat, the ruling élite and the ignorant masses, intelligent and stupid voters who must be bought and so on. All too quickly they become reified groups, what may be hated or loved, passionately supported or opposed, the source of all evil or of good. The next step in the allegory is then a timely warning. The political versions of the Elect and the Damned are in fact not two groups embracing one another in a futile and fatal dance; rather, the two political categories are embodied within ourselves, within our own groups. What appears at first as the Elect turns out to be caught between the two possibilities of the Elect and the Damned. And if *that* is the case, then our mortal opponents, the Damned, are also caught in between, just like us. Now, there are two options at this point. One is to undertake a process of weeding out, of finding the Quislings and informers, of witch-hunting in a brutal search to purify the Elect from the taint of the Damned. Of course, this process never ends until the group destroys itself, for the possibility of the Elect cannot exist without the possibility of the Damned. So the other option is to follow Pascal and treat all as though they are of the Elect. No matter how far away they appear to be, no matter how Reprobate they are, they may well be of the Elect. At this point – dare I say it? – the possibility of a full democracy emerges.

Wagering it all

If the tension between the Elect and the Damned lies deep within, and if we are to treat everyone as though they are of the Elect, then there is one further implication: according to Pascal, we must do all in our power to persuade them to seek God. Hence the need for apologiae, for arguments for the existence of God – in short, for the use of reason to persuade people to search for God. As Goldmann indicates,[16] the contradiction between the Jansenist position on predestination, especially with the emphasis on the utter helplessness of human beings, and the writing of apologies is one that has been pointed out time and again. Even Pascal's colleagues at Port-Royal would have found it strange indeed to appeal to reason. However, Pascal takes the logic of the utter sinfulness of human beings to its logical conclusion and points out that we simply cannot know God's mind on the matter. So we must assume that all people are intermediate beings, that everyone is potentially of the Elect, and so we must do all we can to persuade them to seek God – hence the argument of the wager.

Let me pause at a quiet spot and look at that argument a little more closely. It appears in fragment 233 of the *Pensées*[17] and takes the form of a dialogue

---

[16] Goldmann 1964a, p. 290; 1959, p. 323.

[17] Pascal 1950, pp. 93–7; 1961, pp. 155–9. The arrangement and numbering of the fragments differs from editor to editor. In the text I follow the standard French edition (Pascal 1950), which was first established by Léon Brunschvicq in the mid-nineteenth

between Pascal and an imaginary interlocutor, about whom we learn that he is so made that he 'cannot believe'.[18] Pascal begins the relevant section by pointing out that since God is infinitely unknowable [*infiniment incomprehensible*], we cannot know who he is or indeed whether he exists. How then to proceed? To a series of objections from his imaginary interlocutor, Pascal pushes one reason after another to argue that you cannot not wager on God's existence. If it is a question of reason, then either choice is reasonable enough. If it is a question of happiness, then 'if you win, you win everything; if you lose, you lose nothing'.[19] To the objection that one may lose too much by betting at all, Pascal points out that you lose nothing at all by making the wager: to win is to gain infinite life and happiness; to lose is to be as you are now. But still the interlocutor objects, saying he just cannot believe, for that is the way he has been constituted. At this point comes the reply that Goldmann quotes:

> You wish to come to faith, but you do not know the way; you wish to cure yourself of unbelief, and you ask for the remedy: learn from those who have been tied like you, and who now wager all they have; they are the people who know the way that you wish to follow and have been cured of a sickness for which you want a cure.[20]

Goldmann is keen to establish that the argument of the wager is not window dressing for someone who actually has faith; rather, it is central to Pascal's thought. More important is his question as to who the interlocutor might be: a free thinker perhaps, a sceptic whom Pascal seeks to persuade. Goldmann takes a different line and argues that the interlocutor is Pascal himself, indeed that the two voices are internal to Pascal. He both believes and does not believe. He is the one who now wagers all he has. In other words, the wager is between the voice that doubts and resists and the one who sees that the wager is an exceedingly good bet.

---

century. The English translation by J.M. Cohen (1961) follows the arrangement of the fragments by Jacques Chevalier (Pascal 1954). The catch is that Cohen's numbering of the fragments does not refer to any other numbering system, of which there are many.

[18] Pascal 1950, p. 96; 1961, p. 158.
[19] Pascal 1950, p. 95; 1961, p. 157.
[20] Pascal 1950, p. 96; 1961, p. 158, translation modified; see Goldmann 1964a, p. 286; Goldmann 1959, p. 318.

All the same, Goldmann's argument that the wager is internal is not the only element of Pascal's wager. Another (and, here, I go beyond Goldmann) is the introduction of the element of doubt. Here is truly an element of the dialectic of grace that is almost entirely lacking in Calvinism. All of the elements I have discussed so far – the internalisation of the tension between the Elect and the Damned, the intermediate being caught between these possibilities, the uncertainty of determining who is of the Elect and the wager itself – all of these are unthinkable without doubt. If we never know who is of the Elect (thereby treating everyone as though they are), then we too must fall into that universal group. We too can never be certain, and so we must wager, no matter how good the odds may seem to be.

At this point, Jansenism differs from Calvinism, for in that version of the high doctrine of grace, there is no uncertainty: you are either in or you are not. That means there is no such thing as apostasy. Someone may backslide, may show all the signs of the Damned and yet because they are of the Elect, they will come back. God has decided and there is nothing we can do about it. However, before we can charge Calvin with a certain arrogance, with having been able to climb into God's mind and gain a few morsels of precious knowledge about eternity, he also made sure to insist that we should be slow to judge. Not that he always lived up to such a precept, burning the odd heretic or two at the Genevan stake.

All these fine distinctions are not merely 'metaphysical subtleties and theological niceties',[21] for they have a number of profound political implications. I am, however, underwhelmed by Goldmann's championing of the wager as the key to the philosophy of Kant and the sciences.[22] To be fair, he does give this argument a twist: Pascal, the sciences, Marxism and even Augustine all share common ground, not merely because they all have the trappings of 'scientific' rigour (and Goldmann does use the epithet as often as he can for Marxism), but above all because they are all based in an act of 'faith'. The content of that 'faith' may differ,[23] but it is the act itself that counts. For all its ingenuity – Marxism and indeed Pascal's theology are scientific but only because they are based on acts of faith – this is hardly a new argument. I find myself

---

[21] Marx 1996, p. 81.
[22] Goldmann 1964a, pp. 91–5; 1959, pp. 100–5.
[23] '(Evidence of the transcendent, wager on the transcendent, wager on an immanent meaning)' (Goldmann 1959, p. 104, translation mine).

wanting to say, 'but of course, so let's move on'. But Goldmann is writing in the 1950s, and it may have been a breakthrough argument to make then, especially in a Europe where attaching the word 'scientific' to the study of society or literature or indeed the study of sacred texts such as the Bible allows one to lay claim to a host of associations – rigour, empirical evidence, the absence of extraneous items such as theology, revelation or faith. Half a century later, the point is hardly stunning.

More intriguing is his argument that Marxism as a political movement might do well to see itself in terms of the wager, although not quite in the way he sees it. Like Jansenism with its wager on individual salvation, or Pascal's wager on God's existence, for Goldmann Marxism also operates with a wager: 'in the alternative facing humanity of a choice between socialism and barbarity, socialism will triumph'.[24] Rather than 'triumph', might not doubt be a greater political insight, especially for Marxism? Of course, there is nothing like a little historical hindsight, for the element of doubt is crucial to the wager; no matter how good the odds might be, the risk can never be dismissed. In the current context of rampant and troubled global capitalism, even in China, one would have to say that the wager of Marxism is at best still open and that the odds are not necessarily stacked in its favour. Marxism may have its own wager, but it is a far more doubtful wager than when Goldmann penned this book.

In the world and yet not

One contradiction remains, and that is the one between living in the world and yet not being of the world, between the hermit and the one who continues to live among people in the world. In many respects, Goldmann makes this tension the determining feature of Jansenism as a theological and political movement, with regard to its internal debates, the attitudes to politics, education and so on. But I have a more personal interest as well, for I too constantly feel this tension. On the one hand, I know well the attraction of the ascetic life of a hermit. I longingly seek out my own company, cycle and walk and camp on my own, celebrate pure silence or talk to myself, dodge any responsibility that forces me to deal with people, to organise, engage and talk. Asceticism

---

[24] Goldmann 1964a, p. 301; 1959, pp. 335–6.

is, after all, a deeply pleasurable way to live. And yet, I revel in the bursts of intense interaction with other people, with the to and fro of rapid conversation over a beer or three, with the passion of collective political engagement, with the thrill of flirting and seduction, the tenseness of an argument or a fight. But I could certainly not live in the world in such a way all the time, and all too soon I hanker for the life of a hermit once again.

At this personal level, then, I am interested in how Goldmann's reading of Pascal and Jansenism might explain these two contrary attractions. As before, this personal concern does not exclude a distinctly political angle in my reading of Goldmann, something in which I am also vitally interested. Of course, given the tension itself between living in the world and yet not, the two domains – usually designated by the old but inadequate opposition of the personal and the political – are intimately connected.

To his credit, Goldmann emphasises again and again (perhaps too often) that the tension between the refusal and affirmation of the world is the *lived* contradiction of Jansenism. We can approach such a contradiction in two ways: either the doctrines of grace and predestination were the ideological articulations of such a tension, or this tension between living in and out of the world was the outcome of those theological positions. Both are true, it seems to me, in the fashion of that old Marxist point of the interplay between theory and practice. Goldmann also points out that at its most creative points (Pascal and, to a lesser extent, Racine), this tension became not an either/or but a both/and: it entailed a simultaneous affirmation of knowledge of both the world and of God. In short it was a refusal of the world from within the world – *le divertissement*.[25]

This lived tension raises a crucial question for politics, one that Goldmann touches upon obliquely in his rush to show how close Marx is to Pascal, or rather, how Pascal lays the groundwork for Marx. And that question is what I will call the contradiction of a secular political programme like Marxism. Here, we face a deep contradiction: in eschewing any religious or transcendent reference point, Marxism seems to draw all its insights and ammunition from this world. The economic, political and social realities of existence on this globe are the grist for the Marxist mill. And, yet, Marxism is not bound by

---

[25] Pascal 1950, pp. 64–70; Goldmann 1964a, pp. 50–2, 215–18; 1959, pp. 60–2, 241–4; 1981, pp. 6–7.

this world. It sets its sights on the end of capitalism, on the expectations for a world that is qualitatively different and, we hope, better, whatever its name and shape might be. On this score, Marxism rejects the world, this world of capitalism, in favour of another. To my mind, this is a contradiction, indeed a paradox, that may be expressed in terms of the paradox of Jansenism: a refusal of the world from within the world.

With this question in mind, let us see what Goldmann does with the lived contradiction of Jansenism. To begin with, it enables him to make sense of the theological, social and philosophical differences within Jansenism. The two main streams may be characterised as centrist and extremist, or, in Goldmann's overblown terms, 'dramatic centrism [*centrisme que nous appellerons dramatique*]' and 'tragic extremism [*l'extrémisme tragique*]'.[26] Both were based on the belief that the world is irredeemable; in no way can it be changed through one's actions within it. Where they differed was on the level of one's involvement: the centrists sought to stand up for truth and goodness within the world, where they actually had a small place; the extremists also wished to speak out for truth and goodness, but they believed their words would fall on deaf and hostile ears. In other words, the centrists saw a role for Christians within the world, within which they could stand as lights on the hill, whereas the extremists tended all too readily to retreat from the world in disgust and despair. The name that attaches to the moderates or centrists is Antoine Arnauld (1612–94), the theologian who effectively became leader of the Jansenists after the death of Saint-Cyran in 1643, eventually fleeing to the Netherlands in 1679 to escape persecution. The main proponent of the extremists was Martin de Barcos (1600–78), who succeeded Saint-Cyran as abbot in 1643, corresponding furiously with the other Jansenists,[27] until he condemned Port-Royal's acceptance of the 'Peace of Clement IX' in 1669 and thereby broke with the Jansenists as hopeless compromisers.

Goldmann is careful to point out that both embodied the tension between refusing the world and living within it. Their differences were matters of

---

[26] Goldmann 1964a, p. 148; 1959, p. 164; see also Goldmann 1981, pp. 31–6. Goldmann also espies two positions at the further ends of moderation and extremism: the one sought to comes to terms with the lies and evil of the world, and the other retreated into complete silence before the absolute sinfulness of the world. Neither was a real option, although Pascal's sister, Jacqueline, belonged to the most extreme wing; see Goldmann 1964a, pp. 143, 148; 1959, pp. 158, 164.

[27] See Goldmann 1956.

emphasis, the one more prepared to make a fist of it in the world and the other less so. But these differences had profound consequences.[28] For Arnauld and the moderates, the task of Christians was to struggle within the world and within the Church, albeit with little hope of success. Thus, on social and political matters, the moderates devoted a good deal of attention to the role of the Christians in relation to the powers that be. They ought to be involved and stand up for truth whenever they found it, for there could in fact be good kings and ministers of the government. Similarly, with regard to philosophy, one should give it due attention as another means for locating the truth, for it may have its own value apart from any religious concerns.

By contrast, Barcos and the extremists saw human beings as thoroughly corrupted by original sin, including Christians; since it was therefore impossible to achieve any significant reform, all one could do was proclaim the truth and retire from the world. The extremists were far more concerned over theological issues such as grace, predestination and original sin, but had little interest in questions of a social, political or philosophical nature. These matters were far too much of the world, having no value in themselves since they are irredeemable.

A difference or two in emphasis can go a long way, it seems. What are the implications for my preliminary comments concerning the analogous tension within a Marxism that is of the world and yet refuses it? Its more secular tendencies begin to sound distinctly like the centrists or moderates: capitalism is a fundamentally unjust system, but we had better make the best of it all the same and use what we can. For example, the parliamentary system is one that can indeed be worked in a Marxist direction, whether through a broad left front, or through coalitions with other parties in order to bring some pressure to bear on the exercise of power. And a moderate position would also argue that capitalism may have its good moments along with the bad, and then search for what might be salvaged in a Marxist programme. The risk is that such a position slips into social democracy, opting for a gentler, kinder capitalism with the various safety nets of medical cover, old age care, unemployment benefits and so forth. A more radical Marxism, by contrast, rejects this world of capitalism and all that goes with it. Nothing much in this world of capitalism is redeemable, for it is at its very basis an unjust and exploitative

---

[28] Goldmann 1964a, pp. 150–60; 1959, pp. 166–79.

system. Politically, this radical position becomes all too often the extra-parliamentary Left, eschewing any involvement in a system of government that is far too closely tied in with capitalism, which must be swept away *in toto*. All one can do is condemn predatory capitalism and work for its demise. I must admit that I have more sympathy with this radical position, especially in the way Alain Badiou rejects capitalist parliamentary 'democracy' and argues for true politics as that which operates outside the state. The models here are the soviets, or Mao's collectives or indeed his own Organisation Politique. It is politics without a party, a politics outside the parliamentary system.[29]

I would not want to push the analogy too far, since the danger – like Goldmann – is to make the division between the two groups too sharp. Or, rather, I prefer to follow Goldmann's emphasis on the continuum: just as the moderates and extremists within Jansenism operate within a continuum that has some assumed positions, so also Marxism's various emphases fall into a continuum. In other words, to pick up a point I have stressed earlier: the division or tension lies within. It is not so much a split between two absolute positions, between two radical alternatives, but rather a strained and difficult effort to keep the two together. The hermit must still live in the world.

What this continuum between the moderate and extreme Jansenists allows Goldmann to do is locate Pascal, and indeed Racine, within a continuum. If Pascal moves from a moderate position in his *Lettres provinciales* of 1654[30] to the extreme position of his *Pensées* in 1662, then Racine moves the other way in his plays and his personal and political positions.[31] I am less interested in the details of Goldmann's mapping of Pascal's biography, lurching as it did from one spiritual crisis to another (especially the major crisis of 23 November, 1654). What is far more attractive is the way he is able to make this tension – refusing the world and yet living within it – the key to that biography.[32] On

---

[29] See especially Badiou 2005b.
[30] Pascal 1967.
[31] Goldmann 1981, pp. 55–6.
[32] 'Until 1654 Pascal looked for truth in the natural world and in the abstract sciences; from 1654 to 1657 he hoped that truth would triumph in the Church and religion in the world, and played an active part in trying to bring this triumph about. But towards the end of his life he learned that man's true greatness can lie only in his awareness of his weakness and limitations, and saw the uncertainty which characterises any human life, both in the natural world and in the Church Militant.... In doing so, he discovered tragedy, the complete and certain uncertainty of all truth, paradox, the refusal of the world by a man who remains within it and the direct appeal to

this level, Goldmann draws me right in. For the desire to renounce the world and all that is therein is a very strong one for me. All it need be is a corner away from everyone, the ability to retreat into my own world, or an isolated hill from which I scan around in order to affirm that there is no one in sight or earshot, or deep in the bush that absorbs me quickly, realising that I am alone and able to relax. One of my favoured places is in the mountains at the back of my home. All it is takes a day's steep ride and I am alone in the old growth forest. And the desire strengthens with age.

This tension, this retreat from the world from within it makes an awful lot of sense to me at a deeply personal level. Yet I am never away from the 'world'. Until now, I have let Goldmann get away with his usage of the term without questioning it. He is quite consistent, for 'world [*le monde*]' means the realm of public, political life, the affairs of state and business. A renunciation of the world is the refusal of such a life, and the tension of which he writes is the tension, or as he prefers, the paradox of refusing that public and political world while yet remaining part of it.

All the same, the tension has more to it than Goldmann perhaps realises. If I focus on the question of renunciation that is dear to me, it is not so hard to realise that retreat is really a retreat from one world to another world. For the nuns of Port-Royal such as Pascal's sister Jacqueline, it was a retreat into the cloistered world of the convent. For a hermit, it is the retreat into the world of one's own mind, body and soul, and (if one is so inclined) of God. Even Zuster Bertken in the Netherlands, who lived from the age of 30 until her death at 87 (1457 to 1514) in a narrow cell about 4 metres long, moved from one world to another. Built for her at the permission of the bishop of Utrecht beside his church, the cell had two curtained windows through which food was passed, but which were never opened so that people could see her face. Upon her death, she was buried in the cell that had been her own world for most of her life.

So also in the forested mountains: it is not merely a world of animals and plants and earth and water, but it is a forest that is there only because human beings have preserved it and decided not to cut it down and feed the global

---

God. It was by extending paradox to God himself, and making Him both certain and uncertain, present and absent, that Pascal was able to write the *Pensées* and thus open a new chapter in the history of philosophical thought' (Goldmann 1964a, pp. 182–3; 1959, pp. 204–5).

timber industry. And the bicycle I ride in order to get there, the tent in which I sleep, the mug from which I drink tea all come from that world I seek to escape. So refusing the world from within the world means more than Goldmann seems to think, although we should perhaps reframe it as refusing one world for the sake of another. Is my retreat from the world a resignation and recognition that it is thoroughly 'sinful', totally depraved and irredeemable? In part it is, although at an economic and environmental level more than a theological one. For all my desires to see the end of an economic system that is exploitative at its deepest level, no matter how many achievements have been made, my retreat is a recognition that it will be here for a good while yet. It is also a recognition, in a heterodox way, that the ultimate contradiction between the unlimited growth of capitalism must come up against the reality of a limited planet, that capitalism will only come to an end when it comes up against this limit and can grow now more, or rather capitalism ultimately will destroy the world it has created.

Yet here comes the tension, for I want to resist that sort of fatalism and fashionable catastrophism. If it is not a meteorite, or a new plague out of the jungles of Africa, or overpopulation, then it is the return of Christ on the clouds. So I find myself drawn back into this 'world' of which Goldmann writes, working, thinking and writing tirelessly for a world without capitalism and all that it entails. The reason why Goldmann's take on Pascal, especially this tension of refusal within the world, makes so much sense is not merely because of the Marxism I share with him (although not so triumphalist or indeed moral[33]), but also because Pascal was wrestling with the same problems that are part of my own heritage. My version was Calvinism, which has its own anticipatory features for Marxism, but it too dealt with the problems of an absolute focus on grace, human inability and depravity, and the stark doctrine of predestination.

Neither Goldmann nor I are going to leave such questions at the level of personal desires, except perhaps for the way the personal turns out to be an internalisation of what goes on in the economic and social context. Goldmann's solution is what has been called – and castigated – as homology. The paradoxes of Jansenism, between the Elect and the Reprobate, between the

---

[33] Especially when he comments that capitalist society is 'based upon individual selfishness' (Goldmann 1964a, p. 278; 1959, p. 310), Goldmann lines himself up with a distinctly moral Marxism.

world and its refusal, are a direct expression of the situation in which the Jansensists found themselves.

Theory: the tight fit of homology

Goldmann's answer to the question of context is rather simple: Jansenism was the expression of a distinct group or sub-class within the specific political environment of the rise of the absolute monarchy in seventeenth-century France.[34] Or in more detail: the key political contradiction was that the *officiers* of the *ancien régime* (from whose ranks the Jansenists were primarily drawn) were economically dependent upon a monarchical state whose growth they opposed from an ideological and political point of view. They were opposed to a form of government they could not destroy without destroying themselves. This contradiction explains the contradiction of Jansenism – the essential vanity of the world and salvation in solitude and withdrawal, and yet a continued involvement in the world.[35] In short, the contradiction of Jansenism is a direct expression of the contradictory situation of these political *officiers* (legal functionaries with government posts who went by the collective title of the *noblesse de robe*).

---

[34] As a theological and political movement, the origins of Jansenism are usually marked by the publication of Cornelius Otto Jansenius's *Augustinus* (1640). Jansenius may have been the ideologue of the movement, but his friend and collaborator, Jean-Ambroise Duvergier de Hauranne, more commonly known as Abbé de Saint-Cyran (1581–1643), was its organiser. Originally abbot of Saint-Cyran, he became in 1633 the spiritual director of the nerve-centre of Jansenism, the convent of Port-Royal. The movement grew swiftly, with two outcomes. First, Port-Royal established a second convent in Paris apart from its one in the marshes south of Paris, and it attracted more and more nuns, including Jacqueline, Pascal's sister. Second, it came under persecution. Saint-Cyran was imprisoned by Cardinal Richelieu in 1637 until his death, and one pope after another sought to condemn Jansenism as heretical until Pope Clement XI's Bull 'Unigenitus' in 1713 outlawed it completely and persecuted the Jansenists, many of whom fled to The Netherlands.

[35] See especially Goldmann 1964a, p. 120; 1959, pp. 133–4; 1981, pp. 28–9. Or, in Goldmann's own words, he seeks to provide 'a general picture of the effect which a certain aspect of the evolution of royal absolutism in France had upon legal circles, and in particular upon lawyers closely connected with the *parlements*. I suggested that this evolution gave rise to an attitude of reserve towards social life and the State – "the world" – but that this attitude was free from any element of active political or social opposition to the monarchy. It was this attitude which in my view, provided the background of ideas and feelings against which any Jansenist ideology developed'. Goldmann 1964a, p. 142; 1959, p. 157.

Homology

I have no desire to dwell on the problems of Goldmann's homologies, especially since others have done so.[36] All the same, two elements are worth noting: a literary work, philosophical system or indeed theological position expresses and reflects the interests and aspirations of a distinct social group and class; in order to find such a direct connection, a Marxist analysis must embroil itself in the minutiae of historical detail. Now, Goldmann does his best to avoid slipping into a rather mechanical Marxism (as Cohen shows, he reacted against it), especially in his argument that cultural works express the worldview of a distinct group.[37] Yet, it all too easily does slip into the assumption that the superstructure is the expression of the base. Now, if one is going to engage in vulgar Marxism, then there is no need to pin it to an elaborate theoretical and historical discussion. In the end, it seems to me that Goldmann is able to climb up to one or two striking conclusions – the best of which I have discussed at length in the preceding section – by means of a very rickety ladder, one that collapses somewhere on the way up.

The key words for Goldmann are 'express [*expliquer*]' and 'reflect' or 'correspond [*correspondre*]', which turn up time and again in the chapter on 'World Visions and Social Classes'.[38] Such an approach may take two forms: either a text or philosophical system reflects the general conditions of a particular place and time, so much so that one may read those elements off from the text, or the text in question gives expression to the opinions and beliefs of a distinct author or group. If the former is a more general approach that assumes a reasonably direct correlation between text and context, the latter is more specific and conscious – the text becomes little more than propaganda espousing a platform. Goldmann plays with both options. Not only does Jansenism reflect the specific conditions of a sub-class (the legal officers of the French

---

[36] For example, Jameson 1981, pp. 43–4; Evans 1981, pp. 154–5.

[37] Or, as he puts it somewhat later: 'Genetic structuralism, as I have used it so far, presupposes: (1) The bringing to light of a work's *global* semantic model, the formation of which constitutes *the schema of a global system* of relationships between men and between them and the universe; (2) The sociological study of the genesis of this model within the dynamic tendency of the collective consciousness of particular social groups; (3) The extension of this global semantic structure into an aggregation of partial and more strictly formal structures, on all levels which the study of a written text involves' (Goldmann 1980, p. 142).

[38] Goldmann 1964a, pp. 89–102; 1959, pp. 97–114.

parliament during the rise of absolute monarchy), conditions that may be read from the text, but it is also the conscious and deliberate expression of its authors (Goldmann goes to great lengths to argue that Pascal knew exactly what he was doing and executed it brilliantly). It seems to me that even if Goldmann did not have the historical detail at hand, however mediated it might be, he would have been able to read it off the text without too many problems.[39]

Goldmann's distinct preference for texts and ideas that correspond to particular groups and classes becomes even tighter with his desire for specificity. He wishes to lock them in, to identify 'their fit within [*leur insertion dans*] the intellectual and emotional climate which is closest to them'.[40] This desire for a distinct fit or insertion into a time and place leads him into a detailed and ultimately frustrating analysis of the phases in the rise of the absolute monarchy, the changing allegiances between king, aristocracy and bourgeoisie, the different roles of the varying government apparatchiks, the rise and fall in prices for purchasing hereditary offices (*La Paulette*), all in ever more movements of three stages, down to pinpointing the moment when Jansenism as an ideology emerges.[41] The devil is in the detail, it seems to me; or rather, the detail is a blessing and a curse. As a blessing, Goldmann shows how a detailed political and economic analysis is a must for any Marxist historical study. As a curse, he gets lost, for the detail feeds a rather crude theory of the relation between base and superstructure: the latter expresses and reflects the base.

To be fair, once Goldmann has this tight fit, he then wishes to locate this unit within the broader social, political and economic climate of the time – seventeenth-century France. But he does very little of that work, preferring to remain buried in the ever more specific details of what happened on what date. In fact, what he really presents in this book is primarily a political analysis, and there is precious little of the social and economic situation. When he does raise the question of class, especially concerning the shifting alliances between aristocracy and the bourgeoisie in relation to the king, it is strangely divorced from economics. So it seems that, on top of the problems of corre-

---

[39] Indeed, in another discipline in which I have dabbled from time to time (biblical studies), critics do this all the time – read the conditions and intentions of authors from the texts alone, without any historical information outside the text.
[40] Goldmann 1964a, p. 99; 1959, p. 110.
[41] Goldmann 1964a, pp. 103–41; 1959, pp. 115–56.

spondence (homology) and the desire for a tight fit, Goldmann has also fallen into the trap of substituting political analysis for economic analysis. We end up with the strange picture of an isolated group, drawn from disappointed legal functionaries [*officiers*] of the *noblesse de robe*, which spawns Jansenism. Denied the advancement they expected, opposed to the rise of the absolute monarchy and yet still dependent on it for their livelihood, this group produces Jansenism as an effort to cope with their disappointment.

Dialectics?

For all his talk of a dialectical method, there is not much of it in his historical analysis. It does, of course, turn up in the rather banal opposition of the part and the whole,[42] and then more fruitfully in his discussion of the contradictions between the Elect and Damned within Jansenism. Yet, he seems to have used up all his energy for that discussion, for there is little of the dialectic when he gets to the historical context – a direct and tight fit between a subclass and its ideas is not really an example of the dialectic at work.[43]

On this point, Goldmann may be following Pascal further than he thought, for just as Pascal falls short of the full dialectic, so also does Goldmann when he turns to the question of history. Let me explain: Goldmann can never decide whether Pascal is the genuine creator of the dialectic or whether he merely set up its possibility, a possibility that was to be completed by Marx. At times, he goes overboard with his hero and Pascal turns out to be a full practitioner of the dialectic. For instance, in the dialectic embodied in the wager, between God's existence and absence, between the Elect and the Damned, between particular and universal, but above all in the interplay between reason and emotion, Pascal shows that he was, according to Goldmann, thoroughly familiar with the idea of *Aufhebung* even if he does not use the term.[44] Human existence, in other words, is made of antagonistic elements, such as body and mind, good and evil, reason and passion, and yet the catch is that human

---

[42] Goldmann 1964a, pp. 3–21; 1959, pp. 13–31.

[43] The schematic analysis of 'world visions' as ideological expressions of social realities, changes and movements is hardly dialectic as well. Here we find that dogmatic rationalism, sceptical empiricism, the tragic vision, dialectical idealism, the animalistic view of nature, and mechanistic rationalism all become phases of bourgeois thought (Goldmann 1964a, pp. 14–21; 1959, pp. 24–31).

[44] Goldmann 1964a, p. 251; 1959, p. 281.

beings can neither accept one of these opposed elements nor live in a state of tension. What is needed, then, is some form of synthesis that overcomes the tensions. At times, Pascal is, for Goldmann, so close to Marx that he may as well be an earlier incarnation. But then Goldmann holds himself back, pointing out that Pascal was unable to make the final step beyond paradox to genuine dialectical thought in which equal and opposite truths come into contact with one another, largely due to the social circumstances of the seventeenth century. The mark of this limit is that Pascal sought a theological solution, resorting to God and faith as the way to sublate the tensions, rather than the materialist sublation of Marx.[45] Pascal came so close, but did not quite get over the line to genuine dialectical thought. Goldmann may not resort to God, but unfortunately he too does not quite make it to the line of genuine dialectical historical analysis.

If we were going to offer such an analysis, then we would need to begin on a different note. In asking how the texts of Pascal and the thought of Jansenism respond to their economic and social context, I would suggest that a better approach is that such texts give off signals and hints of their context rather than any direct expression. One way in which such hints appear is by seeing texts as efforts to solve intractable contradictions in the social and economic spheres (an approach championed by Fredric Jameson, among others). The catch is that the contradictions do not disappear; they are displaced in the literary and intellectual work in question in all manner of ways, not least of which is that form of the work. Thus, the ongoing debate about the order of the fragments that make up the *Pensées* (especially since they were not ordered by Pascal), the fact that they are fragments and not a complete work, indeed that Pascal was unable to turn this contradictory collection into a coherent and logical work,[46] all suggest that the disruptions of the time manifest themselves obliquely in Pascal's text. And, if we were to include the

---

[45] Goldmann 1964a, pp. 215, 218–19, 258–9; 1959, pp. 240–1, 244–5, 289–90.
[46] For all his discussion of paradox and fragment, Goldmann misses the opportunity to make something of the disorder of the fragments, preferring to seek coherence and order: 'The order in which the *Pensées* are presented does nevertheless affect the reader's understanding of the work, and there does seem to me to be one particular order which is better than the others: the one which begins by insisting upon the paradoxical nature of man (wretchedness and greatness), leads us to the wager, and concludes by the valid but not compulsive reasons which Pascal gives, in his discussion of miracles and of the Bible, for believing in Christianity' (Goldmann 1964a, p. 201; 1959, p. 226).

broader economic and social context, then surely it must be the ruptured transition from feudalism and its all-too-strong relics (aristocracy and so forth) to the capitalism championed by the bourgeoisie. That the absolute monarchy, playing off old and new, should arise at this time is no accident, for the era of the absolutist state was itself the crucial vanishing mediator of the larger economic transition under way.[47]

However, there is a final feature of such a method: the responses of texts to their contexts are often unexpected. The answers may be negative or positive, offer a complete alternative, block parts of the context, and so on. That is, texts are semi-autonomous: they may metaphorise their context, they may provide efforts to overcome intractable social and economic contradictions, but they do so in unanticipated ways. For example, a story of kinship or tribal conflict does not necessarily mean that such a text comes from a tribal situation. The text's tribal world may be an imaginary creation in a different context, perhaps to provide an alternative model of human relations or distribution of resources. Or, in the case of Pascal, the way he deals with the problem of being faithful to God while living in an utterly sinful world can hardly be said to be the expression of disappointed hopes, the frustrated thoughts of a jilted public servant. Rather, the dialectic of the Elect and the Damned from the perspective of human beings as intermediate beings who must treat all as though they are of the Elect, or indeed the ingenious effort at a solution through the wager, are unexpected and creative responses to rather than mere expressions of their context. In their form of paradox and contradiction, they may respond to the social and economic contradictions from which they arose, but the specific content is not what one would expect. A more expected response might be the high ground of total refusal in some Jansenists or the pragmatic accommodation of others – as one might expect from disappointed and disaffected public servants – but not Pascal's response.

Is Pascal among the Marxists?

The actuality (in the French sense) of Goldmann's study some fifty years after it was first published turns out to be its insights into the contradictions within Jansenism and especially Pascal. I am, like many others, far less taken with

---

[47] See Anderson 1974a, especially pp. 85–112.

Goldmann's method, which singularly fails to live up to all the dialectical huffing and puffing. But then the rickety ladder seems to have done its work.

At this point, a curious anomaly appears, one with three features: the method of homology or genetic structuralism is not up to the task; Goldmann claims elsewhere that this *method* derives from Georg Lukács; and he makes use of the *content* of some of Lukács's work to uncover some features of Jansenist thought. I have provided my reasons already as to why the method of homology is not up to the task, so let me focus on the other two points. As far as developing his method from Lukács, Goldmann claims that Lukács's *The Theory of the Novel*[48] is the source of his approach to the sociology of literature.[49] Apart from the problem that this text is one of Lukács's pre-Marxist and rather Kantian works, Lukács argues that a *genre* functions as a response to a distinct social and historical formation. In *The Theory of the Novel* and the more Kierkegaardian *Soul and Form*,[50] he goes so far as to argue that literature gives a clear voice to the tumult and chaos of a world 'abandoned by God' (see my chapter on Lukács). Even in these early works, Lukács already has (perhaps under the influence of Kierkegaard) a rather sophisticated dialectical understanding of the relation between literature and its context. The problem with these works is that the social context is rather vague; by the time of the Marxist work, *The Historical Novel*,[51] he would specify this in specific economic and social terms.

Goldmann is no fool, so what he does with this pre-Marxist work by Lukács is seek to tighten it up. Yet the path he chooses is one that runs in a different direction to Lukács: he seeks to lock in specific texts to distinct groups or subclasses, or he ties a particular genre into the various phases that he organises within a social formation. As for the former, the argument concerning Jansenism as the reflection of the disaffected legal *officiers* within the rising absolute monarchy of seventeenth-century France is an example. As for the latter, the argument in *Towards a Sociology of the Novel* concerning the novels of André Malraux seeks to lock those novels into the various phases of commodity fetishism and reification (not surprisingly, there are three – expansion-

---

[48] Lukács 1971b, 1994.
[49] Cohen argues that Piaget is also important, especially in Goldmann's idea of the 'transindividual subject' (Cohen 1994, pp. 132–7).
[50] Lukács 1974, 1971a.
[51] Lukács 1983a, 1965.

ist liberal capitalism of the late nineteenth and early twentieth centuries, the structural crises between 1912 and 1945, and state-regulated capitalism after 1945).[52] While the desire for tightening up Lukács's earlier work is admirable at one level, the way Goldmann goes about it loses the dialectical workings of Lukács's approach.

The third feature of this anomaly is that Goldmann's real insights into Jansenism derive not from the method of homology but from the explicit content of Lukács's texts. What he does is quote a specific text from Lukács when he needs to make a specific point concerning Jansenism. It really is a case of juxtaposing Lukács's arguments concerning different modes of thought or different genres in a different time to the situation and beliefs of Jansenism. Thus, in *The Hidden God*, we find a string of quotations from *Soul and Form*, so much so that the key insights into the tensions of Pascal and Jansenism are in fact provided by Lukács. So, we find the theme of *deus absconditus*, the world abandoned by God (that was also crucial in Lukács's *Theory of the Novel*),[53] the tension between faith and reason, between living in the world and yet refusing it, and even the dynamics of conversion in order to understand Pascal's crises of faith – all of which are central to Jansenist theology. By the time I managed to get to the end of the chapter on God,[54] I became so used to seeing a quotation from Lukács at each point made that I suspected this was as much a book about Lukács as it was about Jansenism.

Apart from providing a valuable leg-up the methodological ladder that threatens to tumble at any moment, Lukács enables Goldmann to bring off another sleight of hand. Time and again, Goldmann lists Lukács as a third member of a triumvirate that includes Marx and Engels. Lukács is the great successor who carries on the Marxist intellectual tradition and raises it to even greater heights. And, yet, the Lukács who provides the crucial insights into the tensions of Jansenism is the author of *Soul and Form*, a pre-Marxist and even Kierkegaardian text. However much one might want to argue that the later, Marxist, Lukács was able to give his earlier non-Marxist insights greater depth, all is not as Goldmann would have us believe. It is, in the end,

---

[52] Goldmann 1975, 1964b.
[53] Lukács 1971b, 1994.
[54] Goldmann 1964a, pp. 22–39; 1959, pp. 32–49; see also Goldmann 1981, pp. 10–11.

a pre-Marxist Lukács who hands Goldmann his insights into the workings of Pascal's texts.

However, what this sleight of hand allows Goldmann to do is connect Pascal ever more closely to Marx, so much so that they are cousins, if not half-brothers in the same large family. I have commented on some elements of this close association in Goldmann's text above, both in terms of the dialectic (Pascal is a Marxist dialectician, but then not quite) and the tension within Marxism as a programme thoroughly immersed in this world and yet focused on rejecting it in favour of a qualitatively better one. Goldmann develops a number of other comparisons, such as Pascal's search for God being analogous to the socialist search for the ideal community, or, indeed, the rationalist's search for truth and fame – all of which Goldmann's describes as the search for totality and wholeness.[55] Or Christian faith in God is like the Marxist faith in the future: it is a wager that such a faith will, one day, be proved true.[56]

These comparisons between Pascal and Marxism, or indeed between Christianity and Marxism may work at a rather superficial level, and they have been used to castigate Marxism as yet another (secular) religion with a feeble faith. To his credit, Goldman embraces these points to make them a strength rather than a weakness of Marxism. Yet I am less interested in Marxist faith or the search for another 'god'. What is far more fascinating is an insight Goldmann provides despite himself, and that is the tension between a Marxism that rejects the world while being thoroughly immersed in it.

---

[55] Goldmann 1964a, p. 180; 1959, p. 202.

[56] 'Marxist faith is faith in the future which men make for themselves in and through history. Or, more accurately, in the future that we must make for ourselves by what we do, so that this faith becomes a "wager" which we make that our actions will, in fact, be successful. The transcendent element present in this faith is not supernatural and does not take us outside or beyond history; it merely takes us beyond the individual. This is sufficient to enable us to claim that Marxist thought leaps over six centuries of Thomist and Cartesian rationalism and renews the Augustinian tradition. It does not, of course, do this by reintroducing the same idea of transcendence, but by affirming two things: that values are founded in an objective reality which can be relatively if not absolutely known (God for Saint Augustine, history for Marx); and that the most objective knowledge which man can obtain of any historical fact presupposes his recognition of the existence of this reality as the supreme value'. (Goldmann 1964a, p. 90; 1959, p. 99.)

By way of conclusion: Marxism as a secular and anti-secular project

Let me bring the various elements I have drawn from Goldmann – the tension between the Elect and the Damned as an internal tension of an intermediate being, the treatment of everyone as though they are of the Elect, the element of doubt, but above all the tension of refusing the world from within – together in the following manner: the tension within Marxism between being immersed in the world and yet not of it may be put in terms of a tension between secularism and anti-secularism. If we define the base sense of secularism as a system of thought and action, indeed a way of living that draws its terms purely from this age and from this world, then Marxism is both thoroughly secular and anti-secular. Other, popular senses of secularism may derive from this basic sense, especially the idea that secularism is an anti-religious programme, that it entails the separation of church and state, and that one must keep theology well and truly away from the proper scientific disciplines.[57] But let me stay with the prime meaning of secularism: as a way of acting and thinking that draws its terms from this world, the implication is that a fully secular programme does not draw its reference point from something beyond this world, whether that is a god or the gods above, or a better society and economic system in the future. On the first count, religion is disqualified; on the second count, Marxism is ruled out of order. So we have a delectable paradox: Marxism is thoroughly secular in one sense (did not Marx develop his deepest insights by immersing himself in the study of capitalism?), but, in another, it is not (it takes as its reference point a better society beyond capitalism).

This tension may take various forms, such as that between a reliance on the logic of history and yet taking action to change history,[58] a tension that lies at the heart of Calvinism: on the one hand, we are in the hands of God who has predestined us to salvation or damnation, and yet we must constantly show the fruits of our election by ceaseless activity. Or, indeed, within Jansenism: even though God may have decided between the Elect and the Damned, we mortals do not know what that decision is and so must act as though everyone were of the Elect and seek to bring them around to realise that.

---

[57] The detail of this argument may be found in Boer 2007b.
[58] Goldmann 1964a, p. 303; 1959, p. 338.

The key lies, however, in what Goldmann calls the status of the intermediate being, caught (often unbearably) between the Elect and the Damned. It is not so much that Marxism is either a secular or an anti-secular programme, but that it lies in between these two possibilities. Marxism is engaged in a perpetual negotiation, a dialectic if you like, between rejecting and refusing the world of capitalism and struggling within it. Or, even more tightly, one works within the world in order to bring about its demise.

Chapter Two
The Stumbling Block of Fredric Jameson

>...the biblical stumbling block, which gives Utopia its savor and its bitter freshness.[1]

After Goldmann, the second of the dialectical Marxists is Fredric Jameson. My major concern is the interplay between religion and utopia in Jameson's recent *Archaeologies of the Future*, arguably among the most enjoyable and intriguing of all his works.[2] As the culmination of a lifelong love of science fiction and utopian literature, it brings together many of his reflections concerning utopia over some three decades (indeed, half of the book is a collection of his various essays on science fiction that many have been urging him to gather in one place for quite some time).[3] In this work, Jameson faces a tension. As a Marxist, he assumes that religion has been superseded. Its forms may continue, but its content is a thing of the past. However, he also wishes to operate with a hermeneutics of suspicion and recovery, or what he calls a hermeneutics of ideology and utopia. According to this approach, utopian possibilities

---

[1] Jameson 2005b, p. 180.
[2] Jameson 2005b.
[3] The book has already generated some commentary, although none of it deals with the question of religion and utopia; see Fitting 2006; Cevasco 2005; McNeill 2005. The same applies to the earlier collection of essays in the *Utopian Studies* journal on Jameson and utopia; see Fitting 1998; Buchanan 1998; von Boeckmann 1998; Alexander 1998; Wegner 1998; see also Jameson 1998a.

emerge from even the most retrograde material – religion included. Although these two approaches to religion were first formulated in his earlier work, both of them appear in *Archaeologies of the Future*.

So I begin by outlining this tension in some of Jameson's earlier work (upon which I have written elsewhere). From there, I trace what I call his sidelining of religion when dealing with utopia, a move that we would expect if we assume that religion is no longer relevant. Then I pick up the various moments in which he brings his hermeneutics of ideology and utopia into play. These include his discussions of the role of magic within fantasy literature and of apocalyptic. While the first leaves him open to criticism in his use of Feuerbach and the small sample pool of fantasy (I contrast his reading with the work of China Miéville), the second comes all too close to his own argument that utopia entails rupture. I close by pursuing the dialectic of religion and utopia further, picking up and expanding his comments on medieval theology and the utopian role of religion (both Catholic and Protestant) in Thomas More's *Utopia*. My underlying agenda is to retrieve from Jameson the utopian possibilities of some aspects of religion, especially since religion provides – with all the expected ambiguities – a vast store-house of utopian dreams, wishes and stories. The catch is that these possibilities are rather wily and I need to work a little to track them down.

Before I sink into my main argument, a comment on the stumbling block, or *skandalon* as it is in Greek or *michshol* in Hebrew: they are not uncommon words in the Bible, referring almost universally to what makes one miss the mark, err or sin. And more often than not someone puts a stumbling block in your way, as Leviticus 19:14 shows brilliantly: 'You shall not curse the deaf or put a stumbling block before the blind'.[4] The stumbling block is, then, what trips you up, what breaks the path you are following, what you would rather avoid but cannot. I am not, of course, suggesting that Jameson's stumbling block causes him to sin, or indeed that he must deal with Christ crucified, but that religion trips him up more than once.

---

[4] There is but one semi-positive use, and that comes in 1 Corinthians 1:23: 'But we preach Christ crucified, a stumbling block to Jews and folly to Gentiles'.

Supersession versus a dialectic of ideology and utopia

Out of a range of earlier engagements with religion,[5] two items bear directly on my discussion here: Jameson's line that religion is really an earlier and inchoate language for political and social debates; his appropriation of Paul Ricoeur's theologically inspired hermeneutics of suspicion and recovery.

As for the first point, Jameson makes the intriguing comment in his essay on Augustine that 'religion is a figural form whereby utopian issues are fought out'.[6] One reading of this statement is that religion really means something else, that it is a language or code for other issues and battles, whether cultural, political, social and so on. Add to this comment another of his arguments, namely that religion is a fore-runner for something more complex such as the completion of the Christian doctrines of providence and even predestination in historical materialism,[7] and we end up with a position like this: although religious forms have carried through in our language and thought, religion itself has been superseded. Religion may once have given expression – in an inchoate fashion – to certain economic and political realities, but now we have better ways of dealing with such matters. Engels had argued as much in his essays on Thomas Müntzer and early Christianity[8] and it ties in rather neatly with the rather conventional Marxist (and, indeed, tired old secular) position that one should oppose any transcendent reference point.

Unfortunately, there is always a danger of reductionism in approaching religion as a language or code. So let me draw on another of Jameson's earlier strategies to read somewhat differently the statement, 'religion is a figural form whereby utopian issues are fought out'. This strategy comes from the important discussion of Paul Ricoeur's hermeneutics of suspicion and recovery in Jameson's *Political Unconscious*.[9] Drawing upon Ricoeur's early

---

[5] These include the background of medieval biblical allegory and Northropp Frye for his own three-level method of Marxist interpretation, which Jameson explores in *The Political Unconscious*, 1981, pp. 69–74 (see my discussion in Boer 1996, pp. 3–41 and Boer 2005a), the engagement with Walter Benjamin in terms of the same allegorical schema in *Marxism and Form*, Jameson 1971a, pp. 60–83, the historicising of religion as the ideology or 'cultural dominant' of that imprecise period known as 'pre-capitalist formation' in Jameson 1986 (see also Boer 1996, pp. 58–68), and a study of Augustine in which heretical sects become analogous to insurrectionary groups in Jameson 1996.

[6] Jameson 1996, p. 161.
[7] See the essay on Milton, Jameson 1986.
[8] Engels 1978, 1990. See my detailed discussion in Boer in press-a.
[9] Jameson 1981, pp. 282–6.

Freud and Philosophy,[10] Jameson wishes to turn this double hermeneutics into a more Marxist one, now in terms of ideological and utopian hermeneutics.[11] For Ricoeur, the key is not to overturn the moment of suspicion but to find what is positive in that moment in order to move onto recovery. So, also, with Jameson's reworking: utopian interpretation seeks out the utopian dimensions of even the most reactionary, resistant and degraded material, searching for the point where, especially in the very act of avoidance and concealment, the wish for something vastly new and better shows through.[12]

Although Ricoeur frames his discussion in psychoanalytical terms – the negative moment unmasks the repressive surface and the positive moment releases the fantasy – Jameson is all too aware that theology lies just below the surface in Ricoeur's thought. Rather than following Jameson's path and arguing that religion has been superseded and all that remains are its figural traces – such as Ricoeur's method – I would like to suggest a different take on religion. And this involves nothing less than interpreting religion in light of Jameson's hermeneutics of ideology and utopia. In other words, it becomes possible to locate the utopian possibilities of religion from within the negative, ideological moment. It is in this sense that I read his prescription:

> a Marxist negative hermeneutic, a Marxist practice of ideological analysis proper, must in the practical work of reading and interpretation be exercised *simultaneously* with a Marxist positive hermeneutic, or a decipherment of the Utopian impulses of these same still ideological texts.[13]

Indeed, Jameson has argued on more than one occasion that, rather than the sparring partners they are so often represented as being, Marxism and reli-

---

[10] Ricoeur 1970.

[11] In fact, Jameson argues that the equivalent to Ricoeur's hermeneutics of recovery may be found within the Marxist tradition. Apart from Bloch's 'principle of hope', there is Bakhtin's notion of the dialogical and the carnival and then the Frankfurt School's concept of *promesse de bonheur*. In 'Science Versus Ideology' from 1983 – a text sprinkled with eschatological passages from the prophet Isaiah – Jameson reworks a traditional Marxist opposition in terms of a similar dialectical understanding of ideology. In this case, 'science' becomes 'ideological interpretation', or the negative hermeneutic, while 'ideology' is reinterpreted as positive or 'utopian interpretation'.

[12] As Jameson puts it, '*all* class consciousness – or in other words, all ideology in the strongest sense, including the most exclusive forms of ruling-class consciousness just as much as that of oppositional or oppressed classes – is in its very nature Utopian' (Jameson 1981, p. 289).

[13] Jameson 1981, p. 296.

gion, or, more specifically, Christianity, both gain rather than lose from their affinities with each other: 'any comparison of Marxism with religion is a two-way street'?[14]

In *Archaeologies of the Future* – the major focus of this chapter – we find both of these approaches operating in some tension with each other. While Jameson will often sidestep religion in his discussion of utopia, thereby following his line that religion has been superseded, at others this double hermeneutic of ideology and utopia shows its face. In what follows, I explore this tension, concluding with some suggestions as to what a dialectical reading of religion and utopia might look like in light of Jameson's own suggestions.

Sidestepping religion

Usually, Jameson seeks to sideline religion. He keeps religion on the edges of his discussion, constantly skirting it, occasionally sidling up a little closer, alighting on it here and there, absorbing it or – more often – sidestepping it by one stratagem or another. One phrase in particular functions unwittingly as a programme for this strategy of sidestepping. In discussing the call to abolish money, he writes: 'As a vision, it solicits a return to those older, often religious, anti-capitalist ideologies which denounced money and interest and the like; but *as none of those are alive and viable any longer in global late capitalism...*'.[15] Here, he continues an older argument which I noted earlier: religious ideologies are not even quaint; they are simply dead and buried, no longer viable in the context of late capitalism. One might want to contest this point rather strongly, given the resurgence of religion as a major factor in global politics. But I can agree with the more modest version: the motivations provided by religious ideologies for programmes such as the abolition of money do not inspire people any longer, so we will need to look for others. However, my interest in this statement lies at another level, for it does provide a slogan of sorts for sidelining religion in his discussion of utopia.

A rather telling example of this side-stepping of religion comes in the midst of a longer reflection on the various permutations of Plato's very useful

---

[14] Jameson 1981, p. 285. See also Jameson 1971a, pp. 116–18.
[15] Jameson 2005b: 231, italics mine. For a longer discussion of how he sees theological categories thoroughly secularised in (especially German) philosophy, see Jameson 1998b, p. 79.

opposition between opinion and truth (*doxa* and *episteme*, which also includes Marx and then Althusser's recasting of the opposition in terms of ideology and science). Here is Jameson:

> If the conceptual frameworks outlined above have any relevance, we ought to be able at the very least to register Utopian opinion or doxa by our own readerly reactions, by the *barely perceptible movements of irritation or annoyance that are aroused by this or that detail* of the Utopian scheme, by momentary withdrawals of credibility and trust, by punctual exasperation that can only too easily be turned against the writer in the form of contempt or amusement.... Thus, for example, More's account of the Utopian churches may startle us, owing to the seemingly gratuitous character of the choice of feature and the explanation given it:
>
>> The temples are all rather dark. This feature is due not to an ignorance of architecture but to the deliberate intention of the priests. They think that excessive light makes the thoughts wander, whereas scantier and uncertain light concentrates the mind and conduces to devotion.
>
> The reader at once tends to transfer this opinion to More himself.... Some commentators have interpreted this detail as a taste for Romanesque churches over Gothic ones, thus adducing a further sign and symptom of the medieval cast of More's imagination: if so, our reaction can only thereby be strengthened.[16]

For Jameson, this is an example of More's own opinion rather than utopian truth. (Opinion, as Alain Badiou has reminded us recently, is, after all, cheap and common; truth is rare.) Note what Jameson writes: this particular detail is irritating, annoying and exasperating, leading to a potential withdrawal of trust. And that detail is nothing other than the 'minor blemish' of the utopian churches. It is, of course, intriguing why this particular example should be chosen as an annoying blemish, and not some other.

I would suggest that this example of the utopian churches is symptomatic of what goes on throughout *Archaeologies of the Future*, specifically concerning the uncomfortable interplay between utopia and religion. My suggestion is not merely that Jameson would prefer it if religion was not an issue in utopian

---

[16] Jameson 2005b, pp. 49–50.

thought, that its presence is somewhat irritating.[17] I also want to argue a much stronger point: religion, at least those more eschatological types so beloved by Ernst Bloch, comes uncomfortably close to Jameson's own argument, namely, that utopia is concerned with disruption.

I will return to the question of disruption, especially in terms of of eschatology and apocalyptic, a little later, but now I offer one other example of the way the religious element of utopias is (perhaps unconsciously) sidelined. This one appears in a discussion of the various utopian dreamers and schemers, the makers of imaginary constitutions and city plans in the time since Thomas More's *Utopia* of 1516.[18] Not merely social critics, they were also intellectuals, Jameson points out, with 'a supplementary taste for schemes of all kinds'.[19] In Jameson's main text, he does not, however, mention what those schemes were. But we do find out in a rather long footnote.[20] Thus, during the English Revolution, there was a 'proliferation of *revolutionary-religious "sects"'*, which were regarded by the authorities as 'heresies *theological* and social', such as the 'Muncerians, Apostolikes, Separatists, Caharists, Silentes, Enthusiasts, etc.'.[21] And these were merely variations within one group out of many, namely, the Anabaptists. Why place such an observation about the religious nature of these utopian groups in a footnote rather than the main text? It is a somewhat convenient strategy for sidelining an issue. A similar pattern is operating in this case as with the one concerning Thomas More's utopian churches: an element of utopias that recurs often enough to be a consistent feature is something that Jameson would rather put to the side.

Magic and fantasy

These two examples – one concerning Thomas More's utopian churches and the other the religious nature of many revolutionary and utopian sects –

---

[17] A little later, he suggests that religion has staged an (unwelcome) recent return to written utopias. That return, especially in light of its small role in written utopias from the time after More's religious tolerance through until the 1960s, may be attributed to the current opposition between fundamentalism and Western political tolerance. See Jameson 2005b, p. 146.
[18] More 1989.
[19] Jameson 2005b, p. 43.
[20] Most of the footnote is a quotation from Frank and Fritzie Manuel's book, *Utopian Thought in the Western World* (Manuel and Manuel 1979).
[21] Jameson 2005b, p. 43.

are sufficient to establish a pattern in Jameson's treatment of religion and utopia.[22] They are consistent with the line I noted earlier – religion has been superseded. However, at other points, we begin to see a glimmer of his other strategy, namely the hermeneutics of ideology and utopia.

The most interesting treatment of religion comes in the face-off between the genres of science fiction and fantasy.[23] Here, he acknowledges the way fantasy has overtaken science fiction in popularity, and that nothing much is going to change that situation in the foreseeable future. But I wish to pay close attention to the way he sets up the opposition:

> In the grand opposition between Enlightenment and religion, we find the former taking history, especially in anthropological SF as 'the rise of 'civilization' across the historical ages; while the other pole of religion will eventually...migrate into fantasy and provide the Enlightenment paradigm's mirror image: history as the loss of magic and the decline of the 'old world' of the village and the order of the sacred.[24]

This is a rather well-worn contrast between science fiction and fantasy: science fiction trails the dust of the Enlightenment, history and the question of the rise and fall of civilisations, whereas fantasy is the inheritor of (medieval) religion, especially its underside, magic, and its narrative tends to follow the course of disenchantment, the fading away of magic and 'the sacred'. Jameson will go on to build up the opposition in various ways – religion versus science, magic versus technology, nature versus history, organic versus machine, Middle

---

[22] I cannot help but provide one further moment where an off-the-cuff example reveals far more than at first appears. In his proposal for a federation of diverse utopias, modelled heavily on Kim Stanley Robinson's *Mars* trilogy, Jameson writes the following: 'A plurality of Utopias? But what if one misguided group embraces patriarchy, or something even worse? According to this fundamental principle, you simply leave, and go to another Utopia, one in which *strict religious doctrine* is maintained, like Geneva, or secular republicanism, in imitation of the Roman Republic, or simple hedonism and licentiousness, or a traditional clan structure (into which you would probably have to intermarry or enter as a dependant or a slave)' (Jameson 2005b, pp. 220–1, emphasis mine). The reference to 'strict religious doctrine...like Geneva' is of course an allusion to John Calvin's utopian experiment in Geneva (1541–64) where city government was in the hands of pastors, elders, deacons and a consistory court. The severest punishments were for purely religious aberrations, but Geneva was also a refuge for English Protestant refugees. Again, I want to ask why this rather negative example is used among the others. Is it recognition of the religious dimension of many utopian schemes, but also a blockage of that feature by the negative example?

[23] Jameson 2005b, pp. 60–7; see also Jameson 2002a.

[24] Jameson 2005b, p. 95.

Ages versus industrial capitalism – but my interest is in what he does with fantasy and religion. He argues that the medieval world saturates fantasy – aristocratic and peasant, binaries of Good and Evil, radical otherness (Islam) and peasant egalitarianism, but, above all, religion, running all the way from the tortured god, sin and punishment of wealthy Christianity of the aristocracy to the survivals of older nature religions among the peasantry with their ribald festivals and pilgrimages – except that these elements are rearranged in all sorts of ways.[25] And nothing is rearranged more than religion, for fantasy picks up the underside of medieval religion, namely the pervasive but perpetually repressed world of the occult and magic. So we find fantasy full of sword and sorcery, good and bad magic, powerful stones and rings and whatnot.

Feuerbach versus Marx

My interest is what Jameson does with religion and magic (which he really treats as the same thing) within fantasy. This is where it starts to get interesting, for he provides the first glimpse of what a utopian reading of religion might look like. It should come as no surprise that he will do so by means of a dialectical interpretation: rather than leaving the opposition as it is, he gets to work on the dialectical interaction of the two poles of the opposition.

To begin with, he asserts that magic is the 'fundamental motif' of fantasy,[26] although he also discusses its relation to history and the problem of the

---

[25] A negative example, for Jameson, is Tolkien's anti-Enlightenment and anti-modern construction of a somewhat homey village atmosphere (the 'Shire') along with homogenous nature spiritualism that cuts across castes, a spiritualism that appeals to 'know-nothing American fundamentalisms all the way to the higher-toned Anglican reactionaries' (Jameson 2005b, p. 61).

[26] Jameson 2005b, p. 66. The opposition is, of course, too neat, for science fiction does engage with religion in some notable cases. Rather than magic, he suggests that what we find is that in science fiction 'religion is a kind of mediatory space; it is the black box in which infrastructure and superstructure mysteriously intermingle and celebrate an enigmatic identity – at one with mode of production and culture alike (both of whose concepts it ambiguously anticipates). Religion was perhaps the most ancient organizing concept in the emergence of anthropology as a discipline: the ultimate determining instance for national or racial character, the ultimate source of cultural difference itself, the marker of the individuality of the various peoples in history (a role it still plays in Hegel and whose revival today we can witness in ideologues like Samuel Huntingdon). It can thus provide the most facile solutions for SF, as a kind of ready-made thought of the other; and at the same time stage the most interesting conceptual dilemmas and form-problems' (Jameson 2005b, p. 95). Later

ethical binary of Good and Evil. But what are we to do with magic? In short, it becomes the locus of the utopian potential of fantasy, and the way it does so is drawn from Feuerbach, especially his theory of projection. For Feuerbach, religion is a projection of 'unalienated human creativity'.[27] Religion projects the best possibilities of human activity – labour and productivity, intelligence, imagination and so on – only to hypostatise them all into an entity or force that is exterior from human beings. That entity becomes a figure, a 'god' who appears to human beings as a being in his own right, one that returns to command, punish and save. This, for Feuerbach, is the source of the attraction and continued potency of religion. For Jameson, this pattern of projection and return applies directly to magic in fantasy literature. It is the secret to the appeal of magic in fantasy, a 'figure for the enlargement of human powers and their passage to the limit, their actualization of everything latent and virtual in the stunted human organism of the present'.[28] Magic is, in short, a figure for un-alienated humanity.

A clear instance of Jameson's hermeneutics of ideology and utopia, such an argument provides a wonderful dialectical inversion of the relation between fantasy and science fiction: it is precisely the magical and apolitical element of fantasy that enables this utopian leap to un-alienated existence. Even more, it is precisely because fantasy is somehow freed from all those constraints of history – explored by science fiction at great length – that it is able to make that leap. And, if we have not quite had enough of such dialectics, Jameson offers one further move at the end of the chapter on the 'Great Schism' between fantasy and science fiction. Here, he suggests that since fantasy is so wedded to magic, it must also trace the disenchantment of the world that comes with the decline of the world in which it held sway. But this is precisely the moment when some Novum (to echo Bloch) can emerge: 'when the world of magic

---

on, he observes that, in Lem's *Solaris*, religion is 'as much an allegory of the scientific process – the final discovery of its nature serving the narrative of the revelation of the Absolute – as a projection of our perplexity before a closed and conscious single-celled being.... And yet there remains the possibility that, like us, Solaris is itself an imperfect being, an imperfect or sick god, like that insane deity of Schelling who has to create the world in order to save himself: in that case, we understand Solaris better than we know' (Jameson 2005b, p. 122).

[27] Jameson 2005b, p. 65.
[28] Jameson 2005b, p. 66.

becomes little more than nostalgia', he writes, 'the Utopian wish can appear in all its vulnerability and fragility'.[29]

I must admit that I find this a curious move. To begin with, it does valorise magic, religion, and thereby the genre of fantasy as a whole. And the ingenuity comes from Jameson's commitment to dialectical thinking, whereby he does not merely dismiss fantasy but seeks to read its contrast to science fiction in a productive fashion. Even more, it stays true to his oft-repeated adage, that all manner of ideological and political projects bear within them a utopian seed.

But the first question I want to ask is: why such a step back to Feuerbach? Feuerbach does give us the original theory of religion as projection, one that Durkheim, for one, would shape into a collective rather than individualist theory.[30] However, the deeper impetus for the choice of Feuerbach comes, as Jameson hints,[31] from Marx himself, especially in the fourth thesis on Feuerbach:

> Feuerbach starts out from the fact of religious self-estrangement, of the duplication of the world into a religious world and a secular one. His work consists in resolving the religious world into its secular basis. But that the secular basis lifts off from itself and establishes itself as an independent realm in the clouds....[32]

---

[29] Jameson 2005b, p. 71.

[30] For Durkheim, religion gathers up the best elements of collective, social life and renders them in an ideal form that acts as guide for society for a time. Thus, for religion, 'upon the real world where profane life is lived, he superimposes another that, in a sense, exists only in his thought, but one to which he ascribes a higher kind of dignity than he ascribes to the real world of profane life' (Durkheim 1995, p. 424). Like science, religion for Durkheim is a 'collective consciousness', one that is a 'fundamental and permanent aspect of humanity' (Durkheim 1995, p. 1). One cannot help but notice the echoes of the seventh thesis of Feuerbach: 'Feuerbach, consequently, does not see that the "religious sentiment" is itself a social product, and that the abstract individual which he analyses belongs to a particular form of society' (Marx 1976c, p. 5). Earlier, Jameson argues that Durkheim's theory of religion may well apply to culture as a whole (Jameson 1981, pp. 292–6).

[31] Jameson 2005b, p. 65.

[32] Marx 1976c, p. 4. Here is the version as edited by Engels: 'Feuerbach starts out from the fact of religious self-estrangement, of the duplication of the world into a religious, imaginary world and a real one. His work consists in resolving the religious world into its secular basis. He overlooks the fact that after completing this work, the chief thing still remains to be done. For the fact that the secular basis lifts off from itself and establishes itself as an independent realm in the clouds...'. Marx 1976b, p. 7.

Marx here grants Feuerbach's point: religion is indeed a projection from this world. The 'secular basis lifts off from itself and establishes itself as an independent realm', he writes, and Engels emphasises their agreement with his editorial addition to the fourth thesis: 'He [Feuerbach] overlooks the fact that after completing this work, the chief thing still remains to be done'.[33] At this point, Engels's editorial intervention is spot on. Feuerbach has taken the first step, laying the groundwork for a proper intervention, which is to condemn and overcome the tensions that bring about such a projection in the first place. However, there is far more. I quite deliberately quoted only the first half of the fourth thesis on Feuerbach. The remainder reads:

> Thesis 4:... But that the secular basis lifts off from itself and establishes itself as an independent realm in the clouds can only be explained by the inner strife and intrinsic contradictoriness of this secular basis. The latter must, therefore, itself be both understood in its contradiction and revolutionised in practice. Thus, for instance, once the earthly family is discovered to be the secret of the holy family, the former must then itself be destroyed in theory and in practice.[34]

The whole point in this thesis is not merely that Feuerbach has carried out a necessary first step from which Marx and Engels may advance, but that his analysis is radically incomplete. Without moving on to show how such projections arise from the 'inner strife and intrinsic contradictoriness' of the secular world, and without seeking to uncover and then revolutionise those contradictions, Feuerbach's approach is far too idealistic and individualistic.[35]

---

[33] Marx 1976b, p. 7.

[34] Marx 1976c, p. 4. Once again, here is Engels's edited version: 'For the fact that the secular basis lifts off from itself and establishes itself in the clouds as an independent realm can only be explained by the inner strife and intrinsic contradictoriness of this secular basis. The latter must itself, therefore, first be understood in its contradiction and then, by the removal of the contradiction, revolutionised in practice. Thus, for instance, once the earthly family is discovered to be the secret of the holy family, the former must then itself be criticised in theory and transformed in practice' (Marx 1976b, p. 7).

[35] The subsequent theses charge Feuerbach with individualism, although it might be worthwhile asking whether this criticism is a fair one: 'Thesis 6: Feuerbach resolves the essence of religion into the essence of *man*. But the essence of man is no abstraction inherent in each single individual. In its reality it is the ensemble of the social relations. Feuerbach, who does not enter upon a criticism of this real essence, is hence obliged: 1. To abstract from the historical process and to define the religious sentiment [*Gemüt*] regarded by itself, and to presuppose an abstract – *isolated* – human individual. 2.

All the same, it would be worth asking what Feuerbach does indeed say. Jameson quotes the following sentence: 'In the religious systole man propels his own nature from himself, he throws himself outward; in the religious diastole he receives the rejected nature into his heart again'.[36] I found I had to read this sentence a few times to see the point, but I was still puzzled by the use of biological terms – systole and diastole refer to the heart and its beating – to speak of religion. It does, however, make a little more sense in its context:

> God is the highest subjectivity of man abstracted from himself; hence man can do nothing of himself, all goodness comes from God. The more subjective God is, the more completely does man divest himself of his subjectivity, because God is, *per se*, his relinquished self, the possession of which he however again vindicates to himself. As the action of the arteries drives the blood into the extremities, and the action of the veins brings it back again, as life in general consists in a perpetual systole and diastole; so it is in religion. In the religious systole man propels his own nature from himself, he throws himself outward; in the religious diastole he receives the rejected nature into his heart again. God alone is the being who acts of himself, – this is the force of repulsion in religion; God is the being who acts in me, with me, through me, upon me, for me, is the principle of my salvation, of my good dispositions and actions, consequently my own good principle and nature, – this is the force of attraction in religion.[37]

Even more, in religion – although Feuerbach continues a long tradition in which 'religion' really means Christianity – human beings project what is best in themselves into the divine. As for the worst, that is the non-divine.[38] One way of putting it is that religion is an expression of the unrealised wishes of self-transcendence that each human being harbours, that they have not quite realised themselves in full. Again, Feuerbach:

> In religion man frees himself from the limits of life; he here lets fall what oppresses him, obstructs him, affects him repulsively; God is the

---

Essence, therefore, can be regarded only as "species", as an inner, mute, general character which unites the many individuals *in a natural way*' (Marx 1976c, p. 4).

[36] Feuerbach 1989, p. 31; quoted in Jameson 2005b, p. 65.

[37] Feuerbach 1989, p. 31.

[38] 'What man praises and approves, that is God to him; what he blames, condemns, is the non-divine. Religion is a *judgment*' (Feuerbach 1989, p. 97).

self-consciousness of man freed from all discordant elements; man feels himself free, happy, blessed in his religion, because he only here lives the life of genius, and keeps holiday.[39]

If we replace the words 'religion' and 'God' in this passage with 'magic', or rather 'magic in fantasy', then we come rather close to Jameson's argument. As I wrote a little earlier, I find this extremely curious. Either Jameson wishes to champion a pure Feuerbachian position, leaving Marx, for all his efforts to overtake Feuerbach, back in the rear of the pack with those who see religion as some 'pie in the sky'. Or, as I suspect, this role of magic in fantasy does not help fantasy all that much. For what happens is that fantasy ends up with Feuerbach, a precursor to a more complete Marxian move that seeks to uncover and overthrow the contradictions and alienations that generate religion in the first place.

What we have then is a Feuerbachian fantasy over against a more Marxian science fiction. This assumption, it seems to me, lies behind the following crucial sentence:

> If SF is the exploration of all the constraints thrown up by history itself – the web of counterfinalities and anti-dialectics which human production has itself produced – then fantasy is the other side of the coin and a celebration of human creative power and freedom which becomes idealistic only by virtue of the omission of precisely those material and historical constraints.[40]

Precisely because it is not held back by the material constraints of history, fantasy may lift off into the heavens and project an un-alienated and utopian human existence – what we might call a 'fantasy' in the sense of a wish or dream. The implication is that fantasy is certainly not going to get us there, to help us realise our dream, if I may put it that way. Rather, the path to that dream will emerge back here on the ground, through the contradictions of history. This is, of course, a standard Marxist move, namely that it is only through the tensions of lived economic history that we are able to step forward, however much it may seem that the path is blocked at times by various

---

[39] Feuerbach 1989, p. 98. And so, 'The fundamental dogmas of Christianity are realised wishes of the heart' (Feuerbach 1989, p. 140).
[40] Jameson 2005b, p. 66.

constraints. For Jameson, at least, it is science fiction's task to explore those tensions, constraints, blockages and so on.

The politics of fantasy

I would like to take this grudging appreciation of fantasy further, but before I do, there is one last problem with Jameson's treatment. This is a problem that other commentators will no doubt pick up, namely, the selectiveness of Jameson's examples. In his discussion of fantasy, Ursula LeGuin is the main exemplar, although Samuel Delany's *Nevèrÿon* series[41] and Anne McCaffrey's multi-volume *Pern* series[42] do make the odd appearance. However, at the crux of his Feuerbachian move, it is LeGuin's *Earthsea* tetralogy[43] that becomes the focus. LeGuin is, of course, a wonderful writer and an abiding interest of Jameson, especially her more political novels such as *The Left Hand of Darkness* and *The Dispossessed*,[44] but the politics always seem to dip below her Taoism when it comes to the crunch. Even more, in the *Earthsea* series, magic is very much what makes the world go round.

In light of this limited sample of fantasy, I wonder what Jameson would have made of China Miéville's *Bas Lag* novels,[45] beyond one ever-so-slight engagement,[46] or, for that matter, Jeff VanderMeer,[47] Kirsten Bishop[48] and the rest of the 'New Weird'. Let me stay with Miéville, whose wonderful alternative world, with the imperial, oppressive and capitalist New Crobuzon, the floating free city of Armada, or the revolutionary train in perpetual motion called the Iron Council, along with all manner of species of which human beings are only one among a number – the insect-like Khepri, the frog-like Vodanyhoi, the Cactus people, the scab-mettlers, cray, Remade and so on – operate in an economic and political world in which oppression and revolution are only a moment away. Magic is also woven into the fabric of this world, but a reader would be hard-pressed to see it as either a central feature or as a projection that

---

[41] Delaney 1983, 1993, 1994a, 1994b.
[42] McCaffrey 1968 and so on, almost endlessly.
[43] LeGuin 2001 – although by now it is a sexalogy: LeGuin 2003a, 2003b.
[44] See Jameson 1975; 2005b, pp. 267–80.
[45] Miéville 1998, 2000, 2002, 2004; see also Miéville 2005.
[46] Jameson 2002a.
[47] Vandermeer 2003, 2004, 2006.
[48] Bishop 2003.

lifts beyond the historical and economic limits of human existence to offer a utopian glimpse. Rather, magic functions much more like Lévi-Strauss's *pensée sauvage* – a category Jameson likes to invoke – which designates not merely 'thought gone wild', but a distinct and coherent alternative to science.[49] Except that, in Miéville's novels, magic is very much part of science, indeed part of the empirical fabric of Bas Lag, so much so that the university has its departments of the various magics, with their long history of research and teaching, and the contracts with industry, government and the military merely indicate how interwoven magic is with a world that feels all too familiar. Above all, the possibilities for redemption lie not in some meditation upon magic, or in harnessing good magic against bad magic, but in the dynamics of exploitation, class and revolutionary groups. If Armada and the Iron Council (the latter far more revolutionary than the former) make use of magic in their quests for survival, then so too do the militia and the New Crobuzon government include magic in their means of suppressing revolt. In this thorough reworking of fantasy, Miéville breaks the bounds of the genre, comprehensively recasts it and thereby renders it deeply political.[50] What we do not find is that this fantasy is ahistorical, or caught up in the struggle of Good and Evil, and it is especially not enamoured of magic as the un-transcendable horizon of fantasy. The utopian possibilities lie squarely with the constraints and contradictions of history, no matter how alternative that history might be.

I do not, however, want to discard entirely Jameson's argument concerning the utopian role of magic within fantasy. In many cases, magic does seem to operate in the way he suggests, especially when items within the genre become reflections on the possibilities of magic as un-alienated human existence, rather than a mere plot device. What I want to retrieve from Jameson is something a little different. Let me focus on the form of Jameson's argument rather that the content. Unwittingly, Jameson points to a role for fantasy-like narratives among the Left. In projecting what a complete and un-alienated life might be like, fantasy produces what I have elsewhere described as political

---

[49] Lévi-Strauss 1966.
[50] Variously called 'weird fiction' or 'fantastic fiction', his works fall mainly into the intersections between fantasy and science fiction with a good dose of horror (he has won both the Arthur C. Clarke and British Fantasy awards for his work). However, any creative new direction like this operates both through the intersection of various genres and their reshaping in the process.

myths.[51] By political myth, I mean an alternative language, one that is figurative and metaphorical, one that projects – to use Feuerbach's terms – stories of better worlds. In its own figurative way, political myth throws such worlds out from human desires and wishes. There is, however, a second moment in Feuerbach's analysis, when the projection returns to earth. For Feuerbach, such a return comes in the form of religion, with its god or gods, with its doctrines and beliefs. In the process of return, what is forgotten is that the initial projection comes from the best within human beings themselves. It seems to me that political myth works in a similar fashion, for the world it projects comes back as a distinct entity, a possible world for which one may strive and struggle. In other words, such political myth becomes a motivational and inspirational force that may actually have it own historical effect.

It soon becomes clear that the form of Feuerbach's argument, one that Jameson borrows in order to make a point concerning magic, may also apply elsewhere. That is to say, the pattern of projection and return is not restricted to magic within the genre of fantasy. The form of the argument applies just as well to the work of Miéville, who is in the business of producing an occasional political myth or two. Rather than the idealist and individualist argument concerning magic, in Miéville's case it becomes decidedly collective and political. I think, in particular, of the Iron Council in the book of the same name or Armada in *The Scar*, as precisely such projections. But the content of those projections are as political myths rather than magic, however ambiguous and troubled these utopian spaces might be. Even more, they are not merely narrative devices that render these novels 'political', especially in a deeply Marxist fashion, but they are the focus of meditations on the nature of political myth itself. Let me cite Miéville at this point:

'They say Iron Council's coming back'.

Her face had taken on such joy.

'It's coming back'.

All the things Ori could think of to say were obvious. He did not want to insult her, so he tried to think of something else to say, but could not.

'It's a fairy tale', he said.

'It ain't'.

---

[51] Boer 2008b.

'A fable. There's no Iron Council'.

'They want you to think that. If there's no Iron Council then we ain't never took power. But if there is, and there is, we did it before, we can do it again'.

'Good jabber, listen to yourself...'

'You telling me you never seen the helios? What do you think that was? You think they built the bloody train by marching alongside each other, women, *whores*, at the front? Children riding the damn cab hood?'

'Something happened, of course it did, but they were put down. It was a strike is all. They're long dead –'

She was laughing. 'You don't know, you don't know. They wanted them dead, and they want them dead again, but they're coming back...It's coming back, and even just knowing that's a godsdamned inspiration'.[52]

Within the novel, the Iron Council (with its echoes of Trotsky's famous armoured train)[53] is the stuff of myth, at all levels of the word. Beginning as a strike at the construction head of the transcontinental railway, a strike that turns into open rebellion, the rebels – a mix of railway builders, guards, scientists, prostitutes, Remade and whoever wishes to join – take the train with all of its railway construction material beyond the end of the line. They continue to lay tracks for the train which they then pull up after it, in order to keep it moving. Soon enough, the Iron Council – the name for the revolutionary group and the train – becomes the stuff of legend and myth. Never quite sure whether the Iron Council is a figment of the revolutionary imagination (the ruling powers have a distinct interest in insisting that it *is* pure fiction), it becomes the basis of hopes and fears, inspiration and dread, depending on which side of politics the various characters and groups happen to sit. It is the inspiration for the Collective, a Paris-Commune-like free zone that clears a space for itself in the midst of New Crobuzon. The rumoured return of the Iron Council to the city produces apocalyptic anticipation. However, it is the very movement of the Iron Council, out from the edge of the railway (which subsequently becomes disused as the corporation behind it goes bankrupt) and into the warped Cacotopic Stain that echoes most closely Feuerbach's projection. As it passes from everyday knowledge, it gains a life of its own,

---

[52] Miéville 2004, pp. 393–4.
[53] See Boer 2008a.

one that it then lives up to on the return to the city some decades later – Feuerbach's return of an entity that was initially a projection. And it holds that status, embalmed on its final run into the city in a frozen moment of time before it can be destroyed by the militia – a perpetual entity.

So it does indeed seem as though we can get some political mileage from fantasy, although not quite in the sense that Jameson initially suggested. Rather than its use as an implicit quarantining of fantasy from the political possibilities of science fiction and utopian literature, Feuerbach's model comes in rather handy. Like religion, and indeed magic within fantasy, political myth may be seen to operate in a similar fashion, as the fantasy novels of China Miéville show only too well. Fantasy, it seems, may be just as politically valuable as science fiction and utopian literature.

Apocalyptic

The other great feature of Jameson's dealings with religion, at least in the context of the broader discussion of utopia, is his skirting of the question of apocalyptic. I must admit to being surprised by the lack of attention to apocalyptic,[54] especially since the category of utopia trails a long history in religious thought, and much of that history lies in the various traditions of apocalyptic with its fervent dreams and hopes. Ernst Bloch, of course, realised this history, and in his work the story of the utopian impulse includes the bright lights of Joachim de Fiore and Thomas Müntzer.[55] Indeed, when Jameson does talk about Bloch's deep and founding influence on utopian thought in the first pages of *Archaeologies of the Future*, he manages to omit religion, not to speak of the Bible. Along with Goethe's *Faustus*, the Bible was, of course, Bloch's great inspiration and he returns to it again and again to make yet a further point concerning utopia. By contrast, Jameson makes use of Wayne Hudson's summary of Bloch's project, who, in his otherwise salutary study, finds Bloch's interest in religion and the Bible highly problematic.[56] Indeed, he would

---

[54] Apart from the sparse texts I discuss here, there is one other passing reference to apocalyptic: 'The stars in the night sky are just such an apparition suspended in time, a multiplicity stretched immobile across space, whose other face is that firmament as the scroll of which Apocalypse tells us that it will be rolled up in the last days' (Jameson 2005b, p. 94).
[55] Bloch 1985, Volume 2; Boer 2007a, pp. 1–56; 2007b.
[56] Hudson 1982.

prefer that Bloch had not been so interested in the Bible or religion. Thus the quotation from Hudson in Jameson's text begrudgingly manages a reference to 'religious mystery' in its last two words.[57]

The problem, as far as Jameson is concerned, is that what passes for apocalyptic today – 'the increasingly popular visions of total destruction and of the extinction of life on Earth'[58] – is quite distinct from either the utopian concern with catastrophe or the genre of anti-utopias, whose agenda is to discount utopia as such. However, just when we think Jameson has conveniently sidelined apocalyptic as a concern, he then turns it on its dialectical head. Here is the relevant section:

> Yet this new term oddly enough brings us around to our starting point again, inasmuch as the original Apocalypse includes both catastrophe and fulfilment, the end of the world and the inauguration of the reign of Christ on earth, Utopia and the extinction of the human race all at once. Yet if the Apocalypse is neither dialectical (in the sense of including its Utopian 'opposite') nor some mere psychological projection, to be deciphered in historical or ideological terms, then it is probably to be grasped as metaphysical or religious, in which case its secret Utopian vocation consists in assembling a new community of readers and believers around itself.[59]

What Jameson is trying to do here is avoid the argument that apocalyptic includes the two extremes of complete obliteration and the inauguration of a new age, of the end of history and its beginning anew on an entirely different plane. In its place he attempts an alternative dialectical move: rather than focus on what will take place during the cataclysm and afterwards, the utopian import lies elsewhere, namely in a new community that is formed around the apocalyptic vision. While this is a good example of Jameson's hermeneutics of ideology and utopia, albeit with his usual ability to look awry and find an alternative utopian reading, the question I would like to explore is why he needs to do so. Why avoid the initial point that it includes both what would

---

[57] Jameson 2005b, p. 2. The only other reference to Bloch's passion for the Bible comes in the parenthetical comment, '(which are themselves ultimately theological ones as well)' – referring to Bloch's aesthetic categories (Jameson 2005b, p. 6).
[58] Jameson 2005b, p. 199.
[59] Ibid.

later be called utopia and anti-utopia within its own purview? And why cannot this dialectic include the new community of readers (and surely agents)?

In answering those questions, let me consider this section more closely. The section I have quoted really seems like an afterthought, and that impression is reinforced by the long footnote appended to its end, a footnote that is really a collection of notes and possible thoughts concerning apocalyptic. Two things strike me about this footnote: it elides the various distinctions he has just made, and it actually begins to develop a dialectic of apocalyptic, one that he has just said is not possible. On the first point: while Jameson is keen to distinguish between the recurring theme of science-fictional catastrophe and that of apocalyptic in the main text, in the footnote we find them merging. Thus, John Wyndham (of *Day of the Triffids* fame) and J.G. Ballard, who have both more than dabbled in science fiction, become exemplars of the catastrophe-rebirth pattern of apocalyptic. On the second point, Jameson does precisely what he initially felt was outside the scope of apocalyptic – begin a dialectical reading. Bouncing off Frank Kermode's suggestion that apocalyptic is a projection of the fears of one's own death and Freud's point that dreams about one's own death actually conceal a wish fulfilment, Jameson postulates that

> the end of the world may simply be the cover for a very different and more properly utopian wish-fulfillment: as when (in John Wyndam's novels, for example) the protagonist and a small band of other survivors of the catastrophe go on to found some smaller and more liveable collectivity after the end of modernity and capitalism.[60]

At this point, I am surprised that Philip K. Dick has not made an appearance, for here is a writer on whom Jameson has commented more than once and for whom one narrative sequence was precisely that of catastrophe-cum-renewal, although that renewal is hardly one to get excited about it, given the grim life on the other side of the catastrophe. I am equally surprised that the founding text of utopia as a modern genre – Thomas More's *Utopia*, to which Jameson gives extended attention – does not register here. I would suggest that More's

---

[60] Jameson 2005b, p. 199. Its historical conditions, he suggests, may provide 'the expression of the melancholy and trauma of the historical experience of defeat', which is how he suggests we 'interpret the immense eschatological jouissance of the greatest of modern apocalyptic writers, J.G. Ballard (1930–), as the expression of his experience of the end of the British Empire in the Second World War' (Jameson 2005b, p. 199).

work is a sustained and largely successful effort to secularise the category of apocalyptic and free it from the weight of its religious associations.

Apart from the content of the argument, to which I will return in a moment, I am intrigued by the way apocalyptic appears in Jameson's text. One long paragraph – largely a suggestion concerning genre (which apocalyptic in its original form most certainly is) – has an even longer footnote hanging off it. As I mentioned earlier, it really seems to me that apocalyptic needs a chapter on its own.[61] There is also something very symptomatic about the structure of this paragraph and heavy footnote, and that is the side-stepping of questions of religion that runs through his discussions of utopia. They hang around the edges, hats down and cigarettes glowing in the rain and the dark, but they hardly ever emerge from their murky hideaways. However, there is a deeper reason for such a treatment of religion, and in particular apocalyptic: Jameson's championing of the rupture as crucial to utopia is one that we also find in the religious literature of apocalyptic. The closeness shows up when he advocates the abolition of money, an old anticapitalist and largely religious programme:

> Thus the revival of the old Utopian dream of abolishing money, and of imagining life without it, is nothing short of precisely that dramatic rupture we have evoked.... The lived misery of money, the desperation of poorer societies, the pitiful media spectacles of the rich ones, is palpable to everyone. It is the decision to abandon money, to place this demand at the forefront of a political program, that *marks the rupture and opens up a space into which Utopia may enter, like Benjamin's Messiah,* unannounced, unprepared by events, and laterally, as if into a present randomly chosen but utterly transfigured by the new element.[62]

The invocation of Walter Benjamin's Messiah, and indeed Benjamin's concern with rupture, the break, the explosive flash that may wake us up from our nightmare, is telling. For, as I have argued in another place,[63] Benjamin sought to rework the biblical pattern of creation and eschaton into a theory of history

---

[61] Such a chapter would need to begin with the generic distinctions between apocalyptic, eschatology and messianism, for they are initially all genres of biblical literature. See my discussion of Agamben in Chapter 7.

[62] Jameson 2005b, p. 231; emphasis mine.

[63] Boer 2007a, pp. 57–105.

that would challenge the theories of progress on both Left and Right. His continual return to the first chapters of the Bible and his fascination with the messianic, and indeed the messiah are all part of this programme. For all his confusions, Benjamin shows how deeply the notion of rupture, or, as Antonio Negri has recently argued,[64] the *kairos*, is also a theological, indeed biblical category. And it comes straight out of those texts that belong to the genre of apocalyptic. Jameson's closing argument for disruption as a key feature of utopia is part of the same semantic field.

To sum up: as far as apocalyptic I concerned, Jameson falls back on his strategy of leaving a significant dimension of utopian thought on the sidelines. Eager for some play, it ends up with a few minutes tagged on to the end of the game. This is a shame, since it seems to me that, once again, the possibility of a dialectical reading of religion within utopia has been by-passed. Such a reading would begin with the point that apocalyptic bears within it the opposition of utopia and anti-utopia, especially in the way dire forecasts of annihilation have within them the seeds of a hope for something far better.

By way of conclusion: towards a dialectic of religion

Up to now, I have criticised Jameson for the way he sidelines religion in his treatment of utopia, particularly since religion may be seen in one sense as a store-house of utopian images and stories. And then I suggested that one reason for doing so is that Jameson's position on utopia-as-rupture shares more than he would care to admit with the apocalyptic material that he touches on but largely leaves alone. However, I have also noted where he offers a few hints as to the possibilities of a dialectical reading of utopia and religion. It is these half-buried elements of his thinking that I want to pick up in this conclusion. The first moment was with his argument concerning magic and the Feuerbachian projection of un-alienated existence that magic suggests, and the second was with the all-too-sparse and occasionally contradictory hints at what a dialectical reading of apocalyptic might look like.

But, now, I would like to bring these various hints at a dialectical reading of religion and utopia into the spotlight. My argument is that such a dialectical reading leads to an expansion of religion beyond its narrow confines of belief

---

[64] Negri 2003, pp. 147–80.

and practice. At this point, I move from one aspect of Jameson's approach to religion to another, namely from his assumption that religion has been superseded (and therefore may be sidelined) to the hermeneutics of ideology and utopia. While the former tends to be a reduction of religion to a bygone era or to a code for other issues, the latter enables a dialectical expansion of religion from these narrow confines.

In order to bring about such an expansion, I want to pick up one of Jameson's other tactics mentioned in his *Postmodernism* book, namely transcoding, which designates the process of leaping from one method or mode of analysis to another, the activity of 'measuring what is sayable and "thinkable" in each of these codes or ideolects' in order to 'compare that to the conceptual possibilities of its competitors'.⁶⁵ In the case of religion within utopia, it becomes possible not merely to expand religion into its cultural, political, economic and epistemological spheres, but to read the same phenomena in the different registers that we like to distinguish with such labels.⁶⁶

This approach is really a more generous reading of what I have until now criticised Jameson – his sidestepping, or, if you like, his search for another explanation so as to avoid one that takes account of religion. There is always a risk that the transcoding or expansion of religion might slip back down the slope to a simple quickstep⁶⁷ to get past some conservative backlash that he has excoriated on more than one occasion, a backlash that shows up in the

---

⁶⁵ Jameson 1991, p. 394.

⁶⁶ At other moments, Jameson transcodes an item into theology, as with his latest and most extensive statement on the theological nature of ethics and the binary of good and evil (Jameson 2005b, p. 58), or boredom as a theological category (Jameson 2005b, pp. 192–3).

⁶⁷ An example of such a slip may be found in his discussion of the work-ethic, along with a dig at Max Weber: 'One could, indeed, go on to identify a Christian and ascetic, self-punishing and guilt-ridden impulse in that requirement of work specified in many early Utopias; an impulse – the curse of the lost garden, the punishment of the "sweat of your brow" – that seems richly to validate Weber's religious specification of his modern work ethic.... Yet one can also adduce very different explanations for such "productionism" (*and even, perhaps, for the religious traditions thus alleged to motivate it*). Indeed, any inspection of contemporary right-wing materials often enough betrays the deepest anxieties as to what might happen to the social order if its institutions of repression and discipline, of obligatory labor, were to be relaxed; while any alert Lacanian will readily observe that envy of the *jouissance* of others, of the slackers and the allegedly 'non-productive' members of society, is an explosive force indeed'. (Jameson 2005b, pp. 152–3, emphasis mine; repeated in Jameson 2005a, p. 24.)

returns of political philosophy, or the concern with the subject and the body, or ethics, or, indeed, religion and theology in its most objectionable forms.[68]

I have chosen two examples of such a dialectical reading, although I should emphasise that it remains very much in fragments, offering shards of further possibilities.[69] The first comes from Jameson's brief comment on medieval theology. Terry Eagleton has also emphasised the complexity and value of medieval (which we need to read as Roman-Catholic) theology, but that is part of Eagleton's return to his roots in the Catholic Left.[70] For Jameson, the appeal of medieval theology lies in a number of other areas. To begin with, it is nothing other than a version of Lévi-Strauss's *pensée sauvage* – a thought gone wild, a system of knowledge that operates in a comparable fashion to but without the apparatus of science and philosophy. Except that there is one important difference: it comes after 'linguistic subtleties' and rich formulations of classical philosophy. I must admit to finding that argument a bit of a stretch, since it is precisely this feature which is absent from Lévi-Strauss's concept.[71] But what Jameson wants is the figural element of medieval theology, a feature it does share with *pensée sauvage*. The praise for medieval theology comes thick and fast – 'unique conceptual resources', 'remarkably sophisticated', 'an extraordinarily elaborated and articulated system of thought', a 'remarkable language experiment'[72] – but only because he wishes to expand it beyond its explicit content, as an expression of faith seeking understanding (in Anselm's terms). This is where the expansions take place: theology is figurative, in a way that acts as a precursor to psychoanalysis and *Ideologiekritik*. Even more, it is a 'language experiment' whose great contribution lies in its mechanisms. And those mechanisms show up in no better place than allegory.[73] Jameson has, of course, evoked without saying as much his well-worked and fruitful distinction of form and content. But he runs the risk here of resorting to a sidestepping

---

[68] Jameson 2002b, pp. 1–5; 1998b, pp. 95–6.
[69] Another example is his suggestion that the early Christian sects may be read as the equivalent of far-left groups for whom Augustine is then the social democrat who sees to negate and annihilate them (Jameson 1996). This essay, however, is more of a coming to terms with Foucault, who ends up the worse for the encounter.
[70] See Boer 2007a, pp. 275–333.
[71] Lévi-Strauss 1966.
[72] Jameson 2005b, p. 61.
[73] Jameson's deep connections with medieval biblical allegory is the subject of another essay (Boer forthcoming c), but see some of my earlier forays into this area: Boer 1996, pp. 9–42; 2005a.

that characterises his other treatments of religion. Why dismiss the content of medieval theology so readily in the search for its formal features? Surely a more dialectical reading would seek to interpret that content in its own way. This is where I can expand Jameson himself and suggest that not merely the form but also the content of medieval theology functions as a distinct epistemology. In fact, it is nothing other than a complex ideological system as such that can be understood only in the context of a feudal social and economic system. In all its complexities and sophistications, in all its dealings with paradoxes and contradictions, medieval theology is the heavily mediated mode in which that social and economic world was thought and puzzled over.

The second example is found in Jameson's lengthy treatment of Thomas More's Protestant and ascetic proclivities, especially as they show up in his *Utopia*.[74] In Jameson's search for one of those wonderfully complex semiotic squares with its multiple layers, religion shows up at two points of the square that seeks to lay out the various impulses that went into the writing of *Utopia*. At one of those points (s2), the contradiction of the primary term which is humanism, we find Protestantism, which includes features such as the Hebrew (including the Bible and Jewish kingship). Over against Protestantism along the diagonal axis (-s1) comes monasticism (which also includes the church hierarchy, community and egalitarianism). Monasticism appears not merely in the way utopia has more than one echo of the medieval monastery, the enclave of developing rationality in the Middle Ages, but also registers a sense of loss as the monasteries were systematically closed down under Henry VIII's reforms.

Now we come to the various expansions that Jameson brings about with these terms. Firstly, with monasticism he suggests that monasticism may be read, at least in More's appropriation, as a collective life, the face-to-face community and its inherent egalitarianism.[75] It is this collectivism (a socio-economic communism that has as its other ingredient the state communism of the Inca empires) that shows up in the social organisation of utopia. The

---

[74] Jameson 2005b, pp. 25–33.
[75] Here Jameson follows in Kautsky's footsteps to some extent. As I will argue in Chapter Four, for Kautsky, monasticism not only kept alive the communist impulse of early Christianity, but it also became part of the heritage of primitive communism upon which More drew. Jameson gives all of this a twist of his own that sublates Kautsky's key terms and yet carries on the insight of his reading (without, however, any acknowledgement of Kautsky's argument).

second expansion lies with Protestantism, which is not merely 'individualist inner-directedness',[76] not even the expansion of reason and the ordering of everyday life (Weber turns up frequently in these pages), but, above all, the revolutionary excitement of the Novum. That enthusiasm was expressed above all in the rediscovery of Hebrew. Combined with the rediscovery of Greek in humanism (Erasmus, who knew both languages and produced the first critical edition of the Greek New Testament, which was in itself a revolutionary act, was a close friend of More), Jameson points out:

> ...it is crucial to grasp the way in which both these revivals (of the classics and of primitive Christianity) are felt to be avant-garde causes. Together they constitute the Novum of the day: that is to say a conceptual and an ideological revolution whose innovation constitutively includes passion and excitement within it.[77]

Jameson also suggests, in another moment of transcoding, that such a revolutionary passion had a distinctly cultural flavour. This cultural dimension (no less than a cultural revolution) shows up in the rediscovery of what was felt to be the spirit of early Christianity, which he suggests 'is rather to be understood in the cultural sense', which is at the same time 'a discovery and a new intellectual enthusiasm'.[78]

Jameson's reading draws nigh to Antonio Gramsci's celebration of the Reformation as a revolutionary movement that transformed society from the bottom up.[79] Indeed, Gramsci's catch-cry of moral and political reform, a code for the communist revolution, is drawn straight from his passion for the Reformation. Gramsci goes as far as to champion the Reformers Luther and Calvin (Jameson is content to stay with the more humanist elements in Erasmus and More). For Gramsci, the large-scale transformation the Reformers wrought in Northern Europe, in terms of culture, politics, economics and social organisation provides a paradigm for communist revolution in Italy and elsewhere. It is one of the only models for social change that worked its way through all levels of society. It is not for nothing that Gramsci, in his desire for a communist Reformation in Italy, speaks of Machiavelli as the 'Italian Luther'. If

---

[76] Jameson 2005b, p. 31.
[77] Jameson 2005b, p. 26.
[78] Jameson 2005b, p. 24.
[79] See Boer 2007a, pp. 215–74.

Jameson does not quite exhibit Gramsci's enthusiasm for the Reformation, he has pointed out that Marxism and Christianity are the two great systems of thought and praxis that have captured the imagination of the masses.

What has happened in all of this is that religion has been expanded, or, rather, transcoded as a revolutionary moment, an explosive possibility for the new that finds expression in More's *Utopia*. Note what has happened: religion has become a collective and egalitarian programme (the Roman-Catholic element in More's utopia), and then an intellectual and cultural movement (the Protestant moment), one that is also distinctly political and revolutionary.

In the end, then, what I pick up from Jameson are the moments when he makes use of his hermeneutics of ideology and utopia. What we find are the beginnings of various dialectical possibilities for religion, specifically in terms of utopia. These include: his promising use of Feuerbach in regard to magic in the genre of fantasy, which I extended to understand both political myth and the political fantasy of China Miéville; the glimpses of a re-reading of apocalyptic, in which the genre of apocalyptic (initially a biblical genre) provides the dialectical relation of utopia and anti-utopia, and in which catastrophe functions as a code for utopia; the delectable enticements of the forms of medieval theology; and, finally, Jameson's expansion of religion as both a collectivity and a cultural revolution, particularly in Thomas More's monastic and Protestant moments. How these fragments might come together is a matter for another study.

Chapter Three
The Christian Communism of Rosa Luxemburg

'A curious piece of historical sophistry' – that is how J.P. Nettl in his classic biography[1] describes Rosa Luxemburg's treatise, *Socialism and the Churches*.[2] A rather convenient dismissal, is it not? It does allow Nettl to sidestep the whole issue of religion in Luxemburg's work and get on with what he regards as the more important issues in her life and thought. By contrast, I want to give this neglected text a little more justice than Nettl does. This chapter, then, is a sustained engagement with that work by Luxemburg, along with her essay, which originally appeared in French in response to a questionnaire, 'An Anti-Clerical Policy of Socialism'.[3]

Despite all the beguiling simplicity of her style, the fascination that still surrounds her, or even the freshness of her work that makes it seem as though it were for today's struggles, the reception of Rosa Luxemburg is bedevilled by two problems. Firstly, the vast majority of work on Luxemburg has focused on her biography; I was able to find at least eight biographies in the last four decades.[4] That she was a woman is one obvious reason for focussing on

---

[1] Nettl 1966, Volume 1, p. 323; 1969, p. 221.
[2] Luxemburg 2004b, 1982.
[3] Luxemburg 2004a, 1903.
[4] Frölich 1969; Nettl 1966, 1969; Florence 1975, pp. 79–158; Ettinger 1986; Jacob 2000; Abraham 1989; Shepardson 1996; Cliff 1980.

her biography, especially the intimate and personal details. Another reason is that biography seems to be the fate of those on the Left who meet a grisly end or are visited by some scandal. For Luxemburg, it was a sordid murder at the hands of *Freikorps* on 15 January 1919 after a failed insurrection. For Gramsci, it was his incarceration by Mussolini and subsequent death from dreadful prison conditions, for Althusser the murder of Hélène, for Benjamin his fateful and bumbling suicide at the Spanish-French border, and so on. Mainly due to my deep suspicions concerning biography and the personality cult that it feeds,[5] I will avoid the temptations of biography as an all-encompassing explanatory framework for Luxemburg. The other engagement with Luxemburg is to republish selections of her letters and essays.[6] As for critical engagement, that remains another story, still woefully intermittent and rarely, if ever, going outside her major work, *Accumulation of Capital*.[7]

So I will leave Luxemburg's biography on one side,[8] preferring to engage critically with her writings on religion, or rather, Christianity and the Church. Luxemburg appears first in this collection of Marxists who have dealt with religion in some capacity or other, mainly because she is chronologically at the head of the list. But she also opens up some of the issues surrounding the reconstruction of early Christianity from a Marxist perspective, delving into the New Testament no less. Karl Kautsky follows, since he takes up these questions a little further. As for Luxemburg, I am most interested in her evocation of what I call the political myth of an early Christian communism, as

---

[5] Boer 2007a, pp. 433–4.
[6] Looker 1972; Howard 1971; Waters 1994; Hudis and Anderson 2004; LeBlanc 1999; Ettinger 1979.
[7] Luxemburg 1970, 2003.
[8] Apart from her early and quite distant relationship with the Algemener Yiddisher Arbeter Bund (Bund for short), Luxemburg does not seem to have had any great interest in religion, whether personal or cultural. Finally formed officially in 1897 and based in Vilna in Lithuania, the Bund was a Jewish socialist movement whose roots lie in the response to the counter-revolutionary repressions in Russia and the Russian part of Poland in the 1880s. Such a repression, of course, had the effect not merely of forcing large numbers of Jews to emigrate, but also led to the rapid rise in popularity of Zionism and Jewish socialism. Due to her background in a fully assimilated Jewish family in the agricultural centre of Zamość in south-eastern Poland (which went from Austrian to Russian control in 1815), Luxemburg was put under pressure to join the Bund, but she resisted fiercely any specifically Jewish socialism, in part at least because of her internationalist position, one that opposed any socialist movement that had a strong nationalist flavour (which was to clash more than once with Polish nationalism). See Nettl 1969, pp. 27, 31–2, 54–5, 174–6; Luxemburg 1976.

well as her arresting argument for freedom of conscience regarding religion in the socialist movement. On the way to those two points, I wish to explore and critique the following: her call for a politics of alliance between socialist and Catholic workers; her Reformer's zeal, especially in terms of her scathing criticisms of the venality of the Catholic Church; the argument that the Church has betrayed the communist spirit of early Christianity, and her historical narrative that seeks to show how the Church became part of the ruling class; her enthusiastic valorisation of Christian communism, pointing out that socialism is closer to early Christianity than the Church, that socialism will complete what was begun then, and that what was a limited communism of consumption must be transformed and completed by a communism of production; finally, her startling argument that socialism is not opposed to religious belief and practice, since they are matters of freedom of conscience.

Tactics

A deeply running motive of Luxemburg's works on Christianity is to win the allegiance of the religiously faithful workers, especially the wave of new members that flooded her Polish party, Social Democracy of the Kingdom of Poland and Lithuania, in the revolutionary upsurge of 1904–5. With the diatribes of the Church against socialism in one ear and the socialist broadsides against economic and social exploitation in the other ear, these workers found themselves split, torn between faithful obedience to the Church and a gut feeling that capital really was squeezing out 'their own blood'.[9] What Luxemburg wants is a common front of all workers, Catholic, socialist or whatever: 'The Social-Democrats[10] have placed themselves the objective of drawing together

---

[9] Luxemburg 2004b, p. 2; 1982, p. 19; translation modified.
[10] In this text Luxemburg uses 'Social Democrat', since at the time she was still part of the broader Social-Democratic movement. The sharp distinctions, especially between Social Democrats and socialists/Communists, were not to emerge until a few years later. She was a member of various parties that called themselves Social-Democratic or Socialist. Initially, she joined the united Polish Socialist Party (PPS) when it was formed in 1892, then the alternative Social Democracy of the Kingdom of Poland (SDKP) which broke away over the nationalist question after the third congress of the Second International (6–12 August 1893), and which then became Social Democracy of the Kingdom of Poland and Lithuania (SDKPiL) in 1899. She also joined the Social-Democratic Party of Germany (SPD) in 1898, although she was always an uncomfortable member. The watershed between Social Democrats and socialists came in a double blow: on 4 August 1914 the SPD delegates in the Reichstag voted

and organising the workers in the struggle against capital'.[11] And the drive of that front is to challenge and overthrow the various forms that the exploiting and ruling classes might take.

As one would expect, her unwavering targets are the owners of capital. These owners may be the bourgeoisie, or the remnants of the landed aristocracy, or the Church. The situation was, of course, deliciously complex and it is important not to confuse political power with economic control. Thus, if, at the turn of the nineteenth century, the bourgeoisie were the dominant owners of capital, if they had the upper hand in economic power, they were engaged in a life-and-death struggle with the aristocracy and the Church over political power. In that tussle over control of the state, those older feudal orders might strike a blow at the bourgeoisie, only to find that they were on the back foot not long afterwards. Add to this the fact that the Church and the aristocracy had also transformed themselves into owners of capital, and the situation becomes even more complex.

As Marx showed so well in *The Eighteenth Brumaire of Louis Bonaparte*, in these struggles all manner of tactical allegiances were made. Thus, the bourgeoisie might enlist sections of the working class, with a raft of promises, in order to overthrow the *ancien régime*, only to find that the working class itself had its own programme that was not in line with that of the bourgeoisie. The revolutions of 1848 constitute the moment when the working class, denied what was promised it, turned on the bourgeoisie, which was then forced to crush its former allies. Or, the Church, in its continual efforts to win back lost ground, in education, the care of the sick and the poor, and in pure temporal power, might make alliances with the bourgeoisie or the aristocracy to further its own agenda. And so on it goes, with all the different groups seeking to further their own positions in whatever way possible.

Into this situation come the socialists. For Luxemburg, their main drive leads to some surprising and apparently contradictory positions. At one moment, she will attack the Church in a good old dose of anti-clericalism, advocat-

---

in favour of war credits, much to the dismay of Luxemburg and many others who went on to form the explicitly communist Spartakusbund, and then on 15 January 1919 the Social-Democratic government that came to power in the closing days of World War I tacitly approved the murder of Luxemburg and her long-time partner and then associate, Leo Jogisches. Even though it comes from hindsight, I will use 'socialist' and 'communist' to designate Luxemburg's position.

[11] Luxemburg 2004b, p. 2; 1982, p. 19.

ing the total abolition of ecclesiastical privilege, the complete separation of Church and state, the removal of all educational and welfare institutions and so on. She attacks the venality, exploitation and corruption of the clergy as any good Reformer might – but only when the purpose is to wrest economic and political power from the Church. As she puts it: 'we will assail all efforts attempted by the Church to become a dominating power in the State'.[12]

At other times, she takes a completely different tack and seeks to enlist the clergy and the faithful in the struggle against the depredations of the bourgeoisie. Indeed, she goes so far as to argue that the clergy should in fact be on the side of the socialists. She points out that socialists are not against the clergy who have been fulminating against them, but rather against exploitation at the hands of capital and state: 'never do the Social-Democrats drive the workers to fight against clergy, or try to interfere with religious beliefs; not at all!'.[13] Even more, she argues, if the Church was true to its roots, especially in the New Testament and early Christianity, then it could not help but support the socialists. As she writes,

> Therefore it would seem as if the clergy ought to lend their help to the Social-Democrats who are trying to enlighten the working people. But that is not enough. If we understand properly the teachings which the Social-Democrats bring to the working class, the hatred of the clergy towards them becomes still less understandable.[14]

Yet, her real wish in these efforts to bring the clergy on side (which she realistically knew would never work, except perhaps with the odd clergymen who were as rare as 'white blackbirds', *weisse Raben*)[15] are really directed at the workers faithful to the Church. On this matter, she wants to show that, if the Church were true to itself, it would support the workers in their dissatisfaction with and struggles against exploitation. Even if the Church is not on their side in economic matters, it should be.

These are the twists in her arguments concerning Christianity and the Church that interest me in this chapter. On the one hand, there are stirring denunciations of the Church that should warm anyone's heart with at least

---

[12] Luxemburg 2004a, p. 1; 1903, p. 29.
[13] Luxemburg 2004b, p. 2; 1982, p. 19.
[14] Luxemburg 2004b, p. 2; 1982, p. 20; translation modified.
[15] Luxemburg 2004b, p. 4; 1982, p. 21.

some social conscience, and yet, on the other hand, she is remarkably open to the value of religion within socialism. So much so that she will come out in favour of freedom of conscience regarding belief and even stresses the revolutionary and communist roots of Christianity itself. In what follows, I discuss and subject to critique her diatribes against the Church first, before moving on to do the same with her far more sympathetic treatment of the Church and its history.

A Reformer's zeal

When reading Luxemburg's criticisms of the Church, I cannot help being reminded of the zeal of the Protestant Reformers, especially those among the Radical Reformation such as Thomas Müntzer. For them, the Church was corrupt to the core, run by self-serving and lascivious priests whose only desire was earthly gain and pleasure. The sheer wealth of the Church, the temporal power of the pope, the demand for indulgences in order to finance vast building projects – all these and more were signs for the Reformers that the Church had lost its higher, spiritual vocation.

Often, Luxemburg writes in a similar vein, saturating her texts with a heavy moral tone. In a loud echo of the Reformers' criticism of indulgences, she condemns the clergy for being more interested in their fee than in the needs of the faithful: 'Again, everyone knows how often the priest himself makes a profit from the poor worker, extracting the last penny on the occasion of marriage, baptism or burial'.[16]

Apart from this overweening concern with their own pockets, the priests more often than not side with the rich and powerful: 'The majority of priests, with beaming faces, bow and scrape to the rich and powerful, silently pardoning them for every depravity, every iniquity'.[17] One would be forgiven for thinking that these rich and powerful are somehow external to the Church. Reading Luxemburg, one gets the impression that the churches are full of poor workers. Or, to give her a little more credit, the workers are the only genuine believers. The catch is that the Church counted itself part of the rich and powerful, of the owners of capital and the key figures of the state. To be

---

[16] Luxemburg 2004b, p. 3; 1982, p. 21; translation modified.
[17] Luxemburg 2004b, p. 4; 1982, p. 21.

perfectly vulgar (in a good Marxist sense), the Church needed to ensure that it did not bite the hand that fed it. Favourable treatment (she writes especially of Poland, her home country), state funds for the churches, the maintenance of Church property – all these came from the state, from that same coterie of the wealthy and powerful to whom Luxemburg was so strongly opposed. When it came to the crunch, the Church would first ensure this support base.

It should come as no surprise, then, that the Church should view the socialists' attacks on capital and the state as attacks on the Church itself, or at least on its current livelihood. No wonder the clergy call fire and brimstone down on the socialists:

> It is with extraordinary vigour that our clergy fight against the socialists and try by all means to belittle them in the eyes of the workers…the priests fulminate against the workers who are on strike or struggle against the government; further, they exhort them to bear poverty and oppression with humility and patience.… The clergy storm against the Social Democrats, exhort the workers not to 'revolt' against the overlords, but to submit obediently to the oppression of this government…[18]

She is not afraid of a biblical reference or two to back up her argument: 'The bishops and the priests are not the worshippers of Christ's teaching, but the worshippers of the Golden Calf and of the Knout[19] [*Knute*] which whips the poor and defenceless'.[20] Her reference is to the incident of the Golden Calf in Exodus 32. In this mythical story, Aaron, the patriarch of the priesthood, responds to the request of the people to make gods for them, since Moses had been gone for an eternity, chatting with God up on Mount Sinai about the interior design of the Tabernacle, a sort of chapel on camelback. So Aaron calls on them all to give him their gold and it turns into a 'molten calf' – a young bull, as the Hebrew has it – with an engraving tool (in explicit contrast to the ban on making graven images in the second commandment (Exodus 20:4) that Moses is about to bring down the mountain with him). As the people dance and sing

---

[18] Luxemburg 2004b, pp. 1–3; 1982, pp. 19–20; translation modified.

[19] The knout is a distinctly Russian invention of corporal punishment, made of leather strips attached to a long handle with various additions such as hardened leather, rings and hooks. The English term, although cognate with knot, derives from a French transliteration of a Russian word. It became synonymous with the cruelty of the Russian government.

[20] Luxemburg 2004b, p. 3; 1982, p. 21; translation modified.

and celebrate, Moses returns and in anger smashes the tablets of the law and only just manages to hold God back from destroying the people completely. As one would expect with a biblical story like this, it is deeply ambiguous – is Moses really the upholder of the true faith, and of law and order, and is this a rebellion that has been cast as 'sin'?[21] – but Luxemburg takes it at face value as the condemnation of wayward and corrupt religious practices.

It is but a passing reference, and she will have much more to say about biblical texts from Acts in the New Testament, but what strikes me is the exegetical move she makes. Like the Reformers, the wayward practices of the Church are analogous to those of corrupt and self-serving priests in the Hebrew Bible. Figures such as Moses (and especially Jesus for the Reformers) are reconstructed as the embodiment of true religion over against such priests – precisely the role in which the Reformers saw themselves. Luxemburg's point, then, is very similar: the clergy behave like those wayward priests of ancient Israel. Even more, when we come to her discussions of the communist origins of Christianity, the socialists, who carry on such a tradition (even unknown to themselves), are analogous to the Reformers who sought to return to the *fons et origo* of the early Church.

What, then, is the proper task of the clergy? Here, Luxemburg comes close to a theme we hear *ad nauseam* today: it is to provide religious consolation, to comfort the people who are 'full of cares and wearied by their hard lives'.[22] Instead of providing such consolation, the priests attack socialism in violent political speeches, turning the 'the church and the pulpit into a place of political propaganda'.[23] I can see Luxemburg's point, but it differs little from comments uttered on a regular basis today. If the churches should criticise one government policy or another, the standard response by those criticised is to say that the churches should not meddle in politics; rather, they should focus on the spiritual nourishment of souls. Only the political sides have changed, for it is more often than not conservative politicians who are apt to respond in such a way when the churches condemn a reactionary social policy or political decision. Assuming that the churches by and large agree with them, these politicians react by telling the churches they have stepped out of line when

---

[21] See Boer 2003, pp. 42–64.
[22] Luxemburg 2004b, p. 1; 1982, p. 19.
[23] Luxemburg 2004b, p. 2; 1982, p. 19.

they criticise and take an alternative position. I am, in other words, not particularly persuaded by Luxemburg's point. For it is not so much a call for the churches to stay out of politics (an impossible task even if it is a leitmotiv of the separation of church and state), but rather a call on the churches to support the correct political programme, depending, of course, on whom you happen to consult.

In the end, this call for the churches to stick to their business of providing consolation to the faithful is not going to get us very far. However, there is a deeper problem with Luxemburg's criticism of the Church, and that is her heavy moral tone. Her descriptions of the clergy, bourgeoisie and workers are all saturated with moral terms. For instance, while the clergy are 'parasites', infused with 'hatred' towards the socialists, using 'lies and slander', and while the bourgeoisie are 'emasculated' and full of 'hypocrisy' and 'treachery', the workers are 'defenceless', 'despairing' and 'hard-working'. Similarly, when she comes to speak of the Roman Empire in setting the scene for the emergence of Christianity, we find a description that is largely moralistic. The Roman overlords were corrupt, despotic and vile, living on the backs of their slaves who did all the work. She is at pains to show how the situation under the Roman Empire differs little, at least in terms of the patterns of exploitation, from that of her own day under capitalism.

The snares of such an approach are many, but let me begin with what may be called the argument from human nature. Human beings are naturally greedy, selfish and small-minded, looking out only for themselves at the expense of others. In theological parlance, this is, of course, the state of fallen nature: human beings are by default sinful creatures (a point made in its own way by the myth of the Fall in Genesis 3). Now, the immediate objection will be that Luxemburg does not make *that* argument. True enough, although, at a political level, there is some mileage in the suggestion that capitalism is the most thorough systematisation, at both economic and ideological levels, of human greed (it is a good point to make every now and then in response to the argument that human greed is to blame rather than any social formation). But the mileage is not so great, for it then leads to the unwelcome position that what we need is something like communism to forgive our sins, overcome our greed and set us on the path of a right relation with our fellow human beings. However, let me return to Luxemburg and the argument she does make: the Church and bourgeoisie are inherently greedy, corrupt, base and self-serving, whereas the poor, honest and defenceless working class is needlessly exploited by those greedy capitalists. A few years ago, this would have been called an essentialist argument, in which the bourgeoisie, Church and working class are essentially evil or good. At this point, the old anti-essentialist argument has some bite, for, in this form, Luxemburg's position assumes that the positions and predilections of the various classes are unchangeable: it is part of their nature to be so. Or, to make the argument less crude: they have been constructed through economic circumstances to be so.

At this point, too, we come to the second problem with Luxemburg's heavily moral terminology, namely the slide from moralising into ethics. Do we not have in Luxemburg's texts (more than the two I am commenting on here) an ethical binary of good and evil? This is the largest snare of her tendency to take the high moral ground (a well-worn political phrase that now carries an extra loading). Such an ethical opposition comes face to face with objections such as those of Sartre, Foucault and Freud. For each, in their own way, the opposition ensures the centrality of the self (as good) at the expense of others (as evil). For Freud, it is then a narcissistic exercise that imposes the perspective of the self on others in terms of heroes (for Luxemburg, the working class) and villains (the Church and the bourgeoisie). Or, in Sartre's terms, it is a means of ensuring the self and marginalising others as evil; or, in Foucault's terms, the opposition provides the mechanisms of policing the good and securing what is normal and abnormal through institutions.[24] We can go a step further and point out that the introduction of ethics is not so much an effort to deal with one's behaviour towards and treatment of the 'other', whatever that may be – human beings, animals, plants, earth and so on. This perception of ethics has the whole relation topsy-turvy, for the 'other' is not a category prior to ethics. Rather, ethics produces the category of the 'other' in the very act of offering a way of relating to the other. To my mind, that is something we could well do without.

I am, then, not so enamoured with Luxemburg's moral-cum-ethical positions, for they land us in far too many problems. And I am certainly less than keen to take them up in any further discussion of the interaction between Marxism and religion, for what she does here is replicate some of the more reprobate patterns of theological thinking.

---

[24] See Jameson 2005b, p. 58.

Betraying the spirit

While I do not want to remain locked in such an ethical opposition, neither does Luxemburg, it seems to me. Her first step comes in an argument that will gain strength as I move along: the spirit of early Christianity, in its practice and teaching, was a socialist one; however, the Church has, for a number of historical reasons, betrayed this early spirit. Here is Luxemburg: 'the clergy, which makes itself the spokesman of the rich, the defender of exploitation and oppression, places itself in flagrant contradiction to the Christian doctrine'.[25] Luxemburg will use this intriguing argument for a number of purposes: to castigate the Church, to show the faithful workers that their faith is not in conflict with their deeply-felt political and economic desires, and to recuperate a longer tradition of socialism that pre-dates the nineteenth century. The first two reasons are quite explicit in her argument, the latter more implicit.

At first, this argument by Luxemburg may seem like special pleading, or a curious piece of sophistry. Surely the Church was not a socialist movement in its early days! Indeed it was, she argues, following Engels's famous argument.[26] There is still a decent rhetorical effect in a text like the following, where she draws on various biblical quotations to drive home her point:

> The Social-Democrats propose to put an end to the exploitation of the poor working people by the rich. You would have thought that the servants of the Christian Church would have been the first to make this task easier for the Social-Democrats. Did Jesus Christ (whose servants the priests are) teach that 'it is easier for a camel to pass through the eye of a needle than for a rich man to enter the Kingdom of Heaven'? The Social-Democrats try to bring about in all countries social regimes based on the equality, liberty and fraternity of all people. If the clergy really desire that the principle 'Love thy neighbour as thyself' be applied in real life, then they should welcome keenly the propaganda of the Social Democrats. The Social Democrats try, by a desperate struggle, by the education and organization of the working people, to draw them out of the downtrodden state in which they now are and to offer them a better life and their children a better future. Everyone should admit, that at this point, the priests should bless the Social-Democrats,

---

[25] Luxemburg 2004b, p. 3; 1982, p. 21.
[26] Engels 1990. See also Boer in press-a.

for did not he whom they serve, Jesus Christ, say 'What you do for the least you do for me'?[27]

Let me say a little about each of Luxemburg's biblical citations. They are all drawn from the Gospels and all put in the mouth of Jesus by the writers of these texts. The first comes from Mark 10:25, although it is a common text for all the synoptic Gospels (see also Luke 18:25 and Matthew 19:24): 'It is easier for a camel to go through the eye of a needle than for a rich man to enter the kingdom of God' (quoted now from the Revised Standard Version). In each Gospel the context of the saying is the question of the rich young man (in Luke it is a 'ruler'): 'Good Teacher, what must I do to inherit eternal life?' (Mark 10:17). When Jesus tells him – beyond observing the commandments – to go and sell all he has, give the proceeds to the poor and then to come and follow Jesus, the young man goes away in sorrow, since he had many possessions. And then, to his disciples, Jesus says, 'How hard it will be for those who have riches to enter the kingdom of God!' (Mark 10:23). At this point, the eye of the needle saying follows. It is a strong text, and one that Luxemburg uses to make her point that socialists work to end exploitation at the hands of the rich. By adding the point that wealth derives from exploitation, she goes a step beyond the Gospel text, filling in the gap as it were. But what we should note at this point is the command to the rich young man: 'You lack one thing; go, sell what you have, and give to the poor, and you will have treasure in heaven; and come, follow me' (Mark 10:21). This text resonates with those from the book of the Acts of the Apostles that will become the crux of Luxemburg's argument concerning the communism of early Christianity.

The second text, 'Love thy neighbour as thyself', we find sprinkled throughout the New Testament. The greatest concentration comes in the Gospels (Matthew 19:19; 22:39; Mark 12:31, 33; Luke 10:27), but it is also found elsewhere (Romans 13:9; Galatians 5:14; James 2:8). In the Gospels, it is the second of the great commandments, the other being 'You shall love the Lord your God with all your heart, and with all your soul, and with all your mind, and with all your strength' (Mark 12:30; and, with slight variations, Matthew 22:7; Luke 10:27). However, for Paul, this commandment sums all the others (Romans 13:9; Galatians 5:14), and this is the line that Luxemburg picks up: it

---

[27] Luxemburg 2004b, pp. 2–3; 1982, p. 20; translation modified.

really is the summary, the concise statement of Christian belief and practice. If so, then the clergy really should support the socialist campaign of liberty, equality and fraternity of all peoples. Except, of course, that there is nothing particularly socialist or social-democratic about such a programme; is it not the slogan of the French Revolution, of the newly strong bourgeoisie that she despises so much elsewhere? Not her strongest point, it seems to me, and Nietzsche's strictures against Christian love – in which it is a weapon of domination and control over those to whom one shows love, or *caritas* as the Latin has it – should not be forgotten.

Her third biblical quotation is stronger. The full biblical text reads: 'Truly, I say to you, as you did it to one of the least of these my brethren, you did it to me' (Matthew 25:40). The quotation comes towards the end of a parable that remains one of the enabling motifs of Christian communism. It is the third of the so-called eschatological parables in Matthew 25, the first two being the parable of the five wise and five foolish maidens and the parable of the talents. This parable (of the sheep and goats) goes as follows: at the time of the coming of the 'Son of Man', he will, like a shepherd, separate the sheep from the goats. To the sheep he says, 'Come, O blessed of my Father, inherit the kingdom prepared for you from the foundation of the world; for I was hungry and you gave me food, I was thirsty and you gave me drink, I was a stranger and you welcomed me, I was naked and you clothed me, I was sick and you visited me, I was in prison and you came to me' (Matthew 25:34–6). To the question from the sheep as to when they had in fact done these things, the Son of Man replies with the verse I quoted above. However, the goats are not so fortunate: they are banished to the colourful and entertaining realm of eternal fire and punishment, a realm frequented by none other than the devil and his angels.

The stakes in this passage from Matthew are high, for it mixes a rather clear agenda of what would later be called social justice with the scene of the final judgement and all the usual paraphernalia of heaven and hell. What Christian communists tend to do is focus on the more palatable social-justice dimension and quietly drop the stark contrast of eternal punishment and eternal life. The catch is that this story is not merely a prescription for a politics of compassion, one of social justice and of relieving the 'downtrodden', as Luxemburg puts it; rather, it is a full-scale myth. Set in the apocalyptic moment of end-time judgement, it is saturated with the imagery that one would expect with such a myth – heaven and hell, fire and glory, eternal life either with God or in punishment with the devil and his angels. How else to have a viable judgement scene at the end of history if there is no outcome for the judgement? What the myth does do – rather gratifyingly – is turn the whole idea of heaven as the reward for faithfulness, piety and religious commitment on its head, for rather than being fully aware of one's piety as the means of salvation, it turns out that inadvertent acts of justice are what count in the end.

There is one last feature of Luxemburg's use of this text from Matthew 25: the fuller story as I have excavated it here points to the fact that she too trades in mythological themes, albeit now of a distinctly political flavour.[28] Are not the exploiting capitalists, the conniving bourgeoisie and the venal clergy also condemned in their own way to eternal damnation, although it is a damnation of a more economic and political nature? Are they not the goats, to use the image from Matthew's Gospel, the bourgeoisie and the Church, and are not the working class, with the socialists at their head, the sheep – the ones who gave food and drink to the hungry and thirsty, who clothed the naked, welcomed the stranger, visited the sick and came to those in prison? In Luxemburg's hands, the early church, or at least a few texts from the Bible have taken on a distinctly red colour.

A little church history

Now I turn to Luxemburg's rather intriguing re-reading of church history, which seeks to provide a thumb-nail sketch of the way the role and place of the Church changed within the shifting economic formations of some 1900 years. And the reason for Luxemburg's step into church history lies in her desire to find the way out of an anomaly: if the New Testament presents a picture of the first Christians as devoted to justice for the poor, to communism in living and to providing refuge for the oppressed, how did the Church end up as it is now, as a friend of the rich and powerful, as a supporter of the status quo, as an institution with a distinct financial and political interest in ensuring its place within the economic infrastructure? The answer lies in history: 'In order to understand this strange phenomenon, it is sufficient to glance over

---

[28] See Boer 2009.

the history of the Church and to examine the evolution through which it has passed in the course of the centuries'.[29]

Luxemburg's reconstruction is, quite simply, that the Church of the exploited became the Church of the exploiters. A movement which began with a message of consolation to the poor and as a collective practice of the community of riches gradually changed over time to become part of the ruling classes in the Middle Ages and then changed again to join the ranks of the owners of capital under capitalism.[30] The main features of her reconstruction, which comprises the bulk of her *Socialism and the Churches*, are a reliance on the Marxist modes of production narrative, the outline of the Church's economic and political status within each phase or mode of production, and then the transitions from one mode to the other. Let me say a little more about each one.

To begin with, Luxemburg accepts the structuring role of the sequence of modes of production as they were being defined at the time she wrote; in fact, in some respects, her work assisted in that process of establishing such a sequence. It moves from a slave-based system under the Roman Empire when Christianity emerged, through a feudal system that followed in Europe and then to the more recent transition to capitalism. Within each social formation, she takes as axiomatic Marx and Engels's key to the motor of history: 'The history of all hitherto existing society is the history of class struggle'.[31] And, in the fundamental antagonism between oppressor and oppressed that such a struggle assumes, the Christian Church finds itself firstly among the oppressed in the slave-based system of the Roman Empire, but then it shifts allegiance to become one of the oppressors in the subsequent social formations.

Luxemburg also accepts, albeit implicitly, the class antagonism that Marx and Engels outline in the *Manifesto of the Communist Party*.[32] For instance, the oppositions of freeman and slave, and of patrician and plebeian are drawn from the Greek and Roman eras – the second opposition being specifically Roman. And then the pairs of lord and serf, guild-master and journeyman come from the feudal period.[33] So, if the early Church attracted slaves and

---

[29] Luxemburg 2004b, p. 4; 1982, p. 21.
[30] It is a distinctly European narrative, one that seems to have been an anomaly in terms of world history (see D'iakonoff 1999, p. 56).
[31] Marx and Engels 1976a, p. 482.
[32] Marx and Engels 1976a, pp. 482, 485.
[33] As is well known, Marx and Engels go on to point out that this simple pattern of oppositions really applies only to capitalism, where the conflict is simplified into the

plebeians, then, by the Middle Ages, it formed a class of its own that was closer to the lords than serfs or journeymen.

The crucial moment – or, rather, process – is when the Church moves from oppressed to oppressor, from an organisation that suffers at the hands of the rich and powerful to one that hobnobs with those who have acquired wealth on the backs of others. Here, Luxemburg follows a variation of the conventional Marxist narrative of differentiation (which we will find in more detail in Kautsky's work): from an original community of equality, where everything was held in common, differentiation insinuates itself so that we end up with the old opposition of rich and poor, powerful and powerless. So it was with the early Christian community. But every narrative of differentiation needs a trigger, and, for Luxemburg, that is size: as the Christians grew in number, it was no longer possible to live in small communist groups. Eventually, the rich traded the sharing of their wealth for almsgiving to the poor, which became only a portion of their wealth and not all of it, and then they absented themselves from the communities and the common meals, which were left to the poor church members. Size also becomes the trigger of another feature of differentiation, namely the clergy as a leadership structure, which became necessary to manage the ever-increasing numbers of the movement. And so, the goods that were once shared in common, and which were then given to the poor, were devoted more and more to maintaining the clergy and church buildings.[34] Once this process of differentiation was under way, the next step was the adoption of Christianity as the state religion, with state funding for buildings and a hierocratic structure under Constantine (some time between the battle of the Milvian Bridge in 312 and his death in 337). From there, the path leads to the Church's feudal privileges, ruling class status, accumulation of wealth and property, and role as a rich exploiter of the poor through tithes and labour dues.

'two great hostile camps' Marx and Engels 1976, p. 485) of bourgeoisie and working class. In the earlier phases, there were more complex arrangements of patricians, knights, plebeians, slaves (Rome), and then feudal lords, vassals, guild-masters, journeymen, apprentices, serfs (Middle Ages), along with further gradations within these classes.

[34] As she points out, 'Already, in the 5th Century, the revenues of the Church were divided into four parts; one for the bishop, one for the minor clergy, one for the building and upkeep of the churches, and it was only the fourth part which was distributed among the needy' (Luxemburg 2004b, p. 16; 1982, p. 33; translation modified).

But what happened to the Church when the feudal order crumbled and was swept away? Did it not lose its status and landed wealth along with the deposed feudal lords? Did not the bourgeoisie wrest control of education and learning, as well as the care of the poor and the sick, away from the Church? Like the rest of the old aristocracy, the Church did not merely resign itself to its fate and crawl away to lick its wounds. It was much wilier than that, transforming itself into an owner of capital. Despite its apparent loss of temporal power (here she speaks directly of the Roman-Catholic Church), it became a business enterprise in its own right – Luxemburg provides some telling figures on the capital of the Church in Austria and France to back up her argument.

There are a few problems with her narrative. I am less interested in the charge that she is a bit thin on the details and resources, for it was a pamphlet designed for popular consumption. More of a problem is her characterisation of the Roman Empire of the early Christian era as corrupt and collapsing (a view that Kautsky shared). In part, this was a rather conventional narrative, which argued that Rome collapsed due to corruption, the loss of civic and manly virtue, and a few too many peccadillos and lax morals.[35] If the picture of the Roman Empire is a little schematic, then her rapidly-drawn picture of the medieval Church also suffers from tendency towards ideal types. While the Church loses any sense of its communist roots to become an exploiting class, the peasants are poor, defenceless people taxed and worked to the hilt. It would, of course, water down her story, but some sense at least of the complexity of medieval life would have helped. I think here of the whole area of peasant religion, with its incorporation of pagan elements into an earthy Christianity, its carnivals and license, its celebrations of fertility and magic. In other words, some sense of peasant resistance would have helped. So also would the re-emergence, from time to time, of that utopian image of the early Church from the book of Acts in one movement after another, from the communities of monks living in poverty such as the Franciscans, to the rebellious Hutterites, Albigensians and the followers of the apocalyptic Joachim of Fiore.

---

[35] This argument dates back to the influence of the Roman moralists of the fourth and fifth centuries C.E., and was recycled in works such as Gibbon's 6-volume masterpiece, *The History of the Decline and Fall of the Roman Empire* (1776–89), and then carries through until the twentieth century.

Yet, for all its shortcomings, it is not a bad narrative. Its genius lies initially in the appeal it made at the time it was written (1905) to the many who flooded into her Polish socialist party, the Social Democracy of the Kingdom of Poland and Lithuania. In the revolutionary mood of that period, the mass strikes, the street protests, and the swell of support for the socialists, Luxemburg was at the forefront of making Marxism understood by all the new recruits who knew virtually nothing about it. Rather than the characterisation of a godless, anti-clerical political movement, she sought to reassure those who held religious beliefs that socialism was not incompatible with those beliefs.

A further reason for its genius is that it is a bold act of rewriting history. As Foucault has shown us so powerfully,[36] a crucial way of recasting and challenging the present and future is by telling different stories of the past – or, rather, by telling a different narrative of how we got here and where we are going. Let me put it more strongly: one of the most effective political tools is to rewrite history, for the future rests upon a narrative of the past that sets up such a future in the first place. Thus, when the future seems to be set along a certain inevitable path, then retelling the story that led to that future opens up the possibility of an alternative future or two. In other words, to generate a different future, rewrite the past. This is precisely what Luxemburg is doing in her reconstruction of church history.

Anti-clericalism

In light of such a reconstruction, one would expect that Luxemburg would take every opportunity to condemn the Church, for its exploitation of the working

---

[36] Foucault's brilliant challenge was to take certain assumptions about contemporary society and rewrite their history. So he studied the development of the medical clinic, or the prison, or intellectual disciplines, or sexuality. For example, in his famous study of medical institutions (Foucault 1975), he showed that they were not merely an organised and enlightened response to people's medical problems, a sign of the grand advance of science, but that those problems were very much invented and produced by the creation of the institutions. For instance, old age, poverty and the body itself were pathologised, becoming the site of medical problems. Thus anatomy becomes pathological anatomy and the cutting up of corpses now happens for the sake of identifying disease. As part of this shift to the medical clinic, a new story arose. In the case of pathological anatomy, Foucault points out that it developed the legend of the battle of valiant doctors digging up corpses from graveyards in the wee small hours in order to avoid religious and moral objections, all for the sake of the glorious march of science. That such a story plays very loosely with the facts is, of course, one of the common criticisms of Foucault.

class, for its enmeshment with capitalism, for its hypocrisy in betraying its roots, and so on. Although she does let loose on the Church on more than one occasion, she is still not willing to make anti-clericalism into a plank of socialist politics. In order to see how she refuses to do so, we need to consider her essay, 'An Anti-Clerical Policy of Socialism'.[37] Apart from the interest of the argument itself, it also provides another angle – alongside the argument that the Church has betrayed its original spirit – for her valorisation of Christian communism.

In that essay, Luxemburg makes two points, namely that socialism should not endorse anti-clericalism as an absolute aim, for, in doing so, it loses sight of the class struggle; and that the bourgeois programme is slippery and inconsistent, in contrast to the consistency of socialism. Let me take the second point first: for Luxemburg, the bourgeoisie espouses anti-clericalism as a fundamental platform and yet does not live up to its high-flying ideals. Focusing on France, she points out that anti-clericalism is a distinctly bourgeois strategy, one that derives from the French Revolution. And France, with its battles between a middle-class parliament and a reactionary Church, is the paradigm which shows that anti-clericalism is distinctly bourgeois. In its drive for purely secular power and secular state institutions, especially education, the bourgeoisie is the natural enemy of the Church: 'care of the poor, the sick, the school, all these functions belong at present to the modern State'.[38]

All the same, the bourgeoisie is inconsistent, for it does not actually carry out a full programme of secularisation. Instead, it seeks to split the Church by approving some religious orders and not approving others. Funds may continue to flow to those sanctioned by the state, and the secular bourgeois state wages war only against the non-authorised orders. Or, in the case of education and care of the sick, the state seeks to wrest control away from the Church, while allowing the Church to continue in its other functions. What actually happens is that middle-class anti-clericalism 'really consolidates the power of the Church'.[39] By contrast, socialism has the only consistent approach: it wants the complete abolition of all state support for and recognition of the Church. Only in this way will the Church cease to have a major hand in the

---

[37] Luxemburg 2004a, 1903.
[38] Luxemburg 2004a, p. 5; 1903, p. 34.
[39] Luxemburg 2004a, p. 7; 1903, p. 37.

ruling classes. Over against the fickle approach of the bourgeoisie, the socialists should actually push the bourgeois state to carry out its secular principles completely: it should not merely take control of education along with the care of the poor and the sick, but it should confiscate all church property and abolish what is left of ecclesiastical privilege.

At this point, it would seem that despite its political rhetoric, the bourgeoisie's anti-clericalism is completely hollow, while that of socialism is far more radical. Luxemburg goes on to argue what appears to be a contradictory position – that socialism sees anti-clericalism as a red herring. Before I turn to that argument, let me tarry for a moment with her charge of inconsistency against the bourgeoisie. She has moved a little too quickly in making that accusation. If we come at the problem from the side of the consistency of socialism, then that consistency is due to its focus on class conflict, on the need to overcome the ruling classes and their abuse of power in order to exploit workers. In other words, socialism has a distinct political programme that is at its heart economic: the relief of working-class exploitation. In this light, the middle class may seem inconsistent, but does it not also have an underlying programme? Is that not one of gaining, holding and securing its position as the new ruling class? In this light, the bourgeoisie's inconsistencies become apparent rather than real: in its drive to ruling power, it seeks whatever allegiances will further its programme and that includes the Church when such an alliance gives the bourgeoisie an advantage. Even more, the hoary adage of politics – divide and conquer – applies all too well to bourgeois relations to the Church: a divided Church, one part on side and one part not, warring within itself, is far easier to conquer than one united and hostile.

Both options are also relevant to the bourgeoisie's dealing with the Left. If it is to the advantage of the bourgeoisie, then it will seek alliances with the working class; and then, if that alliance is with a part of the working class, it all too successfully divides the working class and weakens it as a foe. This is where I move to Luxemburg's second argument, namely that, in putting its weight behind bourgeois anti-clericalism, the working class loses sight of the class struggle. On this point, she is quite astute, for by gaining socialist support for anti-clericalism, the bourgeoisie splits the working class and shifts the emphasis of its battles from class exploitation to taking on the Church. Reluctant to give the bourgeoisie so much credit, what Luxemburg does not say is that this is a very clever strategy: anti-clericalism looks like it should be an item in the working-class programme, for under feudalism the Church was very much part of the ruling classes, and it continues to struggle as hard as it can to regain such a position. So it would seem natural that the working class should side with the bourgeoisie in order to cut down the Church's efforts to remain part of the ruling classes.

What Luxemburg does say is that, if socialists place all their eggs in the basket of anti-clericalism, thinking that it is the basis of radical politics, they lose sight of their main objective, which is to free the workers from economic exploitation. Indeed, for Luxemburg, anti-clericalism is 'one of the best ways of turning away the attention of the working-class from social questions, and of weakening the class struggle'.[40] The unwelcome result is that the bourgeoisie manages to enlist the working class in its campaign against the Church, thereby obscuring the more fundamental differences between the middle class and the working class. For, if it is the bourgeois who are the new exploiters, they are the ones the working class needs to overthrow.

At this point in her argument, she seems to come to a glaring contradiction. On the one hand, she has argued that socialists should call on the bourgeoisie to realise their secularising programme, abolish all church privilege and confiscate all church property; on the other hand, she argues that anti-clericalism is not a core socialist position, indeed that it dilutes the proper focus of socialist agitation. There is, of course, a deeper consistency: insofar as a full secularisation, specifically in the form of a full separation of Church and state, is the removal of one powerful section of the ruling classes, then it should be supported. However, such a policy should not blind the working class to the other reality, namely that the dominant new ruling class is the bourgeoisie. So, they too should be overcome, and socialism should not skew that effort by allying itself wholly with bourgeois anti-clericalism.

Anti-clericalism, then, is a valid policy for two reasons: it shows up the inconsistencies of the bourgeoisie, who should be pushed to realise their anti-clerical policy in full, and it challenges the Church's enmeshment with capitalism. It is not, however, a fundamental platform of socialist politics. This position opens up the possibility of Luxemburg's valorisation of Christian socialism. And the reasons for such a valorisation boil down to three: if

---

[40] Luxemburg 2004a, p. 6; 1903, p. 35.

anti-clericalism is not a basic factor in socialist politics, then, in other circumstances, socialism may well have a more positive approach to the Church, and indeed religion more generally; even if the Church is now an owner of capital and thereby an exploiter, it was not always so; if the Church has betrayed its original spirit, then that original spirit was obviously something rather different. It is to that different picture that I now turn.

Christian communism

Let me say up front what I want to do with Luxemburg's argument for an early Christian communism: I take this reconstruction as a political myth, and such a myth has an enabling and virtual power with historical consequences. In other words, the myth of Christian communism may initially be an image, using figurative and metaphorical language that expresses a hope concerning communal living, but once it becomes an authoritative and canonical text, it gains a historical power of its own. It becomes the motivation for repeated and actual attempts at Christian communism. In this sense, it is possible to say that the myth of Christian communism will have been true at some future moment.[41]

As for Luxemburg, the whole argument of her long essay, *Socialism and the Churches*, hinges on the idea that the first Christian communities were communist, even though it was a communism of consumption rather than production. The key text comes from the Acts of the Apostles 4:32–5:

> Now the company of all those who believed were of one heart and soul, and no one said any of the things which he possessed was his own, but they had everything in common. And with great power the apostles gave their testimony to the resurrection of the Lord Jesus, and great grace was upon them all. There was not a needy person among them, for as many as were possessors of lands or houses sold them, and brought the proceeds of what was sold and laid it at the apostles' feet; and distribution was made to each as any had need.

---

[41] For a fuller discussion see Boer 2009.

We can see here a distinct echo of the famous slogan, 'from each according to his abilities, to each according to his need!',[42] although what Luxemburg picks up are two other features of this text: that 'they had everything in common' and that those who had lands and houses sold them and brought the proceeds to the apostles. Acts 2:44–5 summarises these two points rather nicely: 'And all who believed were together and had all things in common; and they sold their possessions and goods and distributed them to all, as any had need'. Add to this both the practice of having meals in common and the abolition of family life,[43] as well as the story of the rich young man from the Gospels, where Jesus tells him, 'You lack one thing; go, sell what you have, and give to the poor, and you will have treasure in heaven; and come, follow me',[44] and we have a theme that has become a powerful current in Christian political thought and practice.

Now, Luxemburg takes this description as a report of real and general communal practice among the early Christians. She goes so far as to back it up with a quotation from an unspecified writer,[45] a church historian (albeit from 1780),[46] and then some quotations from the Church Fathers, Saint Basil in the fourth century, John Chrysostom (347–407) and then Gregory the Great from

---

[42] Marx 1989, p. 87.
[43] Luxemburg 2004b, p. 8; 1982, p. 26.
[44] Mark 10:21; see Matthew 19:21 and Luke 18:22.
[45] 'A contemporary wrote, "these do not believe in fortunes, but they preach collective property and no one among them possesses more than the others. He who wishes to enter their order is obliged to put his fortune into their common property. That is why there is among them neither poverty nor luxury – all possessing all in common like brothers. They do not live in a city apart, but in each they have houses for themselves. If any strangers belonging to their religion come there, they share their property with them, and they can benefit from it as if it their own. Those people, even if previously unknown to each other, welcome one another, and their relations are very friendly. When travelling they carry nothing but a weapon for defence against robbers. In each city they have their steward, who distributes clothing and food to the travellers. Trade does not exist among them. However, if one of the members offers to another some object which he needs, he receives some other objects in exchange. But each can demand what he needs even if he can give nothing in exchange".' Luxemburg 2004b, pp. 7–8; 1982, pp. 24–5.
[46] 'In 1780, the German historian Vogel wrote nearly the same about the first Christians: "According to the rule, every Christian had the right to the property of all the members of the community; in case of want, he could demand that the richer members should divide their fortune with him according to his needs. Every Christian could make use of the property of his brothers; the Christians who possessed anything had not the right to refuse that their brothers should use it. Thus, the Christian who had no house could demand from him who had two or three to take him in; the owner kept only his own house to himself. But because of the community of enjoyment of

the sixth century. None of these count all that well as evidence, since they show how the story in Acts gained a distinct historical effect – they believed it happened and sought to enact Christian communism later on. And the church historian Vogel is no evidence at all, for he was merely offering a paraphrase of Acts itself, assuming it to be a somewhat accurate report of the early Church.

In order to back up her argument, Luxemburg tries to situate the early Church within the Roman Empire, at least as she sees the situation. It is a rather loose reconstruction, locating the early appeal of Christianity among impoverished peasants. Losing their small holdings to the ever-increasing estates of the absent landlords, who then worked those estates with slaves, these freemen either succumbed to debt slavery or fled to cities like Rome. However, without a manufacturing base, there was little work for them, so they relied on the insufficient corn dole to feed themselves and their families. In this situation, she argues, Christianity 'appeared to these unhappy beings as a life-belt [*Rettungsplanke*], a consolation and an encouragement, and became, right from the beginning, the religion of the Roman proletarians'.[47] Given their economic situation, these early Christians demanded an equal share of all resources, especially those that the rich hoarded for themselves. It was a communism born of dire economic circumstances.

Luxemburg's picture of the Roman Empire is a little thin on detail (where are the slaves in this early Church, for instance?), and she is keen to draw as many parallels between the Roman Empire and Czarist Russia, where a despotic régime sought to keep the lid on revolutionary currents. But I am more interested in two features of this reconstruction of the early Church: the tactical effort to show that the economic situation of the early Church is analogous to the situation in which she writes; and the argument that the early Church was a lower-class phenomenon.

As far as the first feature is concerned, I pointed out earlier that Luxemburg writes for the mass of new members of the Social-Democratic Party of Lithuania and Poland, for which she functioned as the main ideologue from her base in Berlin, in order to show that the socialists provide a viable social and economic response to dire economic circumstances in the same way that the

---

goods, housing accommodation had to be given to him who had none".' Luxemburg 2004b, p. 8; 1982, pp. 25–6.

[47] Luxemburg 2004b, p. 6; 1982, p. 24.

early Church did during the Roman Empire. Her deliberate use of the Latin term 'proletarians' is a ploy in this argument: in the same way the lowest class of Roman citizens, freemen without property or ready income, was known as proletarian, so also are the workers under capitalism (for whom the term was appropriated and reworked). Not only does she draw upon Engels here,[48] but she characteristically pushes her argument as far as it will go: making use of an argument from origins that is close to the agenda of radical groups throughout the history of Christianity, she argues that the socialists embody the socially salvific agenda of the early Church, so much so that should Jesus appear in her time, he would side with the socialists:

> And, if Christ were to appear on earth today, he would surely attack the priests, the bishops and archbishops who defend the rich and live by the bloody exploitation of millions, as formerly he attacked the merchants whom he drove from the temple with a whip so that their ignoble presence should not defile the House of God.[49]

As I will point out in a moment, she will take a step further to argue that socialists will complete what was begun by the early Christians.

Secondly, she argues that the early Church appealed to and drew its membership from among the poor. In Marxist studies, this idea goes back to Engels, who writes in his *On the History of Early Christianity*: 'Christianity was originally a movement of oppressed people: it first appeared as a religion of slaves and freedmen, of poor people deprived of all rights, of peoples subjugated or dispersed by Rome'.[50] Surprisingly, Engels is also the source of the idea in New-Testament studies and church history. Able to read Koine Greek, having renounced with difficulty his Calvinist faith, and keeping up with biblical studies, Engels was no amateur on these matters. By the early twentieth century, it became the consensus among New-Testament scholars[51] and among sociologists,[52] holding sway until the 1960s. From then, however, reaction set in and more conservative scholars reclaimed the older argument that pre-dates Engels: Christianity drew its membership from the middle and upper

---

[48] Engels 1990.
[49] Luxemburg 2004b, p. 26; 1982, p. 43; translation modified.
[50] Engels 1990, p. 447.
[51] See, for instance, Deissman 1978, 1929.
[52] See Troeltsch 1992.

strata of Roman society.⁵³ In the end, the evidence is rather slim and not at all conclusive. And one cannot help but be a little suspicious about such swings of the pendulum in biblical studies.

All the same, these developments show up two slips in Luxemburg's argument. The first is that the very text from Acts upon which she relies also mentions those who were 'possessors of lands or houses'.⁵⁴ Even this mythical story includes at least a few of the wealthier citizens. Further, there is a distinct difference between the image in Acts, which paints an ideal picture of the early Christian community in Jerusalem, and the later communities in other cities of the Roman Empire such as Corinth and Rome. (Most of the studies of the class composition of early Christianity focus on these later communities and tend to leave alone the account in Acts.) Luxemburg's mistake, then, is to assume that the story in Acts applies to all Christian communities.

This is where the more recent studies of early revolutionary and messianic movements in first-century Judaea come into play, for the 'Jesus movement' was one of these. For example, Richard Horsley argues that these revolutionary movements drew their numbers from the rural poor suffering under a Roman yoke, engaging in slowdowns, sabotage, scribal writings, counterterrorism, and revolts.⁵⁵ If this is the case, then Luxemburg's question is still valid: when did the change from a messianic peasant movement to a respectable social movement drawn from the middle and upper strata of Roman society take place? For some, such as Jorunn Økland,⁵⁶ the first signs of this shift come very early indeed, particularly with that central ideologue Paul. Keen not to alter the status quo – slaves and women should accept their lots in life and not seek to change anything⁵⁷ – Paul develops the idea of a 'spiritual messianism' and a heavenly kingdom. Removed from the earlier revolutionary messianism and the earthly kingdom of Jesus and company, this spiritual messianism was to become profoundly influential in the early Church. Even at this very early point, a decade after the death of Jesus, and in the earliest written texts in the New Testament, Paul represents a second movement of

---

⁵³ See the work of the 'rational-choice' theorist, Rodney Stark 1996, pp. 29–48. For a critique of the whole 'rational-choice' approach, see Goldstein 2006.
⁵⁴ Acts 4: 35.
⁵⁵ Horsley 1989, 1992, 1995, 1996; Horsley and Hanson 1985.
⁵⁶ Økland 2005.
⁵⁷ 1 Corinthians 7:21–3, 39.

early Christianity that sought to moderate and modify the Christian movement in light of the more well-to-do economic and social circumstances of the Church's Jewish members and proselytes. No wonder the early Church became respectable.

In light of these developments – that Paul marks the first moderating effect and that the early Christian communities in the Roman Empire were rather respectable – we find ourselves with arguments that undermine Luxemburg's historical assumptions. Add to that the extremely unreliable nature of the book of Acts as a historical document at all[58] and her argument begins to look rather thin. Even without the issue of the unreliable nature of Acts, the early Church turns out to be less like the workers to whom she addressed her essay and far more diverse, including a sprinkling of wealthier members of Roman society, indeed a little like the bourgeoisie to whom she is so vehemently opposed – although I am extremely wary of drawing such analogies across vastly different social and economic systems such as the Ancient mode of production of the Roman Empire and capitalism.

Strangely, these historical arguments do not seem to have much impact on the effect of texts such as those in Acts 4:32–5 and Acts 2:44–5. What I mean is that they have become influential political myths, especially outside the small circle of biblical scholarship, a status that may even be enhanced by the unhistorical nature of these texts. For the communist nature of that mythical early community – a paradise-like myth of origins if ever there was one – has continued and continues to influence movements throughout Christian history, such as the Franciscan order within the Roman-Catholic Church, or the communist efforts of Gerrard Winstanley and the Diggers in seventeenth-century England,[59] or the Icarian communes of Étienne Cabet (1788–1856) in the USA, or the various Christian communes that exist today. Their virtual power as political myth shows up in a somewhat different context as well: I have found that when – for my sins – I used to speak to church groups about these texts, especially those from secure and leafy middle-class suburbs, the

---

[58] Penner 2004; Koester 1982, Volume 2, pp. 98–9, 315–23.
[59] In Winstanley's own words: 'And when the Son of man, was gone from the Apostles, his Spirit descended upon the Apostles and Brethren, as they were waiting at *Jerusalem*; and Rich men sold their Possessions, and gave part to the Poor; and no man said, That ought that he possessed was his own, for they had all things Common, *Act.* 4.32'. Winstanley, et al. 1649.

listeners found them profoundly uncomfortable. With their status as founding myth of the Christian Church, they seemed a far cry from the self-serving and nuclear lives that most of these people led.

However, I do want to insist on the point I made above concerning the unreliability of this image in Acts, an image that is so important for Luxemburg. Rather than her effort to fix such a moment historically, or indeed for New-Testament scholars to do so, I prefer a different tack. It may be stated in terms of the following contradiction: the less historically reliable such a story is, the more powerful it is as a political myth. Even further, it is important to insist that this picture of the early Christian community rests on the flimsiest of evidence – the book of Acts – since only then can we avoid the tendency of trying to restore some pristine state that has been disrupted by a 'Fall', whenever that moment might have taken place. The more the belief holds that Acts presents what was once a real, lived experience, the more efforts to restore that ideal early church become reactionary. For any effort at restoring what was lost, of overcoming a 'Fall', is reactionary in the first degree. Such efforts have bedevilled movements within the Church over two millennia, movements that have sought in their own ways to return to that first community. What happens in these efforts is that the mythical early Church becomes a desirable point of origin that needs to be retrieved. However, if we insist that the communal life of the early Church is myth, that it projects a wish as to what might be, that it gives us a powerful image of what may still be achieved, then we are able to overcome the reactionary desire to return to the early Church in the book of Acts and perhaps turn it to radical ends.

Consumption versus production

For all her misdirected efforts to recover an authentic original Christian communism, Luxemburg is not so overcome with a romanticised image of the early Church not to see problems. For her, the major problem is that the image we find in Acts is a communism of consumption rather than one of production. In the end, she argues, such a communism of consumption will not get us very far. It is both limited in the potential size of the commune and in duration, for a communism of consumption is possible only as long as there are riches to share and goods to sell. Here is Luxemburg:

> But this communism was based on the consumption of finished products and not on the communism of work, and proved itself incapable of reforming

society, of putting an end to the inequality between people and throwing down the barrier which separated rich from poor.... Suppose, for example, that the rich proprietors, influenced by the Christian doctrine, offered to share up between the people all their money and other riches which they possessed in the form of cereals, fruit, clothing, animals, etc. what would the result be? Poverty would disappear for several weeks and during this the time the people would be able to feed and clothe themselves. But the finished products are quickly used up. After a short lapse of time, the people, having consumed the distributed riches, would once again have empty hands.[60]

Apart from the Christian communities themselves, nothing has in fact changed within the economic structures as a whole. It would rely on the rich producing more, by means of their slaves, so that they could once again share their wealth with the Christian community – 'That would be to draw water in a sieve!'[61] Should they also sell their means of production, then the Christian communities would quickly starve. Already within early Christian communism, the logic of giving alms to the poor arose, for such a system could only be maintained if the rich kept making surpluses and kept on giving them to the poor.

At this point, argues Luxemburg, the socialists differ from early Christian communism, for the socialists demand a more fundamental change in the means of production. While the Christian communists 'did not demand that the land, the workshops and the instruments of work should become collective property, but only that everything should be divided up among them, houses, clothing, food and finished products most necessary to life', the socialists seek to make into common property the actual 'instruments of work, the means of production, in order that all humanity may work and live in harmonious unity'.[62]

Completing Christian communism

What all of this means is that socialism will complete what Christian communism began. Its intention may have been right – an ardent belief in communism

---

[60] Luxemburg 2004b, pp. 9–10; 1982, pp. 26–7; translation modified.
[61] Luxemburg 2004b, p. 10; 1982, p. 27.
[62] Luxemburg 2004b, p. 7; 1982, p. 24.

– but it needs to go a step further: not merely the products of an economy need to be held in common, but the means of production themselves. Luxemburg's rather arresting conclusion is then that socialism is, in fact, the logical outcome of Christianity:

> What the Christian Apostles could not accomplish by their fiery preaching against the egoism of the rich, the modern proletarians, workers conscious of their class-position, can start working in the near future, by the conquest of political power in all countries by tearing the factories, the land, and all the means of production from the capitalists to make them the communal property of the workers.[63]

If it is not quite Ernst Bloch's argument that atheistic Marxism is the messianic realisation of the rebellious stream in Judaism and Christianity,[64] it certainly comes close.

In contrast to Christian communism, with its alms and charity, with its taking from the rich and giving to the poor, socialism points out that a proper communism is possible only when the land and all other means of production are placed in the hands of the producers themselves, the workers, who will produce what each one needs. In other words, to the Christian communists the socialists say, 'You want communism? We'll give you real communism!'

Freedom of conscience

Not so much a 'curious piece of historical sophistry', for all its flaws, Luxemburg's story of Christian communism and her effort to account for its disappearance in the history of the Church taps into a powerful political myth, one that she in fact had a good hand in embellishing and perpetuating. It was, of course, also a tactical ploy in the circumstances in which it was written, seeking to show how socialism has more in common with certain – especially subversive – elements of Christianity than one might think. That such an argument should have made more than one 'godless communist' uncomfortable goes without saying. It has also made more than one 'good Christian'

---

[63] Luxemburg 2004b, p. 23; 1982, p. 40; translation modified.
[64] Bloch 1972, p. 240; 1985, Volume 14, p. 317.

uncomfortable. Rather than seeking to distance socialism from Christianity, she has not merely acknowledged the affinities but made them a virtue.

Yet, her argument has one more surprising outcome, namely the argument for a freedom of conscience regarding religious belief:

> The Social-Democrats, those of the whole world and of our own country, regard conscience [*Gewissen*] and personal opinion [*Überzeugung*] as being sacred. Everyone is free to hold whatever faith and whatever opinions will ensure his happiness. No one has the right to persecute or to attack the particular religious opinion of others. Thus say the Social-Democrats.[65]

Luxemburg is astute enough to see that 'liberty of conscience' cuts both ways. If she challenges the thought police of the Czarist régime in Russia and Russian-controlled Poland, which persecuted Catholics, Jews, heretics and freethinkers, and if she challenges the efforts of the Church to control what people believe by whatever means available, from state power to the Inquisition, then she will not argue that the socialists should exercise the same type of censorship and control. And the logical outcome of such an approach is that freedom of conscience also applies to religious belief.

There is, as always, a tactical element to her argument, namely that, in contrast to the Church's propaganda, the large number of those with religious commitment in her party need not worry about the incompatibility of their beliefs with the programmes of the party. But there is also a deeper issue here. I, for one, had always taken the idea of freedom of conscience as much a fiction (no one does in fact have full freedom of conscience) as a central element in the ideology of liberalism with its valorisation of the private individual. I must admit to being not so enamoured with Luxemburg's statement that 'religion is a private affair [*la religion est une affaire privée*]',[66] for this slips too far into such a liberal ideological position. Since it is so much a part of the realm of the sacrosanct individual, I have always been profoundly suspicious of and opposed to the idea of freedom of conscience.

However, there is a double paradox in such an idea that Luxemburg shows up somewhat unwittingly. The first one is that the slogan of 'freedom of conscience', especially in the hands of those who propagate it these days, produces

---

[65] Luxemburg 2004b, p. 2; 1982, p. 19; translation modified.
[66] Luxemburg 2004a, p. 2; 1903, p. 28.

the opposite. Thus, in the hands of a Friedrich von Hayek or a Milton Friedman,[67] the link between freedom and capitalism, or freedom of conscience and freedom of speech with the so-called 'free market', always ends up being oppressive, producing widespread exploitation, poverty and environmental destruction. Or, in the hands of an imperial power such at the United States, 'freedom' becomes the ideological justification for invasion and occupation – without even seeing the contradiction, they seek to impose 'freedom' on countries (most recently Afghanistan and Iraq), with disastrous consequences. This first paradox is perhaps best caught up in a slogan of the political Right, 'freedom through firepower'.

There is, however, a second and far more interesting paradox. Rather than throwing out the baby of freedom of conscience with the bathwater of liberal ideology, it seems to me that socialism too has a paradox that turns on freedom of conscience. As a movement that operates primarily from a collective perspective, one would expect that freedom of conscience would be far from such a programme – at least if one believes the critics of socialism such as Hayek, for whom collective will is actually a cover for the imposition of dictator's will. By contrast, a fully collective programme is precisely one that does not seek to impose the will of one over the other. It is, if you like, the complex effort to allow each one in the collective to express her or his beliefs, foibles and obsessions without the imposition of control and censorship. So I end with a dialectical point: only a fully collective programme will enable the full realisation of freedom of conscience. And that applies as much to religious belief as to anything else. To me, at least, this is one of the deepest lessons from Luxemburg's *Socialism and the Churches*.

---

[67] Hayek 1960; Friedman 2002.

Chapter Four
The Enticements of Karl Kautsky

I must admit that, when I first opened Karl Kautsky's *Foundations of Christianity*, I was expecting a dated and doctrinaire materialist polemic against Christianity.[1] After all, the book is a century old, being first published in 1908. Even more, Kautsky often comes across as one of the scholastics of Marxism, a lesser intellect who followed in the path laid out by the founders. As one who had met the 'old man' himself during his stay in England from 1885 to 1890 and who had become a good friend of Engels before his death in 1895, he seemed like an apostle whose job it became to consolidate and develop what Marx and Engels had laid down. The image I had was a Marxist scholastic, an urbane and civilised politician (with the dreadful taint of having voted for war credits in the Reichstag in 1914, although he did change his mind later) whose writings were too voluminous to have the desired depth.

By contrast, *Foundations of Christianity* is well worth a read, for there are a good number of insights that repay some consideration. The great value of that work, for all its flaws, is that it begins what is still an unfinished project, namely a detailed Marxist reconstruction of the social and economic context

---

[1] Kautsky 2001, 1908. Steenson calls it 'little more than an intriguing period piece and a monument to Kautsky's doctrinal commitment' (Steenson 1978, p. 165).

in which the Bible arose. He also carries on the task first attempted by Engels to reconstruct a longer history of communist thought and action that pre-dates Marx and Engels.[2] As for the first, it is nothing less than a reconstruction of the history of ancient Israel, the ancient Near East and the early Church. As for the second, he argues for the crucial role of religion in these pre-Marxist forms of communism, however incomplete they may turn out to be. While Kautsky raises some of the crucial questions in these projects, his work on religion is only a (somewhat flawed) beginning. In other words, Kautsky's work is full of enticement, since, in its incompleteness and false paths, it beckons one to go further – which is precisely what I will do on more than one occasion.

Why did Kautsky want to reconstruct this history? Here I can let him speak for himself:

> Whatever one's position may be with respect to Christianity, it certainly must be recognized as one of the most titanic phenomena in all human history.... Anything that helps us to understand this colossal phenomenon, including the study of its origin, is of great and immediate practical significance, even though it takes us back thousands of years.[3]

How is it that a phenomenon such as Christianity arose? What were the economic, political and social conditions in which it began? And how are we to understand the texts that Christianity (and for that matter, Judaism) regards as sacred? It is less a case of trying to understand the enemy better, or indeed, like Gramsci, to learn something from the first and most enduring global movement; rather, in the act of rewriting or recasting that history, Kautsky both challenges the received histories of Israel and the Church and opens up new possibilities from that history. In other words: rewrite history and you rewrite the possible paths of the future.

I have organised my analysis as follows. After a brief synopsis of his argument, I focus on the troubled use of unreliable ancient texts like the Bible for the sake of historical reconstruction, an issue that is still very much at the centre of biblical scholarship. If they are chronically unreliable sources, then what historical use (if any) do they have? At this point, I bring Kautsky

---

[2] See Engels 1975, 1978, 1990.
[3] Kautsky 2001, p. 13; 1908, p. 1.

into conversation with a major current debate in biblical scholarship over this issue. Secondly, I engage critically with Kautsky's reconstruction, seeking out both problems and insights that are still pertinent today. I am particularly interested in his use of the narrative of differentiation, in his discussion of modes of production, in what a reconstruction in Kautsky's spirit might look like, and in the problem of transitions between modes of production. Third, I pick up an argument he shares with his sometime friend and comrade, Rosa Luxemburg: if early Christianity was a communist movement, then what sort of communism was it? Yet, Kautsky's interest was much wider than Christian communism, for one of his projects was to recover a much greater tradition of socialist thought and practice, one that predates Marx and Engels's 'modern' socialism. Christian communism becomes an important moment in this longer tradition. At this point I bring in his *Thomas More and His Utopia*[4] as well as *Vorläufer des neueren Sozialismus*.[5] If Thomas More is the first modern socialist with a deep religious motivation, then the various revolutionary movements during the Middle Ages and the Reformation are other moments in the extensive history of religiously inspired communism. Like Christian communism, these various movements dip into what I want to call the myth of primitive communism, but they are also incomplete anticipations of the full communism of Marx and Engels. In this respect, Kautsky draws close to Ernst Bloch's *Atheism in Christianity*.[6] Although Kautsky is far more interested in historical reconstruction, he shares an interest in the utopian possibilities of Christianity, albeit without Bloch's irrepressible enthusiasm. Above all, Kautsky manifests a fascination with distinctly religious forms of communism.

Text, history, context

In Kautsky's effort at historical reconstruction, what interests me most is his argument that the Bible is a cultural product of a distinct socio-economic context and history. This may seem an obvious point now, but it took a long struggle for this position to gain credibility, doing so only in the 1980s with Norman Gottwald's Marxist-inspired *Tribes of Yahweh*.[7] Such an argument is

---

[4] Kautsky 2002, 1947.
[5] Kautsky 1976.
[6] Bloch 1972; 1985, Volume 14.
[7] Gottwald 1999 (originally published in 1979).

far more possible within a Marxist framework in which culture, economics, society and so on are inter-related parts of a whole. Thus, the Bible does not provide factual data about the supposed 'events' of which it speaks; it is instead the product of a culture (or cultures) within a social and economic formation. Let us see how Kautsky gets to this point.

Foundations of Christianity is an ambitious book, beginning with the person of Jesus in both pagan and Christian sources. Carefully assessing the information in light of New-Testament scholarship of his time, Kautsky argues that, around this everyday rebel, a whole cluster of superhuman stories grew, stories that became the New Testament. Needless to say, Kautsky wants to cut through the mythical and legendary accretions and offer a historical-materialist analysis. That analysis focuses initially on reconstructing the economic, social and political context of Jesus within the slave mode of production of the Roman Empire, invoking some key Marxist points concerning the technological limits of such a mode of production and the reason for its breakdown. From there, Kautsky tracks backwards to offer a history that runs from the origins of Israel through to the early-Christian movement. Here, again, he reconstructs the underlying social formation, arguing that it was another form of the slave mode of production. The final section comes back to Christianity, where he expands on the famous argument concerning early-Christian communism, how it fell short and how it was subverted in the later history of the Church, only to carry on a half-life within monasticism. But what it does do, quite refreshingly, is break with the linear narrative assumptions of so much historiography which still falls under the spell of moving from origin to close. At another level, Kautsky's arrangement makes more sense, for his concern is Christianity, particularly how it arose and how it became a worldwide movement. In this light, the logical point at which to begin is the figure of Jesus of Nazareth. From there, he can spread his analysis in order to seek the economic and social context, the prehistory and post-history of the Jesus-event.

The slipperiness of sacred texts

There is, however, a preliminary question. When Kautsky comes to the socioeconomic reconstruction of ancient Israel, he bumps up against an old and persistent problem:

> It is impossible to outline a picture of ancient Israel with any certainty, given the scarcity and the unreliability of the sources that have come down to us.... Basically we are reduced to hypotheses when we try to form an idea of the course of the development of Israelite society.[8]

The same applies to the Christian sources regarding Jesus, which manifest a 'complete indifference to the truth'.[9] However much he falls away from this point, resorting to the treacherous terrain of biblical narrative too often in his search for a historical core when all else fails, it echoes loudly in present day debates in biblical criticism. If we take the Hebrew Bible, some would grant greater credence to the reliability of the biblical material,[10] while others argue that it is entirely useless for such a reconstruction, and anyone who relies upon it produces pseudo-history in the shape of rationalist paraphrase.[11] And these are all critical biblical scholars and not some fundamentalist variety that takes the Bible as the inerrant 'word of God'.

Let me say a little more about this very contemporary and heated debate in biblical studies, for it sets the context of Kautsky's own scepticism regarding the biblical text as historical evidence. At the moment when a status quo had been achieved in historiography of the Hebrew Bible – the assumption being that we could in fact come up with some history from the monarchy of David and Solomon onwards (although no earlier) – a group of biblical scholars who would later be dubbed the minimalists (I prefer to call them simply critical scholars) thoroughly disrupted the consensus. They challenged the interpretations of the scarce pieces of archaeological evidence, the heavy reliance on some very shifty biblical texts, the tendency to rationalist paraphrase of those texts, and the construction of an ancient 'Israel' that was really a castle in the clouds. What can we say about the Hebrew Bible? Well, it was probably written and collated very late, most likely in the Hellenistic era (after 331 B.C.E. when Alexander the Great conquered the Near East). The mythical and legendary narratives, which run right through the monarchies and the exiles at the hands of the Assyrians and the Babylonians, and even to the so-called

---

[8] Kautsky 2001, p. 151; 1908, p. 185.
[9] Kautsky 2001, p. 19; 1908, p. 8.
[10] For example, see Dever 2001; Day 2004; McKenzie 2000.
[11] Lemche 1988, 1998a, 1998b; Thompson 1992, 1999, 2005; Davies 1995.

restoration after the exile, have little if any historical basis. They are nothing more than the various elements of a comprehensive political myth (to use a phrase I have explored elsewhere)[12] that did excellent service at the time of the only real independent Jewish state under the Hasmoneans (165–3 B.C.E.).

It is a curious debate all the same, for it is by no means new. Indeed, Kautsky would feel quite at home within it, and it is a debate that has bedevilled modern biblical historiography for at least a century and a half. The only difference is that the current wave of critical scholars is among the most sceptical of the lot. All that can be said for certain, they argue, is that there was a Persian province called Yehud in the fourth century B.C.E. Further, the texts we have are a fanciful production from that period. In fact, it seems as though the 'minimalists' of today have taken Kautsky's comment to heart: 'Bible criticism by Protestant theologians has already shown that a great deal of it is spurious and fictitious, but tends far too much to take as gospel truth everything not yet proved to be obviously counterfeit'.[13] Kautsky is referring to the German biblical scholars of the nineteenth century, whose work he knew rather well. But what scholars of our own day like Philip Davies, Niels Peter Lemche and Thomas Thompson have done is challenge what has 'not yet proved to be obviously counterfeit', seeking to show that it too is spurious and fictitious. If we shift perspective, it would seem that these critical scholars are the heirs of Kautsky's own welcome scepticism regarding the reliability of the Bible for historical reconstruction.

It is, however, a tough standard to set oneself, and Lemche and Thompson have admitted to me that, every now and then, they slip and refer to given dates and events of earlier scholarship. For instance, the exile of the people of Judah in 587 B.C.E. by the Babylonians has been such a staple of Hebrew-Bible scholarship that Lemche has at times referred to it, and yet he has argued strenuously that such an exile is the product of literary imagination.

So also Kautsky: for all his comments regarding the spurious and fictitious texts, when he has nothing else to rely upon, he resorts to biblical texts to back up a point. As a few examples among many, there is the citation of Genesis 13:2 regarding Abraham's wealth,[14] or Ezekiel 27:17 concerning the trade of

---

[12] Boer 2009.
[13] Kautsky 2001, p. 151; 1908, p. 185.
[14] Kautsky 2001, p. 158; 1908, p. 194.

Tyre,[15] or Isaiah 5:8–9 and Amos 4:1–2 on the question of class struggles in ancient Israel,[16] or the rational paraphrase of the story of the twelfth-century conquest of Canaan found in Joshua and Judges.[17] And on it goes. In the end, he wants it both ways, showing scepticism regarding the text and then using it to back up his argument. Too often, he resorts to a paraphrase of the text, at times backing up his reconstruction with quotations from biblical scholars who themselves resort to the same practice.

The Bible as a cultural product

I have, however, not been entirely fair to Kautsky, for he is trying to approach the biblical texts from a very different direction. In a nutshell, he argues that, although we can find very little concerning specific events or details concerning characters such as Jesus, we can learn 'very valuable things about the social character, the ideals and aspirations'[18] of both early Israel and the primitive Christian communities. The point applies particularly to ancient texts such as Homer or the Bible.

This solution to the relation between biblical texts and history is as disarmingly simple as it is missed by that strange breed known as biblical scholars who like to focus on questions of history. The texts are not more-or-less reliable sources of evidence for historical 'facts' and events; rather, they are products of a culture that has a complex relationship with its social and economic context. They give voice to all manner of cultural expectations, hopes, fears and beliefs. But let me extend Kautsky here, since it is a valuable point: biblical texts are historical, then, but in a different sense from that often assumed to be the case. We can argue forever about whether a particular text tells us what actually happened or not, for history cannot be read off the texts as though they were directly referential. Rather, as a collection of cultural products, the texts respond to, block out, seek alternatives to, and are saturated by the images and metaphors of the contexts from which they arise. And that context is unavoidably economic and social. In other words, we need to shift gear and move away from the search for explicit historical events – the exile to Babylon,

---

[15] Kautsky 2001, p. 161; 1908, pp. 197–8.
[16] Kautsky 2001, pp. 178–9; 1908, p. 221.
[17] Kautsky 2001, pp. 173–4; 1908, pp. 214–16.
[18] Kautsky 2001, p. 32; 1908, p. 25.

the return from exile, the kingdoms and battles of David, Solomon et al. – and focus on the wider social formation in which the texts were produced.

Such an approach to biblical texts – one that Kautsky pursues – boils down to a methodological preference. Rather than the scouring of texts in order to construct a political history, Kautsky's Marxist approach focuses on the economic and social history. It is less a search for the chronicle-like sequence of major events in which the political leaders are actors and more an effort to locate the deeper logic of an economic system. And, within such a system – or rather, mode of production – a collection of texts like the Bible is a collection of cultural responses. How it responds is often unexpected, since these cultural products are not mere effluvia of the economic base but are the result of various (now largely unknown) authors exercising a fair degree of agency.

On that score, Kautsky's reading is fascinating, especially the section concerning 'thought and sentiment' in the Roman era.[19] While we might find his constant efforts to draw parallels between the ancient world and his own – such as between the Roman era and the nineteenth century,[20] or between ancient Palestine and modern Poland and Italy[21] – a bit of a stretch, the basic point he makes is worth retaining: periods of economic and social upheaval generate a host of cultural and ideological responses as old structures begin to break down and people search for new structures. The Christian Church was one such structure that provided an answer in a period of turmoil. I will have more to say on how Kautsky sees the early Church later, but, for now, I am interested in the cultural manifestations – the 'thought and sentiment' – of the time. He identifies seven themes that arose in that time of change: insecurity in the face of massive change, credulity (in terms of supernaturalism and the craving for miracles), untruthfulness and deception for religious ends, apparent 'humaneness' (in reality, necessary doles for the poor and the need to keep slaves alive and fit for work), internationalism (as far as the Mediterranean can be counted as 'international'), piety and an increasing number of religious sects, and monotheism (of which Christianity was not the only variety). The list may be incomplete and it may miss the point in some respects. For example, his emphasis on individualism and his vulgar-Marxist explanation for

---

[19] Kautsky 2001, pp. 90–150; 1908, pp. 102–83.
[20] Kautsky 2001, p. 91; 1908, p. 104.
[21] Kautsky 2001, p. 176; 1908, p. 218.

monotheism – as a reflection of imperial politics – are at least two questionable points.[22] Yet the underlying assumption concerning the nature of texts cannot be gainsaid. In my discussion of Kristeva in the next chapter, we will see how she gives a more distinct form to these features of the Roman era. For Kristeva, what we find is a whole range of psychological pathologies – from masochism to psychosis – to which Christianity provides the answers.

Reconstructing economic history

The real achievement of Kautsky's study is that it is the first book-length effort to reconstruct the economic history of ancient Israel and the early Church using Marxist methods. For that reason alone, it is worth renewed attention, as much for the questions raised as for the answers provided. He may have been hampered by a relative scarcity of information, at least compared to the situation at the beginning of the twenty-first century. But, then again, what looks to some like a glut of information[23] is only so when compared to other ancient civilisations. It is still a very small amount for a period of about three millennia (3000–331 B.C.E.). While Kautsky had very little information to go on, we have not quite so little.

Differentiation and slaves

Three items draw my attention in his reconstruction: the narrative of differentiation, the vital role of the slave-based mode of production, and the perpetual question of the transition of modes of production. As for the narrative of differentiation, for Kautsky it is a fundamental resource; he resorts to it in regard to the mode of production in Rome and in ancient Israel, and then again when tracing the dissolution of Christian communism in both the early communities and then the monasteries.[24] At its most basic level, the narrative moves from a given un-differentiated state to one of differentiation. With differentiation comes the division of labour, exploitation and class.

---

[22] Kautsky 2001, pp. 91, 147; 1908, pp. 103–4, 177–8.
[23] Van De Mieroo, p. 2007, p. 7.
[24] Kautsky 2001, pp. 33–5, 177–8, 352–9, 384–91; 1908, pp. 26–9, 219–22, 441–50, 481–93.

With regard to Rome, it goes like this: under certain conditions, such as the varying quality of soil and rainfall, or the possibilities and quantities of trade or booty, the differentiation of wealth and power sets in and is concentrated in the hands of certain astute and unscrupulous individuals. Economic differentiation is the beginning of exploitation and therefore of class, in which a certain group is disconnected from the production of essential items for survival such as food and clothing. This class then relies on those who do produce these essentials and must extract it from them in some fashion, whether by coercion or persuasion or some mix of the two. With more and more people removed from production as exploiters, whether wealthy landowners, chieftains, clergy, or a scribal sub-class, a labour shortage arises: there is simply not enough manpower to till the soil, especially since production was primarily agricultural. The first full mode of production arises from this problem of labour shortage, and the resolution is slavery at the expense of freemen. In the case of Greece and Rome, the response was to resort to conquest in order to find more people to put to work as slaves. The result: a slave-based mode of production in which surplus was extracted from slaves.

With ancient Israel, the beginnings may be slightly different, but the result is largely the same. Kautsky buys into the biblical picture that the early Israelites were desert nomads, accepting the theory that they were probably Bedouin tribes (a theory discredited now). Such a life on the move provided a vital and relatively simple life. However, when these nomads settled in Canaan, they took on an agricultural life on the land. From here, differentiation sets in, with some gaining wealth on the land at the expense of others. Wealthy landowners began appropriating more and more land, which they then rented out to landless peasants at the obligatory punitive rates. When these peasants inevitably failed to meet the exorbitant requirements to repay their debts – usually a portion of the produce of the land – they forfeited their rights to the land and were driven to the position of debt-slaves of those same landowners. From here, the move into a slave-based mode of production was inevitable. In short, although the actual mechanism was slightly different, producing chattel-slaves in Greece and Rome and debt-slaves in Israel, the overall narrative of differentiation is largely the same, running from chance distinctions through to a full-blown mode of production and its mechanism of exploitation. The result is the same as well, namely a slave-based mode of production.

Underlying Kautsky's narrative is an assumed primitive communism: the undifferentiated agricultural life of early Rome or the nomadic life of the Israelites before they settled down in Canaan. This assumption becomes more explicit when he turns to the story of Christian communism. In this case, the early proletarian movement adopted a form of communism based on having all goods in common and sharing a common meal. However, in order to maintain such a commune, it required some with wealth who were able to distribute it. From here, the slide begins, slipping into further differentiation; before long, having all goods in common turned into charity from the rich for the poor, who then became dependent on them. Further, since Christian communism only worked with a small group, as the movement grew in size, differentiation became marked. The movement required organisation and structure, with the result that a hierarchy of leadership developed. Since the leaders and the organisation required material support, the goods that used to be held in common were now provided to maintain the leadership and church structures. Once again, division of labour leads to class difference and economic exploitation. A similar path shows up with monasticism: initially, it carried on the spirit of early Christian communism, although now based on agriculture in the countryside, but, eventually, the monasteries became wealthy (through the ban on marriage and passing of all possessions over to the monastery), developed leaders who became the new exploiters of the monks and nuns, and so on.

I will return to the question of a slave-based mode of production and the nature of Christian communism below, but, first, let me tarry for a while with the narrative of differentiation. What continues to surprise me is how pervasive this narrative is. Kautsky may use it to develop his position of the slave mode of production, in which surplus is extracted from slaves by the slave-owners, or indeed to account for the breakdown of Christian communism. However, a far more common usage of this narrative, especially in biblical studies, is for the rise of the state. So what we also find is that with the concentration of wealth and power, chieftains and towns arise and then, at some vague point when the extraction of essential items becomes sufficiently complex and requires some form of defence for such wealth, we get the city and the state and its ruler, whether a king, despot or tyrant. For example, this narrative turns up in the work of biblical critics such as Niels-Peter Lemche,

Philip Davies and Norman Gottwald, as well as the Marxist work of Perry Anderson, to name but a few.[25]

The narrative itself has a number of features: a progression from a non-differentiated to a differentiated state; a move from simplicity to complexity; a versatile narrative that accounts for economic exploitation, class structures, the end of primitive communism, and the formation of the state; and the need for a trigger that sets differentiation under way. Let me say a little more concerning each item. The narrative assumes a state of non-differentiation and simplicity as its starting point. In this respect, it has deep resonances with two other narratives that are still powerful today, the one from evolutionary theory and physics, and the other from creation stories in the Jewish and Christian traditions. Evolutionary theory postulates a simple origin for life on earth, from which more complex organisms develop over time through natural selection. So also in physics, the theory of the 'singularity' from which the universe (or indeed universes if we take account of string or membrane theory) began is a move from a simple one to a complex multiplicity. And so also in the creation narrative of Genesis 1 (although less so in Genesis 2). Here, we begin with an earth that was 'without form and void'[26] and then move through stages of differentiation until creation is complete – light and dark as day and night, the firmament that separates the waters above and below, the seas and the dry land, which then produce their swarms of creatures and so on. To a lesser extent, the creation story in Genesis 2 begins with simplicity, with an earth devoid of plants, animals, rain and human beings only to be rendered far more complex with the introduction of each of these items.

Given the pervasiveness of such a narrative of differentiation, whether in myth, science or history, one could argue that this is the way things are or that Marxism merely gives the narrative its own twist. So it may be reshaped to provide a story of the origins of exploitation, class and, indeed, the state. And Marxists might also want to note that this version of the narrative has become a staple of much study of both the ancient Near East and ancient Israel. However, a little ideological suspicion never goes astray. Has Marxist analysis merely taken over a mythical biblical narrative for its own pur-

---

[25] Lemche 1988, pp. 22–4; 1998a, pp. 94–5; Davies 1998, pp. 59–73; Gottwald 2001; Anderson 1974b.
[26] Genesis 1:2.

poses, a narrative that does service just as well in science or indeed in stories about the emergence of capitalism? Now, one might want to argue that the evidence points incontrovertibly towards such a narrative, but that is nothing more than special pleading. In the case of ancient Israel and the ancient Near East, the narrative really tries to put the relatively scarce pieces of evidence in a coherent and progressive relation to one another. In that respect, it is no different from any other imaginative narrative, but it is worthwhile recognising it as such – Kautsky's included. But it also means that another narrative may do just as good a job, for instance, one that notes the cycle of crises in the ancient Near East that staggered from one collapse to another in terms of increasing differentiation and then increasing simplicity. Or perhaps one that argues against any narrative that moves from simplicity to increasing differentiation, arguing that what we have is a good deal of complexity and differentiation right from the beginning. This last position is in fact my preference and one I seek to develop elsewhere.[27]

One of the reasons for taking such a position is that it avoids what I would like to call the 'problem of paradise'. What I mean here is that the simple, non-differentiated state is invariably a paradise: in that simple original state, we find mythical stories of a natural harmony before the arrival of sin and disobedience to the deity, or indeed before exploitation in terms of economic relation, gender, ethnicity and what have you. In Marxist terms, this is nothing other than primitive communism, a theme that pervades a significant argument concerning the origins of ancient Israel,[28] let alone Kautsky's own narratives. It is also one to which Kautsky reverts in his analysis of Thomas More.[29]

Further, there is the problem of the trigger for differentiation that then leads to exploitation, class, conflict and the oppression of the state. What exactly is the trigger? Kautsky resorts to a naturalist argument, citing the quality of the soil, differences in climate (which we might put, for the ancient Near East, in terms of irrigation or rainfall agriculture), and the role of natural disasters such as drought or flood affecting crop yields. These natural differences then produce relatively greater yields for some, healthier and more numerous cattle, and less for others, and so we find the first moments of economic

---

[27] Boer 2007c.
[28] Gottwald 1999; Meyers 1988; Yee 2003; Jobling 1991; see Boer 2005c.
[29] Kautsky 2002, 1947.

differentiation. Or he makes use of the simple trigger of size with the early Christian Church: once it moved beyond the small communist groups, the Church had to find some structures to manage the larger movement. The problem of the trigger for differentiation is, however, generated by the narrative itself; without a simple non-differentiated state, we do not need a trigger for differentiation in the first place.

Slaves and other modes of production

At the end of Kautsky's narrative of differentiation comes the slave-based mode of production. On the one hand, the argument for such a mode of production in Greece and Rome remains, even despite the criticisms of Hindess and Hirst, a staple of Marxist reconstructions of the Hellenistic world (and indeed many other approaches influenced by Marxism). On the other hand, it was and is controversial in regard to the ancient Near East, for, here too, Kautsky argues for a slave-based mode of production. On this score, there is an ongoing and fascinating debate, and so I would like to see how his argument fares in light of developments in that debate.

To begin with, he challenges what would at the time have been the Marxist consensus concerning the ancient Near East. He was no mere scholastic, refining the positions of his forebears; Kautsky makes a few bold moves of his own. When he was writing the book in the early years of the twentieth century, the dominant Marxist position was that the ancient Near East was one instance of the Asiatic mode of production, a mode that also included India and China before British colonialism, as well as ancient South America. To see what Kautsky was challenging (and for readers not familiar with this aspect of Marxist thought) let me outline the key elements of such an Asiatic mode of production. The relevant material from Marx and Engels is dispersed in their work over a thirty-year period. It includes newspaper articles, letters, critiques of political economy and ethnological research.[30] Out of this collection, the key features of the Asiatic mode of production are as follows:[31]

---

[30] An early sustained attempt comes in *The German Ideology* (Marx and Engels 1976, pp. 32–5), but the most complete discussions are from *Grundrisse* (Marx 1986, pp. 399–439) and the Preface to *A Contribution to the Critique of Political Economy* (Marx 1987, pp. 261–5).

[31] A number of such distillations exist, such as Bailey and Llobera 1981, Krader 1975, Lichtheim 1990 and Shiozawa 1990. See also Pryor's survey of the Western literature

common rather than individual private property in land, often personified in the figure of the god-ruler; centralised control of public works by the government (irrigation, building, roads and so on); a self-sufficient and decentralised economic world of villages with their resilient combination of agriculture and handicrafts over against the imperial state; the social division of labour in terms of usefulness. Marx is not always consistent on the Asiatic mode of production, most (in)famously describing it as a stagnant economic form that changed little over millennia, and yet elsewhere he writes of far greater complexity, especially the exchange, surplus, rent (in labour and in kind) and tax operating within the village community, between communities, between communities and the state and then between the state and the limited long-distance trade generated by manufacturers. This was the position Kautsky comprehensively challenged with his argument for a slave mode of production in ancient Israel.

All the same, Kautsky's reconstruction has an extraordinary resonance with Soviet studies of the ancient Near East that spanned the decades from the 1920s to the 1980s, the implications of which have yet to be fully appreciated today. Kautsky's argument for a slave-based mode of production became the default position in Soviet scholarship from the 1930s until the 1960s. The strange thing is that none of this work – at least work that I have been able to find[32] – refers to Kautsky, for he was branded as a deviationist for other matters in the Soviet Union, especially after he and Lenin disagreed.[33]

As far as that debate in the Soviet Union was concerned – a debate that provides an extraordinary example of the dialectical interplay between data and theory rarely matched in the West – it falls into a number of clear stages. The early position that the ancient Near East, of which ancient Israel was a part, was characterised by the Asiatic mode of production. That position gave way briefly to feudalism which then fell beneath the sweep of the slave-based, or ancient mode of production, which in its turn begrudgingly allowed the return of a revived Asiatic mode of production. The 'anti-Aziatchiki', as the

---

up until 1980 (Pryor 1990). The problem is that these summaries tend to lose sense of Marx's dialectical approach in dealing with precapitalist modes of production.

[32] As I write I am engaged in a large project to make the best of this work from the 1920s to the 1980s available in English translation. What exists at the moment is rather piecemeal. I am at this point heavily dependent on Dunn's useful summary (Dunn 1981), as well as the collections edited by D'iakonoff (D'iakonoff 1969a, 1991).

[33] See Lenin 1972–6, Volume 28, pp. 104–12.

opponents of the Asiatic mode of production were called, swept the field early in the debate and the Asiatic mode of production disappeared as a viable category. For a few years, feudalism became the preferred descriptor – a position that held sway long afterwards in non-Marxist scholarship on the ancient Near East[34] – but it soon fell away. The crucial moment in Soviet scholarship was the influential lecture (four hours!) delivered in 1933 at the Academy of the History of Material Culture in Leningrad by V.V. Struve. He dismissed feudalism as a way to describe the mode of production in the ancient Near East, pointing out, 'If we say that everything is feudalism, then we get a feudal porridge in the literal sense from Babylon to Napoleon'.[35] In a careful survey of all the crucial and available texts for ancient Mesopotamia and Egypt, Struve persuaded most scholars that the evidence incontrovertibly suggested a slave mode of production. Struve's argument was ingenious, for he pointed out that, although slaves were not as numerous as classes, especially free labourers or landholders, the slaves were owned collectively by the state and temple complex, worked the year round and were therefore the dominant means for the extraction of surplus.

Struve may have been more of an expert on the ancient Near East – an academician no less – and Kautsky more of a politician and populariser, but it is remarkable how Kautsky anticipates the dominant position in the USSR by a good three decades. In the end, the reconstruction of a slave mode of production was to crumble, but not until the 1960s and even the early 1970s. After much argument, that I have traced in more detail elsewhere,[36] including refinements, challenges and qualifications, Struve's argument finally gave way, only to see a refined and refreshed Asiatic mode of production re-emerge from the wings.

However, neither the slave nor the Asiatic modes of production have fared all that well with regard to the ancient Near East. If the former faces the insurmountable problem that slaves were only a minority of the population and that the primary location of production was the village-commune, then the latter runs aground in the argument that the state was the prime exploiter by means of tribute. For one of the staples of Marxist historiography is that the

---

[34] See Schloen 2001, pp. 187–9.
[35] Quoted in Dunn 1981, p. 44; see Struve 1969.
[36] Boer 2007c.

state arises in the context of class struggle: it is an outcome and manifestation of class struggle and not one class in that struggle. And as Hindess and Hirst have shown in their strictly theoretical work,[37] tribute or tax is neither a unique nor a primary means for extracting surplus.

The sacred economy: prolegomena to a reconstruction

Kautsky's is by no means the only effort to produce a systematic and workable reconstruction of the economy of ancient Israel or, indeed, the ancient Near East as a whole. The efforts since Kautsky have been characterised by two features: the search for the motor of the whole system and the multiplication of modes of production. For Kautsky, the key was the production of surplus (although he is astute enough to see that this was not the surplus-value characteristic of capitalism) and he found that in slavery. Others have differed, offering multiple models. To cull a few examples from later studies, some have argued that tribute was the key,[38] or that it was really a feudal system,[39] or, as with Kautsky, that it was slavery, or patron-client relations,[40] or, most anachronistically, a 'market economy',[41] or that we can also find what is variously called a communitarian or domestic mode of production for which the motor was the extended household and which was opposed to a dominant tributary system.[42] Faced with the difficulties of reconstruction, some have simply given up and refused to propose a distinct mode of production for the ancient Near East at all.[43]

So, it seems to me that we need to begin again, giving equal attention to the available data along with a robust attention to economic modelling. The building blocks of such a reconstruction include the following, although to go into detail would take me too far from my concern with Kautsky. To begin with, we are mistaken if we focus on imperial economic structures as the basis. This is all too easy to do, since most of the records available come from imperial sources, whether Babylonian, Assyrian, neo-Babylonian, Persian or

---

[37] Hindess and Hirst 1975, pp. 183–200.
[38] So, for example, Gottwald 1999; Briant 2002.
[39] See my earlier discussion of the Russian debates.
[40] Simkins 1999a, 1999b, 2004.
[41] McNutt 1999, pp. 195–6; Thompson 2000, p. 233; Silver 1983.
[42] Meyers 1988; Jobling 1991, 1998; Yee 2003.
[43] So Anderson 1974b; de Ste. Croix 1981.

Greek. Such a focus leads to an emphasis on tribute gathering, but the catch is, as Marx was fond of pointing out, there must be something from which tribute can be drawn. And that leads to the economy of the village-commune, which was overwhelmingly agricultural. Indeed, 95 per cent or more of the population was engaged in agricultural production, so this is where any economic reconstruction must begin.

On this matter, we can distinguish three areas for analysis: the old Marxist question of ground-rent and what I call the regimes of allocation and extraction. A starting point for ground-rent is the long discussion in the third volume of *Capital*.[44] Yet, for all the discussion of both differential and absolute rent, or indeed the differences between surplus-product in precapitalist formations and surplus-value under capitalism, the basic issue for ground-rent is how one accounts for and distributes the productivity of the soil and its variations. The issue for an agricultural system like the one of the ancient Near East is how the soil produces, to which I would add the productivity of animals and, indeed, women, who were regarded as part of this system of production.

As far as distribution is concerned – or, as I prefer, allocation – the issue is how one goes about allocating agricultural produce. There are four modes or regimes of allocation that can be discerned in the ancient Near East: complex family or clan structures, overlapping patron-client relations, the role of the judiciary and constant warfare. Inserted within, and often in conflict with, these systems of allocation, we also find tribute and trade, both of which may be designated as régimes of extraction. Tribute was a feature of the imperial economy and trade was a limited process restricted to luxury goods for the ruling élite (although this has not stopped more than one historian being mesmerised by trade as the key). It seems to me that the economy of the ancient Near East is distinguished by a contradiction between these régimes of allocation and extraction. It was a contradiction that both enabled that economy to exist and also led to the pattern of crisis and collapse.[45]

---

[44] Marx 1998, pp. 608–800. See also Hindess and Hirst 1975, pp. 188–93; Mandel 1968, pp. 271–304; Harvey 1999, pp. 330–72; Lenin 1972–6, Volume 13, pp. 217–429. Despite his important work on the whole question, Kautsky does not connect the two matters of ground-rent and the economy of ancient Israel; see Kautsky 1988, 1899.

[45] For a preliminary outline of this argument, see Boer 2007c.

Transitions

Back to Kautsky: although I differ concerning the reconstruction of the economy of ancient Israel, I do share a deeper assumption with him, and that is the narrative of modes of production. Now, that narrative has a number of implications well-known to those who work with Marxist theory. Its starting point is difference, for the theory of distinct modes of production operates on the assumption of qualitative differences between each mode of production: feudalism is as distinct from capitalism as the slave (or ancient) mode is distinct from hunter-gatherers, and so on. The question of continuities – such as private property or money – then becomes a crucial issue. How does one account for the role of private property in slave, feudal and capitalist modes of production?

Further, the theory of modes of production more often than not generates competing narratives of the progression of modes of production. Initially Eurocentric, that narrative moved from hunter-gatherer through tribal, slave, and feudal modes to capitalism. However, as D'iakonoff has argued,[46] the European situation is an anomaly when one takes a global perspective. So what we find is that various complexities, alternative tracks, intersections and disruptions have entered into the narratives, so much so that we have numerous narratives.[47] All of them end, however, with a global capitalism. Rather than seeing these various narratives as internal debates within Marxism, it may be better to take them as an effort to deal with the way various parts of the globe have arrived at capitalism.

Each of these mode-of-production narratives cannot avoid the tricky question of transitions. If modes of production are qualitatively different – in terms of their distinct combinations of certain features rather than the originality of those features – then the way one replaces another becomes crucial. For Kautsky, there is no problem with a transition from whatever mode of production prevailed in the ancient Near East to that of the Hellenistic world, for they were both slave societies. Where the problem does arise is in the transition from slavery to feudalism.[48] In Kautsky's case, the question is more

---

[46] D'iakonoff 1999, p. 56.
[47] For example, see Melotti 1977.
[48] A problem that also concerns, among others, Perry Anderson in his fascinating study, *Passages from Antiquity to Feudalism* (Anderson 1974b).

interesting than the answer: the inherent decadence and technical backwardness of slavery (the second point he derives from Marx, the first from Gibbon), as well as the depredations of the barbarian invasions of the Roman Empire, led to the decline and collapse of the slave mode of production. Already embodied in the *colonus*, a tenant farmer that first arose in Egypt, feudalism emerged as an answer to the bankruptcy of slavery.[49] In short, it is a classic Marxist narrative, relying upon the internal contradictions of a mode of production that eventually lead to its stagnation and collapse as well as external factors such as the invasions of a weakened Roman Empire.

There is little to fault in this reconstruction, except for a detail or two. The combination of internal contradiction and external forces is one of the great Marxist contributions to historiography, and Kautsky provides as good an example as any, although I do have a problem with his tendency to moralise concerning the corruption and decadence of the Roman Empire (Gibbon's legacy is indeed persistent). However, in order to show how Kautsky's reconstruction of this transition still holds up, let me refer briefly to Perry Anderson's reconstruction of the transition, which really is a model of Marxist analysis.[50] Anderson tracks feudalism's emergence from the intersections between Roman slavery and a Germanic primitive communal mode of production in which the Roman *servus* becomes, via the *colonus* or dependent peasant tenant, the feudal serf. Yet these relations of production are part of a more fundamental shift in the mode of production in which the extraction of surplus moves from the vital role of the ubiquitous slaves (only slaves in fact 'worked') to that of the serfs, indentured to the lord but no longer 'owned' by him.

However, there is a point in Kautsky's discussion of transition that provides both an unwitting insight and potentially undermines his argument for the similarity of the ancient Near East and the Hellenistic world. It comes in his discussion of the turbulent state of the Roman province of Judea at the time of the early Christians.[51] Here, he points out that Judea was riven with competing groups, some of them decidedly insurrectionist. While the Pharisees and Sadducees struggled over cultural and religious accommodation and resistance to the Romans, the proletarian Essenes withdrew from the

---

[49] Kautsky 2001, pp. 51–65; 1908, pp. 50–70.
[50] Anderson 1974b.
[51] Kautsky 2001, pp. 226–68; 1908, pp. 283–337.

world to await divine intervention. The proletarian Zealots, by contrast, took the armed struggle up to the Romans with an early form of guerrilla warfare. For Kautsky, all of this is a sign of 'the spectacle of woe and blood that constitutes the history of Judea in the epoch of Christ'.[52] It is in this context that the Jesus movement, or early Christianity, first arose.

However, the only reason Kautsky can give for such violence and bloodshed was that it came as a response to Roman imperialism. Not quite, it seems to me. Rather than merely the turmoil of Roman imperial expansion and control, what we have are the distinct signals of a tension, if not a shift, between two very different modes of production. Needless to say, this argument runs against Kautsky's position on the two slave-based modes of production in the ancient Near East and the Hellenistic world; these two comparable systems merely bumped into one another at the flashpoint of Judea. How, then, do we account for the widespread blood and woe?

Here, the recent work of Richard Horsley fills in some of the details in light of more recent research.[53] Horsley, and those who follow him, focus on the extraordinary transformations brought about in the Roman Empire by Augustus: the full-fledged development of the cult and gospel of the Emperor, the centralisation of patron-client relations in the emperor, and the profound impacts of such changes in regional cities such as Ephesus in Asia Minor and Corinth, where the Christian movement took root. Above all, the infamous *pax Romana* turns out to be a system of violence, bloodshed, systematic destruction and enslavement in order to expand and maintain the empire. Here is Horsley:

> During the first century B.C.E. Roman warlords took over the eastern Mediterranean, including Judea, where Pompey's troops defiled the Jerusalem Temple in retaliation for the resistance of the priests. The massive acts of periodic reconquest of the rebellious Judean and Galilean people included *thousands enslaved* at Magdala/Tarichaea in Galilee in 52–51 B.C.E., *mass enslavement* in and around Sepphoris (near Nazareth) and thousands crucified at Emmaus in Judea in 4 B.C.E., and the systematic devastation of villages and towns, destruction of Jerusalem and the Temple, and *mass enslavement* in 67–70 C.E. In the area of Paul's mission, the Romans ruthlessly sacked

---

[52] Kautsky 2001, p. 255; 1908, p. 322.
[53] Horsley 1997.

and torched Corinth, one of the most illustrious Greek cities, slaughtered its men, and *enslaved* its women and children in 146 B.C.E.[54]

Yet it seems to me that even Horsley does not go far enough either. Was it merely the Emperor, warlords and the Romans themselves who are responsible for such acts? Such a concern with their agency loses sight of the political and economic issues at stake. One of the basic signs of change in social formations is a high level of violence, social unrest and conflict as a new system imposes itself on an older established one. Such troubled transitions produce displacement, tension and violence, in demographic, economic, social, political and psychological terms. I have highlighted the references to enslavement in my quotation from Horsley, for the Greeks and especially the Romans brought a new economic system to their Empire, a slave-based economic system in which the slaves did all the work and the relatively few 'citizens' did not.[55] In other words, what the Romans brought to the 'East' was a rather different mode of production than the one that prevailed there, one that I have outlined briefly above in terms of the sacred economy.

But, then, Horsley is no slouch as a Marxist biblical scholar, for he goes on to point out that while the Greeks under the Seleucids and then the Romans may have imposed their economic and cultural system on the cities of Judea and Samaria, the rural areas still operated according to the older system. All these rural areas found themselves doing was rendering tribute to a new empire. However, what was that older, different mode of production that the Greeks and then Romans gradually replaced in a pattern of systematic brutality? This is none other than the sacred economy (see above), which was gradually replaced by a slave-based system in piecemeal fashion through systematic violence and disruption, especially in the three or four centuries at the turn of the era. The genius of Christianity in this brutal environment was to provide a psychic, intellectual and emotional narrative that enabled people to make sense of such a massive and brutal transition. This took place particularly through the story, developed by Paul in the New Testament, of the violent

---

[54] Horsley 1997, pp. 10–11, emphasis added.
[55] See the useful studies of Sheila Briggs on Paul and slavery and of Jennifer Glancy on slavery and the New Testament (Briggs 2000; Glancy 2006), although a more systematic treatment indebted to Marxist analysis would have strengthened both works.

crucifixion and resurrection of a certain Jesus of Nazareth, one who suffered all the violence of the system and yet rose beyond it.

While my reconstruction may seem to be some distance from Kautsky, it carries on in his spirit at a basic level. For Kautsky argues that Christianity arose as a response to economic and social conditions, specifically the brutally oppressive one of Roman rule in Judea. I have merely extended this position to argue that the context of early Christianity marks the transition from one mode of production to another, from the sacred economy to the slave mode of production of the Hellenistic era.

Christian communism

The crucial question then becomes: what kind of movement was early Christianity? Here, Kautsky follows and extends Engels: it was a proletarian, militant response to Roman rule, an urban movement that mediated between the militancy of the anarchistic and disorganised Zealots and the communist escapism of the Essenes who escaped to the countryside.[56] As a proletarian movement, early Christianity gave voice to a hatred of the rich, expressed in an image of rebel Jesus who condemns the rich and powerful, is anti-establishment and anti-clerical, identifies with the poor and oppressed, and loves a communal life with the disciples who gave up all to join the group.[57] Well-known sayings still have bite, such as, 'It is easier for a camel to go through the eye of a needle than for a rich man to enter the kingdom of God'.[58] Or the words of the Son of Man, when he identifies with the poor and hungry in the parable of the sheep and the goats:

> I was hungry and you gave me food, I was thirsty and you gave me drink,
> I was a stranger and you welcomed me, I was naked and you clothed me,
> I was sick and you visited me, I was in prison and you came to me.[59]

---

[56] Kautsky 2001, pp. 268–72; 1908, pp. 338–43.
[57] Kautsky 2001, pp. 272–80, 305–12; 1908, pp. 343–53, 384–92.
[58] Mark 10:25.
[59] Matthew 25:35–6. If we thought that the arguments over Jesus as a revolutionary figure date from the 1960s and especially from liberation theology, then Kautsky shows that such a debate is not all that new. Kautsky's engagement with an unnamed theologian whom he calls 'A.K.' on precisely this question shows that it was already an issue a century ago.

Above all, Kautsky is probably most remembered for his claim that the early Christian community, beginning with Jesus and then reflected in the Acts of the Apostles,[60] was a communist one:

> At first the community had been permeated by an energetic though vague communism, an aversion to all private property, a drive toward a new and better social order, in which all class differences should be smoothed out by division of possessions.[61]

Indeed, this was the secret of the success of Christianity, for only a 'communistic mutual aid society [*kommunistische Unterstüssungsorganisation*]'[62] would have enough impetus to move beyond the death of its founder. Kautsky was not the only one who saw something here, for people as diverse as Gerrard Winstanley and the Diggers in seventeenth-century England and Étienne Cabet and his Icarian communities in the nineteenth century also found inspiration here.[63]

The reconstruction of a supposed Christian communism is very close to Rosa Luxemburg's own reconstruction. And they share the same argument concerning the demise of this early form of communism, yet, despite the fact that, both texts were written at about the same time (Luxemburg's appeared in 1905 and Kautsky's in 1908), they do not refer to each other. Kautsky argues that, for all its proletarian base and for all its communistic organisation, Christian communism was flawed, for without an agricultural base it remained a communism of consumption rather than production. It is all very well for people to aspire – based on the stories in Acts – to share everything, to sell all they have and own it communally. But that does nothing to change the way such things are produced. What happens when the goods run out? Do people go back to their various professions in order to produce or buy more goods so

---

[60] Acts 2:42–5; 4:32–5.
[61] Kautsky 2001, p. 346; 1908, p. 433.
[62] Kautsky 2001, p. 317; 1908, p. 403.
[63] See Boer 2007b, pp. 105–27. Étienne Cabet argued that communism is in fact pure Christianity. Cabet (1788–1856) was a fiery character and endeared himself neither to the Roman Catholic hierarchy nor the French Government. Soon enough, the deeply Christian but anti-clerical Cabet was found guilty of treason and fled France. In his later years, he attempted to establish socialist – or 'Icarian' as he called them – communities in the United States, basing them on the model of his book *Travel and Adventures of Lord William Carisdall in Icaria* [*Voyage et aventures de lord William Carisdall en Icarie*] from 1840.

that they can sell them again or share them once more? Indeed, for Kautsky, a communism of consumption needs the larger economic system to continue, for the commune's members would need to keep on generating some income in order to distribute it to each other.[64] So we find that early Christianity had no effect on the economic system based on slavery.

Again, like Luxemburg, Kautsky traces the way this initial Christian communism dissipates: having all things in common becomes charity and almsgiving by the rich; the commune becomes a community that is increasingly attractive to the rich; the common meal (a real vestige of primitive communism) was divided into the symbolic Eucharist, and a meal for the poor members who receive alms; as the community grows it develops its own administrative hierarchy of bishop, apostle and prophet. So great was the change that by the time Christianity was adopted by Constantine and became the religion of the Roman Empire, it had become yet another mechanism for exploitation. Yet Kautsky ends his narrative on an ambiguous note: for all the changes that took place, the communist drive could not be eradicated entirely, so it was shunted off into monasticism. Here, we find an obverse of the urban-based communism of consumption, for the rural basis of the monasteries lent themselves to a communism of agricultural production – a communism of production rather than consumption. For all the expansions of the monasteries, their *latifundia* and concentrations of wealth, for all the exploitation of slaves and unpaid workers, they maintained 'uncommon resistance and capacity for development'.[65] All of which was to lead into the Middle Ages and its communist movements.

What are we to make of this reconstruction of Christian communism, especially since it is historically dubious (see my discussion of Luxemburg)? Let me pick up an argument I began in my discussion of Luxemburg. Both of them took the book of Acts in the New Testament as an accurate description of the early-Christian community. (For Kautsky, at least, it was one of the many times he forgot his caution about the reliability of the Bible for historical reconstruction.) But this story functions far better, it seems to me, as a 'founding myth', for the book of Acts is as unreliable as any biblical text for historical data. Here, we face a delightful contradiction: the less historically

---

[64] Kautsky 2001, p. 353; 1908, p. 442.
[65] Kautsky 2001, p. 388; 1908, p. 488.

reliable such a story is, the more powerful it is as a political myth. In fact, it is important to insist that this picture of the early-Christian community rests on the flimsiest of evidence – the book of Acts – since only then can we avoid the tendency of trying to restore some pristine state that has been disrupted by a 'Fall'. As long as the belief holds that Acts presents what was once a real, lived experience, the more efforts to restore that ideal early Church become reactionary. Any effort at restoring what was lost, of overcoming a 'Fall', is reactionary in the first degree. However, if we insist that the communal life of the early Church is myth, that it projects a wish as to what might be, that it gives us a powerful image of what may still be achieved, then we are able to overcome the reactionary desire to return to the early Church in the book of Acts. It might then be possible to reclaim it as a radical rather than a reactionary myth.

This extension of Kautsky actually builds on one his major projects, which was nothing less than the effort to reconstruct a much longer history of socialism of which modern socialism is the culmination. In this light, Christian communism becomes one moment in this longer history. For example, in his great study, *Vorläufer des neueren Sozialismus* [*Forerunners of Modern Socialism*],[66] he looks to the Middle Ages and then the period of the Reformation for various movements, mostly inspired by Christianity, that he identifies as socialist in some sense, although he describes them as 'heretical communists'. Among many others, he discusses the various mystical and ascetic movements, the Waldensians (deriving from the twelfth century and still existing today in Piedmont, they hold to the model of Christian communism in Acts), Lollards (followers of Wycliffe who stressed personal faith, divine election, the Bible and were involved in a series of uprisings in England), Taborites (a fifteenth-century religious movement that championed asceticism, communal living and the establishment of the kingdom of God by force of arms), those around

---

[66] Kautsky 1976. Kautsky could manage only two volumes, one called *Kommunistische Bewegungen im Mittelater* and the other *Der Kommunismus in der deutschen Reformation*. This second volume has been translated into English as *Communism in Central Europe at the Time of the Reformation* (Kautsky 2002). The third volume was completed by Marx's son-in-law, who added Kautsky's discussion of Thomas More to his own sections on Thomas Campanella and the Jesuits in Paraguay (Kautsky and Lafargue 1977). The final in what is now a four-volume set was written by Hugo Lindemann and Morris Hillquit, focusing on socialism in France in the seventeenth and eighteenth centuries and early socialist and communist movements in North America (Lindemann and Hillquit 1977).

the Peasants' Revolt and Thomas Müntzer (who took Luther's reforms to their radical and logical conclusion), the Bohemian Brethren (who believed that the kingdom of God was among them in a communal life and worship and who had a profound influence on Czech literature through the translation of the Bible) and the Anabaptists of the radical Reformation more generally. Ernst Bloch would tread a similar, albeit more philosophically sustained path in his search for the utopian impulse through various heretical religious currents.

However, Kautsky's great hero is Thomas More, whom he calls the first modern socialist.[67] More's *Utopia* is, for Kautsky, one of the major socialist texts before Marx and Engels. But what is it that unites all of these various movements? They draw upon various features of primitive communism, such as the common meal, communal living and sharing all things. Indeed, it is this tradition – of which Christian communism is one of the earliest and clearest expressions – that also inspired Thomas More. For Kautsky, More finds that element in both the 'old, feudal, popular Catholicism [*Volks-katholizmus*]'[68] and the monasteries which kept alive the spark of Christian communism. It was this Catholicism of which More was the last representative and for which More died as a martyr. Yet More also offers sustained criticism of economic exploitation in the England of Henry VIII and offers his *Utopia* as an economic, political and social alternative to what he experienced. At this level, he is also a materialist critic. More, then, becomes the crucial link between the older Christian and primitive communism and modern communism, the one who links medieval religiosity and modern materialism.[69] Or, in Kautsky's words:

> We believe that we have disclosed the most essential roots of More's Socialism: his amiable character in harmony with primitive communism; the economic situation of England, which brought into sharp relief the disadvantageous consequences of capitalism for the working class; the fortunate union of classical philosophy with activity in practical affairs – all these circumstances combined must have induced in a mind so acute, so fearless, so truth-loving as More's an ideal which may be regarded as a foregleam of Modern Socialism.[70]

---

[67] Kautsky 2002, 1947.
[68] Kautsky 2002, p. 72; 1947, p. 104.
[69] See Schwartz 1989.
[70] Kautsky 2002, p. 128; 1947, pp. 228–9.

In Kautsky's reconstruction of this long history of pre-Marxist communism, religion plays a central role. Indeed, it is only with Marx and Engels that a complete materialist communism emerges, for which all of these earlier forms are incomplete forerunners.

This narrative of the forerunners of communism is curious for a number of reasons. It plays a double game regarding both the continuity and originality of socialism. I can see great value in stressing the continuity of revolutionary history, of which Marx and Engels then become the latest exponents. But the catch is that it undermines the efforts by Marx and Engels to distinguish between these religiously inspired movements and their own. The moniker for such movements was of course 'utopian socialism', which took a beating in both the manifesto and Engels's *Socialism: Utopian and Scientific*.[71] Yet Engels himself played the same game, proclaiming loudly against such revolutionary movements and then claiming them as precursors.[72]

Further, I am suspicious of this narrative, not only because it is inescapably teleological – the path leads inevitably to Marx and Engels (a problem that also beset Ernst Bloch) – but also because it operates with a dubious assumption. It assumes that the religious moment and motivation is primary. More often than not, Kautsky takes the religious impulse as the source of these pre-Marxist communist movements. By contrast, I would suggest that the religious nature of these movements is one form they may take, but it is not necessarily their source or original power. What we have, then, is the religious form of a longer and deeper revolutionary and insurrectionary current which at its core is the search for a whole new collective social formation. This is how I would like to read Kautsky's reconstruction, although I will return to the question of the religious moment of this tradition in my discussion of Georg Lukács and Raymond Williams.

Conclusion

I could have focused on the various points where Kautsky falls short in his *Foundations of Christianity*, such as his argument that mercantilism profoundly affected Israel's thought, nationalism and sacred text, as well as being the

---

[71] Engels 1989; Marx and Engels 1976.
[72] Engels 1975, 1978, 1990.

basis for anti-Semitism, or the conspiracy theory concerning the role of the Church in editing and canonising the Bible, or, indeed, his tendency to moralise regarding wealth and its attendant decadence. Yet, his study of the foundations of Christianity is full of enticements and questions, especially the unfinished nature of the projects he inaugurated – a Marxist reconstruction of the economic logic and history of the ancient Near East, ancient Israel and the early Church, as well as his effort to find pre-Marxist forms of communism. His answers may fall away as inadequate, but not the questions raised.

Chapter Five
The Forgetfulness of Julia Kristeva

> We may need to be slightly Marxist...[1]
>
> Now one realizes that one cannot just make the system of a society from the model of ideology. It is necessary to transform it. But not on this side of it, but by passing to the other side.[2]

This chapter is a little different from the others in this book, for I seek to recover a neglected and forgotten Marxist dimension of the work of Julia Kristeva. I do so for two reasons: Kristeva has made a good number of forays into biblical studies and she still reverts to Marxist analysis when her favoured psychoanalysis boxes her into a corner. Indeed, Kristeva has hidden a former (for her) Marx in a dark corner of her mind in favour of psychoanalysis. I would like to recover this repressed Marx in order to revisit some of Kristeva's readings of biblical texts. However, I am not interested in trotting him out, freshly scrubbed and in new gear for the sake of a small point in my argument: I am after a Marxist Kristeva with her memory intact. And there are moments enough in Kristeva's work to encourage me to recover Marx.

Kristeva has also written on the Bible on more than one occasion, along with theologians such as

---

[1] Kristeva 1996a, p. 70.
[2] Kristeva 1996a, p. 45.

Augustine and Anselm. The problem with these biblical reflections is that they are, at best, patchy. There is some very good and there is some absolutely dreadful Kristeva. As far as the Bible is concerned, her readings of Ruth,[3] the Song of Songs,[4] or Hebrew language[5] are ordinary and superficial, if not simply bad. She trots out conventional, even conservative positions as though they are blindingly new discoveries. If we thought that Kristeva's patchiness was restricted to her biblical interpretations – stretching herself a little too far perhaps – then we would be mistaken, for her theoretical work shows a similar oscillation between the good and the dreadful. Given her tendency to offer sweeping analyses of a single theme, too often her work betrays a certain thinness. Thus, we find a theme like melancholia[6] or the stranger[7] or love[8] or the abject[9] traced through signal points all the way from ancient Greece, via the Bible, and into the West. I find myself wanting the tangled materialist complexity of Marxist analysis, not least of which would be to trouble the assumed classicist narrative of such efforts. And, like her biblical readings, some Kristeva is cringingly awful, such as 'Love will save us',[10] as are her naïve political comments[11] or sweeping social analyses based on anecdotes and personal encounters, whether they be of France or Europe or America or Bulgaria, efforts to pinpoint a global social malaise and offer a cure.

At the same time, there is some very good Kristeva. The reading of the Levitical taboos in *Powers of Horror*[12] is one such moment. It contains a distinct insight or two that have been noticed in biblical studies.[13] The same applies to her engagements with Paul, where she focuses on the formation of the individual subject in *Tales of Love*[14] and then on a much more collective agenda from *Strangers to Ourselves*.[15]

---

[3] Kristeva 1991, pp. 69–76; 1988, pp. 102–11; Clément and Kristeva 2001, pp. 101–3; 1998, pp. 163–6.
[4] Kristeva 1987c, pp. 83–100; 1983, pp. 83–98.
[5] Kristeva 1989b, pp. 98–103; 1981, pp. 105–11.
[6] Kristeva 1989a, 1987b.
[7] Kristeva 1991, 1988.
[8] Kristeva 1987c, 1983.
[9] Kristeva 1982, 1980b.
[10] Kristeva 1996a, p. 121.
[11] See Kristeva 2002, pp. 223–68; 1998.
[12] Kristeva 1982, pp. 90–112; 1980b, pp. 107–31.
[13] Black 2006.
[14] Kristeva 1987c, pp. 139–50; 1983, pp. 135–47.
[15] Kristeva 1991, pp. 77–83; 1988, pp. 113–22.

In what follows, then, I track the strategies by which Kristeva sidelines, conceals and bypasses Marx while never really being able to get rid of him.[16] In the process, I bring Marx back into view, especially since Kristeva's work is barely understandable without Marx. Secondly, I turn to consider one of Kristeva's readings of biblical texts – the taboos in Leviticus 11–14 – rereading it in the company of a somewhat more Marxist Kristeva. Thirdly, I focus on another of her interpretations of the Bible, this time her engagements with Paul. Once again, I bring a much more Marxist angle to these texts. In a nutshell, my argument is that, while her psychoanalytical readings of these biblical texts fall short, a Marxist reading is able to offer a more comprehensive assessment of what is of value in her interpretation regarding both the Levitical taboos in the Hebrew Bible and Paul in the New Testament. In short, Kristeva's shortcomings do not incite me to turn away from her work; rather, they encourage me to look further, to seek out Marx and then to see how her incomplete readings of biblical texts might be enhanced.

Flushing out Marx

Kristeva's preferred method, one that she has been reworking consistently for more than three decades, is psychoanalysis.[17] She practises it in her consulting rooms and in her writings, moving from individual to global society with ease, claiming that it offers, through a chance to restart psychic life, the only viable form of human freedom, indeed that it is the vivid, fleshly realisation of Christianity.[18] With such increasingly strong claims, it becomes a struggle to find some sense of the conditions – historical, political or cultural – of psychoanalysis in her work.[19] So what better way to temper these universal

---

[16] Here, she has much in common with Slavoj Žižek, for both of them reflect in their personal and intellectual trajectories the recent history of Eastern Europe (See Boer 2007d).

[17] She will resort to psychoanalysis too when nervous about being identified as a religious person, especially when a few too many interested in feminist spirituality turn to her work. So, not only does she swamp the question of 'faith' in psychoanalysis, but she asserts that she is, after all, 'not a believer' (Kristeva 1987a, p. 23; 1985, p. 35).

[18] See also her translation of the biblical and theological elaborations on the death of Christ in psychoanalytical terms (Kristeva 1989a, pp. 130–5; 1987b, pp. 138–45).

[19] When asked this question, Kristeva sidesteps it by asking questions in response or showing some political or social benefit of psychoanalysis – not quite the same thing (Kristeva 1996a, pp. 24–5).

claims for psychoanalysis than through Marx? However, there is no need to introduce Marx from outside, for he resides deep within her work.

We need to work backwards to find Marx in Kristeva, a little like her native Bulgaria that she claims to have all but lost. Here, I would like to focus on a key essay written in 1968, 'Semiotics: A Critical Science and/or a Critique of Science',[20] an essay that is an extended engagement with Marx. At the end of the essay, we find a Marx who is trumped by Freud. Although Kristeva remains faithful to Marx's critical perspective, she needs to move past him, to show where he falls short. Two parts of 'Semiotics' interest me. Firstly, Kristeva identifies what she sees as Marx's great insight, namely the immanent method. Secondly, she argues that, for all his insight, Marx is inadequate when he comes to discuss the key categories of production and work. At this point, according to Kristeva, Freud provides a far better analysis.

I deal with these two points in reverse. Marx falls short, argues Kristeva, by focusing on the questions of production and work. This is fine as far it goes, but it does not go far enough. Freud's great insight was to draw attention to the realm of *pre*-production, and that is located in nothing other than the unconscious. To bring home her point, Kristeva focuses on Freud's category of the 'dream-work'. Here, Freud reveals a different type of work that precedes and pre-conditions Marx's notion of work. In the dream-work, where the unconscious and scattered patterns of the dream take on a definite narrative sequence, where the unconscious and conscious intersect, semiotics takes root in the play of signs in the dream. And, for Kristeva, at this point in her thought, a semiotics indebted to Freud is the way forward from Marx.

In this early essay, Kristeva trumps Marx by identifying a more original cause – the dream-work – that lies beneath Marx's categories of work and production. Now, while we might suspect that she has fallen into the trap of identifying original causes, at least with Marx she is not content to rest with such an argument. In her later work, she asserts time and again that psychoanalysis outruns Marx in the final stages, providing a more comprehensive answer than he ever could. Thus, Freud achieves Marx's programme of trying to unite the increasingly fragmented fields of human activity, or at least those separated fields of theory and action.[21] Further, Freudian social analyses and

---

[20] Kristeva 1986, pp. 74–88; 1969, pp. 27–42.
[21] Kristeva 1996a, pp. 151, 198.

solutions outperform an exhausted socialism.²² For Kristeva, then, psychoanalysis is not only more comprehensive than Marxism, but it also provides the personal, social and political healing that socialism fails to provide.²³

I am, however, reading Kristeva's 'Semiotics' essay backwards. Earlier in the essay, she identifies Marx's great insight, what she calls his crucial 'epistemological break'.²⁴ And that is the immanent method, a method that emerges from the item or work in question rather than from outside. It also means that criticism must arise from the object under criticism. Thus, if we want to interpret the work of someone, say, like Kristeva, it means that we will use their own methods to interpret them. For Kristeva, Marx is 'the first to practise' this method.²⁵

Kristeva's interest, at least at this moment in her thought, is on the implications of Marx's insight for semiotics. Thus, 'No form of semiotics, therefore, can exist other than as a critique of semiotics'.²⁶ Or, in the dense detail of her early writing, semiotics is the very act of producing models. Let me quote Kristeva again:

> It is a formalization or production of models. Thus, when we say semiotics, we mean the (as yet unrealized) development of *models*, that is, of formal systems whose structure is isomorphic or analogous to the structure of another system (the system under study).²⁷

Marx, it seems, could not be more important, marking a fundamental break in the history of knowledge. In effect, Marx subverts 'the terms of a preceding science'²⁸ in the terms of that science itself. So, he overturns economics by means of economics. For instance, he takes the term 'surplus-value' from Smith, Rodbertus, Ricardo et al. and shows how the term means not the 'addition to the value of a product' but the extraction of surplus – both constant and variable – in the wage-relation. The key is that he does so *from within* the theories of these political economists. Like their own noses, they

---

[22] Kristeva 1995, pp. 209–10; 1993, pp. 252–4.
[23] Kristeva 1996a, pp. 24–5.
[24] Kristeva 1986, p. 79; 1969, p. 32.
[25] Kristeva 1986, p. 78; 1969, p. 31. In her early *Revolution in Poetic Language*, she also gives Marx his due for pointing out that the signifying process lies outside the sphere of material production (Kristeva 1984, p. 105; 1974, p. 153).
[26] Kristeva 1986, p. 78; 1969, p. 31.
[27] Kristeva 1986, p. 76; 1969, p. 29.
[28] Kristeva 1986, p. 80; 1969, p. 33.

simply cannot see the proper origins of surplus-value. Once this is done, we get the generation of a whole new set of terms that marks the rise of a new science.[29]

Marx is even more important for Kristeva than at first appears to be the case. This essay on semiotics is not the only place where Kristeva must rely on Marx. Let me give a few of examples where Kristeva cannot dispense with Marx, especially at a sticky spot in her argument. The first is historical, the second political and the third deals with feminism. In an effort to deal with the rise of the avant-garde in literature – the moment of modernism from the end of the nineteenth century and embodied in the work of Lautréamont, Mallarmé and Bataille – Kristeva is able to mix good Marxist social theory with the best of them. At moments like these, her efforts to depict the big picture with a few firm, rapidly drawn lines, work extremely well. Thus, the avant-garde is a signal and effort to deal with the massive changes that took place with the comprehensive onset and spread of capitalism:

> A new phenomenon has arisen since the rise to power of the bourgeoisie, the onset of the free market, the inflation of capital permeating relationships of production and reproduction and dominating them, and the crisis of the patriarchal family.[30]

At this moment of crisis in state, family and religion, capitalist excess and restructuring take precedence over restraint and structure. Everything must give way! Here, of course, she is paraphrasing the famous statement concerning the constant revolutionising of capitalism in *The Manifesto of the Communist Party* – 'All that is solid melts into air, all that is holy is profaned, and man is at last compelled to face with sober senses his real conditions of life, and his relations with his kind'.[31] Psychoanalysis, then, becomes one of the new

---

[29] Kristeva herself is rather well-known for a series of new terms – semanalyse, abjection, intertextuality and so on – at the emergence, or even the hint or semblance of an emergence, of a new method or idea.

[30] Kristeva 1996a, p. 96.

[31] The full paragraph reads: 'The bourgeoisie cannot exist without constantly revolutionising the instruments of production, and thereby the relations of production, and with them the whole relations of society. Conservation of the old modes of production in unaltered form, was, on the contrary, the first condition of existence for all earlier industrial classes. Constant revolutionising of production, uninterrupted disturbance of all social conditions, everlasting uncertainty and agitation distinguish the bourgeois epoch from all earlier ones. All fixed, fast-frozen relations, with their train of ancient and venerable prejudices and opinions, are swept away, all new-formed

modes of dealing with such profound social and economic changes, especially the relationship between the unconscious and the social restrictions Freud argued were crucial for any society to function.[32]

Secondly, on a more political note, Kristeva's definition of the 'Left' is a moment of sheer insight. Rather than seeing it as one side of the eternal shifting binary of Left and Right in our current political landscape, she sees the Left as 'the locus where the question of politics, and above all of the limits of the political (from the viewpoint of symbolic formations, that is, the acquisition of culture and knowledge), can be formulated and dealt with'.[33] A psychoanalytical version, if you will, of the Marxist notion of the 'withering away of the state'. But it is also an extraordinary recognition of the Marxist point that politics is, after all, part of the domain of culture and religion and knowledge and ideology, *and* the point that this is what Lacan's notion of the Symbolic – of language and society and culture – is really about. In the crossover, then, between Lacan's Symbolic and Marx's superstructure, we find politics. But it is not only a point where political battles are fought, but where the Left identifies itself by identifying the limits of politics and thinking beyond them.

Finally, and crucially for my engagement, when she faces difficulties in her dealings with feminism, Kristeva reverts occasionally to Marxism. She has, infamously, kept feminism at an arm's length, especially US liberal feminism. She teases such an audience with comments like the one concerning the phallus, which, as 'numerous scholars' have shown, is indeed the basis of signification and religion.[34] More substantially, in her trilogy, *Female Genius*, she focuses on three women who were independent from and placed themselves, like Kristeva herself, above and beyond feminism as well as Marxism – Hannah Arendt, Melanie Klein and Colette.[35] From this perspective, Kristeva can then view feminism in terms of three overlapping stages: the demand for political rights by the suffragettes; the assertion of ontological equality; and,

---

ones become antiquated before they can ossify. All that is solid melts into air, all that is holy is profaned, and man is at last compelled to face with sober senses his, real conditions of life, and his relations with his kind' (Marx and Engels 1976a, p. 487).

[32] For other examples, see Kristeva's argument for a different social context for gender relations in China (Kristeva 1996a, pp. 100–1), or the analysis of the dilemmas faced by Mitterand's socialism in France (Kristeva 1996a, p. 154).

[33] Kristeva 1996a, p. 174.

[34] Kristeva 2000, p. 88; 1996b, p. 111. She also claims to despise anything that is politically-correct (Clément and Kristeva 2001, p. 12; 1998, p. 24).

[35] Kristeva 2001, 2004a, 2004b, 1999.

since May '68, the search for sexual difference. The problem, as far as Kristeva is concerned, is that feminism is trapped between two dogmatisms,[36] either the dogmatism of 'leftism', as she tends to call it, or a conservative dogmatism of patriarchy and the Right. Feminism tends either to mirror this second dogmatism, the one that it opposes, or take up communist dogmatism in its drive for liberation for all women. Caught between a rock and a hard place, it will not be long before she trots out the conventional argument, following Hannah Arendt, that we need to avoid the two totalitarian extremes of fascism and Stalinism – a refrain from her earliest texts[37] – by means of some mythical middle way. Otherwise, feminism finds itself slipping into either form of totalitarianism.

Her answer to this problem is as important as it is intriguing. In response to feminist agendas for social change based on gender, she states:

> ...what is happening now, in Eastern countries, is that the collapse of the Marxist and socialist idea is showing something else. It shows that we can arrive at a better society not before bourgeois individualism but after. I think they ought to revise their ideas, seeing what is happening in the East now. Because many feminist ideas were unconsciously calculated and modeled on the image of communist and Marxist countries, as if a progressive and communitarian ideology could produce the economy of bourgeois society. *Now one realizes that one cannot just make the system of a society from the model of ideology. It is necessary to transform it.* But not on this side of it, but by passing to the other side.[38]

Just when I began to suspect that Kristeva was yet another liberal in disguise, or perhaps even a conservative who bemoans a supposed religious crisis generated by the deterioration of belief[39] and thereby the end of viable revolt,[40] she produces an extraordinarily central Marxist point. Too often, Kristeva invokes terms such as freedom and democracy (without any qualifiers), or 'plurality of consciences'[41] or the importance of the individual, and dismisses

---

[36] Kristeva 1996a, p. 7.
[37] Kristeva 1980a, p. 23; 1977, p. 357; see also Clément and Kristeva 2001, p. 13; Clément and Kristeva 1998, p. 25.
[38] Kristeva 1996a, p. 45, emphasis added.
[39] Kristeva 1995, p. 221; 1993, p. 267.
[40] Kristeva 2000, 1996b.
[41] Kristeva 1996a, p. 51.

communism as inherently totalising. But, here, she produces a statement that would have been heresy in the countries of 'actually existing socialism' such as Bulgaria, but one that is deeply faithful to Marx. Firstly, against any notion of idealism, she states bluntly that an ideology – here, feminism – cannot a society make. Secondly, feminism, understood as a progressive and communitarian ideology, is incompatible with bourgeois society.[42] You cannot just take a Marxist ideology and graft it onto a capitalist one. Thirdly, the society desired by feminism *and* communism must come *after* bourgeois individualism – i.e. liberalism – and not before. This flies in the face of the argument that became increasingly common in former Communist countries, namely that it was possible to bypass fully-fledged capitalism and move straight to communism.[43] Here, Kristeva calls on the Marx who argues that the full run of capitalism must be experienced first before anything different may come into being. One might argue that, with globalisation, brought about by the collapse of Communism in Eastern Europe, we are only beginning to glimpse what a full capitalism might be, what a fully commodified world might look like.

This is the Marxist Kristeva who interests me. So, let me list the points that I want to take with me in my rereadings of her readings of Leviticus and Paul: no gender without political economics; no ideological change without social and economic change; no mismatches between bourgeois ideology and feminism; a communitarian rather than an individual feminism; in short, Marxist feminism rather than bourgeois feminism, but a Marxist feminism willing to bide its time and let capitalism run its course. Given the variety of feminisms that make up a multifaceted movement, Kristeva clearly sides with a communitarian and progressive feminism rather than an individualist and liberal feminism that focuses on rights. In other words, the individual has a place but only when one begins from the collective.

---

[42] She makes a very similar point concerning the incompatibility between Mitterand's socialist agenda and France's capitalist economy in the context of the European Common Market (Kristeva 1996a, p. 154).

[43] In a further twist that echoes Chinese arguments, it is sometimes asserted in post-Communist countries that there are many capitalisms, and there a gentler form might grow.

Monocausality, or, the taboo of the mother

From this more Marxist Kristeva, I turn to her better efforts at biblical interpretation. Here, my concern is her interpretation of the food taboos in Leviticus 11–14 in the Hebrew Bible.[44] After identifying the core of her own argument, particularly the moment where it falls short, I ask what it might look like with a decent dose of Marxism. Among her most well known biblical interpretations, Kristeva argues that, at the heart of all the various taboos that we find in Leviticus – food taboos (crustaceans, pigs, carrion eaters and so on), menstrual taboos, taboos over skin diseases, to name but a few – lies what she calls the 'taboo of the mother'.

Although Kristeva argues that a psychoanalytical reading goes all the way, far beyond the historian of religions (by which, I suspect, she means biblical critics of a historical bent), who stops at the point of identifying loathing as the key to the taboos, and the anthropologist (here, she really means Mary Douglas), who stops a little further on the way by pointing to the role of symbolic systems as markers of social boundaries, I want to argue that Kristeva's argument is merely the first step. It is an astute observation about the logic of the Levitical taboos, and yet she too stops far too short.

Let us first see what she argues. The 'mythème originaire' of the Levitical taboos, she concludes, is the 'taboo of the mother' that manifests itself in the prohibition of incest.[45] The key text is: 'You shall not boil a kid in the milk of its mother'.[46] Boiling a kid in its mother's milk is a metaphor of incest,[47] she argues, but incest itself points to the fundamental taboo of the mother, by which she means the abomination of the fertile female body. This is the foundation for her notion of the abject, that which is abhorred and vital, rejected and inescapable at the same time – in short, her version of the constitutive exception. There are, then, three steps, each one pointing to the next: the prohibition against boiling a kid in its mother's milk, the incest taboo, and then

---

[44] Kristeva 1982, pp. 90–112; 1980b, pp. 107–31; see also Kristeva 1995, pp. 116–17; 1993, pp. 142–3; Clément and Kristeva 2001, pp. 96–7; 1998, pp. 156–8.
[45] Kristeva 1982, pp. 105–6; 1980b, pp. 123–4.
[46] Exodus 23:19; 34:26; Deuteronomy 14:21.
[47] Unfortunately, Athalya Brenner's useful essay 'On Incest' (Brenner 1994) does not refer to Kristeva. In fact, Brenner closes out most psychoanalytical readings since they are inescapably androcentric. Her preference is for Melanie Klein's theory of subject-object relations.

the taboo of the mother. Once there, we have the foundational taboo that provides the interpretive key to all the others.

How does Kristeva get to this point? Leviticus 11 contains the dietary regulations made famous by Mary Douglas.[48] Here, the thoroughly carnivorous Israelites may eat the cud-chewing cloven-footers on land, the finned and scaled in the waters, four-legged winged insects with legs above their feet,[49] but not those who break or mix these categories, such as camel, pig, and those swarming things with many or no feet.[50] Kristeva espies three overlapping and determining features of the taxonomy of the food laws: the extension of the commandment 'You shall not kill' to food laws (carnivorous animals are forbidden, except, of course, human beings); admixture between the categories such as cud-chewing and cloven-footed; and then confusion between the fundamental elements of earth, water and air.[51]

The key to Leviticus 11, at least for Kristeva, is Chapter 12, but, before pondering her reading more closely, let me jump past these two chapters and consider the obsession with skin diseases in Chapters 13 and 14. In two long chapters, we find all manner of swellings, eruptions, spots, boils, burns and itches,[52] discussions of their colours, depths, whether they have hair in them or not and what colour that hair might be,[53] whether they have raw flesh in them or not,[54] whether they spread or not,[55] whether garments or indeed houses are infected,[56] and then the endless assessments, rituals and sacrifices at the direction of the priest.[57]

While Kristeva notes that the issue of disease itself is a problem, she is more concerned with the type of disease, namely disease of the skin. And the problem here is that the skin is an 'essential if not initial boundary of

---

[48] Douglas 1966.
[49] Respectively, Leviticus 11:3, 9, 21. The birds do not gain a positive identification: all we find is a list of those banned, such as eagle, vulture and ostrich (Leviticus 11:13–19). One may imply that they are rapacious or carrion eaters, but the text gives no reason, unlike the other groups.
[50] Leviticus 11:29–31, 41–3.
[51] Kristeva 1982, pp. 98–9; 1980b, pp. 117–18.
[52] Leviticus 13:2, 18, 24, 29, 38–9.
[53] Leviticus 13:3–4, 19–20, 24–6, 30–1, 36–7, 43.
[54] Leviticus 13:10.
[55] Leviticus 13:6–8, 22–3, 27–8, 32–6.
[56] Leviticus 13:47–59; 14: 33–53.
[57] See especially Leviticus 14:1–32.

biological and psychic individuation'.[58] Break that boundary and we have, like the dietary taboos of Leviticus 11, the problem of admixture and the threat to identity. But what is really going on here, argues Kristeva, is that breaks in the skin become another version of childbirth. Like the various emissions from male and female bodies in Leviticus 15, the eruptions, breaks and openings in the skin of Leviticus 13–14 indicate a much darker view of childbirth itself. These chapters present a decayed body that breaks forth, a signal for Kristeva of her key category in *Powers of Horror*, namely, the abject. Note carefully, however, that she does not rest with the simple point that giving birth is pathologised by being connected with disease and emissions. Rather, her point is that the generative power of women is the key to these other abominations and regulations. At the basis of the abhorrence of skin diseases and their different pusses,[59] as well as the various emissions from female and male bodies,[60] lies the abhorrence of the fertile, generative, offspring-emitting bodies of women.

Now we can see why Leviticus 12 is the key for Kristeva. For, here, we find the taboo of the mother manifested in the regulations concerning uncleanness and purification around childbirth:

> Yahweh said to Moses, 'Say to the people of Israel, If a woman conceives, and bears a male child, then she shall be unclean seven days; as at the time of her menstruation, she shall be unclean. And on the eighth day the flesh of his foreskin shall be circumcised. Then she shall continue for thirty-three days in the blood of her purifying; she shall not touch any hallowed thing, nor come into the sanctuary, until the days of her purifying are completed. But if she bears a female child, then she shall be unclean two weeks, as in her menstruation; and she shall continue in the blood of purifying for sixty-six days'.[61]

In this brief account of the purity rules for childbirth, the birth of a male child produces uncleanness for seven days until his circumcision on the eighth day, whereas for a female child the initial uncleanness is two weeks. The doubling also applies to the period of purification, or 'the blood of her purifying [*dheme*

---

[58] Kristeva 1982, p. 101; 1980b, p. 120.
[59] Leviticus 13–14.
[60] Leviticus 15.
[61] Leviticus 12:1–5; translation mine.

taharah]',[62] after this initial time: for the boy child it is 33 days, whereas for the girl child it is 66 days. At the completion of either period, the mother is to offer a yearling lamb (a pigeon or turtledove if too poor) as a burnt offering and a pigeon or turtledove as a sin offering.[63]

After pointing out that the mother is the one defiled rather than the child and that circumcision sticks out in this passage (the violent severance and thereby sacrifice and purification of the boy from the mother),[64] Kristeva moves to her main argument: the abomination of the fertile feminine body is the foundation of the other abominations.[65] Or, rather, the separation between the sexes enacted in this abomination is the primary cause that makes sense of all the other abominations, and even extends to the nature of language and social organisation. The mother – fecund, archaic and phantasmatic – must be separated, identified, objectified and located in a distinct place.[66] Through that act everything follows:

> ...that evocation of defiled maternality, in Leviticus 12, inscribes the logic of dietary abominations within that of a limit, a boundary, a border between the sexes, a separation between feminine and masculine *as foundation for the organization* that is 'clean and proper', 'individual', and, one thing leading to another, signifiable, legislatable, subject to law and morality.[67]

Her distinct insight is that this logic finds its most succinct formulation in the text I noted earlier: 'You shall not boil a kid in the milk of its mother'.[68] Initially, we might object that Kristeva has used a text from outside, from Exodus and Deuteronomy to make sense of Leviticus 11–14, but our objection would miss the psychoanalytical move that the key lies with what is

---

[62] Leviticus 12:4, 5.
[63] Leviticus 12:6–8.
[64] This is the only point Exum draws from Kristeva's discussion (Exum 1993, p. 127).
[65] Kristeva assumes a universalising function of these priestly texts, but see Ilana Be'er 1994, who argues that Leviticus provides a priestly ideology of purity at odds with a more relaxed approach to matters such as menstruation in wider Israelite society. The problem here is that her only evidence is other biblical texts, especially narratives. Rashkow 2000, p. 16, however, argues that the purity laws apply to the whole people.
[66] Elsewhere, Kristeva suggests that this 'abjecting' of the mother is 'an essential movement in the biblical text's struggles against the maternal cults of previous and current forms of paganism' (Kristeva 1995, p. 118; 1993, pp. 144–5). I am grateful to Judith McKinlay 2004, p. 91, for pointing this out.
[67] Kristeva 1982, p. 100, italics added; 1980b, p. 119.
[68] Exodus 23:19; see Exodus 34:26 and Deuteronomy 14:21.

excluded – with the constitutive exception no less. In the same way that the taboo of the mother is the hidden logic of these chapters, so also a text found outside the chapters of Leviticus reveals the logic of those chapters. Now, all of this is insightful and swift, and, as far as I can tell, the first time such connections have been made.[69]

However, I did emphasise the phrase 'as foundation for the organization' in the quotation above for a reason. Indeed, what we have here is another version of the primary cause, the first mover, and all the appropriate suspicions of mono-causal explanations come to the fore at this point. The terms are telling: the ban on boiling a kid in its mother's milk is the 'unconscious foundation' of the logic of separation that runs not merely through the Levitical abominations, but through the 'whole biblical text [*tout le texte biblique*]'.[70] This text on boiling a kid in its mother's milk is the key, and its taboo is the cause of all the others. In fact, the taboo of the mother is dietary, incest and maternal taboo all in one. The main problem with this mono-causal explanation is that it marks an analysis that stops far too short. It is merely a first step – an insightful one, but a first step all the same. It is possible to take such an analysis much further, above all to situate it within a wider context, but, for that, we need Marx.

If we allow Kristeva's repressed Marxism to speak, then the argument begins to look somewhat different. In particular, I would like to pursue the implications of the two elements in her work that I identified in the previous section: no gender without political economics and a preference for communitarian over against individualist feminism. In light of these principles, Kristeva's mono-causal argument concerning the taboo of the mother becomes decidedly untenable.

The problem with mono-causal explanations such as the one proposed by Kristeva is the first half of the term, the 'mono'. In isolation, the taboo of the mother takes on an overarching role, but such a mono-causal approach is not consistent with that dimension of Kristeva's feminism that I am stressing

---

[69] Kristeva gains a crucial hint from Jean Soler (Soler 1979) concerning the connection between eating and sex in the ban on boiling the kid in its mother's milk. I find it strange, however, that Rashkow's psychoanalytical reading (Rashkow 2000, pp. 38–42), which follows Soler as well as Eilberg-Schwartz (Eilberg-Schwartz 1990), makes the same point without any reference to Kristeva, whose work predates hers, even in translation.

[70] Kristeva 1982, p. 105; 1980b, p. 123.

here, namely the communitarian agenda and the connection with economics. In short, I want to suggest that the taboo of the mother is but one element of what may be called a sacred economy.

What happens to the taboo of the mother when it is understood in such a wider context? To begin with, that taboo of Leviticus 11–14 is closely connected with the obsession over the womb. Time and again, Yahweh closes and then opens wombs, whether in Pharaoh's court when Abram and Sarai visit,[71] Sarai's own womb, and those of Rebekah, Leah and Rachel.[72] This obsession over the womb, along with the taboo of the mother, is part of a wider concern with fertility, not only of a woman's body but also of the soil and domestic animals. The over-riding metaphor that links them all is one of a receptacle for seed, whether that is a woman for a man's seed, the ground for crop seeds, or female animals with the seed of male animals. The catch is that Yahweh in his various names ultimately controls and thereby *allocates* such fertility, as the legislation that separates the producing mother indicates, as do the narratives of opening and closing wombs of both women and animals, as does the fear of famine and celebration of plenty.

I suggest that the theme of fertility operates according to a logic of allocation, indeed that it can only be understood within the framework of an allocative economics. This allocative economic logic – characteristic of the ancient Near East – attempted to account for production outside human control and knowledge by attributing both the production itself and its allocation to the gods. The deity or deities were responsible for the fertility of the soil, rains, open wombs and so on, and for the various mechanisms of allocation, which include kinship, patron-client relations, warfare, and the judiciary. As the gods provide the ideological glue to the system, I suggest that we use the term *theo-economics* to designate the ideological logic behind such an allocative economics.

In this light, the taboo of the mother is hardly an isolated element, nor indeed is it a primary cause: it is but one part of a larger item, that of fertility, within an even broader context, that of theo-economics or the sacred economy. Women, but also animals, crops and land, are part of what may be

---

[71] Genesis 12.
[72] Genesis 24–5 and 29.

called a régime of fertility.⁷³ The taboo of the mother, or, as I have renamed it, the régime of fertility, is neither isolated nor the prime cause of the system as a whole. Rather, the economic logic of fertility is similar to other parts of that economy: if the deity (re-)allocates land, just as he allocates fertility to animals, women and soil, then the (re-)allocation of the produce of such items takes place through the channels of clan structure, the patron-client relationship, the war machine and the judiciary.

This, I would suggest, is the context in which Kristeva's taboo of the mother operates. Rather than the prime cause of the system as whole, the taboo of the mother is but one element in a wider concern of fertility, a concern that includes those of animals and land. The key is that all of them produce by themselves, and so we find an over-riding effort to control that auto-production. Of course, that economic system is threaded through with all manner of contradictory patriarchies that ultimately cannot hold the system together. If the ideology is one of sacred control, where the deity is the one responsible for controlling fertility and for allocating the products, then the economic system relies on kinship structures, warfare, the patron-client system and the judiciary to ensure such allocation. That ideology may be called a 'sacred' one, and its purpose is to justify an economic system or (re-)allocation – hence the 'sacred economy'.

I have sought to bring a repressed Marx out in Kristeva's work and then to bring a more Marxist Kristeva back to one of her most influential readings of the Bible, the taboo of the mother in Leviticus 11–14. Her psychoanalytical reading of this text brings to the fore that taboo as the key to the text, if not the whole Hebrew Bible. However, when Marx returns to Kristeva's analysis, we find that her delineation of such a taboo is but the first step. For it turns out that the taboo is merely part of a wider socio-economic system.

Paul the Apostle, both ways

From the taboos of Leviticus in the Hebrew Bible, I turn to the New Testament, especially the letters of Paul. On two occasions, Kristeva deals with Paul, the first concerning the themes of *agape* [love] and Paul's narrative that cuts

---

⁷³ For more detail, see Boer 2007c.

through the various psychological pathologies[74] and the second with the collective role of the *ekklesia* in dealing with psychosis.[75] As with my discussion of the taboo of the mother, I argue that, while her psychoanalytical readings of Paul fall short, a Marxist reading is able to offer a more comprehensive assessment of what is of value in her interpretation, especially on the questions of *agape* as something that comes from completely outside the human realm, the social and historical context of the pathologies cured by Paul, and the political implications of her focus on the collective.

My primary concern is to uncover the repressed Marxism in Kristeva's work on Paul, but I read her interpretation at the intersection of two very different approaches to Paul. Since this chapter on Kristeva and the next two on Alain Badiou and Giorgio Agamben deal with Paul to some extent, the following survey of Pauline scholarship provides the necessary background for those less familiar with this arcane corner of scholarship.

The two approaches to Paul are biblical scholarship on Paul and political philosophy. Even if they hardly talk to each other, they are my conversation partners. To begin with, there lies the unruly thicket of biblical commentators on Paul. In that jumble a couple of things are striking about Pauline studies at the moment, one extremely familiar, the other an anomaly of New-Testament studies. On the first count, readings of Paul are no different from readings of other biblical texts: the text is either good for you, or it is not (or perhaps a rare mix of the two). And if it is not, you try to detoxify it. Feminist scholarship on Paul is a good example of this approach, as – to name but a few – the efforts towards a liberating potential of Romans 8:22–3,[76] or the possibilities that emerge from Paul's use of birthing metaphors,[77] or the search for an anti-hierarchical strain in Paul's thought,[78] show only too well. I might add the efforts to come up with an anti-colonial[79] or liberating Paul,[80] or the eradication of anti-Semitism and sexism through a recasting of Paul as one element in that 'Jewish book', the New Testament.[81] Kristeva falls into the same trap:

---

[74] Kristeva 1987c, pp. 139–50; 1983, pp. 135–47.
[75] Kristeva 1991, pp. 77–83; 1988, pp. 113–22.
[76] Rehmann 2004.
[77] Gaventa 2004.
[78] Hawkins 2004.
[79] Wan 2000.
[80] Callahan 2000.
[81] Schottroff 2004.

Paul's writings can be good for you if you read him in the right way. The work of Økland[82] and Fatum,[83] who argue that the fundamental images and constructions of space in Paul's work are inescapably male, come as welcome corrections to this tendency to detoxify Paul. Indeed, the biblical Left has been and continues to be wary of Paul. He is, after all, the one who is responsible for ensuring a distinct structure of patriarchy was locked into the very ideology of Christianity, for the dangerously conservative text in Romans 13 about being obedient to one's rulers, and who denigrated and argued for the sublimation of the libidinal dimensions of human existence in his idealisation of celibacy in 1 Corinthians 7, to name but a few of his more stellar achievements.

The second element of New-Testament studies is such a given of the 'megatext' of Pauline studies that it is now hardly questioned: the key to understanding Paul is his Hellenistic context within the Roman Empire. This is the latest phase of Pauline scholarship that may be called the 'new new perspective' on Paul. Let me explain: for much of the twentieth century, German scholarship held sway in biblical studies, as it had done since the middle of the nineteenth century. Given the weight of Lutheran assumptions, for this scholarship, Paul was very much a theologian and an introspective one at that. The key names include Karl Barth with his neo-orthodoxy and the argument that God addresses us here and now, Rudolph Bultmann and his demythologising of the New Testament and recasting in existentialist terms, and Ernst Käsemann, the last of the great German scholars.[84] They presented a Paul who was, above all, concerned with the universal concerns of one's inner relationship with God through Christ.

However, with the exodus from Germany to the United States before and during World War II, German biblical scholarship dramatically gave up its international leadership. A few hung on until the 1960s and 1970s, but the majority had bolted and German scholarship turned inward, aided by a conservative academic system. The break with the old hegemony came in the 1970s with a couple of works, one by Krister Stendahl and the other by James Sanders,[85] which challenged this introspective and theological Paul. While Stendahl argued that Paul simply did not share what he called the 'introspec-

---

[82] Økland 2005.
[83] Fatum 1995.
[84] Barth 1985, Bultmann 1948; Käsemann 1980.
[85] Stendahl 1976; Sanders 1977.

tive conscience of the West' (which really stems from Augustine), Sanders in great detail placed Paul within his Jewish context. Soon enough, this contextual shift was dubbed the 'new perspective' on Paul and dominates much Pauline scholarship today. However, we can detect a third phase, still very much concerned with context. The difference is that Paul is to be understood not so much in his Jewish context but in his relation to the Roman Empire. So we find an increasing number of studies that have 'empire' in the title, seeking to show how much or how little Paul responds to and challenges Rome.[86] I have dubbed this emerging third phase the 'new new perspective' on Paul, since it is not that new after all. The basic assumptions remain largely in place, for context remains the key. What one needs to do is locate an as yet neglected feature of Paul's context, a feature that then becomes the secret passage to a new understanding of Paul.[87]

The other conversation partner is a group of sundry philosophers of a Marxist bent. In a flurry that has not yet abated, Slavoj Žižek turned to Paul in developing a distinct political position, especially in *The Fragile Absolute, On Belief* and *The Puppet and the Dwarf*.[88] For Žižek, Paul is the purveyor of the radical political core of Christianity. (Kristeva will in fact come closest to Žižek at certain points.) But Žižek was responding at first to Alain Badiou's magisterial *Being and Event*[89] and then later to his reading in *Saint Paul: The*

---

[86] Elliott 1994, 1997, 2000, 2008; Carter 2006; Horsley 1997, 2000, 2002, 2003.

[87] This search for context has led other scholars to seek that key to Paul in all manner of places, none of which have gained the hegemonic position of Paul's imperial context. For example, there is the ideological place of the androgyne as the answer to the tension between universalism and dualism in Paul's writings (Boyarin 1994, 2004), or the Stoics who provide the inescapable philosophical and social background for Paul's thought (Swancutt 2004), so much so that he is a philosopher first (Engberg-Pedersen 2000), or the various *encomia, progymnasmata, physiognomics* and other rhetorical treatises that provide us with a picture of collective 'Mediterranean' notions of personality that must not be confused with 'Western' individualist notions in our understanding of Paul (Malina and Neyrey 1996), or inheritance rights throughout the ancient Near East, Greece and Rome which give some sense to Paul's theme of adoption (Corley 2004), or Hellenistic perceptions of sexuality and the body that become the necessary background for reading Paul (Martin 1995), or the *psychagogia*, the 'leading of souls' that runs through the moral philosophy of Greece and Rome which give us a sense of what Paul is on about in Philippians (Smith 2005). I cannot help the thought that Paul must have been extraordinarily astute to be in touch with all these various currents of Hellenistic thought and culture.

[88] Žižek 2000, 2001, 2003.

[89] Badiou 2006a, 1988.

Foundation of Universalism.⁹⁰ For Badiou, with whom I deal in the next chapter, Paul is the first militant who outlines the structure of event via his doctrine of grace, and who thereby establishes a political group faithful to that event. In Italy, Giorgio Agamben (my focus in Chapter Seven) also responded to Badiou's interpretation with a very different take that focused on the messianic and remnant themes in Paul, themes that keep alive the possibility of political disruption.⁹¹ Standing at a variance to all of these, there was the 'spiritual testament' of Jacob Taubes, his last lectures that were transcribed from an audio tape and translated as *The Political Theology of Paul*.⁹² All of this activity sent people scurrying back to Heidegger's lectures on religion where he too focuses on Paul.⁹³

Strangely, there is a distinct lack of fit between my two conversation partners. Biblical scholars, especially of the Pauline variety, are all too quick to dismiss the philosophers for being out of touch with the current debates in Pauline scholarship or of not contributing anything new. One such scholar confided in me that little could be found of use in the philosophical work, although it seems to me that, in light of the megatext of Pauline scholarship – the overbearing concern with historical context, the need to detoxify Paul, the unquestioned assumption that we have access to the *ipsissima verba* of the man himself no matter how little that might be – some blinkers are firmly in place concerning Paul, although no more than one would expect in any other highly specialised sub-discipline. The philosophers, for their part, see no need to saturate themselves in that scholarship, preferring to touch on a few key works here and there. But they are after other things: neither the historical Paul nor the father of a particular ideology (theology) for a particular institution (the Church) draws them, but, rather, Paul's thought as a key moment in *political* theology, indeed political thought as such. For some reason or other peculiar to the discipline and the institutions that sustain them, political theology barely makes the agenda of Pauline scholarship. The fact that these philosophers are all Marxists of various stripes makes them even more intriguing.

To sum up the lack of fit between these two angles on Paul, if Pauline scholarship is fixated on historical context and origins, philosophical work on Paul

---

⁹⁰ Badiou 2003, 1997.
⁹¹ Agamben 2005a; Agamben 2000.
⁹² Taubes 2004.
⁹³ Heidegger 2004; de Vries 1999.

is concerned with his place in the genealogy of Western political thought. While Pauline scholars relegate subsequent interpretations and appropriations of Paul to the realms of *Rezeptionsgeschichte* and *Wirkungsgeschichte* (where this is conscious), trying to ignore 2,000 years of appropriation in the search for Paul in his context, the philosophers understand Paul precisely in that long tradition of appropriation, especially the Reformation and Enlightenment. The Paul of political philosophy comes out of the many variations of this history of interpretation that is largely ignored by Pauline scholarship.

Into the empty space between these two groups comes Kristeva; or, rather, that is where I would like to place her in my following discussion. On one side, the Marxists will allow me to bring out a repressed Marx in her work, while, on the other side, the Pauline scholars will – unwittingly or not – keep her honest, especially when she gets too soppy about love saving us and so on. Before proceeding, let me outline the three points of my rereading of Kristeva's reading of Paul. Firstly, I am interested in the political implications of her argument that *agape* comes from completely outside the human realm. Secondly, I want to ask why Paul's focus on Jesus Christ cuts through all the psychological pathologies. And, lastly, I pursue the implications of her focus on the collective, both in the 'love your neighbour' command and in her notion of the *ekklesia* as an ideal community that soothes psychic stress.

Other-than-human love

In the first of her two texts on Paul, 'God Is Love', Kristeva argues that the 'true revolution' of Christianity was its focus on *agape* as the centre of its message. Elevated over against *eros*, *agape* becomes, in Paul, theocentric: rather than human love of God, the key becomes God's love for human beings (Kristeva forgets the crucial role of *philia* in all of this). In fact, God is the locus of *agape* while human beings become the place of *pistis*: 'God is the first to love; as center, source, and gift, his love comes to us without our having to deserve it – it falls, strictly speaking, from heaven and imposes itself with the requirement of faith'.[94] If Kristeva sounds more like a theologian than a biblical critic, then her reliance on the Swedish theologian Anders Nygren's

---

[94] Kristeva 1987c, p. 140; 1983, p. 137.

Agape and Eros[95] plays a large role. To be frank, I am less than impressed by Kristeva's concern with love. Indeed, given the steady stream of self-help and philosophical books on love, and indeed ethics, we really ought to impose at least a half-century ban on discussions of love.

However, I am more interested in the slips of her argument. One of those slips comes at the point where she speaks of a 'gift-love', of love as a disinterested gift that breaks out of a reciprocal gift-economy. The problem here is that, without naming it directly, she is actually talking about grace, not love. Indeed, we might expect Kristeva to favour texts on love such as 1 Corinthians 13, but it is nowhere in sight. Her preference lies with Romans and its heavy emphasis on grace. In fact, the majority of her references are to Romans.[96] In this light, her efforts to rope the texts on grace in Romans under the banner of love are less than convincing. Is not the gift another term for grace, and is not Paul's great discovery in Romans that of grace? The key texts have been rehearsed often enough, with the canonical decision to place the epistle to the Romans first playing a significant role. Thus, Paul winds himself up in the first chapters of Romans until he gets to the final verses of Chapter 3, where he distinguishes sharply between justification [*dikaiosune*] through works of the law and justification through 'grace as a gift'.[97] This distinction then becomes either the law over against grace[98] or works versus grace.[99] It is no great surprise that Paul's key myth should resonate through the various dimensions of this position, for grace is inseparable from the death and resurrection of Jesus Christ, who was 'put to death for our trespasses and raised for our justification'.[100]

The odd Pauline scholar might be forgiven for thinking that Kristeva has a wholly unreconstructed Paul in her sights. Love? Grace? Justification? Works? Are these not the catchwords of Pauline scholarship before the old 'new perspective' in which Paul was no longer read as a singular, introspective and apolitical theologian, but in terms of his context, especially that of Judaism?[101] As for what we might call the new 'new perspective', in which Paul must

---

[95] Nygren 1953.
[96] Romans 4:6; 5:6–11, 15, 20; 6:3, 5, 14; 8:31–7.
[97] Romans 3:20–6.
[98] Romans 6:14.
[99] Romans 11:6.
[100] Romans 4:25; see further 5:15–17; 6:14.
[101] Sanders 1977; Stendahl 1976.

now be understood in the context of the Roman Empire and its imperial cult, Kristeva's Paul seems very remote indeed. If one were to remain within the rarefied confines of Pauline scholarship, it would be all too easy to dismiss Kristeva. But such scholarship deludes itself if it thinks it is free from the long theological traditions that shape not merely biblical scholarship, but also societies and cultures. A scholar from Denmark will bear indelible traces of the Danish Lutheran Church, while one from Bulgaria would be hard put to deny the Orthodox heritage of reading Paul, and so on. Such influence may operate at a personal level (how many biblical scholars are not also believers and members of a church or synagogue?), an institutional one (the place of biblical studies within an educational establishment) or a cultural level (in the broad framework of the societies in which such scholars work). In their enthusiasm for the various 'new perspectives' on Paul, biblical scholars have lost sight of something more than their own shaping influences. I speak here of the inherently political nature of the old Pauline slogans, indeed their vital contemporary importance, something that the political philosophers have brought unashamedly to the fore.

Paul's few letters are, of course, the great site in which ecclesiastical, cultural and political battles have been and continue to be fought. I need only mention the long political struggles around the Reformation and Counter-Reformation, especially the infamous Thirty Years War (1618–48) between the various alliances of Roman Catholics and Protestants. That the Reformers stressed grace, justification and predestination, while, in response, the Roman Catholics took up Molinism, with its emphasis on giving human beings as much involvement as possible in ensuring their own salvation,[102] shows how deeply these theological slogans provided the language in which these cultural and political oppositions took shape.

If we thought that these days are well and truly past, that the time when the Bible provided the language of politics belongs to a dim and distant memory, then we need to think again. While Kristeva gets to the edge of such analysis, hampered as she is by her devotion to psychoanalysis, other Marxist readers of Paul throw into relief the inescapably political nature of Paul's texts. I think

---

[102] Attributed to Luis de Molina (1535–1600), especially his *Concordia liberi arbitrii cum gratiae donis* of 1588. Over against the Reformers, Molina gave as much room as possible to human works and obedience to the divine commandments. See the discussion of Molina in the chapter on Goldmann.

here especially of the old Maoist, Alain Badiou, for whom Paul is a vibrant political thinker dealing with urgent matters. In his Paul book, Badiou argues that Paul's central message is grace, and that grace can be laicised. Badiou writes:

> The pure event is reducible to this: Jesus died on the cross and resurrected. This event is 'grace' (*kharis*). Thus, it is neither a bequest, nor a tradition, nor a teaching. It is supernumerary to all this and presents itself as pure givenness.[103]

For Badiou, the key text is Romans 6:14, the Reformers' slogan: 'since you are not under law, but under grace'. I will write more on Badiou in the next chapter,[104] so all I need do here is point out that he is not interested in the resurrection per se, for it is a fable or pious myth. Rather, as a Maoist, atheist and one of France's leading philosophers, he seeks to 'extract a formal, wholly secularized conception of grace'.[105] Later, he will variously name this a laicised or materialist grace. In other words, Badiou is interested, firstly, in the way Paul deals with the resurrection, which is in terms of the notion of grace, and, secondly, in the way it can be turned into a materialist, political and militant doctrine. How does he do this? Grace emphasises what is inexplicable, unexpected, what comes from outside human experience and causality. Badiou will call this the Event, over against our everyday world of Being. In Badiou's words:

> it is incumbent upon us to found a materialism of grace through the strong, simple idea that every existence can one day be seized by what happens to it and subsequently devote itself to that which is valid for all.[106]

Badiou, then, reads Paul for the urgent political tasks of today, and, in the process, Paul becomes a militant, acting as the go-between for small cells of the new society, writing letters, thinking on the run. Badiou's great contribution is to remind us that Paul's thought is thoroughly political in and of itself: it does not have political implications; one does not read a politics from it. It is political as such. You might be forgiven for thinking that I would rather

---

[103] Badiou 2003, p. 63.
[104] See also Boer 2006; 2007a, pp. 343–59.
[105] Badiou 2003, p. 66.
[106] Badiou 2003, p. 66.

Badiou's Paul than Kristeva's. True enough, in some respects, but, here, I want to use Badiou to bring out an element in Kristeva's work: what she argues with regard to love in Paul, Badiou presents as central to his notion of grace. But I would not have arrived at this point without a much more visible Marx, whom Badiou has helped me bring to the fore.

Crucifying the pathologies

The catch with the focus on love, indeed on God's love, is that it neatly sidesteps another of Paul's recurring themes – the wrath of God with its own delicious kick. Paul is no hippy, and love is not all there is, but just when we think his diatribes against 'unnatural' passions really wind up to a hysterical crescendo that condemns all those unworthy sinners out there, he gives it all a twist that puts everyone in the same boat.[107] In short, no-one stands above anyone else and each person is subject to God's wrath. So how does Kristeva deal with this other theme of Paul's thought? She does so through Paul's narrative of the death and resurrection of Jesus Christ. For her, the sacrifice of the body of the son is the distinctive and scandalous element of *agape*. But what intrigues me is her argument that Paul's standard narrative about Jesus Christ – the predictions in the Hebrew prophets, his death and resurrection, his designation as son of God, and the gifts of grace and faith – cuts through nearly all the psychological pathologies. As for Paul, he never fails to seize an opportunity to trot it out.[108] For Kristeva, Paul's genius is that this narrative of Christ's temporary death is able to deal with narcissism, masochism, fantasy, repression, death drive and oral sadism.

I suspect there is something in this point, one that comes out of Kristeva's own interests. Let me take masochism as an example and examine it a little more closely. While *agape* goes beyond masochism, it must do so by traversing masochism. There are two steps in Kristeva's argument. To begin with, she dives into Paul's convoluted arguments to come up with nothing other than a variation of the scapegoat. Here is Kristeva: 'Sacrifice is an offering that, out of a substance, creates Meaning for the Other and, consequently, for

---

[107] See Romans 1:18–32 and the twist in Romans 2:1–11.
[108] See, for instance Romans 1:2–6; 3:21–6; 4:24–5; 5:6–11; 6:3–11; 8:11, 32; 10:9; 14:8–9.

the social group [*l'ensemble social*] that is dependent on it'.¹⁰⁹ In other words, you obliterate something concrete – a red heifer, a goat, a human being – in order to produce the abstract sense of the group. The most common way in which that happens is to transfer the group's 'sins' symbolically onto the scapegoat and then cast all this evil out of the community for its own well-being. The catch here is that you create the symbolic notion of the group in the very process of identifying what is good and bad about it. The second step picks up Romans 6:5: 'If in union with Christ we have imitated [*omoioma*] his death, we shall also imitate him in his resurrection'. From imitation, we move via identification with the victim to the internalisation of murder and thence to masochism. Kristeva does not shy away from stating that Paul's logic is masochistic – 'Jubilatory suffering inflicted on one's own body by a supreme and cherished authority probably is the trait they have in common'.¹¹⁰ But Paul goes beyond it by making the masochism analogous rather than real. Just as the initial sacrifice was symbolic rather than real, so the second, masochistic sacrifice is analogous and not real. But, note how Paul does it: Christ intervenes in order to overcome the pathology. Here, Christ is the means by which masochism becomes analogous: believers die in a manner *analogous* to Christ, not *as* Christ.

What about the other pathologies? Paul's writing brings up one pathology after the other, but, in each case, he either negates or goes beyond the pathology in question, and, just as in the case of masochism, each time he does so by means of Christ. Thus *fantasy* is neutralised by making the passion of the cross a universal narrative. This short-circuits fantasy since we can no longer identify ourselves as Christ. Further, *repression* is avoided by means of idealising one's own death; that is, one's death is brought to the fore, rather than repressed, in the narrative of Christ's death and resurrection.¹¹¹ So also do we avoid the destructive path of the *death drive* (unlike Sade or Artaud), since this narrative is a collective one that prevents us from identifying with the Father on our own, of writing ourselves into the story. If repression and

---

[109] Kristeva 1987c, pp. 142–3; 1983, p. 140.
[110] Kristeva 1987c, p. 143; 1983, p. 141.
[111] Or, as Kristeva puts it in *New Maladies of the Soul*, the taboos of Leviticus offer a way to bypass the necessary repression of the desire for murder. Since such a desire is primarily a desire to murder the mother, by enabling a separation from the mother, specifically in terms of transforming sacrifice into a language and system of meaning, the Bible defuses such a desire (Kristeva 1995, p. 120; 1993, pp. 146–7).

the death drive are negated, *narcissism* is appropriated and then overcome. First, the appropriation: the acceptance of death, as the limit of negative narcissism, becomes the way to achieve salvation. Then the overcoming: Paul simply shifts the death onto Christ, and so it ceases to be narcissism, since it is focussed on another.[112] We still have the salvation, but no longer the narcissism. Since narcissism is so close to Paul's logic, Kristeva will later argue that the command to love your neighbour as yourself completes the overcoming of narcissim. Finally, *oral sadism* is conquered by the mediation of Christ: placed in between the self and its destructive hunger, Christ redirects oral sadism. Since oral sadism is primarily directed at the Mother, the Son overcomes this by stepping in between and being eaten himself. Kristeva is of course referring to the Eucharist or the love-feast. There is no sadistic satisfaction in such an eating of the Son of the Father (not the Mother), and so it becomes the means for identification with the Father.

The pattern is remarkably similar: fantasy, repression, the death drive, narcissism, oral sadism and even masochism are either negated or traversed by means of Christ. To some extent, Kristeva has a point concerning these crucified pathologies in Paul. But I find myself longing for some good old history, some of the better versions of those intense concerns with Paul's context that I discussed in the previous section. However, all Kristeva can manage on the historical question is that the success of the new line of thought articulated by Paul answered problems that had arisen within Paul's Hellenistic context. Much more can be said, but, for that, we need the Marx Kristeva has hidden so carefully.

On that score, I am intrigued by the recent focus on the Roman Empire as the context for Paul's thought, and the New Testament as such. Richard Horsley[113] has been instrumental in this work, and I have cited his work in the preceding chapter on Kautsky, so let me summarise. In light of the vast amount of enslavement, mass crucifixions and brutal repression of social unrest that Horsley traces in detail, it seems to me that we have all the marks of a shift in modes of production. In my discussion of Kautsky, I described it in terms of a shift from a sacred economy to the slave-based mode of production of the Hellenistic era. This transition gradually transformed the Roman Empire.

---

[112] Kristeva quotes Galatians 2:20 at this point.
[113] Horsley 1997.

The imposition of a different economic and social formation took place in a piecemeal fashion through systematic violence and the imposition of a different economic and social system, especially in the three or four centuries at the turn of the era. Such troubled transitions produce displacement, tension and violence, in demographic, economic, social, political and *psychological* terms. I would suggest, then, that the various pathologies Kristeva sees answered in Paul's missives may be regarded as the result of such a massive and brutal transition. The troubled genius of Paul, then, is that he may unwittingly have found a myth – the crucified and risen Jesus – that provided a means of dealing with these pathologies.

Collectives

Among the list of the various pathologies, there is one that Kristeva does not mention – psychosis. Or, rather, she does not mention it in *Tales of Love*, but the section on Paul in *Strangers to Ourselves*[114] is a different story, for there we find the idea that Paul's *ekklesia* speaks to psychic distress and soothes psychosis (which is usually divided into schizophrenia and paranoia). To my mind, Kristeva's enthusiasm for the *ekklesia* is where the collective dimension of her feminism comes into its own.[115] I should not need to point out that collectivity is one of Marxism's great contributions to political thought and practice.

As before, I track Kristeva's argument in order to locate its shortcomings. Although she does not raise the question of psychosis in the section on Paul in *Tales of Love*, Kristeva does come around to the collective in that text, even if it is via the individual. Here, she argues that the final step of Paul's reworking of *agape* is love of one's neighbour, or more specifically loving one's neighbour as oneself.[116] And, just in case narcissism should creep in the back door, Kristeva makes sure she points out that the self now includes neighbours, foreigners and sinners in the definition of 'Self'. The capital 'S' is important here, for it is a collective Self. This point comes out much more clearly in the

---

[114] Kristeva 1991, pp. 77–83; 1988, pp. 113–22.

[115] In contrast to her reading in *New Maladies of the Soul* where the focus on 'psychic conflicts that border on psychosis' is of a distinctly individualist focus (Kristeva 1995, pp. 122–3).

[116] Kristeva quotes Galatians 5:14 (Kristeva 1987c; p. 146; 1983, p. 144), but see also Romans 13:8–10.

passage from *Strangers to Ourselves*. The last thing we could say about this text is that Kristeva has an unreconstructed Paul in mind: over against the distinctly Protestant emphasis on an introspective and individualist Paul, or the great polemic of the Enlightenment in which the private individual is the point from which one must consider any group or society, or, indeed, Margaret Thatcher's chilling comment, 'there is no such thing as society', in *Strangers to Ourselves* Kristeva sides firmly with the collective, specifically the *ekklesia*. This *ekklesia* is 'une communauté d'étrangers', 'a community of foreigners'.[117] It is an 'ideal community', 'an original entity', a 'messianism that includes all of humankind'.[118] Note carefully Kristeva's language: although we might suspect she is getting carried away in all the eschatological excitement, what she sees here is the image of a transformed society. This sense of a new society is one of the most Marxist *and* feminist elements in Kristeva's work, as we will see in a few moments.

Indeed, Paul is not only a politician, for he is also 'a psychologist, and if the institution he sets up is also political, its efficiency rests on the psychological intuition of its founder'.[119] And what marks that new community is that it speaks to people's *psychic* distress, or rather spoke to the psychic distress of Hellenistic people and does so presumably today.[120] More specifically, the *ekklesia* soothes psychosis: it answers the schizophrenic split of the foreigner, for the *ekklesia* is by its very nature a foreign collective. But Kristeva goes further, for the *ekklesia* embodies, assumes within itself this psychosis. The way this works is that, instead of trying to insert foreigners into an existing social body, Paul recognises the foreigner's split between two countries and transforms it into the passage between and negotiation of two psychic domains – between flesh and spirit, life and death, crucifixion and resurrection in a body that is simultaneously the group and Christ's body.[121] Their external division becomes an internal one, internal to the collective's construction and the individual's psyche. The way Paul soothes such psychosis is that such a split

---

[117] Kristeva 1991, p. 80; 1988, p. 117.
[118] Kristeva 1991, p. 80; 1988, p. 118.
[119] Kristeva 1991, p. 82; 1988, p. 120.
[120] For Kristeva, this is also a feature of sacred texts more generally: 'If it is true that all texts considered "sacred" refer to borderline states of subjectivity, we have reason to reflect upon these states, especially since the biblical narrator is familiar with them' (Kristeva 1995, p. 117).
[121] See Romans 12:4–5.

is 'experienced as a transition toward a spiritual liberation starting from and within a concrete body'.[122]

I must admit that I find Kristeva's reading appealing, although not quite for the reasons she provides. I will come back to this question, for I need to deal with a few problems. Firstly, Kristeva shares with some critics, feminists among them, the idea that reading Paul can be good for you; or rather, that if we search carefully we can redeem or liberate Paul. For instance, Hawkins argues that we can locate an anti-hierarchical strain in Paul's thought.[123] And Horsley agrees, for in 1 Corinthians Paul finds an *ekklesia* that is an egalitarian alternative society to the Roman patronage system. Texts such as 1 Cor 5:9–13; 6:1–11 and 10:14–22 show up exclusive, eschatological communities that draw from but do not participate in wider imperial society.[124]

The problem with such a reading lies in the language used: Paul uses exactly the same language in modelling an alternative social, political and religious *ekklesia* as that which was used for the Imperial cult. Is it really an alternative, or another of the same? Kittredge, for one, is wary.[125] She argues that, since political language shapes the internal organisation of the *ekklesia*, it threatens to replicate the patriarchal structures of the other bodies on which it is modelled, particularly in terms of patriarchal marriage.[126] Kittredge's hesitation echoes that of Økland,[127] who makes use of Marxist studies of space in conjunction with feminist and ritual studies to reconfigure the domestic politics of the Corinthian correspondence. Focusing on 1 Corinthians 11–14 – the part that deals with ritual gatherings – Økland argues that Paul clearly demarcates the 'sanctuary space' of the *ekklesia* by means of a gender hierarchy of cosmic proportions, the model of the male body of Christ and women's dress and speech. She makes use of ancient literary texts, ritual materials, archaeological evidence on gender roles, as well as some sophisticated theoretical work in Marxism and feminist studies, to argue both that such a 'sanctuary space' is distinct from the Hellenistic context of public and private space, that it is inescapably gendered, and that the Corinthian correspondence begins to mark a

---

[122] Kristeva 1991, p. 82; 1988, p. 121.
[123] Hawkins 2004.
[124] Horsley 1998, 2000.
[125] Kittredge 2000.
[126] Her focus is 1 Cor 14:34–5.
[127] Økland 2005.

shift from gender segregation into a hierarchical integration in which the male was closer to the godhead. Alternative this *ekklesia* may be, but that does not make it any more egalitarian than the bodies it opposes.

The second problem follows from the first. For Kristeva, the *ekklesia* becomes something of a therapeutic device. Thus, if we look at Romans, we soon find Jew and Greek, Greek and barbarian, wise and foolish, mortal and immortal, and so on and on, along with a distinct narrative to account for the passage between these splits. But, what if we give this a Foucauldian twist? What if, in the very act of providing therapeusis for psychosis, Paul's theory and practice of *ekklesia* may in fact be responsible for psychosis and other pathologies in the first place? We need to keep this question constantly in mind, since Paul's soothing *ekklesia* does not provide therapeutics for all – hierarchical and intolerant, it has a history of repressing sexual and gender difference, of denigrating the libidinal, of expelling or absorbing heretics, and of being intolerant to the foreigner.

Thirdly, Kristeva's picture of a great universal collective of happy ex-psychotics is not quite the political collective that emerges from Paul's texts. Here, I would like to introduce an insight from Giorgio Agamben that has a direct bearing on the collective: he argues that Paul continually introduces oppositions that undermine his earlier ones. For example, if we assume that one of Paul's great splits is between Jew and Greek,[128] then he has already unsettled this with the earlier one between Greeks and barbarians.[129] Are the Jews barbarians? Or are the Greeks split themselves? Agamben develops this much further to argue that Paul continually cuts across his binaries in new ways – flesh and spirit, grace and works, life and death, grace and law, sin and law, the law of God and the law of sin, and so on – so that we end up with a highly unstable collective.

This instability intrigues me, for it provides a somewhat different image of the *ekklesia*. Not quite the same of the politico-religious gatherings on which it was modelled, different yet similar, egalitarian, segregated and hierarchical, providing an answer for and yet perpetuating pathologies, it is a curious body indeed. What is going on here? Let me return to my earlier point concerning social formations, especially that of the troubled and violent transition

---

[128] For example, Romans 1:16.
[129] Romans 1:14.

from a sacred economy to a slave system. The problem may be put in this way: what is the question to which Paul provides an answer? We have the answer but not the question. Yet the traces of the question leave their marks all over the answer, especially in the instability of the *ekklesia*. It seems to me that Paul's collective is a political, religious and psychological answer to the brutal changes everywhere apparent in economic and political forms. His response, as the old socio-psychological point would have it, was to provide unwittingly the forms that would facilitate the shift into the different slave-based social formation. It is not for nothing that this answer would become the ideology and practice of the later Roman Empire.

Conclusion

For all her shortcomings, for all my frustrations with the thinness of her analysis, Kristeva does incite me to undertake two tasks: locate the buried Marx within her work and then complete her unfinished insights. When she lets a distinctly Marxist feminism come to the fore, one that is collective, progressive and socially transformative, then I find it possible to enrich her analyses of biblical texts. Let me reiterate the main points of my argument. On the taboo of the mother: with the help of Marx the taboo uncovers a crucial aspect of the regime of fertility within the sacred economy of the ancient Near East. On love: although Kristeva argues that *agape* is a love that comes entirely from outside any human action or causation, and although she also evokes the traditional theological category of grace, she nevertheless falls short on the political implications of her argument. On the pathologies: for all the insight that Paul provides a means for curing, or rather, crucifying the various pathologies, she is woefully thin on why this might have been the case for economic and historical reasons, which I then explored in terms of the transition from a sacred economy to a slave based mode of production. On the collective: her welcome focus, via the *ekklesia* in Paul, on the collective as a new society comes up short when this ideal image of happy ex-psychotics floats free of its economic and political context.

As far as Paul is concerned, Kristeva invests heavily in a Paul who is good for you. Her Paul provides a transformative focus on love [*agape*] and the collective [*ekklesia*], a transformation effected by the myth of the death and resurrection of Christ. In short, she wants a Paul whose thought and collective is innovative and therapeutic. One might be forgiven for thinking that Kristeva is still searching for the redemption in Christianity and psychoanalysis that Marxism failed to deliver.[130] I must admit to being more than a little suspicious of such an agenda, not least because Paul becomes a vehicle for her own therapeutic desires. For instance, while Kristeva regards Paul's invention of the *ekklesia* as a new political and psychological body, it turns out, as I argued above, that this body is only partially and ambiguously innovative, saturated as it is in the social, spatial, gendered and hierarchical space of the Roman Empire; or, as I would prefer, of the slave-based mode of production system violently enforced by the Romans.

The problem is that, while Kristeva brings out some of the political dimensions of Paul's texts, she is in the end not political enough. This is where some of the crop of current Marxist philosophers who have commented on Paul, such as Badiou and Agamben, may be of some assistance. For what they have recovered, in contrast to New-Testament critics who bury themselves in the first century of the Common Era, is the inescapably political nature of Paul's theological slogans in the present. What, then, might be retrieved from a more Marxist and political Kristeva in her reading of Paul? If theology is inescapably political, then her stress on the external and undeserved nature of *agape* (really a code for *charis*, grace) has some mileage. The great political insight here is that political, cultural and socio-economic change does not necessarily rely on human agency. Nearly all theories of substantial and qualitative political change rely in some form on human agency. And most such theories rely on models of past change, such as the shift from feudalism to capitalism. What if, by contrast, the agency for such change was to come from non-human sources? I do not mean the gods or some divine sphere, but rather the vast realm of life on this planet beyond human existence. In particular, I think here of the ultimate contradiction between unlimited capitalism and a limited planet where the natural environment created by capitalism itself begins to break down, bringing with it a whole range of political upheavals.[131]

As for her enthusiasm for Paul's shaky *ekklesia*, Kristeva's collective agenda is something I would rather endorse than discard, but not in the form she presents it. Rather, given that such an *ekklesia* is riddled with gendered,

---

[130] See further Boer 2007d.
[131] See further Boer 2009.

hierarchical, slave-bound and politically conservative elements, it would be worthwhile to invoke Ernst Bloch's dialectic of utopia at this point: even the most degraded collective forms give voice to some utopian impulse. The trick is to extract that impulse from its oppressive content.

Chapter Six
The Fables of Alain Badiou

> [W]hoever enters into this text either abandons it or else grasps its movement and perseveres with it.[1]

A tension runs through the lucidly militant work of Alain Badiou. It takes various shapes, such as the tension between the rigorous ontology of mathematics and the structures of narrative, or between fiction and argument, image and formula, poem and matheme, or Anglo-American analytic rationalism and continental lyricism.[2] However, the shape of that tension that interests me most is between the triumphant banishing of theology via mathematics and its perpetual recurrence in his thought. For all Badiou's efforts to dismiss theology as the philosophy of the 'One', for all his efforts to read Pascal, Kierkegaard or Paul as exemplars of the 'event' without buying into the belief system they purvey, for all his dismissals of the pious myth or fabulous core of Christianity, it seems as though he cannot avoid theology. The question, then, is whether this philosopher who is 'rarely suspected of harbouring Christian zeal'[3] may actually provide an insight or two into theology.

The texts on which I base my reading are *Being and Event*, the short book on Paul, *Logiques des Mondes*,

---
[1] Desanti 2004, p. 63.
[2] See Badiou 2006a, pp. xiii–xiv.
[3] Badiou 2006a, p. 222; 1988, p. 245.

especially the section on Kierkegaard, and parts of the disparate collection, *Theoretical Writings*.[4] A rather formidable collection, to say the least. In what follows, I begin by considering the absolute blockage of theology in Badiou's philosophy, specifically through his banishment of the One. And yet, despite his best efforts to seal his system against theology, it has an uncanny knack of returning. I am particularly interested in the way theology has a ghostly presence in what appears for all the world like a fifth 'procedure of truth' (alongside the four pillars of art, science, politics and love), in his enthusiastic affirmations of Pascal and Kierkegaard, and the play between fable and truth in his engagement with the apostle Paul.

Banishing the One

Badiou's effort to close down theology comes with the opening assertion of *Being and Event* that the one is not – 'l'un n'est pas'.[5] And since theology is the thought *par excellence* of the One, theology is thereby ruled out of order. Let us see briefly how he gets to this point. In saying that the one is not, he seeks to overcome the philosophical problem of the one and the multiple, expecially in the way it asserted the priority of the one and thereby created a problem of the multiple. Rather, for Badiou, the multiple is, not the one. And the way the multiple, the pure multiple, steps to the fore is through the set theory inaugurated by Cantor and then perfected by Zermelo, Fraenkel, von Neumann and Gödel. Cantor's simple definition of the set – 'By set what is understood is the grouping into a totality of quite distinct objects of our

---

[4] Badiou 2006a, 1988, 2003, 1997, 2006b, 2004b. Over the long and slow process of reading *Being and Event*, on various ships and trains throughout Europe, I began to feel as though I was reading a somewhat strange novel: early on there is a death or murder, specifically of the One. Then we meet who is left, the old partner of the One, namely the Multiple. This Multiple is a complex character, bristling with mathematical formulae, a specialist in set theory. In place of the One, we encounter the enigmatic Void, a mysterious character who is both necessary and a danger that sometimes needs to be warded off. The Void brings with it (through the dense thicket of formal language) an event, be it in politics, science, art, or love. The event is the great turning point of the story. Before the resolution of the story, we must face the great challenge of constructivism (it is all language!) which forbids any event for it is unconstructible. Having won through, at last the hero (the 'subject') emerges to claim the event that has risen from the edge of the Void and force the way through to the future of truth.

[5] Badiou 2006a, p. 23; 1988, p. 31.

intuition or our thought'[6] – establishes the fact that only multiples exist and not the one (except for the operation called 'count-as-one', that is, that one may count a set of multiples as one).

How does all of this have a bearing on theology? For Badiou, thought of the one, or indeed an ontology of the one, is the definition of theology.[7] Of course, by the one, he means a singular transcendence, for which 'God' is the usual term. Immediately, we come upon a problem, one that Badiou will partly recognise a little later. That problem is as disarmingly simple as it obvious: theology is by no means excluded to the zone of the one. If we take theology in a broader sense as the development of a distinct discipline that deals with the various ramifications and problems of a religion or of religious belief and practice, then I would point to the many polytheisms for which the multiple is the dominant category. And, if we understand theology in its narrow sense as a distinctly Christian discipline with its own history, language and modes of argument, then even here we come upon two further problems, namely the multiplicity of names for God in the Hebrew Bible and the paradoxical Trinity. In the Hebrew Bible, monotheism is a very late imposition upon polytheistic texts, the most obvious signals of which are the multiple names that turn up – Yahweh, El, El Shaddai, Elohim, Baal, Adonai and so on. As far as Trinitarian theology is concerned, we find a complex interaction of the one and the multiple, for, according to this doctrine, God is both singular and plural, with neither permitted to dominate. As we will see, Badiou notes later that Christianity in fact avoids the problem of the one with its initial split between Two. It is a little problematic, then, that he will continue to connect theology with the one. His only targets end up being strict monotheisms, such as Judaism and Islam, as well as certain forms of Greek philosophy with their unmoved mover and prime cause.

For now, however, let us see how Badiou develops his argument. He goes on to wrest ontology itself from the arms of the one and thereby theology, placing it under the care of the multiple. This is a relatively simple move, for if the one is not and the multiple is, then the concern of ontology – as reflection on being – is the multiple. For Badiou, since it is mathematics that has

---

[6] Quoted in Badiou 2006a, p. 38; 1988, p. 49.
[7] See, for example Badiou 2006a, p. 90; 1988, pp. 104–5, although it is a recurring theme.

banished the one and given us the multiple, then mathematics itself is concerned with ontology; or, rather, mathematics is ontology. All of which means that one cannot shirk the necessity of mathematics in any philosophical endeavour, as Plato showed only too well.[8]

Mathematics, it would seem, provides Badiou with a thoroughgoing way to banish anything that even vaguely smells of theology from philosophy. Apart from the ban on the one and the claim that mathematics is the ontology of the multiple, there are two further steps in this argument. One of those is really a historicising move, where he suggests that theology is tied in with Greek concepts of finitude.[9] When theology first becomes a distinct mode of thought – through the combination of Greek philosophy and biblical narrative – God fits into the whole scene as that which is beyond the known limit of finitude. This is really what 'infinite' means. Thus, theology works perfectly well within a Greek framework of finitude, but, once it encounters the discovery of a proper infinity (of the multiple) with Cantor, Zermelo and Fraenkel's discovery of set theory, it meets its own limit and is no longer viable. At this historical juncture, theology comes to an end.

A final step, which may be seen as the logical step beyond the previous historicising move, is to argue that mathematics absorbs God into its workings, thereby overcoming the divine. Badiou makes this explicit in a rather striking discussion of Spinoza: 'God has to be understood as mathematicity itself'.[10] Indeed, for Spinoza, 'God' is really a place-holder for mathematics. Let us see how this happens. Spinoza's God or Substance is what Badiou calls the 'count-as-one'.[11] Now, this count-as-one is not the one, for the count-as-one marks a mathematical operation, namely the ability to say that a certain group of items constitutes one set. Thus, my bicycle, the statue of Lenin from Bulgaria that was given to me, a 1951 baseball glove from Canada, and Annie Sprinkle's *Post-Porn-Modernist* constitute the one set of things I can see right

---

[8] I am not so troubled by the effort to recover Plato (the more the better), but there is an unexamined classicism at work here. Such a classicism assumes a narrative that runs from ancient Greece to the West. Now, it may well be that the story has become true through its constant use, but it is always useful to note the bump and ruptures such as the fact that Greece is part of the Balkan East, or that the insights of Greek philosophy passed through the Arab world before making their way via Spain into Aquinas's work.

[9] Badiou 2006a, pp. 142–4; 1988, pp. 161–3.

[10] Badiou 2004b, p. 93.

[11] Badiou 2006a, pp. 112–20; 1988, pp. 129–36.

now. So, for Spinoza, God marks an operation of counting as one a whole range of items, whether singular things or multiple individuals.[12] Mathematics, then, consummates the death of God. Or, rather, mathematics is the full realisation of what theology was able to glimpse in a glass darkly. If theology was once the queen of the sciences, Badiou would affirm the slogan of Karl Friedrich Strauss that now 'mathematics is the queen of the sciences'.[13]

So we have reached the point where one of the most formidable materialist philosophers (a former Maoist, no less) writing today, systematically excludes any possibility of theology from philosophy and indeed political thought. And yet... For one who decisively breaks philosophy from its long and tortuous dance with theology, it is surprising how often theology, or indeed God, explicitly turn up in his works. Of course, I will now pick up those moments, exploring their implications not only for his own thought but for theology itself. We come across a scent on the breeze in the discussions of mathematics, and I deal with it first. Yet all that such a foretaste does is point me in the direction of the Event, where there is more theology than we might have expected.

As far as mathematics is concerned, I am less interested in some of the more general problems – the tension between the intrinsic ontology of the Zermelo-Fraenkel system and the 'forcing' of Cohen that he needs to break through to the margins of that system,[14] or the sense that the formidable code of formal language provides an impression of rigour,[15] or Badiou's tendency to follow a 'great-men-of-the-history-of-mathematics' approach.[16] Rather, I am much

---

[12] Badiou's quibble with Spinoza lies in another area, namely that Spinoza tries to close down the void. The trick is that this cannot be done, for there is always an excess of the void.
[13] Quoted by Weintraub 2002, p. ix.
[14] Desanti 2004; Surin in press, pp. 408–10.
[15] In my less charitable moments I begin to wonder whether the dense undergrowth of mathematical formulae provides an impression of a rigorous basis for the erudite (and usually shorter) engagements with the likes of Mallarmé, Hölderlin and Pascal. We are more inclined to believe that Badiou has a formidable system because of those pages of formulae. I must say that this sense comes not from throwing my hands up in despair after an attempt to read and understand. Rather, it comes from a patient and slow reading while on a long journey by ship, train and bicycle through Russia, Scandinavia and The Netherlands, a reading in which I can indeed claim to have understood most of *Being and Event* (or rather Oliver Feltham's Herculean translation), except for the last section on forcing where Badiou really goes overboard.
[16] When dealing with mathematics, or more strictly the history of mathematics, Badiou slips into the age-old practice of focusing on various individuals and their

more interested here in the fact that mathematics bumps into theology every now and then. In fact, it does so at a rather telling point, with none other than the inaugurator of set theory and sometime theologian, Cantor.

For Badiou, Cantor is a curious figure, for he both makes the discovery that, according to Badiou, declares the end of the one and yet he uses his theory to take the path to God. Badiou finds this a wrong turn, for Cantor resorts to the absolute when a set becomes too large or cannot be conceived as a unity (the paradoxical multiple). In the face of this inability to see the totality of a set, he argues that such sets are absolutely infinite. From here, it is a short step to God. In other words, when we reach the limit of a set, we must postulate God outside the system, one who provides a deeper and more powerful consistency. For Badiou, this is a mistake, although he gives various reasons for it.[17] The first is that Cantor fails to see that with such an infinity we reach, rather than the limits of a set, the limits of language, the point at which language can no longer give an adequate description. But this will not get Badiou very far, since this argument has been used by more than one theologian to argue for God. So, Badiou switches tactics and suggests that Cantor, perhaps through a loss of nerve, failed to see the radical implications of his discovery. Indeed, rather than the 'folly of trying to save God',[18] Badiou argues that there is no need to postulate beyond the multiple an infinite supreme being who holds it all together. What if we allow the inconsistency of the pure multiple to be as it is? In this case, we simply do not need God, or the one. At one level, Badiou is perfectly correct, for the set theory that Cantor inaugurated, which was then completed by Zermelo, Fraenkel and Gödel, is a closed system. It is, to use the term of Desanti, an intrinsic ontology that is sufficient unto itself, that simply cannot permit any contact with the margins.[19] In this light, God is out of the question. Yet, towards the end of *Being and Event*, Badiou himself comes to a problem very similar to Cantor's: how does the event break into the given multiples of set theory? Here, he must make use of Cohen's theory of 'forcing'

---

unique contributions to the body of mathematical knowledge. As Weintraub points out (Weintraub 2002, p. 3), this narrative of brilliant 'discoveries' or even events in the hands of Cantor, Zermelo, Fraenkel, Gödel, Cohen and others perpetuates the impression that these discoveries take place in a disembodied vacuum.

[17] Badiou 2006a, pp. 41–3; 1988, pp. 52–4.
[18] Badiou 2006a, p. 43; 1988, p. 54.
[19] Desanti 2004.

to break the boundaries of such a closed system. Perhaps Cantor saw more than Badiou grants him.

I did say earlier that this moment provides a first whiff of a deeper pattern in Badiou's thought, for theology somehow will not leave him alone. He may have killed off the one at the beginning of his story, but it continues to have a ghostly presence in his work. It haunts Badiou, particularly with his theory of the Event.

Theology and the Event

Perhaps the most well-known element of Badiou's philosophy, the canonical account of the Event, goes as follows. In the four realms of politics, art, love or science,[20] an entirely chance, incalculable and unexpected Event smashes its way into the status quo, which goes under various names such as Order of Being, the situation, or even the 'there is'. The terms cluster heavily around the Event, which Badiou also describes as a supplement to or excess of a situation, or as a subtraction from the 'there is'. The catch is that the pure Event – or rather 'Events' since the Event is a multiple and not a one – can never be apprehended directly. It can only be identified after it has happened by its consequences. If someone says, 'that was an event x', then that is a naming after the fact. Thus May '68, the words 'I love you', Galileo's discovery or Mallarmé's poetry are the always inadequate names of an Event that had already taken place. They are traces of something that has abruptly taken place and then passed. An Event, therefore, leaves in its wake what Badiou calls procedures of truth, patterns of language and thought and action through which an Event is identified – and thereby constituted – as a contingent moment. These patterns appear as the 'illegal'[21] naming of the Event, the constitution of the subject as a result of the Event, and an eventual fidelity to which others are attracted. What an Event does, then, is thoroughly rearrange the co-ordinates of the way things are. Like an earthquake or a tsunami, we

---

[20] On these four, apart from numerous references in various essays, see Badiou 2006a, pp. 339–41; 1988, pp. 374–6; 2006b, pp. 18–42.

[21] 'Illegal' because the process of recognising and deciding must avoid drawing its terms from the situation or order of being. Any name for the Event must be made out of an unpresented element – hence 'illegal'. See Badiou 2006a, pp. 202–4; 1988, pp. 224–6.

can know that an event has happened through its effects. The 'there is' will never be the same as the result of the Event, its identification and the truth procedures it generates. It really is a thoroughgoing philosophical elaboration of the category of revolution, or, rather, it subsumes revolution within a much wider philosophical discussion. Indeed, for Badiou, it is possible for something genuinely new to happen, against the adage from Ecclesiastes, 'there is nothing new under the sun'.[22]

The ingenious thing about Badiou's theory is that philosophy is not one of the generic procedures or conditions of the Event. Unlike art, love, politics and science, philosophy does not produce truth, nor is it the bearer of a truth. Should it do so, that would be a disaster: too often throughout its history, philosophy has tried to pass itself off as art, as the means of love, or as politics, or indeed as a science. Truth, therefore, should not be detained and imprisoned by philosophy. Rather, the task of philosophy is what I have just outlined: to discern the procedures of truth generated by Events. Philosophy's proper role comes after the fact of an Event, grasping and organising the procedures of truth. It does not produce truth in and of itself.

Theology, it seems, is nowhere to be found, at least according to this canonical presentation (one that has been propounded time and again by Badiou himself, let alone his interpreters). However, there is more to the Event and its procedures of truth than at first appears to be the case. Indeed, I want to run against this received text of Badiou's thought and argue that he himself opens up a space for theology. There are three moments in such an argument: a ghostly presence of a fifth procedure of truth that is nothing other than theological; an explication of that procedure by means of Pascal's advocacy of the miracle; and then the opening up of the possibility that truth itself, as a result of the Event, is just as much concerned with fable or myth as it is with any propositions of truth. These three moments constitute the real test, for Badiou attempts to read Christianity, Pascal's *Pensées* and the letters of Paul, especially the epistle to the Romans, in a thoroughly secular manner, as a source

---

[22] A point that Badiou makes, offering a loose version of the Latin Vulgate from Ecclesiastes: 'there is some newness in being – an antagonistic thesis with respect to the maxim from Ecclesiastes, "*nihil novi sub sole*"' (Badiou 2006a, p. 209; 1988, p. 231). Apart from pointing out that the text actually reads '*nihil sub sole novum*' (Ecclesiastes 1:10 in the Vulgate), it is a rather telling mark of his Catholic context.

of political insight.[23] In other words, I want to suggest that theology cannot be banished all that easily from Badiou's thought.

A generic procedure of religion?

Among the classic four conditions or 'generic procedures' of truth, theology seems to be far from the scene. It was thus with some surprise that I came across a few pages in *Being and Event* where religion, or more specifically, Christianity, does indeed seem to join the other generic procedures. Badiou does not say so directly, but, by a repeated series of examples, Christianity becomes part of the group.

The context of this underhand appearance of theology is his discussion of the 'theory of the subject' (a reconsideration of his early book by the same name). Here, he deals with the themes of subjectivisation, chance, nomination and forcing. In brief, subjectivisation designates the way a 'subject' appears as a result of an Event, chance designates the way a truth unfolds after an Event (or the way the 'procedures of truth' develop), nomination is the process in which the subject names the Event and certain features associated with it, and forcing speaks of the way those names expect some future fulfilment (they 'will have been true', as the future anterior would have it).

In order to ground these theoretical distinctions and steps, Badiou sprinkles his discussion with a number of repeated examples. As far as subjectivisation is concerned, he mentions '..., Lenin for the Party, Cantor for ontology, Schoenberg for music, but also Simon, Bernard or Clair, if they declare themselves to be in love'.[24] Let me state the obvious: these are the realms of politics, science, art and love – the four generic procedures of truth. Now let me fill in the ellipsis: '*Saint Paul for the Church*, Lenin for the Party, Cantor for ontology, Schoenberg for music, but also Simon, Bernard or Clair, if they declare themselves to be in love'.[25] It seems as though we have a fifth procedure of truth, one that comes at the beginning of the list. In case we might think that this is an isolated occurrence, I provide the rest.

---

[23] Badiou 2006a, pp. 212–22; 1988, pp. 235–45; 2003, 1997. While I would have liked to discuss the whole area of a laicised and militant grace in Badiou's reading of Paul, I should say that I have already done so in Boer 2007a, pp. 372–6.
[24] Badiou 2006a, p. 393; 1988, p. 431.
[25] Badiou 2006a, p. 393; 1988, p. 431; emphasis mine.

Badiou goes on to point out that each moment of subjectivisation also makes a subjectivising split between 'the name of an event (*death of God*, revolution, infinite multiples, destruction of the tonal system, meeting) and the initiation of a generic procedure (*Christian Church*, Bolshevism, set theory, serialism, singular love)'.[26] As he proceeds, Badiou uses various combinations of these examples, such as the evental site for the *first Christians in Palestine* or Schoenberg's discovery in the symphonic universe of Mahler,[27] or the production of names that trail an Event, asking us to think of '"faith", "charity", "sacrifice", "salvation" (Saint Paul); or of "party", "revolution", "politics" (Lenin); or of "sets", "ordinals", "cardinals" (Cantor)'.[28] In order to hammer the point home, one more example, now with the category of 'forcing':

> That such is the status of names of the type *'faith'*, *'salvation'*, 'communism', 'transfinite', 'serialism', or those names used in the declaration of love, can easily be verified. These names are evidently capable of supporting the future anterior of a truth (*religious*, political, mathematical, musical, existential) in that they combine local enquiries (predications, statements, works, addresses) with directed or reworked names available in the situation. They *displace* established significations and leave the referent void: this void will have been filled if truth comes to pass as a new situation (*the kingdom of God*, an emancipated society, absolute mathematics, a new order of music comparable to the tonal order, an entirely amorous life, etc.).[29]

It is quite a collection: 'Saint Paul for the Church', 'death of God', 'Christian Church', 'Palestine for the first Christians', 'faith', 'charity', 'sacrifice', 'salvation', 'religious', and 'the kingdom of God'. To all appearances, it would seem as though we have a fifth generic procedure of truth – the theological – alongside the four of art, science, politics and love.

I am not quite sure what to make of all this. Is this a remnant of an earlier draft in which religion was present, only to be excised rather imperfectly from the collection at the final stages? Or is it, perhaps, an unconscious recognition that his heavy use of Paul and Christianity point to another generic procedure? What I do know is that this ghostly presence opens up the possibility

---

[26] Ibid.
[27] Badiou 2006a, p. 394; 1988, p. 432.
[28] Badiou 2006a, p. 397; 1988, pp. 435–6; emphasis mine.
[29] Badiou 2006a, p. 399; 1988, p. 437; emphasis mine, except for 'displace'.

for religion – it is actually theology – to play some role in Badiou's thought, no matter how much he may wish to banish it.

Pascal's miracle

So let us see how this ghost haunts Badiou's text. The signal moment where theology takes on all the trappings of a procedure of truth is in his treatment of Pascal, which now makes a good deal more sense after I came across the pages I have just mentioned. In short, Pascal's attraction for Badiou is that, through his championing of the miracle, he points to the evental kernel of Christianity itself.

There is, of course, a slightly longer answer as to why this intense Jansenist attracts Badiou so. Badiou writes that although he is 'rarely suspected of harbouring Christian zeal', what he admires so much about Pascal is that he goes 'against the flow [*à contre-courant*]', that he does not go the way of a weak and sceptical world, holding out instead for the possibility of changing the world itself. In other words, Pascal (like Paul) is committed to the 'militant apparatus [*dispositif militant*] of truth';[30] indeed, he writes and acts (again like Paul) as a militant himself. It does help matters that Pascal was quite a mathematician and sprinkles his *Pensées* with the word 'truth'.

Why is Pascal at odds with the world? It is not because he simply rejects the world and retreats into solitude in despair. This was indeed the position of some of the Jansenists, as we saw more fully in my discussion of Goldmann. Nor is it because he falls back on what appears on a first read (which is indeed my own experience) to be the most reactionary and credulous of positions – belief in miracles, the Church's doctrines, the prophecies, and so on. No, the reason lies in a much more difficult path. And that is the effort to find some connection between two stern dialectical extremes: one is the radical assertion of the truth of a miraculous Christianity, and the other is the equally radical embracing of the rush of modern developments in science and mathematics to which he made a few signal contributions himself. The connection he seeks is not via some accommodation to the world, watering down Christianity in the process. Rather, it is through a radical and dialectical affirmation of both. This is why Pascal prefers to address the staunch atheist

---

[30] The preceding three quotations are from Badiou 2006a, p. 222; 1988, p. 245.

rather than any lukewarm believer who has made a home in the world. At this point, we find two of his central means for bringing the dialectic into play – the miracle and the wager.

I will say a little more on the miracle as intervention, the evental truth of Christianity (in Badiou's opinion), and the wager before focusing on a curious vacillation, namely Badiou's switching between speaking of the 'event' of Christianity and the 'emblem of the event'. As for the miracle, Badiou embraces Pascal as follows: 'the miracle…is the emblem of the pure event as resource of truth'.[31] Pascal, after all, holds that 'all belief rests on miracles [*toute la créance est sur les miracles*]'.[32] What Pascal does for Badiou is provide an intricate instance of the workings of the intervention, which boils down to the line – the diagonal of fidelity – that connects a previous Event to the next. It does not lead one confidently to expect an Event, nor does it allow one to calculate when and how it will happen; what it does is to establish continuity from the previous Event to this one so that it becomes possible to intervene in a situation when a new Event happens. Or, in Badiouese, fidelity to the first Event opens up the possibility of the next without making it necessary. What it does is enable those who are faithful to the first to decide a new Event has occurred, intervene accordingly and name it as their own. Indeed, in light of the new Event, the truth of the first Event is clarified.[33]

This is precisely how miracles work, at least in Badiou's reading of Pascal. They provide that crucial diagonal line of fidelity from the prophecies of Christ's coming (suitably interpreted in an ambiguously Christian and typological sense)[34] to the 'Event' of Christ's death and resurrection. Even more, they set up the possibility of the third Event in the sequence, the Last Judgement. Add the faithful avant-garde (the 'spiritual') as the custodians of the Event and we have our agents of decision and intervention in the new Event. By the time we get to the Paul book, Badiou will argue for the *form* of such

---

[31] Badiou 2006a, p. 216; 1988, p. 239.
[32] Pascal 1961, p. 229; 1950, p. 277; quoted in Badiou 2006a, p. 216; Badiou 1988, p. 239. Pascal is, of course, as a Jansenist, faithful to Augustine here: 'I would not be a Christian without the miracles, says Saint Augustine'. Pascal 1961, p. 229; 1950, p. 278.
[33] Badiou 2006a, pp. 216–19; 1988, pp. 239–42.
[34] I write 'ambiguously' since the prophecies have a double meaning: the literal meaning of immediate clarity and the proper prophetic meaning that only comes to light with Christ. There is nothing particularly complex about this since it is a rather old and mainstream Christian way of appropriating Hebrew prophecy.

a sequence – Event, fidelity and intervention. But that is not his take here. Rather, what we have is a translation into Badiou's schema of the classic theological narrative of history.

Now, this is where it all becomes quite interesting, for when he shifts from his discussion of Pascal to Christianity as such, Badiou comes out in favour of certain features of Christianity insofar as they exhibit his own theory. Or as he puts it, 'All the parameters of the doctrine of the event are thus disposed within Christianity',[35] although they are muddied with an ontology of presence. So, let us see what these elements of the Event look like once the waters have cleared. The main Event is none other than the Passion – the suffering, torture and death – and resurrection of Christ, and Badiou has no qualms calling it an Event on a number of occasions. Further, it takes place in what Badiou calls a 'site', namely the Jewish background and the fact of human life at the edge of the void (marked by suffering and pain), and a 'situation', which is none other than the incomprehending and embarrassed state (the province of Palestine and the Roman Empire) that treats this Jesus as yet another nuisance agitator. So far, so good, for all this is rather conventional terminology for Badiou, although it does have the clear point that Christianity is, at root, a revolutionary and militant movement.

Until this point, we have been in what might be called the story of Jesus of Nazareth – the 'historical' story of political revolutionary that is standard fare among Christian socialists, as well as political and liberation theologians. But, now, Badiou shifts gear and drives full speed into theological doctrine. On the way, he links his discussion of Pascal to the creedal affirmation of the three points of what is nothing other than salvation history: the Christ-Event is the fulcrum of two other Events – the Original Sin of Adam and the Last Judgement.[36] This is a curious move on a number of counts. Badiou really produces a sleight of hand here, since he moves from what might be regarded as the historical Jesus to a distinct theory of history. Indeed, he asserts that there is an 'essential historicity'[37] about this periodisation in terms of Original Sin/Christ-Event/Last Judgement. This phrase – 'essential historicity' – is nothing but ambiguous. Does it mean that Christianity is based on verifiable historical

---

[35] Badiou 2006a, p. 212; 1988, p. 235.
[36] It was a pattern that fascinated Walter Benjamin as well; see Boer 2007a, pp. 96–102.
[37] Badiou 2006a, p. 213; 1988, p. 236.

events such as the resurrection of Christ? I suspect not. Perhaps he means that this schema moves in a line from beginning to end rather than in some circular, agricultural pattern? If so, then it is neither original nor correct. Is it the case that Christianity and especially the Bible break with myth? Once again, not an original point and hardly justifiable, for this schema of history is also a mythical pattern. Indeed, it is not so much a biblical pattern, for the Bible is far too diverse for such a uniform view of history; it is a theological extraction of certain elements from the Bible to give us such a schema. What about the point that any idea of history is heavily ideological and schematic? Then, of course, Christianity has an 'essential historicity', but then so does any other schematic story of how things have come about and where they will go. At the heart of this point concerning the historicity of Christianity lies, I suspect, the need for some historical kernel in order to link it with his theory of Event and truth, for they indeed must be 'historical'.

Not his strongest point, it seems. Badiou goes on to stress the way these 'Events' provide both a pattern of fidelity from one Event to the next and the possibility of intervention in a situation by the avant-garde or 'faithful' in light of this fidelity. We have seen this argument in relation to Pascal, so I will not dwell on it here. Rather, what is far more interesting is Badiou's point that Christianity avoids the trap of the one. As we saw earlier, Badiou has pronounced the end of the one, banishing it to the nether darkness where there is much gnashing of teeth. Even more, he will again and again connect theology with the one: all talk of theology is talk of the one, and for this reason theology is no longer viable. Yet, here, he gets Christianity off the hook, if only partially. He writes:

> The ultimate essence of the evental ultra-one is the Two, in the especially striking form of a division of the divine One – the Father and the Son – which, in truth, definitively ruins any recollection of divine transcendence into the simplicity of a Presence.[38]

I hardly need to point out that this is a theological point, honed in the intricate debates of the first centuries when Greek philosophy was harnessed to the biblical stories. But what it does is reveal the deep problem that attaches

---

[38] Badiou 2006a, p. 213; 1988, p. 236.

to Badiou's elision of the one with theology, and that problem is none other than the 'nonsense' of not merely the split between Father and Son, but the Trinity itself. My earlier objection that not all religions have an ontology of the one also applies to Christianity, for here is a curious multiplicity at the heart of the one.

I am no great admirer of the doctrine of the Trinity, but what is fascinating is the way it allows Badiou to retrieve Christianity – understood in his own way – into his theory of the Event. It works even better because of the incarnation: this earthy presence simply ruins any notion of divine transcendence. For one who asserts the end of transcendence (inextricably tied up with the one) in favour of immanence, this is good news indeed.

What we have, then, is a bold appropriation of two dimensions of Christianity into Badiou's philosophy: the Event of the revolutionary Jesus of Nazareth and his death, and the evental schema of Christian theology, with the bonus of sidestepping the one and transcendence. Like others, I get the impression every now and then that the examples – such as Pascal and Christianity – of the Event and its truth are rather neatly moulded to fit the over-arching philosophical framework. But what are we to make of all this?

Badiou seems to have come rather close to affirming Christianity, at least as an authentic case of the Event and its truth procedures. However, just when it seems as though he has paid his dues and received his membership card, he opens up an escape route or two – one via the suggestion that the Church has betrayed its fidelity to the Event, another via Pascal's wager and a third through a vacillation over the authenticity of what he calls the 'Christ-Event'. He is, after all, not noted for his 'Christian zeal'.

To begin with, Badiou dabbles with the possibility that the Church has betrayed the initial Event, that it is no longer characterised by fidelity to the Event that it claims as its own founding moment. The problem lies with a faulty ontologisation, for the Church seeks to contain the effects of the Event (such as fidelity) within its own domain by means of transcendence. In my terms, by referring to God, the Church tries to limit the possibilities generated by an interruption. The most telling examples are heresies: if you cannot absorb them, burn them. Or, in Badiou's terms, the Church limits the set of multiples to the flock of the faithful. It does so by positing transcendence as the maximal point and by locking everything into a hierarchy in which there can be no further errancy. Thereby, like communism and classical metaphysics, it effects a closure to thought.³⁹ This argument is all very well, but all it does is present in new garb the tired old argument that the Church, or indeed the various churches, have lost touch with, or betrayed, or prostituted, the authentic moment of Christ and the early-Christian movement. There are as many variations on the nature of the betrayal (Emperor Constantine the Great, the split between East and West, the venal popes before the Reformation, those wayward churches that ordain women and gays) as there are theories of what the authentic original moment actually was (an existential Jesus who calls us to faith, a revolutionary Jesus, a morally pure movement, and so on). It is no surprise, then, that Badiou makes relatively little of this argument from betrayal.

A more viable escape hatch opens up via his treatment of Pascal's wager. Initially it poses few problems for Badiou (he leaves its treatment until last).⁴⁰ However, if we peer a little closer, he makes two curious moves: he switches from 'wager [*pari*]' to 'choice [*choix*]' and then he opts implicitly for what he sees as the libertine's choice. Now, despite Badiou's impression that choice and wager are interchangeable, choice is a little different from a wager. Pascal argues that one cannot avoid making a wager on Christianity, and that the best wager is one for infinity itself. Yet, if we shift the terminology to choice, the immediate effect is a greater certainty: one may choose clearly and decisively one way or another. Indeed, Badiou later makes choice, of which Kierekgaard is the model, a central feature of his *Logiques des Mondes*.⁴¹ So we find Badiou arguing that, since the Event is itself undecidable, one must of course make a choice.⁴² Indeed, once an avant-garde of true Christians have decided that Christ was the crucial event, then one cannot avoid making such a choice. The catch is that one need not make their choice, for the option of the libertine – Pascal's chosen interlocutor – is also possible, namely to choose not to buy into that Event and its consequences. If we replace each 'choice' or 'choose' in the preceding few sentences with 'wager' or 'bet', the whole sense shifts to far greater uncertainty. Why the shift? I suspect that the reason lies in Badiou's

---

³⁹ See Badiou 2006a, pp. 238, 283–4, 392; 1988, pp. 263–4, 313–14, 430.
⁴⁰ Badiou 2006a, pp. 220–2; 1988, pp. 243–4. See Pascal 1950, pp. 93–7; 1961, pp. 155–9.
⁴¹ Badiou 2006b, pp. 425–46.
⁴² Yet he seems to feel that wager and choice are interchangeable, for he writes a little earlier, 'Since it is of the very essence of the event to be a multiple whose belonging to the situation is undecidable, deciding that it belongs to the situation is a wager [*un pari*]' (Badiou 2006a, p. 201; 1988, p. 223).

own certainty; he certainly does not wager that the one is not, that God is dead and that theology has no content. No, of this he is certain; it is a truth and he has chosen so. For that reason, he can side with the libertine: 'I am forced to wager [read: choose]...and I am made in such a way that I cannot believe'.[43]

A new problem arises in light of his choice not to buy into this Event, as well at its truth and fidelity. Is it a real Event? Is it true? It seems to have the form of an Event, but Badiou cannot assert that it is a genuine Event – unlike the French Revolution, or the Russian Revolution, or Cantor and Cohen's discoveries in mathematics, or indeed falling in love. Is it a semblance or a pseudo-Event, such as the Nazi takeover of power in Germany, or perhaps the attack on the World Trade Center on 11 September 2001? These have the form of Events – nothing will ever be the same! – and yet, for Badiou, they cannot be genuine Events.[44] It seems as though it is neither. He would be loath to put Pascal and Christianity in general in the same boat with the Nazis or the neoconservatives in the USA, and, yet, he will not assert the truth of this Christian Event.

For all its affronting boldness, this claim for Christianity really lies in no-man's land, a vacillation between the Event and the semblance of an Event. This vacillation rises to the surface if we look awry at Badiou's word choice. On the one hand, Badiou writes of the 'Event' at the heart of Christianity 'that is the death of God on the cross'.[45] He will occasionally even use the term 'Christ-Event', *l'événement-Christ*. On the other hand, he speaks of the miracle as the 'emblem [*l'emblème*]' of the pure Event or as the 'symbol [*symbole*]' of an interruption.[46] The effect of both terms is to put some distance between the miracle and the Event. Let me follow the path of emblem first. Badiou uses 'emblem' again when referring to the cross, this time as a synonym for naming the truth of the Event of Christ's death and resurrection that establishes – for the Christians at least – that he is indeed the Messiah.[47] Now, this is

---

[43] Pascal 1950, p. 96; 1961, pp. 158; translation modified.
[44] A pseudo-Event or semblance of an Event follows the following precept: 'I have never said that every transformation or becoming is a truth procedure and consequently dependent upon a founding event and a fidelity to this event' (Badiou 2004a, p. 236). Surin notes the way the Right is all too ready to use the terminology of the Event (Surin in press, pp. 387–9), while Žižek pushes the line that the Resurrection too is a semblance of an Event (Žižek 1999, pp. 143–4).
[45] Badiou 2006a, p. 212; 1988, p. 235.
[46] Badiou 2006a, p. 216; 1988, p. 239.
[47] Badiou 2006a, p. 217; 1988, p. 240.

a tell-tale move, for the lining up of both the cross and the miracle as 'emblems' of the Event merges them together. The initial impression is that Badiou has acknowledged the connection of Christian theology: the cross is *the* central miracle of the Christian proclamation. The other miracles, of healing, of the multiplication of the loaves and fishes, of the water into wine, are supports for this one great miracle. However, implicit in this connection is a double move on Badiou's part that shifts the miracle imperceptibly away from the Event. To begin with, it seems that, for most of the argument, the miracle is another term for the Event. Is not that which breaks into our mundane, everyday existence in an unexpected fashion precisely the miracle? This would be one step too far, for Badiou does after all affirm the libertine's response that he is made in such a way that he cannot believe. So we find the next move, namely to designate the miracle as an emblem of the Event, just like the cross. In this shift, the miracle is no longer on par with the Event; rather, it is one move away, as its emblem or name.

Now Badiou's other term, 'symbol', comes into its own. Although it overlaps somewhat with 'emblem' in French, there is much that lies beneath it. It too shifts the miracle away from the genuine Event: the miracle functions as a symbol that may point to the Event (in the same way that the Bible, according to some interpretations, is a symbol that points to God). The trick here is that the symbol is not the thing itself. Thus, the miracle may be a symbol of the Event but it is not the Event. There is a further connection with the French *symbole*, for it is used not merely to designate a symbol, but it is also used for 'creed' as in *symbole des apôtres* and *symbole de saint Athanase* – the Apostles' Creed and the Athanasian Creed.[48] I assume Badiou is aware of these connections; indeed, it enables him to shift the miracle into the realm of a creed that one can assert or deny.

For all Badiou's affirmation of the militantly unconventional Pascal, for all his assertions that Pascal's thought gives an insight into the Event-based nature of Christianity, he leaves the question very much in limbo. Is the 'miracle' of the death and resurrection of Christ an Event that Christians name as such and to which they are faithful? Or is the miracle an emblem or symbol,

---

[48] In this respect, the French is closer to the Classical Greek sense of the word σύμβολον. Not merely a token, ticket or omen, it was also the term used for the distinctive mark of Christians, which then became the creed or the confession of faith.

a creedal statement which one can freely accept or refuse? This vacillation becomes much sharper in his discussion of Paul, the one who is far more of a radical, a far greater revolutionary than Pascal.[49]

Kierkegaard's encounter

Before turning to Paul, I pick up Badiou's engagement with a theological comrade of Pascal, namely Kierkegaard, in the recent *Logiques des Mondes*.[50] Here, too, we find an ambivalence, for, despite Badiou's systematic translation of Kierkegaard's radical encounter with God into the terminology of a revamped theory of the Event, he will not buy into Kierkegaard's explicitly Christian content. In fact, he finds that Kierkegaard's search for a path to God, along with his heavy reliance on the religious 'sphere' (the other two are the ethical and aesthetic), waters down the full realisation of Kierkegaard's insight.

The only surprise of Badiou's engagement with Kierkegaard is that it comes so late. It seems to me that the inner encounter, the radical disruption of coming face-to-face with God and the decision called for, all seem like the parts of a classic instance of the Event. I would go so far as to say that the whole theory of the Event has a deeply existential feel about it. After all, God's radical interruption in Kierkegaard's system is as unexpected, undeserved and unaccountable as the Event itself.

Systematically, throughout his discussion, Badiou points to the correspondences with his own theory, although that theory now has the elaboration of what he calls the 'point',[51] which turns out to be both the absolute choice generated by the irruption of the Event and the localised place in which it happens. With Kierkegaard, absolute choice is the pivot: 'For Kierkegaard, the key to existence is nothing other than the absolute choice, the alternative, the disjunction without rest'.[52] Other than this item, all the usual suspects turn up. Thus, the paradox of the encounter with eternity in a moment in time is nothing other than the specific and contingent moment of the Event and its truth. The process of Christian subjectivisation in that encounter may be read

---

[49] Badiou 2003, pp. 47–50; 1997, pp. 50–3.
[50] Badiou 2006b, pp. 447–57.
[51] Badiou 2006b, pp. 425–46.
[52] Badiou 2006b, p. 447.

as Badiou's theory of the subject. The identification of truth that comes only from a radically inward gesture for Kierkegaard all too easily lines up with Badiou's procedures of truth that follow an Event. In short, for Badiou, the moment of the impossible intersection between eternity and existence generates the crucial possibility of choice, which is the point where the subject of truth emerges.

It would seem that Kierkegaard, like Pascal, is another embodiment of that ghostly theological procedure of truth that I traced a little earlier. Indeed, Badiou feels that Kierkegaard's position is close enough to his own, mentioning 'the Christian paradox (which is, for us, one of the possible names of the paradox of truths)'.[53] And Kierkegaard, writes Badiou, thinks and understands 'as we do [*comme nous*]'.[54]

Yet, despite the delicious scandal of this self-professed atheist lining himself up with some like-minded theologians, Badiou still holds himself back. He concludes the section on Kierkegaard by pointing to the limits generated by the latter's Christian commitment. The attachment to the highest religious sphere, the dependence on God, the need for repentance and reliance on God's love, the fact that the choice itself is weighted in favour of God – all of these lead to the despair of the being who is not absolute. Let me pick up my earlier comment concerning choice in my discussion of Pascal: implicit in Badiou's assessment of the limits of Kierkegaard's thought is the possibility of another choice, however much Kierkegaard may seem to weigh it in God's favour. Should Kierkegaard free himself from the paraphernalia of Christian doctrine (the content of the religious sphere), then he would indeed find himself with Badiou's own conclusions. In other words, like Cohen, he has taken a wrong turn, thereby vitiating his insights.

Paul's fable

Now, at last, it is Paul's turn. What interests me about Badiou's analysis of Paul, apart from what I take to be a fascinating but unwitting Calvinist flavour, is the way the event that lies at the core of Paul's truth claims is inextricably tied up with a pure fable. Indeed, Paul's central proclamation

---

[53] Badiou 2006b, p. 450.
[54] Badiou 2006b, p. 454.

is that Christ has been raised, a claim that he produces whenever possible.[55] Paul identifies the Truth-Event of Christ's resurrection only after the fact, only in his outright militancy, in occasional pieces written on the run (the epistles). But, the Event in question, the Resurrection, is, for Badiou, pure fable or mythological core; it has no verifiable or historical truth.[56] However, what draws my attention in Badiou's book on Paul is a comment barely made: the Resurrection is not merely a fable, but a *necessary* fable.

At this point, we need to introduce a distinction: the 'Event' in question should be designated a fiction and the 'truth' concerning it is actually a 'fable'. So we end up with parallel sequences: Event-Truth is parallel with fiction-fable. Indeed, Badiou himself insists on this distinction, arguing that, in the realm of religion, we necessarily deal with fiction and fable. Thus, when we are dealing with religion, the Event has the structure of fiction. Even though it is named as an Event, even though it produces all of the procedures of truth, even though we find people who act in fidelity to the Event, the Event itself must be fiction. And so we would expect fable to play a central role in formulating and determining the 'truth' of the Event – as, for instance, in political movements such as the one around Thomas Müntzer. By contrast, in other cases, such as May '68 or the Chinese Revolution, the Event has the structure of fact, so there is no room for fable.[57]

For all its neatness, the distinction is not as clear as it first appears. It all seems straightforward: if one can only know an Event by the truth that declares and names it, then the same applies to the fable in relation to fiction. Yet, how does one know we are in the realm of fact or fiction? We cannot rely merely on the word of those faithful to the Event in question, for they will claim that it really happened, whether that is May '68 or the resurrection of Jesus. If we bring in external criteria of verification (whatever they might be), then we introduce evidence that is inadmissible in the terms of the Event itself – it is, after all, unexpected, unknowable and unverifiable.[58] The distinction is

---

[55] Romans 1:2–6; 3:21–6; 4:24–5; 5:6–11; 6:3–11; 8:11, 32; 10:9; 14:8–9 and so on.
[56] Badiou 2003, pp. 4–6; 1997, pp. 5–7.
[57] Badiou did in fact respond in this vein to a presentation of mine that was a very early version of this chapter. It was at the 'Singularity and Multiplicity' conference at Duke University, 26 March 2005, organised by the Institute for Critical Theory.
[58] For a discussion of this tension in Badiou's thought between the pure externality of the Event and its emergence from the given multiples of the Order of Being, see Boer 2006.

further troubled by Badiou's argument in the Paul book that he is interested not in the *content* of Paul's fable, but in its *form*.[59] This form exhibits a paradigmatic case of the procedures of truth. But then, just as with his discussion of Pascal, the boundaries between fable and truth blur even further. If truth and fable have the same form, then there is even less to distinguish them.

So, I would rather take the stronger line: it is not that truth procedures have some element of the fabulous about them, but that a truth is necessarily fabulous. Indeed, let me push Badiou here and argue that the very strength of Paul's central claim – that Jesus is resurrected – is that it is pure fable, that it is not tied to any element of the 'earthly' life of Jesus, or, more generally, any historical conditions or causes. It is not falsifiable or verifiable in terms of the order of fact, according to any of the canons of scientific or historical enquiry. And this fable of the Resurrection has all of the procedures of truth in a paradigmatic fashion – the naming of the Event as a truth, a militant movement characterised by fidelity and certainty. It seems to me that Badiou's Paul book reveals the truth of his position as a whole: a truth necessarily deals with the fable.

However, I have run on too far in my argument, neglecting to ask what should in fact be the prior question – what is a fable? In terms of genre, the definition is straightforward: a fable is a story that takes place in the world of animals, plants, or inanimate objects with a point to make about human society.[60] However, I am intrigued by Badiou's use of the adjective 'fabulous', *fabuleux*, or indeed 'element of fabulation', *point de fable*,[61] for they break out of the strict confines of the definition of fable I have just given. While 'fabulation' suggests the legendary and mythical, 'fabulous' moves beyond these associations to suggest the tremendous and extraordinary – all of which means that the story of the resurrection of Jesus is not a fable in the strict sense, it is both fabulation and fabulous, or, if you like, a myth. Indeed, the 'fable' of the death and resurrection of Jesus in Badiou's hands actually means myth.

In fact, it seems that, for all Badiou's efforts to keep fable and myth under lock and key so that they will not taint the philosophical task of dealing with the Event, truth, fable and myth constantly mingle and rub up against one

---

[59] Badiou 2003, p. 6; 1997, p. 6.
[60] Yassif 1999, pp. 23–6.
[61] Badiou 2003, p. 4; 1997, p. 5.

another. The first instance comes, tellingly, from mathematics, Badiou's favoured mode of thought. I cannot help but notice that in a variety of texts Badiou broaches what can only be described as a fabulous wonder at the beauty of mathematics, *precisely when he asserts the ontological priority of mathematics*. Out of a number of such moments, those of Mallarmé and Fernando Pessoa (in the persona of Álvaro De Campo) stand out. As for Mallarmé, Badiou writes: 'the injunction to mathematical beauty intersects with the injunction to poetic truth'.[62] A brief poem from Pessoa is even more to the point: 'Newton's binomial is as beautiful as the Venus de Milo. The truth is few people notice it'.[63] It is not merely the oft-made observation that underlying Plato's rigorous philosophy lie the Orphic Mysteries, the music of the spheres and so forth, nor even that Plato struggles desperately with the quarrel between philosophy and art, resorting to images, metaphors and myths at the limit of thought,[64] but that, at the heart of the stark and courageous discipline of mathematics, we happen upon a Platonic wonder at the beauty of mathematics.[65] It reminds me of the mathematician, whose name escapes me, who was overcome with the beauty of the simplest of formulae. Is it perhaps a wonder at the fabulous – and here I take the word in all its nuances – nature of mathematics?

The second instance of fable's unavoidable presence follows from this first example. Let me put a question to Badiou: is mathematics the only way to identify the procedures of truth that follow the Event? How might he respond?

> I have always conceived truth as a random course or as a kind of escapade, posterior to the event and free of any external law, such that the resources of narration are required *simultaneously* with those of mathematization for its comprehension. There is a constant circulation from fiction to argument, from image to formula, from poem to matheme – as indeed the work of Borges strikingly illustrates.[66]

The play of oppositions is crucial here: narration and mathematisation, fiction and argument, image and formula, poem and matheme. And, I would

---

[62] Badiou 2004b, p. 20; see also Badiou 2006a, pp. 191–8; 1988, pp. 213–20.
[63] Badiou 2004b, p. 20.
[64] Badiou 2005a, pp. 19–20.
[65] Badiou 1999, pp. 11–13.
[66] Badiou 2000, p. 58.

add, myth and truth, as Plato's myth of Er the Pamphylian at the end of the *Republic* with all its 'traps and birfurcations'[67] shows only too well. Except that they are not so much oppositions as a series of points in a continual circulation, or, perhaps, an Adornoesque dialectic. So it seems that narration, fiction, image, poem and fable – all of these are as necessary for dealing with the truth of an event as are argument, formula and matheme.

What else would we expect for something that breaks into our everyday multiplicity? After all, the Event is extraneous, unexpected and undeserved, operating at the edge of language and beyond. It is not for nothing that Badiou resorts to poetry, plays and fiction time and again, not merely in his own writing practice but also in speaking of the Event. Indeed, just as speaking about the Event takes place at the moment when 'language loses its grip',[68] so also mathematics at times enters the 'liminality of language'.[69] Poetry is no different, for it signals the instance when language itself starts slipping: 'Poetry makes truth out of the multiple, conceived as a presence that has come to the limits of language'.[70] So also with the fable of the Event that speaks its truth.

Conclusion: necessary fables

Perhaps we can sum up Badiou's take on theology as follows: with the death of God at the hands of Cohen's set theory (even though Cohen himself argued in favour of God), theology turns out to be a distinct language that provides a paradigmatic instance of the Event and its procedures of truth. We can see this model in the letters of Paul, the writings of Pascal and Kierkegaard, and, indeed, in the creedal statements of Christianity. Minus the divine referent –

---

[67] Ibid.

[68] Badiou 2004b, p. 109.

[69] Sometimes Badiou overdoes it. For example, in his discussion of the formal notation of the Void, Ø, he observes that the mathematicians had to search for a sign as far as possible from their usual languages (Greek, Latin and Gothic). So they settled on the old Scandinavian Ø. He writes: 'As if they were dully aware that in proclaiming that the void alone is...they were touching upon some sacred region, itself liminal to language; as if thus, rivalling the theologians for whom the supreme being has been the proper name since long ago, yet opposed to the latter's promise of the one, and of Presence, the irrevocability of un-presentation and the un-being of the one, the mathematicians had to shelter their own audacity behind the character of a forgotten language' (Badiou 2006a, p. 69; 1988, pp. 82–3). Badiou has let himself go a little too far, for Ø is very much part of the vibrant Danish language.

[70] Badiou 2005a, p. 22.

the transcendent one – there is no risk that we will buy into this pious fable.

At one level, Badiou may well come under the suspicion of secularised theology that Adorno expressed so well,[71] for the trace of the former theological use of a term or an idea is not excised so easily. However, there is a slight difference: Badiou does not so much seek to secularise theological concepts and processes as see them in terms of his own system. These concepts then become instances, fully decked in their theological garb, of the event and its truth procedures.

More to the point is the argument of this chapter as a whole, namely that Badiou cannot quarantine his own system of thought from the implications of theology. By that, I mean that the religious fable leaks into Badiou's thought on the Event and truth. For, at the heart of each instance – the ghostly theological procedure of truth, Pascal's miracle, Kierkegaard's encounter and Paul's militant proclamation – there lies that strange thing called the 'Christ-Event' (a term Badiou himself uses). If these various examples are paradigmatic cases of the procedures of truth, we cannot escape the conclusion that truth and fable are inseparably entwined. Indeed, I would prefer to take the strong position and stress the necessary role of the fable. If the procedures of truth set in motion by the Event also apply in the case of a religious fable like the Resurrection, then the fable itself becomes a necessary feature of what Badiou calls a truth. Or, more sharply, a primary mode for telling the story of the Event takes the form of fable and myth.

---

[71] See Boer 2007a, pp. 422–30.

Chapter Seven
The Conundrums of Giorgio Agamben

> ...the Messiah is the figure in which the great monotheistic religions sought to master the problem of law...[1]

I must confess to a certain disquiet over Giorgio Agamben's engagement with theology. To be sure, his political appeal for many lies in his uncanny ability to show how elements sidelined in conventional political wisdom – such as the concentration camp, biopolitics (the inclusion of natural life within the machinery of power), the category of the non-citizen, martial law or the state of exception and totalitarianism – are, in fact, constitutive of capitalist parliamentary democracy. Yet, when we come to his study of Paul, there are some profound problems. This chapter, then, is an effort to bring those problems to the fore: his confusions concerning Paul's letters, his reliance on Christology in order to develop his idea of messianism, his clear decision to make Paul a thinker of the law, thereby sidelining the question of grace, and the shaky category of pre-law as a solution to Paul's arguments.

Yet, in the midst of these problems a usable insight emerges: Agamben tries to relativise the absolute claims made on behalf of theology, specifically by

---

[1] Agamben 1998, p. 56.

reaching back over theology to find the pre-theological usage of political terms that are still with us. In this way, he attempts to negate the argument that most of our central categories – hope, sovereignty, love, promise and so on – are ultimately theological. What he sets out to do – relativising theology – is sorely needed, but the way he does so leaves much to be desired.[2] This is particularly the case when we come to his study of Paul, which is the focus of my discussion. Although I will draw on his other works where necessary, this chapter is primarily a commentary on his commentary on the letter of Paul to the Romans in the New Testament, namely *The Time That Remains*.

In what follows, I focus on the problems before exploring the insight that emerges from their midst. There are four main problems. In the effort to shake up the field of Pauline scholarship, Agamben embarrassingly slips up too often, using non-Pauline letters and making dubious arguments. Second, although he pursues a secularised reading of Paul's letters, especially to develop a theory of messianic time and act, he cannot escape the problems surrounding that Christology so easily, for the idea of the messianic with which he works is inescapably Christological. Third, his decision to take the opposition between faith and law as the central one in Paul's thought may be seen as a direct counter to Badiou's emphasis on grace. While it may be seen as a necessary correction, Agamben ends up going too far, for he can make little sense of Paul's concern with grace, which becomes a mere placeholder of the void between faith and law. Finally, we come to the argument that the key to Paul's thought is the whole realm of Hellenistic (and a little Hebrew) law, or rather pre-law. To my mind, this resort to pre-law in order to understand Paul is the major argument of the book. The problem is that Agamben constructs this category of pre-law on the flimsiest of evidence (linguistic arguments derived in part from Benveniste), he assumes that Paul must make sense and, for that reason, seeks a point of coherence outside Paul, and he gets caught in the quicksand of a narrative of differentiation. However, this trek in search of pre-law also contains a promising insight. In straining and stretching to reach as far back as he possibly can, Agamben attempts to relativise theology's claim to the absolute. At this moment, he marks a transition in the structure of the book, for, in this chapter, we pass from those who engage

---

[2] My unease over Agamben's reading of Paul's stands in sharp contrast to Kroeker's enthusiastic embracing of Agamben. See Kroeker 2005.

with the biblical Paul (Kristeva and Badiou) to the effort to think past theology (Lukács and Williams), or what I call the passing moment of theology. Agamben straddles both.

The search for Paul

Agamben's enthusiasm for Paul is almost infectious. Indeed, Agamben feels that he has happened upon elements of Paul's thought that biblical scholars, locked into their own small worlds, have simply missed. We find comments like, 'Now as much as it may embarrass those theologians…'.[3] Or his own work 'paves the way for a correct understanding';[4] it 'undoubtedly aids our understanding…of the history of Christian theology'.[5] One more example: 'Even the most elementary knowledge of Greek would have shown…'.[6]

While I am perfectly happy to grant that Agamben has been able to identify a few threads that Pauline scholars have missed, indeed that he is able to follow them to places of genuine insight, he runs the risk of missing what may be called the mega-text.[7] This is nothing other than the collection of assumptions, knowledge and positions – a generic common knowledge – with which it is crucial to become acquainted. We have all come across the novelist, for instance, who dabbles in a new genre such as science fiction, thinking that she is doing something breathtakingly new, only to find that it is not so new after all.

So I find it a little embarrassing to come across examples in Agamben's treatment where he makes obvious, if not outmoded, observations on biblical topics. Let me give a few examples. In his comments of the category of 'prophet', he assumes that such figures operated largely as depicted in the Hebrew Bible (rather than being constructs of the texts that bear their names) and that their focus was indeed the future.[8] There is nothing new in his comments concerning the Hebrew term *berit* [covenant] and its basic meaning of

---

[3] Agamben 2005c, p. 117.
[4] Agamben 2005c, p. 121.
[5] Agamben 2005c, p. 124.
[6] Agamben 2005c, p. 96.
[7] I owe this point to Fredric Jameson in a conversation. For a brief sketch of the state of scholarship on Paul, see the chapter on Kristeva.
[8] Agamben 2005c, pp. 60–1.

'to cut'.⁹ The discussion of 'faith in' and 'faith of' Jesus is very ordinary,¹⁰ as is that on *pisteuein eis*, or 'belief in'.¹¹ I suspect, in part, that these observations are targeted at a biblically illiterate audience, but then, instead of claiming that they are insights, perhaps a word or two to indicate that these are introductory and explanatory remarks would have been useful.

The worst case is his search for a historical Paul and his thought.¹² In doing so, he uses the pseudo-Pauline epistles along with the genuine ones. That is, out of the eleven letters to which he refers (there are thirteen in total) four are not written by Paul but by someone else under the name of Paul.¹³ Now, this would not be a problem if he were concerned only with 'Paul's letters', as he claims. Indeed, the Paul of these letters, who we might call the Church's Paul, the one of all thirteen letters, has been far more influential in theology, philosophy and culture than the scholarly Paul of the seven genuine letters. A problem does arise, however, with Agamben's search for a real, flesh-and-blood Paul to whom he can attribute these thoughts. It is, at best, somewhat capricious and mischievous to use four of the pseudo-Pauline epistles as a way into the thought of Paul.¹⁴

---

⁹ Agamben 2005c, pp. 117–18.
¹⁰ Agamben 2005c, pp. 124–6.
¹¹ Agamben 2005c, pp. 126–7.
¹² Despite Agamben's claim that he focuses on Paul's letters (Agamben 2005c, p. 1), he actually wants a real, historical Paul who is responsible for the letters.
¹³ He deals with sizeable pieces of all seven genuine epistles, especially Romans, 1 Corinthians, 2 Corinthians, Galatians, and smaller snippets from Philippians, 1 Thessalonians and Philemon. Out of the pseudo-Paulines we find Ephesians (Agamben 2005c, pp. 75–7, 90, 94, 118), 2 Thessalonians (Agamben 2005c, pp. 96, 111), Colossians 1:29 (Agamben 2005c, p. 90), and he even refers to a pastoral epistle, 1 Timothy 4:7–8 (Agamben 2005c, p. 87), which is a very long way from the Pauline thought world and semantic field. Elsewhere, Agamben continues the same pattern, as the reference to Colossians 1:26 in *Potentialities* shows (Agamben 1999, pp. 39–40). These references are often used to make crucial points. For instance, Agamben challenges one of his main protagonists, Carl Schmitt, especially Schmitt's interpretation of the pseudo-Pauline 2 Thess 2:3–9. Schmitt's doctrine of the exception as the basis of sovereignty turns on the exegesis of these verses from 2 Thessalonians, especially concerning the term *katechon*, holding back or arresting force (Agamben 2005c, pp. 108–11). In response, Agamben argues that '2 Thess. 2 may not be used to found a "Christian doctrine" of power in any manner whatsoever' (Agamben 2005c, p. 111), for it is not the realm of the state that is in question, but the realm of Satan *for Paul*.
¹⁴ This is not the only time that Agamben is somewhat mischievous in his citations. Dimitri Vardoulakis of Monash University noted a similar problem in a seminar on Agamben, Spinoza and the idea of impassivity on 9 August 2006.

I find myself wanting Agamben to shake up the smug and closed world of New-Testament scholarship. Indeed, I would dearly like him to 'embarrass' scholars in the field with an insight or two so that they do indeed engage with philosophers and others outside their own field like Agamben. I just wish he had done a better job of it.

Christology, or the problem of Jesus Messiah

I move now to the explicit content of Agamben's argument, so let us see how he fares. That content has three dimensions: the pervasive concern with messianism, the opposition of faith and law, and the crucial role of what he calls 'pre-law'. Let us begin with the messianic, which is, for Agamben, the name for a dual tension, one in terms of time and the other in terms of act: the name of the first is proleptic messianism, and the name for the second is deactivation. As for proleptic messianism, it is a suspended moment [*kairos*] between an instant of chronological time and its fulfilment. Deactivation is then the mechanism by which the law is deactivated in order to pump up its potentiality so that it may be fulfilled: act [*energeia*] is disengaged so that potentiality [*dynamis*] may flourish – like the scribe whose full potentiality manifests itself when he does not write.

I must admit that I am dismayed by the pervasive presence of messianism in Agamben's text, for it cannot avoid the enticements and traps of Christology and secularised theology. In brief, my criticism of his use of messianism is twofold: firstly, messianism cannot function without a messiah, as Agamben shows all too clearly; secondly, for all Agamben's desires to secularise theology, messianism in this day cannot be thought without Christology, which has its own group of problems.

Despite all the talk about messianism without a messiah, whether that is in Derrida,[15] or in Walter Benjamin, or in whoever follows such a line, Agamben throws into relief the impossibility of speaking of the messianic without a messiah waiting in the wings. It matters not whether such a messiah is purely literary or metaphorical or even thoroughly secularised; it is still a messiah. Agamben's own argument is revealing in this respect. His analysis of the

---

[15] On Derrida, Agamben is absolutely correct: 'Deconstruction is a thwarted messianism, a suspension of the messianic' (Agamben 2005c, p. 103).

temporal logic of messianism is brilliant. Despite Agamben's protestations otherwise,[16] this is one of the best descriptions of proleptic messianism that I have read. Rather than the conventional presentation of proleptic messianism as a time that has been inaugurated and yet awaits its fulfilment, Agamben argues that messianism is 'the time that is left us'.[17] If we live within chronological time as though we are powerless under its control, messianic time (or what Agamben also calls 'operational time') is the time that we seize for ourselves, that we make our own and bring to an end. It is, in other words, *kairos*, the seizure of a moment of *chronos* that brings it to fulfilment.[18] May I suggest that such a notion of time is impossible without the narrative of the 'Christ-Event' – note the terminology – in which Christ comes once, dies and is resurrected, is therefore present with us from that moment on even when he has gone, and yet remains to complete that presence on his return? The *kairos* is then Christ's life and death, one that seizes a moment of *chronos*, but one that can come to fulfilment only with his return.

In its second, juridical aspect, messianism marks a deactivation of the law in order to enable its fulfilment. I want to ask, 'fulfilled through whom?' But I will hold that question for a moment. Agamben must rely on a good deal of imported material here, particularly the Aristotelian distinction between *dynamis* and *energeia* in order to make his juridical argument. He rather likes this distinction, using it also in his discussion of sovereignty in *Home Sacer*,[19] so much so that one begins to suspect it is a template to make sense of a whole range of problems. As for Paul, the crucial verb is *katargein*,[20] which he reads as 'to deactivate' or 'make inoperative'. He then invokes the distinction between *dynamis* and *energeia* in order to try and unravel Paul's contradictions concerning the law. For, Paul both casts the law aside in moments of radical antinomianism and reaffirms the law as good and just.[21] How does all this work? Agamben argues that, once the law is rendered inactive (in Christ),

---

[16] Agamben 2005c, pp. 69–70.
[17] Agamben 2005c, p. 68.
[18] See also Agamben 1999, p. 168. Intriguing as it is, this essay from *Potentialities*, 'The Messiah and the Sovereign' (Agamben 1999, pp. 160–94), is problematic since it follows the false lead that sees the Cabala everywhere in Walter Benjamin's work. For a discussion of this essay, see Mills 2004.
[19] Agamben 1998, pp. 39–48.
[20] Romans 3:3, 31; 4:14; 6:6; Galatians 3:17; 1 Corinthians 1:28; 13:8, 11; 15:24; 2 Corinthians 3:14 and so on.
[21] Romans 3:19–20, 28; Galatians 3:11–12, and then Romans 3:31; 7:12.

then, instead of existing in a dual role of being both active and potential, it shifts completely to the realm of potentiality. From here, it builds up its potential, gaining a *telos* that remains to be fulfilled. Thus, in Romans 10:4, 'Christ is the *telos* of the law', both end and fulfilment. Here is Agamben:

> This is the meaning of the verb *katargeo*: just as, in the *nomos*, the power of the promise was transposed onto works and mandatory precepts, so does the messianic now render these works inoperative; it gives potentiality back to them in the form of inoperativity and ineffectiveness. The messianic is not the destruction but the deactivation of the law, rendering the law inexecutable.[22]

The final triumphant piece of evidence for Agamben is Romans 3:31: 'Do we then make the law inoperative [*kataergoumen*] through faith? No, we hold the law firm [*histanomen*]'. It is, to extend an example Agamben himself uses elsewhere (borrowed from Avicenna), like the scribe who no longer writes. In doing so, his potential to write increases all the more. Or, as I would prefer, like the football player who sits on the bench, breathing in oxygen and sucking down high-energy drinks in order to come on in the last minutes, reactivated and ready to make a crucial spurt in the last minutes of the game.

I am less interested here in Agamben's curious, if not ludicrous, argument concerning the messianic import of the switch from Saul to Paul in Acts,[23] or the equally strange comments on the messianic origins of rhyme in Paul's writing.[24] Nor am I interested in his formal plays with Walter Benjamin, especially the interlinear translation of some Pauline texts at the end of the book that echoes the last sentence of Benjamin's essay 'The Task of the Translator',[25] or his all too clever argument for Benjamin's secret hints concerning his reliance on Paul,[26] or his intriguing argument that Paul develops the messianic remnant through a persistent process of division, each division cutting across the previous one,[27] or even his polemic against Carl Schmitt's use of *katechon*, 'holding back', from 2 Thessalonians 2:3–9 (a Pseudo-Pauline text) as the basis

---

[22] Agamben 2005c, pp. 97–8.
[23] Agamben 2005c, pp. 10–11.
[24] Agamben 2005c, pp. 78–87.
[25] Benjamin 1996, pp. 253–63; Agamben 2005c, pp. 147–85.
[26] Agamben 2005c, pp. 138–45.
[27] Agamben 2005c, pp. 53–7.

for a doctrine of the state.[28] Rather, my interest is in how the temporal and juridical logic of messianism that Agamben explicates is unthinkable without a distinct messiah, namely Jesus Christ.

Actually, I should use Agamben's preferred translation, 'Jesus Messiah'. Not only can messianic time not be thought without the contracted time, the time that remains between Jesus's resurrection and return, not only can the deactivation of the law in order to fill it with potentiality happen except through the Christ-Event, but the Jesus Messiah himself is all over Agamben's text. My initial impression, especially when I came to the third chapter on *aphorismenos*[29] was that all Agamben's talk of the 'messianic' was an effort to deal with the term without a messiah. This seemed highly problematic, but then, by the fourth chapter, the messiah, Jesus Messiah, appeared with a vengeance. This is particularly the case with the definition of *apostolos*, the favoured word of this fourth chapter and usually translated as 'apostle'. Agamben offers instead 'emissary of the Messiah'.[30] As if that were not enough, in the second half of the last chapter,[31] Jesus Messiah is back, whether in terms of faith in him or his own faith, the performative act of faith and, most curious of all, the argument that 'Jesus Messiah' is in fact a nominal sentence. Neither predicate (Jesus is the Messiah), nor epithet (Jesus as Messiah), the nominal sentence shows forth the entwined inseparability of Jesus and Messiah. This, argues Agamben, is the expression of Paul's faith. Perhaps I should let Agamben have his say at this point:

> But what then is this world of faith? Not a world of substance and qualities, not a world in which the grass is green, the sun is warm, and the snow is white. No, it is not a world of predicates, of existences and essences, but a world of indivisible events, in which I do not judge, nor do I believe that the snow is white and the sun is warm, but I am transported and displaced in the snow's-being-white and the sun's-being-warm. In the end, it is a world in which I do not believe that Jesus, such-and-such a man, is the Messiah, only-begotten son of God, begotten and not created, cosubstantial in the

---

[28] Agamben 2005c, pp. 108–11, even though this is a brilliant piece of work, showing how these verses refer to the period of demonic control.
[29] Agamben 2005c, pp. 44–58.
[30] Agamben 2005c, p. 61.
[31] Agamben 2005c, pp. 124–37.

Father. I only believe in Jesus Messiah; I am carried away and enraptured in him, in such a way that 'I do not live, but the Messiah lives in me' (Galatians 2:20).[32]

In this effort to depict Paul's 'experience',[33] what Agamben shows is not only that messianism cannot really operate without a messiah, but that it is, since the emergence of Christianity, inescapably Christological. Indeed, he writes of the 'originary messianic – that is, Christian – experience of the word'.[34]

In a moment, I will return to this inescapably Christological nature of messianism, and draw on Adorno's critique of such secularised theology, but, first, I need to hold Agamben to account for his confusion over eschatology, messianism and apocalyptic. His confusion comes from producing a binary opposition out of what is really a triadic relation. Thus, for Agamben, eschatology and apocalyptic are one and the same: they are concerned with the end of time, the last things, or *eschata*. Messianic time, by contrast, is concerned with the time of the end, or the time that contracts itself and begins to end. The catch is that eschatology and apocalyptic are not the same things.

Let me outline the triadic relation first before making a few comments.[35] Eschatology is the base category; its concern is the process of change from an undesirable present age to another that is qualitatively better, a shift from hardship to peace and plenty. Isaiah 42:9 is as good a statement of eschatology as any: 'Behold, the former things have come to pass, and new things I now declare; before they spring forth I tell you of them'. Indeed, eschatology first emerges as a distinct genre in the prophetic literature of the Hebrew Bible. Its generic signals are an end to social, economic and bodily ills, a new age of freedom and plenty, and an unavoidable use of figurative language, all of which is announced by a prophetic figure.

---

[32] Agamben 2005c, p. 129. It is passages like this that suggest Badiou's comment on the 'latent Christianity' of this 'Franciscan of ontology' may not be far off the mark (Badiou 2006b, pp. 583–4).
[33] Agamben 2005c, p. 129.
[34] Agamben 2005c, p. 134.
[35] See Caird 1980, pp. 243–71, where he gives a good account of the history and uses of the term, although his suggestion that it is a metaphorical way of providing a theological interpretation of history betrays his own heavy theological tendencies.

Messianism is quite simply eschatology plus a messiah. Often confused with eschatology, messianism is, in fact, a subset of eschatology. In the prophetic literature,[36] the messianic genre overlays pure eschatology. The difference is that we now have a divinely appointed individual who brings about the transition from old to new. The messiah, or 'the anointed one', is, in the Hebrew material, mostly a royal figure based around the figure of King David, but then later, especially at Qumran in the Dead Sea Scrolls, we find royal, priestly and possibly a prophetic messiah for whom Moses, Aaron and Elijah become the models. And the Christians simply followed suit with a twist or two of their own.

As for apocalyptic, it too assumes the background of eschatology, and, at times, includes a messiah. The difference here is that now we have a genre of literature marked by a body of revealed knowledge (*apocaluptein* in Greek) about the end times, fevered speculation and calculation of the end, often by means of calendars and numerology, a dualism between good and evil, between God and the Devil and a host of angels and demons, an esoteric method of interpreting the sacred scriptures to find hidden messages, and an overly metaphoric language that provides a coded narrative of the end times. There are but two full apocalyptic texts in the Bible, Daniel in the Hebrew Bible and the Revelation of John in the New Testament. Most of the apocalyptic texts – and there are many – were excluded from the canons of the Bible.

Despite their overlaps, they are distinct categories. Further, although they have their social, religious, political and indeed philosophical dimensions, eschatology, messianism and apocalyptic are firstly literary genres, and Hebrew ones at that. The problem, however, is that, after the New Testament and the history of Christianity, it has become impossible to think these terms without some reference to that history. Messianism is thus indelibly stamped with Christology, and any messianism that is not Christian must set itself over against Christianity. Apocalyptic too has been defined by the one apocalyptic text that was admitted to the New-Testament canon, namely the Revelation (Apocalypse) of John.

Eschatology, too, has suffered this fate of Christian over-writing. Indeed, one might object that I have fudged the meaning of eschatology: does the term not signal a concern with the end, with the *eschaton*? This is where the

---

[36] For example, Isaiah 11:1–4.

Greek terminology falls short, for eschatology's concern is the process to the end, which can be spoken of only in figurative language. What, then, is the source of Agamben's confusion, setting eschatology-apocalyptic over against messianism? I fear that his well-known immersion in the etymology of Greek terms has got the better of him. Let me follow him for a moment: etymologically, eschatology is, as I have just pointed out, the concern with the end. Yet it is not long before he slips up, for apocalyptic means quite strictly revelation, revealed knowledge, and has nothing to do with the end, as he suggests. The slippage continues, for in opposition to this ill-fitting pair of eschatology-apocalytic, he sets a Hebrew term, messianism. So we have one Greek term, eschatology, whose etymology is intact, another Greek term, apocalypse, whose etymology is forgotten, and a Hebrew term. In the end, my point is rather simple: etymology can be a false path, for terms slip and move about, and inadequate terms can signify something that is at odds with their etymology.

Agamben is aware of the problem, it seems to me, when he invokes the Hebrew terms *'olam hazzeh* and *'olam habba*, this world (from creation to its end) and the world to come.[37] Messianism, he argues, is the time in between both. What he means is that *eschatology* is the time in between and that messianism can appropriate that time for itself. To be consistent, either we need Hebrew terms for all three – perhaps the genres of the *nabi*, *messiah*, and *ro'eh*, or prophet, messiah and seer – or we need Greek terms. Or, rather, we need one more Greek term to add to eschatology and apocalyptic, and that should be nothing other than Christology. This is the one term that Agamben deftly effaces, for in the name Jesus Christ he translates *Christos* as Messiah, rather than use *Christos* itself. Nothing, to my mind, shows how inescapably Christian his discussions of the messianic are, and this in itself is a problem.

My point is that Agamben cannot produce a theory of the messianic without the weight of Christianity behind him. It appears in his notion of 'the time that remains' (that is, between Jesus's life-death-resurrection and his coming again), in the argument concerning the deactivation of the law, in the designation of 'apostle' as 'emissary of the Messiah', and in his translation of Jesus Messiah.

---

[37] Agamben 2005c, p. 62.

However, Agamben may well object that this is an unfair criticism, that he is not beholden to Christ, no matter how much Paul might claim him to be the Messiah. Indeed, the Messiah and messianic would seem to function in Agamben as secularised or materialist theology, shorn of its theological content and belief structure. Paul's content is then not so important, for what Agamben really wants is the form of Paul's argument, the logic of the messianic in its temporal and juridical aspects. But this raises a whole new batch of problems that Adorno so sharply identified.[38] For Adorno, the problem with secularised theology is twofold: it replicates the patterns of alienation embedded within theology (the sovereignty of God is then replaced by another, unacknowledged sovereign), and it amplifies the worst of such systems while anything that might have acted as a check is discarded. One cannot take theological language, empty it of its content and refill it with another, for language, argues Adorno, 'molds thought'.[39] This is the problem: it is not as though the content floats free of its container, language, but that language itself has its own content-producing function. Agamben, it seems to me, cannot escape the implications of the content of Paul's thought about Jesus Christ, the Messiah and redeemer.

Perhaps the major implication is none other than the personality cult. For, Agamben runs the risk here of becoming a purveyor of the personality cult, an issue I have dealt with in detail elsewhere.[40] That this human figure, Jesus of Nazareth, should be claimed by Paul to be the Messiah is nothing less than 'pretensions of the finite' of which Horkheimer and Adorno speak.[41] Or of what Paul speaks for that matter: 'I have been crucified with Christ; it is no longer I who live, but Christ who lives in me; and the life I now live in the flesh I live by faith in the Son of God, who loves me and gave himself for me'.[42] Pretension of the finite it is indeed: in the same way that Jesus can become deified as the Son of God, so also can any other human being, and that includes Paul himself. It is this logic of the personality cult that Chistological messianism enables, and Agamben plays into it. I will never forget an observation

---

[38] Adorno 1973; 2003a, Volume 6, pp. 413–526.
[39] Adorno 1973, p. 5; 2003b, p. 416.
[40] Boer 2005b.
[41] Horkheimer and Adorno 2002, p. 145; 2003, p. 202.
[42] Galatians 2:20.

once made by David Jobling, namely that the problem with Christianity is that it relies upon a redeemer figure.

Faith, law and grace as placeholder of the void

The second major feature of Agamben's argument is that he opts for faith and law, or, as he prefers, *pistis* and *nomos*, as the primary opposition in Paul's thought. This decision is significant: rather than grace versus law, within which faith must find its place, Agamben opts for faith as the key term. Bereft of its place at the table, grace must now renegotiate its relatively minor place in Agamben's reading. Here, we find the sharpest difference with Badiou's treatment of Paul: while Badiou stresses that Paul is against the law through his focus on grace, only coming back later to speak of the law of love,[43] Agamben reacts and argues that Paul himself is a thinker of and within the law.

What, then, about grace? As I pointed out in my discussion of Kristeva (which the reader may consult for the necessary background in Pauline scholarship), I find it curious that, just when Pauline scholars feel they have moved away from the idealised 'theological' categories such as law, faith, grace and works, preferring instead either the old 'new perspective' in which Paul was to be understood in relation to his Jewish background,[44] or what may be called the new 'new perspective' in which the key to understanding Paul is felt to be his direct encounter with the Roman Empire,[45] the philosophers seem to be recovering these categories.[46] There is a paradox here: while Pauline scholars feel that they are expunging the last traces of theology from their treatments of Paul,[47] the philosophers are rediscovering the very items that have been rejected as idealised categories. Indeed, one suspects that these philosophers are pointing to dimensions of these concepts that biblical scholars may well have missed in their hurry to move on.

---

[43] Badiou 2003, pp. 75–87; 1997, pp. 79–92.
[44] Following on from Stendahl 1976; Sanders 1977.
[45] For example, Horsley 1997.
[46] For example, Badiou 2003; Žižek 2003; Fadini 2005; Trigano 2004; Sichère 2003.
[47] There is a further paradox: in the name of 'scientific' scholarship, they seek to remove any theological trace while maintaining a religious commitment. See, for example, Engberg-Pedersen 2000, pp. 19–22.

Agamben is one of these philosophers. Now, while I applaud his concern with categories such as law, faith, works, and even grace as philosophical rather than theological items, I do find his treatment of grace wanting. Indeed, in contrast to the crucial role of grace from time to time in major philosophical and political debates (one need only mention Luther, who does appear in Agamben's text, and Calvin, who does not), and especially in his response to Badiou's stress on grace, in Agamben's hands grace has been spectacularly sidelined. It appears as a placeholder of the void between faith and law. And it gains this role only as an afterthought once the grand tension between faith and law has played itself out. Let us see what Agamben says. The primary opposition in Paul is between faith [*pistis*] and promise [*epagglia*] on the one hand and law [*nomos*] on the other. So far, so good. This rupture, however, takes place only after the passage from pre-law to law, that is, after the law's codification. At this point, grace comes into play as the space between, the mediator between the two: 'Having once been united in prelaw in a magical indifference, faith and law now fracture and give way to the space of gratuitousness [*gratuita*]'.[48] Grace is, in other words, a messianic category, a space in between that operates during the time that remains. Yet, a placeholder it is, for grace separates faith and law but never lets them completely break apart.

The implication: the famous opposition of law and grace[49] is a false opposition. Indeed, grace 'is readily misunderstood when not situated in its proper context, that of the rupture of the originary unity between *epaggelia* and *nomos*, law [*diritto*] and religion in the sphere of prelaw [*prediritto*]'.[50] Note what has happened: in the various items of pre-law, grace has quietly disappeared, for it arises only after the passing of pre-law into law.

It seems to me that grace throws a spanner in the works of Agamben's argument. The few pages on grace,[51] a mere add-on to his main argument, show a distinct aporia. Compared with the discussions of faith and law, when it comes to grace he writes without his characteristic clarity and ease. The

---

[48] Agamben 2005c, p. 119. Or, when exegeting Paul's discussion of the two covenants [*diathekai*] from Abraham, one the old covenant of the law via Moses and the other the new covenant of faith through Sarah, in Galatians 4:22–6, Agamben describes grace as follows: 'The space that opens up between the two *diathekai* is the space of grace' (Agamben 2005c, p. 122).
[49] As found, for example, in Romans 3:21–4 and 6:14.
[50] Agamben 2005c, p. 119.
[51] Agamben 2005c, pp. 119–21.

reasons, I would suggest, for such an aporia with regard to grace begin with the observation that Agamben has spent a good deal of his work immersed in the philosophy of law.[52] The philosopher of law has found another of his ilk. Now, while such immersion will open up some possibilities, especially with regard to the theory of pre-law, it also closes down others. Perhaps Agamben's radar is just too attuned to questions of law. Note his various formulations: Paul's work may be characterised, he argues, as an opposition between antinomianism[53] and affirmation of the law;[54] or he writes of the real tension between the promissive, or non-normative, and normative aspects of the law.[55] Thus, what seems to be a tension between faith and law turns out to be a tension within law, between faith-promise (Abraham) and law (Moses), or between the 'law of works [*nomos ton ergon*]' and the 'law of faith [*nomos pisteos*]',[56] or between the law of sin and the law of God.[57]

In the end, Agamben has opted for law and pre-law as the key to Paul. Grace then takes on a shadowy existence, a placeholder of the void between faith and law, or at best a spatial counterpart to the messianic time that remains. This then raises the final problem for Agamben: how is the law to be overcome? He can hardly avoid this question, for it saturates Paul's texts. Christ has nullified, overcome, fulfilled the law. He is its end in all senses of the word *telos*. In his reading, Agamben cannot resort to grace as the way in which the law is overcome.

This is a shame, since it seems to me that a greater engagement with grace would have been helpful. The underlying drive of grace is that it is thoroughly undeserved, unearned and unexpected, breaking into an ordinary life and thoroughly re-orienting it. For Paul, grace is an unexpected gift from God, particularly in the death and resurrection of Jesus.[58] In other words, the source of grace is God through Jesus. But what if we take the underlying logic of grace rather than its explicit reference to God? In its concern with the unexpected and unearned that breaks into human life, two items stand out: firstly, it is thoroughly anti-anthropocentric. Rather than the assumption that human

---

[52] Agamben 1998, 2005b.
[53] Romans 3:19–20, 28; Galatians 3:11–12.
[54] Romans 7:12; 3:31.
[55] Agamben 2005c, pp. 94–5.
[56] Romans 3:27.
[57] Romans 7:22–3.
[58] Romans 3:24; 5:1–2, 15–21; 11:5–6.

beings are the source and end of all events and acts in history, the idea of grace stresses that this is not so. Human beings are but a small part of a much larger whole, whether that be the earth itself or indeed the universe. Secondly, grace may come from an entirely different quarter than its assumed divine source. Under the weight of Paul's influence, grace inevitably winds its way back to God. But that is not necessarily so, for the logic of grace is that it may be any unexpected and undeserved moment or event. It may be a moment or revelation that strikes one out of the blue, or a natural event (catastrophe or not) of global or universal proportions that entirely redirects life.

For Agamben, however, there is nothing that comes from outside the system, unexpected and undeserved. So it must come from within the system. He provides a number of angles on this question: it is, to begin with, a release or overcoming of the tension between non-normative and normative law, between promise-faith and law, or, if you like, between justice and the law: 'Justice without law is not the negation of the law, but the realization and fulfilment, the *pleroma*, of the law'.[59] Further, it is also a restoration or reunion that goes back to the moment of pre-law, before the differentiation between these two halves: 'The messianic is the instance, in religion and equally in law, of an exigency of fulfilment which – in putting origin and end in a tension with each other – restores the two halves of prelaw in unison'.[60] The messianic, of course, plays a crucial role in such a restoration/overcoming of the tension within law. Finally, as we saw earlier, the law may be overcome through its deactivation and potentiality: deactivated in the messianic time that remains, the law retires only to come into its own in the fullness of time. But what does this mean? Here, it seems to me, we find the barest hint that perhaps it is not possible to overcome the law by means of its own bootstraps: Agamben writes, finally, of moving beyond the dialectic of faith and law, beyond pre-law, towards 'an experience of the word, which...manifests itself as a pure and common potentiality of saying, open to a free and gratuitous use of time and the world'.[61] It seems to me that this is the smallest opening to grace, one that enables merely a free use of time and the world. Should he open it up

---

[59] Agamben 2005c, p. 107.
[60] Agamben 2005c, p. 135. In *The Open: Man and Animal* (Agamben 2004), he gives such a reunion an ingenious twist, now in terms of the separation between man and animal that awaits its messianic overcoming.
[61] Agamben 2005c, pp. 135–6.

any further, should he understand grace as the unexpected breaking-in from outside the system, he would need to go outside the law entirely. But that would entail an entirely different reading and he would need to start again, for it cannot be theorised from within the law.

Pre-law, or trying to make sense of Paul

At a number of points in the preceding section, I have mentioned pre-law, or what Agamben also calls 'the law in its originary structure'.[62] Pre-law is the other lane of the royal road that cuts its way through the jungle of Paul's argument. Agamben argues that the solution to the tension between faith and law, *pistis* and *nomos*, may be found in the realm of pre-law, an amorphous moment before the differentiation of law, politics and religion. This is where his argument becomes quite interesting, for now a dilemma emerges in my close tussle with him. Agamben's argument concerning the pre-law has a number of problems and yet, in its midst, something valuable rises to the surface. So, while I have deep misgivings with his dubious reconstruction of an undifferentiated ur-law, I also find that the effort to leap back before the theological moment of Paul's thought has its appeal. I explore the problems first and then turn to that athletic effort from a rather out-of-condition Agamben in the conclusion.

Let us return to Agamben's distinction between faith [*pistis*] and law [*nomos*]. In brief, he argues that the only way to solve the tension between faith and law is by recourse to the misty realm of pre-law. In order to track this argument, we must start with faith. Here, Agamben's characteristic move of using etymology to gain access to pre-history comes into play.[63] The original sense of *pistis* (or *fides*) is of an oath, a keeping of faith that may be described as reciprocal personal loyalty (here, Agamben relies on Benveniste). It is therefore linked with 'oath [*horkos*], 'promise [*epaggelia*]', 'pact [*diatheke*]' and the Hebrew 'pact' or 'covenant [*berit*]'. He uses the example of 'giving over in faith [*dounai eis pistin* in Greek, *deditio in fidem* in Latin), in which a city surrenders to an enemy at the gates, a surrender that carries with it the understanding that the enemy will not massacre the inhabitants and

---

[62] Agamben 1999, p. 167.
[63] Agamben 2005c, pp. 113–19.

raze the city to the ground. Rather, the people give themselves over to the *pistis* of their conquerors, who, in turn, exercise *pistis* and preserve the city, albeit subject to the general, king or emperor in question. In other words, *pistis* involves a mutual obligation, both from the ones who surrender and from those who conquer. At this level, *pistis* is an inescapably (pre-)legal term. Or, as Agamben writes:

> If we want to comprehend the meaning that underlies the opposition between *pistis* and *nomos* in the Pauline text, we should keep in mind this rooting of faith in the sphere of the law – or rather, in prelaw, that is, where law, politics, and religion become tightly interwoven. In Paul, *pistis* retains something of the *dedition*, the unconditional self abandon to the power of another, which obliges the receiver as well.[64]

There are a few major hitches with this argument: the reconstruction of this realm of pre-law lies on some rather shaky foundations; it assumes that Paul must make sense; and it falls foul of the vain search for a point of differentiation. On the first matter, Agamben sets out on his quest for the hazy region of pre-law by calling on Homer and then the somewhat generic 'ancient Greece' in order to see what 'oath [*horkos*]' might mean.[65] Once we get into the realm of the gods or immortals, who are also subject to the oath, we find ourselves introduced to the realm of 'pre-law'. The next moment is the 'most ancient Indo-European institution' of 'personal loyalty', one that is designated by 'faith'.[66] However, the only evidence for such an ancient institution is the reconstruction by Emile Benveniste from linguistic data alone. It is from this flimsy evidence that Agamben draws his argument. In order to add a political aspect to this institution, he then turns to the example of the city that surrenders 'in faith [*pistis* and *fides*]' to its conqueror: just as the inhabitants of the city trust him to spare them, so he must honour that faith. This was, it seems, a Greek and Roman practice, although of no specified period. Finally, we have the discussion of Hebrew covenant [*berit*], which, he argues, is a similar item from the era of pre-law. His only evidence for this, however, is the Hebrew Bible, a shaky source of evidence if ever there was one. Now, the selection of Homer, ancient Greece, a most ancient Indo-European institution, Greek

---

[64] Agamben 2005c, p. 116.
[65] Agamben 2005c, p. 114.
[66] Ibid.

and Roman practice in warfare, and Hebrew is no accident, for it provides a comprehensive background in all of the traditions that one might expect to have influenced Paul. However, not only are they impossibly vague, not only are the institutions reconstructed from purely linguistic data, but they also assume that the key to Paul's thought may be found on some hitherto neglected feature of his context or background.

Why has Agamben chosen this path, especially with regard to the opposition of law and faith in Paul? To begin with, Agamben unwittingly shares the assumption with Pauline biblical scholarship that Paul must be consistent and coherent. Paul, it would seem, is one of the few who must make perfectly logical sense all the time. It is a terrible burden to bear. Rather than being like us – formulating ideas, rethinking them, changing them, contradicting himself, and being simply confused – he must make completely consistent sense.[67] However, since he does not seem to do so on his own, we must import a lot of extra information into his argument.[68] In other words, the secret to Paul's coherence must lie outside his letters.

But there is another reason for seeking out pre-law: Paul himself has provided the lead. Let us see how this works. In the pages I have been considering in Agamben's text,[69] there is a curious feature that requires some further attention: Agamben does not once refer to the biblical texts he is in fact exegeting. Paul's texts in question are Romans 4 and Galatians 3, where he discusses the relationship between Abraham and Moses on the question of faith and law. Yet, in pursuing the question of pre-law as a way of explaining faith and law, Agamben's references are Deuteronomy 26:17–19, Genesis 31:44–54, Exodus 24:8, Deuteronomy 7:9, and Genesis 15:18 – all from the Hebrew Bible. From the New Testament, we find Matthew 26:28 and Ephesians 2:12.[70] There is a sole Pauline text in the whole discussion, or rather

---

[67] For a discussion that highlights Paul's delightful inconsistency, see Räisänen 1983.
[68] See my discussion of Kristeva in Chapter Three for some examples of this overwhelming tendency to refer to Paul's context.
[69] Agamben 2005c, pp. 113–19.
[70] The purpose of the citation of Ephesians 2:12 is merely to note the phrase 'pacts of the promise' from that verse as an instance of the link between the pre-juridical pact and faith.

a pseudo-Pauline text. When Agamben finally does come to discuss Galatians 3 and 4, it is when he has moved on from the question of pre-law.[71]

What is so strange about this search for pre-law is that the texts one could conceivably use for such a pursuit – that is, Galatians 4 and Romans 4 – are simply absent from Agamben's discussion. I suspect the reason he carries on such a curious practice is that these texts by Paul act as signposts to the past. Agamben takes his cue from Paul, for the latter goes back to Abraham, before Moses the lawgiver, in order to stress Abraham's faith. And this, for Agamben, is the realm of pre-law, the shady realm before the (Mosaic) law itself. Agamben, however, falls into a trap, for just when he thinks he has located the necessary tie between law and faith in the realm of pre-law, Paul turns the whole thing on its head in Galatians 3:23–9, where faith follows law! Up until that point, Agamben is somewhat persuasive: Paul talks about Abraham's justification [*dikaiosyne*] by faith and not justification by the law. Justification is, in part at least, a (pre-)legal term. And Paul himself points to the pre-empting of the law with a simple piece of spurious chronology: 'the law [*nomos*], which came four hundred and thirty years afterward, does not annul a covenant [*diatheken*] previously ratified by God, so as to make the promise [*epaggelian*] void'.[72] So we do seem to have the time before the law, the time of covenant and promise and faith that Agamben stresses. Then, when everything seems clear, Paul writes:

> Now before faith [*pistin*] came, we were confined under the law [*nomon*], kept under restraint until faith should be revealed. So that the law was our custodian until Christ came, that we might be justified by faith.[73]

Everything has been turned on its head: faith is no longer in the realm of pre-law, but quite clearly post-legal. Or is it both? Here, faith is precisely the 'new and luminous element'[74] that Agamben denies it is. A moment earlier, faith preceded law through Abraham, but now faith succeeds law, becoming possible only with Christ. It seems to me that any reading of Paul ultimately founders on these tensions in his thought, no matter how much such readings might twist and turn or seek to import extra information in an effort to make

---

[71] Agamben 2005c, pp. 120–3.
[72] Galatians 3:17.
[73] Galatians 3:23–4.
[74] Agamben 2005c, p. 114.

sense of Paul. Even with an immersion in context, Paul's texts eventually come to an unbearable tension as he tries to explicate his thoughts.

I have run on ahead of myself, for I have not yet asked a basic question: what is pre-law? For Agamben, pre-law, or *pré-droit*, is 'a prejuridical sphere in which magic, religion, and law are absolutely indiscernible from one another'.[75] In this light, *pistis* is 'both juridico-political and religious, and originating in the most ancient sphere of prelaw'.[76] Pre-law is, then, the moment before the differentiation of the spheres of magic, law, politics and religion. Such a position assumes a narrative of differentiation, which I discussed in some detail in the chapter on Kautsky. Characteristic of Marxist discussions of the move from primitive communism to exploitative economic and social formations, it identifies an undifferentiated moment that then moves on through a gradual process of differentiation until we find ourselves with the state, class, exploitation and so on. The problems with all such narratives lie both with the initial trigger for differentiation and when the differentiation into distinct realms becomes clear. As for the trigger, what we face is the paradox of paradise. If it is truly paradise, then there is no need for it to break down. If it does break down, then it is a flawed gem: the mechanism for its collapse must be embedded within paradise, but then it would no longer be paradise. Unless, of course, paradise functions as the beginning of a narrative; in this case, paradise, by definition, must be flawed so that the narrative may get under way. The story of Genesis 2–3 is paradigmatic in this respect: the tree in the garden is the trigger for the end of paradise. It is necessary for the narrative to get moving, but it hardly leaves one with a sense that paradise is an ideal moment or place.

Identifying the trigger for differentiation may be one problem; finding the point in the narrative where the various items are clearly differentiated is another. Thus, in narratives of the formation of class and the state, the trigger may be uneven patterns of fertility of the soil, animals and women: some people have better crops, larger herds, more children, and others do not. However slight, distinct levels of wealth creep in, and with it power. Eventually one becomes a chieftain, the leader out of a group of powerful men, and from there we move to the state, to kings and despots and emperors. However, in

---

[75] Agamben 2005c, p. 114.
[76] Agamben 2005c, p. 116.

Agamben's case, the trigger and the clear differentiation of different spheres – religion, magic, law and politics – are closely bound together, if not one and the same. And that moment of simultaneous trigger and clear differentiation turns out to be the codification of law.

Let us look at what Agamben says more closely. He writes that pre-law comes from an 'obscure prehistoric background'.[77] Is 'prehistoric' not another term for the time before history was written, when there are written records of whatever type? This would mean that pre-law signals the time before law becomes written, before it is codified? In Mesopotamia, that moment famously comes with Hammurabi's law code, while in Athens the name of Solon becomes the inaugural moment. Of course, in the Hebrew Bible, it is the mythical codification with Moses, or is that King Josiah as older biblical scholars thought,[78] or is it with Ezra and Nehemiah in the books by their name, or is it even later, in the Persian or Hellenistic eras? All these positions have been held in biblical studies. Agamben is not as specific, preferring to cite Germanic, Greek and Roman practices as examples of the general sphere of pre-law. I find myself wanting some more specificity, some attention to Mesopotamia, Egypt and Palestine. Be that as it may, the deeper problem is that codification of the law is both the trigger for differentiation and the sign of the clear distinctions between magic, religion, law and politics, so much so that, by the time Paul is writing, these distinctions must be assumed. I am not so sure. Is it really so clear that Paul assumes such distinctions and therefore needs to go back to the pre-law of Abraham in order to make his arguments concerning faith and law? To take one example, in the era of the emperor cult, with its gospel [*euaggelion*], its churches [*ekklesiai*] and its clergy,[79] can we really speak of a distinction between religion and politics, or church and state, to put it in post-Enlightenment terminology?

Pre-law, then, is a curious category, based on dreadfully weak foundations, triggered by a desire to make sense of Paul and yet following his directives, trapped in Paul's own twisting arguments and then falling foul of narratives of differentiation.

---

[77] Agamben 2005c, p. 114.
[78] See 1 Kings 22.
[79] See Horsley 1997.

Conclusion: relativising theology

Yet, there is something to be said for this search for pre-law, not so much in the content of Agamben's argument but in its form. That content is riddled with so many termites that you would not want to step on it for fear of falling through. But the form has something going for it, which I have described as a leap back over the theological moment. This jump into the hazy past in search of pre-law may be read as an effort to locate the non- or pre-theological usage of terms that have come to be associated closely with theology. When we make that move, theology becomes but one moment, one way to use a term out of many.

Why do I find this a valuable move, even if I am not persuaded by the particular results of Agamben's search? The reason is that relativises theology's claim to the absolute. The effect of Agamben's strategy is to undermine the claims that theology is the ultimate source of this or that idea in politics, or philosophy, or the social sciences, or literature...No matter how 'secularised' these ideas might now be, goes the claim, they all pour forth from that spring in the lofty heights of theology. For example, we find the argument that sovereignty as exception is of the same ilk as the exceptional miracle, so much so that all political concepts are, in the end, theological.[80] Or our notions of society, hope and history have in their murky basements the theological categories of the Church, the messiah or the schema of creation and redemption.[81] Or, the existential categories of Being and Thrownness [*Geworfenheit*] are really secularised theological categories.[82] Or, indeed, love as a political category may be traced back to the Bible.[83] And on it goes.

Agamben's strategy is not to dispense with theologically tainted terms entirely (which we will see in my discussion of Lukács in the next chapter), but to launch himself back over some two millennia and try to land in the pre-theological time of these terms. I keep imagining a stunt cyclist who revs up his bike, hits the ramp at an impossibly high speed in order clear a pile of buses or perhaps a huge gulf between two high-rise buildings. So, in the case of Paul in the New Testament, this leap takes Agamben back to an inchoate and

---

[80] So Schmitt 2005.
[81] So Milbank 1990.
[82] So Adorno 1973, 2003b on Heidegger.
[83] So Hardt and Negri 2004.

undefined pre-law. He uses the same strategy on a couple of other occasions. For example, he makes a similar move in his search for the original sense of *homo sacer*, where he invokes 'the memory of a figure of archaic Roman law'.[84] Again, like his search for pre-law with Paul, the form of the argument is more persuasive than the content. Perhaps the most effective use of this strategy appears in his engagement with Carl Schmitt in *State of Exception*. In tackling Schmitt's contention that the constitutive exception draws its logic from the theological concept of the miracle, Agamben argues that the paradigm is, in fact, the ancient Roman *iustitium*, the standing still or suspension of the law when the state was under dire threat.[85] The effect is to negate Schmitt's resort to theology as the ultimate source and thereby relativises theology's claims.

It is not a tactic Agamben uses all the time and it should not be confused with his tendency to resort to classical sources in many of his philosophical engagements. That classicism is a common feature of much Western philosophy. We find in standard introductory classes on philosophy which begin with Socrates and the pre-Socratics, or in the arguments of Badiou or Butler or Adorno. The problematic assumption of such a move is to posit a reasonably continuous narrative that begins with ancient Greece and Rome and then passes through into the 'West'. The constant return to the classical philosophers is as much a reinforcement of that classicist narrative as it is a sign of its instability, for it busily applies filler with a large spatula to the gaps, ruptures, dead ends and devious tracks that philosophy takes.

However, when Agamben does take the approach I have identified, it has the potential to show that the theological usage of these terms is but one moment in a much longer trajectory. Despite the problematic content of his arguments, the strategy is extremely valuable, since it punches the wind out of inflated claims by theology, relativises it and makes it much more workable. When theology becomes what I call a passing moment in the history of such political and philosophical terms, it must take its place beside all the others. And, in doing so, it also gives up the resort to some ultimate arbiter.

---

[84] Agamben 1998, p. 71. See also Agamben 1998, p. 89, where he mentions the 'ancient Roman custom' whereby a prepubescent boy placed himself between the magistrate and the lector.

[85] Agamben 2005b, especially pp. 41–51.

Chapter Eight
The Self-Exorcism of Georg Lukács

> Above all my messianic utopianism lost (and was even seen to lose) its real grip on me.[1]
>
> Things now face us in a clear, sharp light which to many may seem cold and hard; a light shed on them by the teachings of Marx.[2]

Georg Lukács spent a lifetime trying to exorcise the last traces of romantic, idealist and religious categories from his thought. While I admire the ascetic and militant discipline of the later Lukács, especially since he was most critical of his own earlier work, it seems to me that his premise is mistaken. For, in the act of self-exorcism, he assumes that these themes function as an original source that must be overcome and excised. So, he sought to dispense with his earlier 'romantic anti-capitalism', 'messianic utopianism', the sense of a 'world abandoned by God' or an 'age of absolute sinfulness'. I do not argue that Lukács is trying to overcome some earlier moment of religious commitment or faith – unlike Louis Althusser, Henri Lefebvre or Terry Eagleton. Rather, his affectation of religious themes seems to be something he picked up in the various circles he frequented and types of thought that appealed to him at the time, such as Jewish mysticism via Martin Buber, Kierkegaard's

---

[1] Lukács 1988, p. xxvii; 1968, p. 30.
[2] Lukács 1972b, p. 1.

Christian introspection, or Bloch's messianic Marxism.[3] Rather, the argument of this chapter is that, despite Lukács's own perception, such themes are not necessarily religious, or indeed romantic or idealist, but that the time of their religious occupation is but a passing moment, however delayed it might be. In this respect, my treatment of Lukács fills out some of the comments that appeared in the closing section of my discussion of Agamben.

In what follows, I trace Lukacs's attempts at self-exorcism along two overlapping paths, the one critical and the other autobiographical. As for the first, we find a curious relationship between *The Theory of the Novel* and *The Young Hegel*. In the former, Lukács argues that the novel could arise only in a world abandoned by God, but his solution is to search for a revival of the lost and integrated classical world, and he finds that in Dostoevsky. In *The Young Hegel*, he takes Hegel to task for making largely the same argument, except that now, for Hegel, the alienating 'positivity' of Christianity must be overcome in favour of the recovered republican freedom of ancient Greece and Rome. In dispensing too readily with Hegel's idealism, I wonder not only at the need to exorcise his own past, but also whether he has not missed something in the form of the youthful thought of both Hegel and himself: rather than some original idealistic-cum-theological core that needs to be cut out, the effort to leap back to a pre-Christian moment suggests that the theological filling is not necessarily original or determining. On the autobiographical path, we have become accustomed to the lengthy prefaces – often written much later for reprints, or translations, or, in some cases, first editions – that seek to assess the limits and insights of the text in question. But what interests me in a select number of prefaces – particularly those of *The Theory of the Novel* and *History and Class Consciousness* – is the continuing autobiographical narrative, especially where that narrative touches on questions of religion. For, here too, we find a more intimate effort at exorcising the spirits from his thought and life. However, there is a difference between the two prefaces: while that in *The Theory of the Novel* categorically discards his sense of 'an age of absolute sinfulness', and thereby his romantic and idealist pretences which underlie that text, the preface to *History and Class Consciousness* gives voice to a nostalgia for

---

[3] Löwy 1979, pp. 93–6; Kadarky 1991, pp. 58–9, 62–4, 115–16. For this reason I do not find it particularly interesting to try to uncover the theological corpse in Lukács's basement, as Maier tries to do (Maier 1989), or, for that matter, Kadarky in his overblown and painfully written biography (Kadarky 1991).

that book's 'messianic utopianism'. I close by suggesting that such nostalgia may be read at another level, namely, for the form rather than the content of the argument in *The Theory of the Novel* and *The Young Hegel*.

A world abandoned by God

I begin with *The Theory of the Novel*, where the first attempt at self-exorcism begins. More than most, Lukács was given to looking back at an earlier, youthful piece of writing and cringing at what he later regarded as crude moves and naïve assumptions.[4] His pre-Marxist works came in for particularly heavy treatment and *Theory of the Novel* was no exception. Yet, I am interested in this work for two reasons: at one level, it marks an effort to indicate a distinct malaise to which the novel is then the response, the attempted solution to that illness. Lukács then offers his own solution since he finds that of the novel itself problematic. At a second, and perhaps more important level it is precisely this attempted solution that he seeks to excise from his later Marxist thought.

The malaise to which the novel genre is a response is none other than 'historico-philosophical' question of apostasy, or as he puts it, divine abandonment: 'The novel is the epic of a world that has been abandoned by God'.[5] And the solution? As far as the novel is concerned it is twofold: through the device of a coherent individual life, that of the hero, the novel attempts to locate an abstract aesthetic continuity in place of the one that was lost.[6] Secondly, by means of irony (the very result of abandonment by God), we find an effort in the novel to glimpse a God who no longer exists. But this can happen only by looking awry, by avoiding the knowledge of God, or even its desire. However, for Lukács, this is a solution doomed to failure. So, he seeks a 're-awakening of spirit' in theological terms, namely, a recapturing of the lost totality of the Golden Age of classical antiquity through a miraculous

---

[4] As he puts it in *A Defence of 'History and Class Consciousness'*: 'I have broken with my past completely, not only socially but also philosophically.... I consider the writings that I wrote before my entry into the Hungarian Communist Party to be mistaken and wrong in every way' (Lukács 2000, p. 93).

[5] Lukács 1971b, p. 88; 1994, p. 77. Goldmann, of course, picks up this theme, albeit via *Soul and Form* (Lukács 1974, 1971a), in his study of the 'hidden God' in Pascal, Racine and Jansenism more generally (see Chapter One).

[6] Lukács 1971b, pp. 70–1; 1994, pp. 60–1.

and apocalyptical process of spiritual renewal, as prefigured in the novels of Dostoyevsky, the Homer of the new world.[7] Later, Lukács would come to criticise what he called his residual messianic utopianism.[8]

I want to unpack this paragraph, since it shows a Lukács very much saturated in theological thought. As far as the abandonment by God is concerned, if we shift the agent from God to human beings, abandonment turns out to be nothing other than apostasy. And this abandonment or apostasy both organises the novel itself and provides its conditions. So, abandonment by God draws a number of other features of the novel in its wake – interiority, adventure and irony. Even if there are other losses that the novel laments, such as youth, 'inner voice,' or home – the loss of faith or abandonment by God is the one that binds the others together. But what does it mean for apostasy to provide the conditions of the novel? For Lukács, the signal of a world sadly come of age is that we have put away our childish faith and the enthusiasm of youth, losing faith in our heroes, the gods. This is the historico-philosophical condition of the novel.

In a manner that became characteristic, albeit with a Marxist twist, Lukács constructs a typology of the novel by means of a generic contrast – here, the novel stands over against tragedy and epic. Thus, in contrast to the over-arching destiny of both epic and tragedy, the novel marks a shift to adventure, to the realm of risk and uncertainty: we do not know for certain whether the hero will win through. With the loss of destiny for the sake of adventure, the novel also exhibits a move from the unity of soul and world (exteriority) to antagonism between them (interiority). The novel is then characterised by the presence of adventure and interiority. Yet, such transitions are not without their problems; the traces of the newer social tensions show up in the cultural product of the novel. And, so, the two features of the novel, adventure and interiority, sit uneasily together. Or, to put it in terms of a second opposition, soul and work become incommensurable with each other, a tension that

---

[7] Lukács 1971b, pp. 152–3; 1994, pp. 137–8.
[8] His later reassessment would also bring about a fascinating twist in his appreciation of Dostoyevsky (Lukács 1973, pp. 179–97). In this case, the conservative Dostoyevsky gives voice to the deeper questions of human existence through the violent despair of his agonised heroes. That despair becomes a masked protest against bourgeois society. But what is remarkable about this interpretation is that the hope for a harmonious and integrated society becomes a dream, albeit a necessary dream for it expresses the hope for a better society and revolt against this one.

determines the nature of the novel itself. Thus, interiority may dominate the hero's soul, becoming narrower and thereby overcome by the outside world of work and adventure (so Don Quixote); or, the soul of the hero may surpass his context of adventure and work, becoming wider and larger than what life can offer (Balzac's *Comédie humaine*).[9] But, then, the question arises as to how the hero may outstrip his world, how he may overcome his situation and triumph in adventure. Without God, the only possibility is a demonic one: 'because of the remoteness, the absence of an effective God, the indolent self-complacency of this quietly decaying life would be the only power in the world if men did not sometimes fall prey to the power of the demon and overreach themselves in ways that have no reason and cannot be explained by reason, challenging all the psychological or sociological foundations of their existence'.[10] But not every hero triumphs, and, here, the crumbling world of adventure overcomes him so that he finds himself facing 'a glass wall against which men beat in vain, like bees against a window, incapable of breaking through, incapable of understanding that the way is barred'.[11]

Now, all of this may be very well, and I could argue that, despite the melancholy note of Lukács's analysis, he is in fact welcoming a world abandoned by God, a world that must face the reality of maturity and putting away of childish superstitions. But not so, for the novel has its own strategy for recovering God, albeit a complex and paradoxical one – irony. The paradox is that God does indeed provide the coherent substratum of the novel, but only because he is no longer present. For Lukács, this is at heart a formal question that takes on the specific features of irony. Irony is both the mark of the novelist's freedom 'in his relationship to God'[12] and an effort to glimpse the God who no longer exists. But – and here is the dialectical twist – such an effort can work only through the very avoidance of the knowledge of God or even its desire. A little like apophatic theology, the key lies in an absolute refusal to acknowledge or know God, for only then will He manifest himself: it is precisely in not knowing God, in the inability to make contact with the transcendent, in

---

[9] The later preface is scathing about the results of this 'far too general' and abstract typology, without a stronger sense of the specific historical and aesthetic nature of the novels in question; see Lukács 1971b, pp. 13–14; 1994, pp. 7–8.
[10] Lukács 1971b, p. 90; 1994, p. 79.
[11] Ibid.
[12] Lukács 1971b, p. 92; 1994, p. 81.

God's abandonment (and, here, he echoes the cry of Jesus from the cross in the Gospels), that one may encounter God. So also with the novel: precisely when the historico-philosophical context witnesses God's departure does it become possible to subsume God into the 'material authenticity' of a form. This is what the novel achieves. When the novel achieves its perfect form 'God himself becomes the substratum of form-giving, homogeneous with and equivalent to all the other normatively given elements of form, and is completely embraced by its categories'.[13] Thus, 'irony, with intuitive double vision, can see where God is to be found in a world abandoned by God'.[14]

What intrigues me about this argument – the novel constitutes an attempted resolution that continually abolishes itself – is that it applies just as much to Lukács's own solution to the problem that the novel signals despite itself. That solution is a thoroughly mystified resort to the supposed Golden Age of classical antiquity, particularly of ancient Greece. The grand historical schema with which Lukács works is based on the sheer difference between the world of the Greeks and of our own: their achievement was an integration of soul and world that generated both epic and tragedy. Over against this integrated civilisation is our (or rather, that of Lukács in a Europe, or indeed *fin de siècle* Hungary of the early twentieth century) problematic one, of which the novel is the cultural marker. Once the Greek world collapsed, only Christianity was able to provide an alternative integrated civilisation more complete than the one it surpassed:

> the world became round once more, a totality capable of being taken in at a glance...; the cry for redemption became a dissonance in the perfect rhythmic system of the world and thereby rendered possible a new equilibrium no less perfect than that of the Greeks.[15]

It will come as no surprise that Lukács's solution is not one that harks back to the last great integration of Christianity, but to the classical pre-Christian world itself. In the last brief paragraph of the book, he speaks of the creative vision of Dostoevsky, either the harbinger or occupant, like Homer, of the new world. A visionary and apocalyptic tone suffuses this last paragraph,

---

[13] Lukács 1971b, p. 91; 1994, p. 80.
[14] Lukács 1971b, p. 92; 1994, p. 81.
[15] Lukács 1971b, pp. 37–8; 1994, p. 29.

a call for a renewal of spirit.[16] It is not for nothing that the Marxist Lukács would savage his own earlier work (see the 'Preface'), for this is hardly a progressive solution. Yet, what is interesting here is that it is precisely this argument that he would criticise in the early Hegel many years later. Reading *The Young Hegel*[17] after *Theory of the Novel* you get the uncanny sense that Lukács is exorcising a demon or two. So let us turn to the second book.

Leap-frogging Christianity

For Lukács, Hegel is anti-theological and anti-Christian in his early works, criticising the 'positivity' of Christianity, the alienating externalisation of religion into imposed norms by an institution. But the problem is that Hegel opposes theology with an idealised version of the republican freedom of classical Greece. In form, at least, this is the very strategy of Lukács in *Theory of the Novel*, with some minor modifications in detail. In both cases, they see no solution in an earlier more pristine form of Christianity, whether that may be found in the words of the founder or in the last integration of soul and world; rather, they leap-frog to an earlier pre-Christian moment for inspiration, namely classical Greece. Lukács's criticism of Hegel becomes then, implicitly at least, a criticism of his own earlier position.

So let us see how he goes about this in *The Young Hegel*. To my mind, five strands may be untangled from Lukács's argument. The first comes from the importance of Hegel in the early history of dialectic. It is crucial for Lukács to establish that the origins of the dialectic lie not with theology, but with a profound criticism of theology, or indeed an anti-theological thrust.[18] Second, the positive element of this argument is that the dialectic, in Hegel's hands, is due to both the political conditions of Germany at the time (its political and cultural backwardness in relation to France and the rest of Europe, its struggles to achieve national unity) and to Hegel's engagement with economics.[19] The catch with this argument is that economics forms something of an absent cause, since Hegel's economic manuscripts were lost at the time Lukács was writing. Third, against the arguments of many of his interpreters, Hegel is, in

---

[16] Lukács 1971b, pp. 152–3; 1994, pp. 137–8.
[17] Lukács 1975, 1967.
[18] Lukács 1975, pp. xviii–xxii, 217–18; 1967, pp. 18–23, 285–6.
[19] Lukács 1975, pp. xxvii, 168–78; 1967, pp. 29, 225–39.

fact, on the Left. For Lukács, the early Hegel, who read deeply in classical literature as well as that of the German and French Enlightenments, 'finds himself increasingly on the democratic left-wing'.[20] Fourth, Lukács blames Hegel's editors and biographers, such as Nohl, Lasson and Hoering, for emphasising the theological nature of Hegel's early writings – 'the belief in Hegel's "theological" early period remains a legend created and fostered by the reactionary apologists of imperialism'.[21] Indeed, he suggests (a not uncommon suggestion) that these interpretations are part of the irrational and mystifying interpretations that lend themselves to fascism.[22] Finally, as for Hegel himself, the 'unprejudiced and attentive reader will find precious little to do with theology in them [Hegel's early works], indeed as far as theology is concerned the tone is one of sustained hostility'.[23]

I am particularly interested in the last two strategies, for, in order to tackle those interpreters who emphasise Hegel's debts to theology, Lukács must show a somewhat different Hegel. And he does so by means of the central text, *The Positivity of the Christian Religion*.[24] I remember reading this text, as well as Lukács's commentary on it, for my Master of Theology thesis on Hegel and Marx in the late 1980s, and it struck me then as it does now on a re-read that Hegel's thought is perhaps a little more subtle than Lukács gives him credit for – or, rather, than the use to which Lukács wishes to put it. The argument that appeals to Lukács here hinges around the notion of positivity: both regrettable and inevitable, Christianity extends the words directed by Jesus at the individual to society as a whole. It moves, then, from the words of its founder to an objectified and alienating structure, one that constructs doctrines, institutions, a judiciary to keep the wayward in line, commandments and clergy, all of which impose an alien will on the populace. And it is not a case of returning to the words and early community of Jesus, for not only have reform movements been attempting to do precisely this – overcoming the corruption and self-interest of the institution now in favour of return to pristine origins – but Jesus himself laid the seeds of Christianity's full-blown

---

[20] Lukács 1975, p. 5; 1967, p. 37.
[21] Lukács 1975, p. 16; 1967, p. 52.
[22] Lukács 1975, pp. xxviii, 8, 32; 1967, pp. 30, 41–2, 68–9.
[23] Lukács 1975, p. 8; 1967, p. 42.
[24] Hegel 1961, pp. 67–181.

positivity.²⁵ Compared to Socrates, Jesus would have been an object of laughter, the creator of a 'narrow minded, closed sect'²⁶ rather than creating masters and leaders in their own right. In short, Christianity cannot help but be a positive 'religion'. Lukács loves this material, much more than the Frankfurt text, *The Spirit of Christianity and Its Fate*,²⁷ which is full of a contradictory sympathy to Christianity, and he plays it out as much as he can: 'There can be no doubt: these ostensibly theological writings are one long indictment of Christianity'.²⁸

Well, not quite, for Lukács's text betrays a tension, not so much in Hegel (although there are enough of those) as in his own thought. Indeed, Lukács needs to steer a course between the Scylla of Hegel's idealism and the Charybdis of his materialism, his socio-historical observations and emphases. While he is not afraid to criticise Hegel for his idealism, yet he cannot let Hegel become too idealist, since then he would land in the camp of the right Hegelians and those mystifying commentators who wish to see his beginnings in theology. But, then, if Hegel were too materialist – Lukács points to his awareness of the division of labour in antiquity,²⁹ to the importance of seeking the socio-historical roots of religion,³⁰ and his crucial economic research³¹ – we would need to ask why Marx had to stand him, or rather his dialectic, on its feet.

How does this tension manifest itself on the question of 'religion'? The problem for Lukács is that, for all Hegel's polemic against Christianity, his solutions were still very much religious. To his credit, Lukács recognises this: 'His aim is to discover the social prerequisites for a return from the religion of despotism and enslavement to a religion of freedom on the model of antiquity'.³² Lukács goes so far as to praise the dialectical insight that out of the two oppositions of public-private and positive-subjective, Hegel sees the deeper connection between positivity and the private: the very strength of positive Christianity is that it is very much a private affair, a policing of the heart. But

---

²⁵ See Lukács 1975, pp. 63–4; 1967, pp. 103–4.
²⁶ Lukács 1975, p. 48; 1967, p. 89.
²⁷ Hegel 1961, pp. 182–301.
²⁸ Lukács 1975, p. 23; 1967, p. 60.
²⁹ Lukács 1975, p. 40; 1967, p. 79.
³⁰ Lukács 1975, pp. 16, 84–5; 1967, pp. 52, 128–9.
³¹ Lukács 1975, pp. xxvii, 168–78; 1967, pp. 29, 225–39.
³² Lukács 1975, p. 9; 1967, p. 43.

the solution to this problem is in itself religious, if not theological – Hegel wants a subjective and public religion in its place, a 'religion of the self-liberation of the people'.[33] The central cultural and religious model, the living example that fed off and fed into Hegel's utopian picture of a republic of the future, was the republican freedom of Greece and Rome.[34] Lukács, having himself espoused a very similar position in his earlier work, will not have a bar of it. In fact he argues that the over-estimation of the role of religion stays with Hegel for the rest of his life, peaking in the crisis years of the Frankfurt period. When Hegel does let his theological bent come to the fore, he systematically discards all his hard-won and carefully constructed insights.[35] This is, in Lukács's estimation, the fatal flaw of Hegel's mature system: 'History is...the process of religious change, or, to put it in the language of objective idealism: it is the history of God's metamorphoses'.[36] Lukács would much rather see history as a process of gradual emancipation from religion.

So far so good, for, through Hegel, Lukács seems to be excising, systematically, the last vestiges of theology from his thought, even down to the idealised pagan classicism that saturated German thought – and, of course, his own earlier thought.[37] However, in his drive to a thoroughgoing materialist atheism – something he admits Hegel never reached – by means of excising the last traces of theology, I cannot help but wonder whether Lukács has not proceeded a little too rashly here.[38] In fact, in the next step of my argument, I want

---

[33] Lukács 1975, p. 29; 1967, p. 67.
[34] See also Lukács 1970, pp. 89–90. Lukács is not, however, an anti-classicist. Far from it, for he defends the interest in and treasuring of the classical heritage as 'adequate pictures of great periods of human development' and as 'signposts in the ideological battle fought for the restoration of the unbroken human personality' (Lukács 1972b, p. 5).
[35] Lukács 1975, p. 191; 1967, p. 255.
[36] Lukács 1975, p. 80; 1967, p. 122.
[37] A particularly sustained effort also appears in his engagement with Kierkegaard. Thus, his earlier infatuation with Kierkegaard, including an essay in *Soul and Form* and the effort to imitate Kierkegaard's introspective, thinly veiled autobiographical style (Lukács 1995, pp. 11–62), gives way to the self-surgery of the chapter on Kierkegaard in *The Destruction of Reason* (Lukács 1980, pp. 243–305). Here, Kierkegaard's romantic anticapitalism and irrational inwardness are tied up with a reactionary theological agenda, so much so that Kierkegaard becomes a pure apologist of bourgeois decadence. As much as I love such phrases, this brutal exercise of self-exorcism loses the dialectical flair that interests me in this chapter.
[38] On the question of religion, Lukács will not even grant Hegel his dialectic: thus he can only see in Hegel's argument – 'Christianity not only springs from the moral decadence of a people governed by tyrants, but equally tyranny is an effect brought

to draw not so much from Lukács's dismissive polemic regarding Hegel's idealism and religious mysticism but from the moments he lives up to the dialectic he inherits from Hegel. I refer to his argument that in Hegel's crisis-ridden Frankfurt period, when he was most open to Christianity, the dialectic as a fully historical method first emerges from his writing.[39] For Lukács, even the Hegel of the *Phenomenology* is muddled, developing an idealist dialectic that could only begin and end with religion, even to the point of running the major Christian doctrines through the dialectic,[40] and yet he acknowledges Hegel's discovery and runs with it.

This is the Lukács that I want to follow, now with respect to the form of both his and Hegel's arguments in their early texts. For there may, in fact, be something in the form of Hegel's argument rather than the content that is worth considering, and, for that matter, the form of Lukács's earlier argument in *Theory of the Novel*. And that is the curious strategy of leap-frogging over Christianity itself, especially its founder, to a moment before Christianity. For Hegel and the early Lukács, this was, of course, classical Greece and perhaps Rome.

But what the form of their arguments, of both the early Hegel and the early Lukács, suggests is that perhaps the way of considering the persistence of theology in political philosophy is not to pursue the endless and futile effort to excise theology and think non-theologically – for we will always find the theological monster hiding under someone else's bed – but to think of such theological content as but one phase in a much longer history. I am going to leave this observation dangling for a little longer, since, before I tease it out, I want to follow Lukács's other, more autobiographical path of self-exorcism.

Autobiographical exorcism

Again, I am interested in two texts, this time the prefaces to *Theory of the Novel* and the other to *History and Class Consciousness*. Both were written well after the first editions came out, most famously the preface to *History and Class Consciousness* some forty-five years after its initial publication in 1922.

---

about by the Christian religion' – the confused half light of an argument from which he could never free himself (Lukács 1975, p. 79; 1967, p. 121).

[39] Lukács 1975, pp. 191, 233–4; 1967, pp. 255, 304–5.
[40] Lukács 1975, pp. 521–2; 1967, pp. 640–1.

Lukács, as anyone who has taken the time to read these ever more lengthy prefaces will know, was given to endless reflection, obsessing over his own intellectual and political development.[41] And commentators have followed suit: as with Benjamin (as also Marx and Althusser), much has been made of his intellectual, ethical and political turn from a rather mystical romanticist idealism to Marxism.[42] Lukács himself has been in part responsible for this, since he reflects at length on his own intellectual biography, speaking not only of a decisive embracing of Marxism but also a long process of apprenticeship, undertaken in both political and intellectual spheres, in other words, in praxis and theory. Yet, it is precisely this 'conversion', in both the sudden and gradual senses of the term, that interests me here. And one feature of such a conversion was a particular obsession that turns up in these prefaces, namely the perpetual sniffing out of the last faint odour of religious thought from his work. The phrases and terms that turn up in these reflections, such as 'age of absolute sinfulness,' 'romantic anti-capitalism' and 'messianic utopianism', are, at first glance, hardly the signs of sustained theological reflection. Yet, for Lukács, they marked a distinct problem, one that he needed to identify and put behind him. Again, I wonder whether such an exercise in home surgery is the best procedure for the patient.

So, on a first read of the preface to *Theory of the Novel*, we get the distinct impression that Lukács is hardly interested in commenting on its underlying religious tone, that it was not really so crucial to the book as such. But, then, a second reading alerts us to what might best be called a code, where phrases begin to stand in for those he used in the text itself. Thus, the key description of the world abandoned by God disappears and we find in its place a world 'gone out of joint'. At one level, the two mean roughly the same thing, but it is the slippage from the theological to the secular that is peculiar here. But, then, just when we thought that Lukács is trying to squeeze out from under the theological weight of his early text, he offers us the comment that the time of

---

[41] See, above all, Lukács 1983b; 1973, pp. 308–26. This autobiographical obsession also colours his sense of the development of literary criticism: 'the clouds of mysticism which once surrounded the phenomena of literature with a poetic colour and warmth and created an intimate and "interesting" atmosphere around them, have been dispersed. Things now face us in a clear, sharp light which to many may seem cold and hard; a light shed on them by the teachings of Marx' (Lukács 1972b, p. 1).

[42] Kadarky 1991; Löwy 1979; Arato and Breines 1979.

writing was for him and so many others an 'age of absolute sinfulness'.[43] The phrase is borrowed from Fichte and marks Lukács's absolute despair at the enthusiasm of the Social-Democratic parties in Germany for the First World War. But what are we to make of such a substitution? Is not the age of absolute sinfulness precisely the world abandoned by God, albeit the flip side, the human response to or even the cause of God's abandonment?

Once we have keyed in to what is going on, other allusions begin to tumble out. To begin with, there is the admission that his Hegelianism at the time was heavily influenced by Kierkegaard, before he became popular. The excuse, which one becomes accustomed to seeing, is that Marx himself had also fallen under Kierkegaard's sway for a time. The early Marx, Kierkegaard and Lukács then become part of a group characterised by 'romantic anti-capitalism'.[44] And what is the main ingredient of such a romantic anticapitalism? Messianic utopianism, something that also afflicted the early Marx:

> a highly naive and totally unfounded utopianism – the hope that a natural life worthy of man can spring from the disintegration of capitalism and the destruction, seen as identical with that disintegration, of the lifeless and life-denying social and economic categories.[45]

Behind all of this is the desire to identify and burn out any last trace of idealism and its theological core. Here, in the preface to *Theory of the Novel*, this becomes in Lukács's terms a 'right epistemology'. Indeed, as far as Lukács is concerned, this youthful work is the first one that combined a left ethics with a right epistemology. Of course, by the time of the preface, Lukács has moved well past such a combination, but he sees it turning up in Bloch's *Spirit of Utopia* and in his book on Thomas Müntzer, the works of Walter Benjamin, the early writings of Adorno, as well as Sartre in France. The target is distinctly theological: Bloch remained enamoured with the revolutionary potential of the Bible throughout his life, Benjamin sought to rub Marxism and theology together and Adorno's first book in philosophy was, in fact, a theological book – *Kierkegaard: Construction of the Aesthetic* was

---

[43] Lukács 1971b, p. 18; 1994, p. 12.
[44] Lukács 1971b, p. 19; 1994, p. 13. Under the spell of Lukács's own characterisation of 'romantic anti-capitalism', Löwy (1979, pp. 15–90) uses the phrase to describe the whole generation of intellectuals among whom Lukács grew up.
[45] Lukács 1971b, p. 20; 1994, p. 14.

written under the direction of Paul Tillich. Here, the stalwart of the Eastern Bloc, for whom a bad and corrupt Communism is better than none at all, assesses his Western-Marxist contemporaries and finds them wanting. They now join those condemned in his book *The Destruction of Reason*, residing in the Grand Hotel Abyss:

> A beautiful hotel, equipped with every comfort, on the edge of an abyss, of nothingness, of absurdity. And the daily contemplation of the abyss between excellent meals or artistic entertainments, can only heighten the enjoyment of the subtle comforts offered.[46]

And this is where Lukács feels *Theory of the Novel* resides, enjoying a drink at the bar. In this deservedly famous image, the stakes of the idealist, romantic and even religious impulse in this early text become extraordinarily high.

Let me turn to the second preface, this time to the book in which Lukács felt his messianic utopianism gave its last glorious gasp, *History and Class Consciousness*. For one who was so accustomed to speaking of what was true and false, correct or mistaken, even if he was constantly aware of how what appeared to be true in his own work turned out later to be 'false', Lukacs equivocates over his messianic utopianism, and it is this equivocation that I want to explore for a moment. So, in this preface, he states that, after writing the monograph in final form in 1922, 'my messianic utopianism lost (and was even seen to lose) its real grip on me'.[47] The book itself he sees as the conclusion to a period of his own development that began in 1918–19. I will return to look at this statement more closely in a moment, but a little earlier, in the context of providing reasons for his rejection of the reflection theory of knowledge, he writes: 'Against this [mechanistic determinism] my messianic utopianism, the predominance of praxis in my thought rebelled in passionate protest – a protest that, once again, was not wholly misguided'.[48]

These statements are more ambivalent than they seem, for the words run against the overall impression that he has passed beyond this messianic utopianism, that he has in fact excised romantic and theological categories entirely. Let me exegete a few phrases: 'real grip' hints at a less than real or solid grip, a residue perhaps that may have remained with him despite the

---

[46] Lukács 1971b, p. 22; 1994, p. 16; see Lukács 1980, p. 243; 1962, p. 219.
[47] Lukács 1988, p. xxvii; 1968, p. 30.
[48] Lukács 1988, p. xxv; 1968, p. 27.

end of a certain zeal. But, then, 'was even seen to lose' slides the emphasis, by means of the passive, over to the impression given to others: here, a greater sense of finality attaches to shedding this messianic utopianism, for not even an appearance remains. Yet, like one who has gradually come to terms with the abiding influence of earlier passions and commitments, with all their habits, associations, social context and ways of speaking and thinking, he looks upon it as not completely useless – 'a protest that, once again, was not wholly misguided.' Even if it has gone, left behind in a new phase of life, some nostalgia attaches to it, for it was not without some value.

I cannot help but think of his comments about tactical writing, the need to write certain things, such as his self-criticism in 1929 after the failed Blum Theses with their call for a democratic dictatorship,[49] or his subsequent withdrawal from Hungarian politics so that he could continue his writing,[50] or the moves he made under Stalin in order to do the same. Autobiographical comments like this always have such an undercurrent for readers aware of Lukacs's moves over the years. Tied in with all this is the continual role of praxis in his thought and life: the events which shaped his thought and upon which he sought to reflect and provide guidance also produce their sometimes unwanted effects. It is not for nothing that the sentence, 'Lenin died in 1924,' follows the 'real grip' sentence,[51] for this marked the beginning of the iron-broom years of Stalin, the downturn in revolutionary activity and its local failures, as well as the theory of socialism in one country. In other words, his messianic utopianism was part of the great expectations for the communist revolutions throughout Europe between the Wars; battening down for a longer haul also meant dampening revolutionary enthusiasm and turning to more rigorous theoretical work in the interim.

For all the similarities between the two prefaces, especially in terms of Lukács's perpetual exercise of self-exorcism, there are some marked differences. The *Theory of the Novel* is his last officially pre-Marxist text, belonging to the introspective, overly-sensitive, *fin-de-siècle* Lukács, the one of the Thalia theatre, the pretentious 'circles' and so on. Unlike many critics, who prefer the sensibilities of this early aesthete, I prefer the ascetic discipline of the later

---

[49] Lukács 1972a, pp. 227–53.
[50] Lukács 1988, p. xxx; 1968, p. 32.
[51] Lukács 1988, p. xxvii; 1968, p. 30.

Lukács, the one who was able to coin phrases like 'decadent bourgeois irrationalism'. *History of Class Consciousness* is a product of this later Lukács, but it is a book that suffered due to the petty jealousies and vindictiveness of the Stalin years. Lukács clearly liked *History and Class Consciousness*, and his recently discovered defence,[52] vigorously replying to his critics, reinforces the sense of the carefully worded preface that silenced his critics and held on to the arguments of the book. For there is a certain nostalgia in the preface to *History and Class Consciousness* that is not there in the preface to *Theory of the Novel*, a passing recognition that there was indeed some value in his messianic utopianism at the time, despite all its flaws. However, it seems to me that such nostalgia and defence point to something that Lukács himself may not have expected.

Conclusion

This is where I want to loop back to my reflections on *The Theory of the Novel* itself and *The Young Hegel*, for the terms he uses in the prefaces – messianic utopianism, romantic anticapitalism, age of absolute sinfulness – have another echo that is not necessarily theological. In order to explicate this comment, my earlier reflections towards the end of the chapter on Agamben, and the brief observation I left dangling earlier regarding the form of both Lukács and Hegel's arguments – that there was indeed something worthwhile in the early arguments of both that was not necessarily connected to the content – I want to turn now to Michel de Certeau, of all people. Initially, it seems that Lukács seeks to excise, one after the other, basic categories that he feels come out of the theological tradition – hope, sinfulness, abandonment, to which we might now add the political subject, the presumed unity of thinking and being, of deliberation and action. He seeks a dissolution of these terms, a perpetual self-exorcism that can only end up with a complete dismissal of someone like Kierkegaard as irrationalist,[53] or the effort to dismiss religious art as decorative, ornamental or at best allegorical, where there is no necessary connection between the objects depicted and their meaning; in short,

---

[52] Lukács 2000.
[53] Lukács 1980, pp. 243–305.

religious art focuses on a transcendent pseudo-reality rather than the this-worldly focus of proper art.[54]

How does Michel de Certeau offer the beginnings of an answer, a very different strategy to the one that Lukács employs? The key sentence from Certeau that has in fact sat beneath my discussion all along is: 'In a certain way we might consider the time of their religious "filling" as a moment in the history of these cultural forms'.[55] This sentence comes at the end of a long discussion in which Certeau speaks of the extraordinary process in which the various modern disciplines ranging from the sciences through the humanities emerged from theology. His initial point is that, even though this may appear to be the case, we should realise that, however much such disciplines and ways of thought have their origin in theology, they have ceased to be theological. The forms have been re-employed so that what appear to be similar formal elements between theology and the modern disciplines now operate in terms of other practices and systems. As non-religious disciplines that once began in theology, it is now possible to study religion and theology as though from 'outside'. Thus, sociology analyses a form of religion or theology through its organisation, the nature of its hierarchy, its doctrinal themes and so on, as a type of society; sociolinguistics interprets theological language as indices of socio-cultural transformations; individual religious affirmations become representations of psychological categories, and so on – in short, religious claims are understood as symptoms of something else, whether social, historical or psychological, rather than truth claims relating to belief.[56] And, so, we get a transition from an initial theological content to something that is anything but theological.

However, what I find astounding about this argument, for all the detail that Certeau gives to it, is the way the sentence I initially quoted from him undermines the whole argument and thereby relativises theology. What if it were the case that the time of the religious and theological 'filling' of these terms, these modes of thought, was but a moment in a much longer history? This move completely rearranges the relationship: no longer is theology the one who sets the agenda, for it becomes but one sojourner, albeit a long one,

---

[54] Lukács 1963, Volume 1, pp. 132–8, 377–82; Volume 2, pp. 777–856.
[55] Certeau 1988, pp. 175–6.
[56] See Certeau 1987, pp. 192–3.

in the tents of a thinking that goes back well before theology. Instead of granting priority to theology, as Certeau does initially himself before this observation, as Lukács does in a negative register, by trying to exorcise theology from his thought, the question then becomes one of tracking a much longer trajectory of these forms of thought. But the most urgent question asks what terms such as hope, sinfulness, God's abandonment, apostasy and messianic utopianism – I would like to add grace, eschatology and myth for starters – would look like if their theological filling is but a passing and momentary phase.

What I suggest, then, is that Lukács's efforts at self-exorcism are misguided, for they assume an original source – romantic, idealist and theological – that must be overcome and discarded. Rather, it seems to me that we might read Lukács's nostalgia in the preface to *History and Class Consciousness* in a dialectical fashion. At one level, it is a nostalgia for the time when that book appeared, in the early years after the October Revolution in Russia, as well as nostalgia for the content with all of its perceived 'messianic utopianism'. At another level, however, it might also be read as nostalgia for the form of an argument that he had in fact abandoned. And that form appears in the argument he follows in *The Theory of the Novel* and then criticises in *The Young Hegel*. There is little mileage in an argument that harks back to some mythical harmonious Golden Age, whether that is Dostoyevskian classical world or the republicanism of Rome. Rather, it is the form itself – the act of seeking some moment before the long era of theological dominance – that is far more promising: not because it seeks some original moment in a misguided classicism, but because it points to the fact that the theological and religious occupation of these terms is but a passing moment in a much longer and diverse history.

Chapter Nine
The Bible and The Beekeeper's Manual

> God, you might say, is their formula for being neighbourly.[1]

In *Politics and Letters*, Raymond Williams comments, in a symptomatic autobiographical moment, that the only books in his parents' house in Pandy (a home town foregrounded so often in his writings) were the Bible and the *Beekeeper's Manual*, apart from a few children's items.[2] What is interesting here is the bifurcation that this passing note suggests, a split between the making-do of the rural working class embodied in Williams's father and the latent, quietly forgotten religion that the dusty family Bible marks. If the manual was his father's favourite, then the Bible was the mark of his grandmother (his mother remaining, as expected, silent). But this is not merely a neutral comment, for it functions as a signal that locates both books in Williams's childhood and later life. If the *Beekeeper's Manual* was the sign of all that he valued about his background, the social location that he felt was so important for other writers, then the Bible, as the book that was both ubiquitous and forgotten, is that of a grandmother who was far more conscientious about church observance than

---
[1] Williams 1960, p. 223.
[2] Williams 1978a, p. 27.

Williams's parents; a book of a generation fading away, with about as much relevance.³ Yet this reading is all too easy, one that Williams himself was keen to foreshadow. My suspicion is that it is not all that simple for Williams to separate the two.

The specific issue on which I focus is the role of religion in Williams's work. The initial answer is deceptively obvious: very little. For one in whom autobiography seems so close to his written work (and not only in his novels), religion had about as much importance in Williams's life as it had in his critical writing. So why bother with the question of religion and Raymond Williams? Perhaps a few demurrers are needed at this point: I do not want to suggest that Williams was secretly religious, that he drew his inspiration from a deep but hidden spiritual source. Nor do I want to claim him as a thinker of implicit religious motivation, an anonymous Christian.

The reason for considering Williams and religion is that his work raises most sharply a peculiar problem, which may be stated as follows: are Christian theology and the Bible forgotten and yet enabling and empowering elements of Williams's thought and work, or has he realised, in dropping religion to a remote moment in the past, that which is implicit in an older and now thoroughly irrelevant religious structure? In other words, has he denied his roots, or does his work mark an internal logic of religion in the (post)modern world itself? Or, to put it in the terms of Michel de Certeau, was the religious content just a temporary phase in a longer life of certain forms that now show up as various disciplines, political groups, key concepts, themes and practices? Did Williams, then, suffer from a certain tone deafness, as he put it, in regard to religion, or did his consistent sidelining of religion signal an entirely appropriate post-religious development?

---

³ In the eternal return of the autobiographical in Williams's work, the bees reappear, now in a discussion of the pressure upon and decline of classical languages: 'I have often put the charge to myself, since I know that if I had not been good at school Latin I would not, from a working-class family, have entered the kind of higher education which led to my writing *The Long Revolution* and other similarly subversive works. It was not for that, it could be said, that my Latin master took me patiently through the *Georgics*, though as it happens his choice of text – for I was by that stage his only pupil – was made because he knew that my father supplemented his earnings as a railwayman by the extensive keeping of bees and by selling their honey in Abergavenny market, just down the road from the Grammar School, I wish I could say that anything I learned improved his beekeeping' (Williams 1989b, p. 45).

However, let me spend a few moments by looking awry, a glance out of the corner on my eye that assists in seeing things more clearly. What I am thinking about here is the work of some comparable figures from the British Left – Terry Eagleton and Edward P. Thompson – for whom religion plays a distinctly important role. Eagleton, of course, was involved with radical Catholic politics and has recently returned in some way to this past. His early books include *The New Left Church* and *The Body as Language: Outline of a 'New Left' Theology*, the edited collections *From Culture to Revolution* and the *Slant Manifesto*,[4] as well as deep involvement in the journal *Slant*.[5] While Eagleton for long felt that he had moved beyond this kind of Catholic activism, I have argued in another place that this is one dimension of Eagleton's work where there are ghosts aplenty.[6] Thompson also continued to be fascinated by religion until his death, especially sectarian and revolutionary forms. Thus, in his early *The Making of the English Working Class*,[7] religion plays a crucial if negative role, whereas in his last book, *Witness Against the Beast*,[8] he seeks to link William Blake to currents of radical theological and political dissent, especially the Muggletonians. Indeed, Thompson himself becomes part of the Muggletonian heritage, taking over the archives from the last Muggletonian and then declaring himself a Marxist Muggletonian.

Not so Williams. He did write a piece, entitled 'Culture and Revolution: A Comment', for the Slant collection *From Culture to Revolution: The Slant Symposium 1967*, edited by Brian Wicker and Terry Eagleton,[9] but even this says little directly about religion per se. What intrigues me is how we might account for such an absence in those huge slabs of writing; why is religion consistently passed over, even when he was alerted to it by the *New Left Review* interviewers in 1979? There is, to begin with, the self-assessment of a certain kind of tone-deafness, specifically when he was asked why he did not consider religion for a swathe of nineteenth-century British writers, especially when they would have enunciated their own positions in religious terms. Or, it may

---

[4] Respectively, Eagleton 1966a, 1970; Eagleton and Wicker 1968; Cunningham, et al. 1966.
[5] Eagleton and Cunningham 1966; 1966b, 1967b, 1967a, 1968d, 1968b, 1968c, 1968a, 1969.
[6] Boer 2007a, pp. 275–333.
[7] Thompson 1966.
[8] Thompson 1993.
[9] Williams 1968, pp. 24–34.

be accounted for in terms of the conventional Marxist line that when people speak religiously it is, in fact, a code for other issues, be they social, political or economic.[10] Or, again, it may be that religion belongs to the residual features of a culture and a mode of production, on the way out but with a significant continuing presence.[11]

An apparent absence?

Until now, I have followed the general perception of Williams, of one who found no time or interest to discuss religion. But all I am doing is favouring the *Beekeeper's Manual*, leaving the Bible to languish, as Williams would have preferred. Yet, if we look a little closer, at certain moments Williams does consider religion. I will argue below that there is a deeper level where religion works its way through his material, but, first, the more obvious references. Let me begin with what I find to be one of the most interesting texts, *Politics and Letters*. The issue of religion occurs here consistently, although, on most occasions, its emergence is due to the questions of Perry Anderson, Anthony Barnett and Francis Mulhern. Apart from the nature of these questions, it is the mode in which Williams responds that intrigues me. One of the questions relates to the major figures dealt with in *Culture and Society* – Burke, Southey, Coleridge, Kingsley, Arnold, Ruskin, Hulme, Eliot, Tawney – and the absence of any consideration of religion in their lives:

> ...there is one other interesting silence in *Culture and Society*. That is the relative absence of any attention to religion. For if one looks through the figures in the book, one notices immediately how central religion was to the development of the tradition. If you had asked them what their main ideas were in their own time, probably a numerical majority – Burke, Southey, Coleridge, Kingsley, Arnold, Ruskin, Hulme, Eliot, Tawney – would have replied with a centrally religious definition. This was not just an adventitious or extrinsic phenomenon. Christian themes, whether in Anglican, dissenting, evangelical, Catholic forms – the whole gamut of possibilities of Protestant and non-Protestant variance – furnished one of the main ideological repertoires from which an industrial capitalism could be and indeed was

---

[10] Williams 1978a, p. 130.
[11] Williams 1977, p. 122.

criticized. This is very evident in the continental tradition as well....Did you think it would clutter the book too much to refer to religion?[12]

Williams responds by sliding onto other questions – how religion is replaced with literary value, especially by Matthew Arnold, how a book on religion and social thought would be an entirely different effort and not one he could write. It simply does not engage him enough to write about it sympathetically.

This is an extraordinarily curious response on Williams's part, for he does refer to religion in *Culture and Society*, although it is not the book's major focus. Most notably, there are the directly religious works – A.W. Pugin's *Apology for the Present Revival of Christian Architecture in England*, R.H. Tawney's *Religion and the Rise of Capitalism*, and T.S. Eliot's *The Idea of a Christian Society*.[13] In the case of Eliot, Williams draws out the idea that culture is a whole way of life, extracting it from Eliot's religious conservatism as a valuable concept, another side of the man. In other words, over against the conventional understanding of Eliot as a conservative, Williams attributes this tendency to his religious inclinations, pointing to a greater complexity that enables a more radical reading.

And then there is this text:

> That man was so capable, that the pursuit of perfection was indeed his overriding business in life, was of course widely affirmed elsewhere, especially by Christian writers. But for Mill it was Coleridge who first attempted to define, in terms of his changing society, the *social* conditions of man's perfection.[14]

Mill, notes Williams in the following pages, proposes a National Church, a whole class or Clerisy, with theology as the 'circulating sap and life', but the main aim of this new church was the cultivation of civilisation and human perfection. Again, as with Eliot, Williams wants to extract something valuable out of the religious material, but he must pass through the religious in order to get to the social. He does the same with Newman and Arnold, finding more of value in the latter: whereas Newman saw culture as an element of divine perfection (hardly something we can see Williams endorsing), Arnold 'had

---

[12] Williams 1977, pp. 129–30.
[13] Williams 1958, pp. 130–3, 216–17, 231–43.
[14] Williams 1958, p. 62.

commitments elsewhere' Williams points out. Further, 'it may of course be argued that, being thus committed, he was nearer the actual truth'.[15] Outside the Church, Arnold draws nearer to the sort of thing Williams is after, a social or cultural tendency, preferably progressive, that would point to what was coming.

All of which leaves me wanting to see what else he does, hoping that there are more than fleeting references, such as those to Edmund Burke and the influence of Owen and Southey on Christian socialism. One more text: in the *The Long Revolution*, we find a series of references to religion, in relation to creativity, individuals and society, images of society, education, the reading public and the social history of dramatic forms. One of the most sustained discussions is the last time religion appears in the book: in seeking to uncover an alternative history of English drama, one connected in all sorts of ways with society, he cannot avoid beginning with the original role of the Church in the creation of drama.[16] So, medieval drama emerges from the Church's liturgy, an effort to bring to life the stories of the Bible. But this drama evolves out of the worship service into processional drama in which various trade guilds (bakers, tanners, websters etc.) took on particular parts of the story of Christianity from creation to the lives of the saints, especially at the Corpus Christi festival. The search is, of course, for signals of links between the forms of such drama and society, which Williams finds in the processional context of the drama on festival days and in the way ancillary figures become contemporary with the audience. For instance, the nativity shepherds are Yorkshire shepherds, and the major figures in the nativity story, such as Herod, God and Jesus are also very much contemporary in people's individual and social lives. Yet, even this extended discussion is very much a prelude, a beginning that is soon superseded by other forms that leave these religious origins well in the past.

A similar pattern emerges elsewhere: with education Williams traces the origins back to the vocational training for the Church in the cathedral and monastery schools, places for training the monks, priests and scholars of the Church.[17] Along with grammar schools (to read ecclesiastical Latin) and song schools (for liturgy), he reads these as training in the social character and

---

[15] Williams 1958, p. 127.
[16] Williams 1961, pp. 247–50.
[17] Williams 1961, pp. 127–35.

beliefs of Christianity. But, here too, the initial structures break down under the pressure of an expanding curriculum, and the grammar and song schools are gradually shaped by the newer ideology of a liberal education, the move away from church control over certain elements of teaching (especially law, medicine and philosophy) and the universities' fights for independence. This development follows religious lines more closely, with the Reformation and Dissenting churches crucial for the story. Yet, religion fades from view as we get closer to the time of writing, so that, by the end of the chapter, it is only a distant memory.

My final example from *The Long Revolution* concerns literacy and the reading public,[18] where Williams locates the origins of the debate over literacy in the desire, especially in Protestant countries, to enable the poor to read the Bible which would then lead to moral improvement (although how reading the Bible should achieve this is anyone's guess!). The catch here is that it also allowed people to read other material, such as the radical press. But what interests Williams is less this origin than the shift to literacy campaigns and their effects in the nineteenth century. When the ability to read became widespread, the Church became heavily involved in censorship, a task subsequently secularised in the form of 'criticism'. But, in this case, Williams runs against what is implicit in such activities – the devaluation of a widespread reading of popular literature – for this is one of the great values he sees in the developments of literacy and working-class culture.

I could draw on other examples from his critical work,[19] but in light of those I have given, the reference by the interviewers to the 'silence' of Williams on religion as well as Williams's own evasion of the issue take on a strange hue in light of these references. Is it simply that he was not sufficiently engaged to write about religion? But then this assumes some form of religious connection, a commitment perhaps, as a prerequisite for writing about religion. I find a similar response when I mention that some of my work takes place in biblical studies and religion more generally: for some reason, it is assumed that one must be engaged in religious practice in order to study this material. But, then, students of classical Greece do not believe in Apollo, Zeus or Athena

---

[18] Williams 1961, pp. 15–60.
[19] Williams 1958, pp. 6, 11–12, 73–4, 107; 1983, pp. 40–1, 130–1, 193; 1980, pp. 69–73, 157, 198; 1973, pp. 199–204, 248–59; 1993, pp. 35–45.

(as a general rule), art critics are rarely artists, political scientists rarely politicians, students of French literature not necessarily French, and so on. That Williams could not write on religion and society becomes a self-effacement on his part, for he in fact does so, and if anyone could have written on religion, society and literature from a Marxist perspective, then it would have been Williams.

Warm Marxism

Thus far, I have argued that Williams does in fact speak of religion, although in a particular way. He shuffles and shifts when the issue of religion comes up, preferring to historicise religion, in this case the specific form of Christianity, granting it a ghostly presence, well dead but perhaps lingering in some indefinable form, an issue that is no longer of concern in the key political issues of the time. There is, however, another dimension to Williams's work where religion has a more sustained, although covert, presence. I am thinking of what Ernst Bloch called the 'warm stream' of Marxism, the Williams who espoused a politics in which the ideas and practices of neighbourliness, community, humanity, solidarity, trust, faith, and even socialism itself were paramount. And these terms, heavily laden with positive associations, appear in his favoured triad of autobiography, Wales and the working class. But the political values and the places where they appear mean that I will also need to consider what is often felt to be Williams's lesser achievement, namely, the writing of fiction. How all of this relates to the question of religion is the burden of what follows.

Autobiography

Like many others, I assume here that the novels, or at least some of them, are autobiographical or at least draw heavily on the autobiographical. At the same time, I want to register my profound suspicion of the recourse to autobiography. Is it not significant that the realm of fiction is the most appropriate one for autobiography? Let me begin, then, with the widely assumed autobiography of *Border Country*, running through something like seven revisions until it gelled into shape with a father's death (a curious instance for Williams, given his suspicions of psychoanalysis). Even though the contrasting impulses of his own father are split between Harry Price and Morgan Rosser, the one solidly working-class and set, the other entrepreneurial, political and then small capitalist, all of which is then figured in the doppleganger of Will/Matthew, itself an echo of Jim/Raymond. Yet, here, we find the whole panoply of a childhood eventually inoculated against religion: a tension between church, where Matthew/Will was christened, and chapel where he went as a child; a hostile father who cannot stand the uppity Baptist pastor, Watkins, who lives across the lane, seeking a lower person to take out his latrine yet practising his prayers and sermons audibly for the neighbours; a completely ineffectual establishment priest, the vicar Arthur Pugh, whose sadness comes through in every line, his belief in a transcendental being now transferred to seeing 'God' in the social relations and connections of his flock. The training for 'Matthew' or 'Will' once, in a distant past of cathedral schools, would have led to ordination and a place in the vast structures of the Church. Now, Pugh shows Matthew/Will the macro- and micro-universes through his telescope and microscope. The sheer irrelevance of Pugh, except perhaps as a repository of antiquated knowledge, as well as his absence of faith and recognition of the lack of a basis for religious faith of a traditional kind in his community, is of the same type as Williams's more scholarly analyses of religion and society.

There is an important interchange between Matthew/Will and Pugh that signals another pattern in Williams's work. The passage quoted begins with Pugh, the vicar, talking about the village and his opposition, the chapel:

> 'The real life, for these people, is each other. Even their religion is for each other'.
>
> 'Isn't that right, sir?'
>
> 'I'm not saying it's wrong. I'm just looking at it.... The chapels are for people to meet, and to talk to each other or sing together. Around them, as you know, moves almost the whole life of the village. That, really, is their religion'.
>
> 'Is it, sir?'
>
> 'The chapels are social organizations, Matthew. The church here is not. I don't mean their religious professions are insincere, but they could equally, it seems to me, be professions in almost anything – any other system of belief, for instance. What matters, what holds them together, is what their

members do, through them, for each other. God, you might say, is their formula for being neighbourly'.[20]

This, rather than the ancient church itself, with its relics and memories of a very distant and irrelevant age, dating back to the Normans, marks a crucial but rarely acknowledged transition in Williams's work. In this interchange, we find the stress on neighbourliness and social organisation, the solidarity of relations between people, all of which are found in the Baptist chapel rather than the established Church of Wales (itself a branch of the Church of England). And these terms are central to Williams's own work and politics – along with humanity, solidarity, trust and faith. Yet, he consistently locates these socialist values in another place, a triangulation of autobiography, Wales and the working class.

When he is searching for some ideas for his alternative picture of society, Williams becomes distinctly autobiographical, mining a curiously non-conflictual childhood for all it is worth. Here, we find, particularly through a father, all of the values crucial to Williams's politics. Within *Border Country*, these values show up from the most unexpected quarters during the General Strike of 1926, from both strikers and strike breakers, as well as during the more conventional moments of illness and family death. Even his long adherence to a particular form of Marxism that he names 'cultural materialism' is a natural position that he inherits through his working-class family, an 'extension' or 'mode of affiliation' (the pun is more than accidental) to it.[21]

One approach to the material in his novels is to distinguish between religious beliefs and commitment on the one hand, and the various institutions with their attendant social practices on the other. We could then argue that Williams sides, somewhat ambivalently, with the latter, narrating such a shift in novels like *Border Country*. Indeed, Williams seems – at least in the dialogue I quoted above – more interested in the social functions of the Church than its beliefs. If he does speak of beliefs, it is in a negative register, and their effect is to create harsh division rather than the solidarity and community he so valued. Thus, again from a novel:

---

[20] Williams 1960, pp. 222–3.
[21] Williams 1977, p. 1.

Their father, Mervyn, was a furnaceman and a lay preacher, who had found in Christian teaching a way of accepting the hardness of his life. It had given him meaning and dignity, but equally it had cut him off from his sons as it had long cut him off from his wife. Neither Harold nor Gwyn went to chapel after their mother's funeral; the religion, like school, was one of the childish things they put away. It was a deliberate break, against the father as much as anything, but there was no new settlement to break to, for work was hard to some by and it seemed in the end that they would have to move right away.[22]

The Christian teaching comes from precisely the same place that provides the social cohesion in the earlier quotation from *Border Country*, namely, the (Baptist) chapel. The division it causes is the same type as that produced by capitalism itself, one of whose manifestations was Taylorisation in manufacturing.

Yet it seems to me that the distinction between Christian beliefs and the social organisation of the Church is a little too easy, for are not the teachings themselves, along with their attendant religious faith, part and parcel of the institution? Or, to use the Marxist terms with which Williams was familiar: the various dimensions of religious ideology are inseparable from the institution itself. One cannot disconnect social and economic forms from ideology so easily.

Williams himself tended more towards the established church, of all things, than the chapel. The autobiographical register of the *Border Country* quotation above sees him prefer the church's vicar and his liberal deism. He returns to this preference in the interviews of *Politics and Letters*. Thus, in response to a question about the role of religion in his life, Williams responds briefly, pointing out a shifting family allegiance between chapel (Baptist) and church. And his preference at the time was the latter. The discussion ends with his refusal to take confirmation, an item he selected to include in his annals.[23]

The decision to include the moment of his refusal of confirmation in his annals, out of a host of other events that might have been listed, points to a fascinating link between the autobiographical narrative of Williams's own

---

[22] Williams 1978b, p. 29.
[23] Williams 1978a, pp. 24–5.

rejection of Christianity and his way of dealing with the Church in his own historical reconstructions. For what he does, time and again, is speak of the Church in the past tense, as something that was once powerful but whose time has passed. I want to suggest that one function of this relegation is to provide a framework, now in terms of the sweep of history, for his own personal rejection.

This historicising move also turns up in his responses to the interviewers in *Politics and Letters*. Asked about the crucial role of the Church in precapitalist England, Williams replies by mentioning the vast numbers of stone churches built in England in times when very few people lived in stone houses. The question is: why would people take time out – a mix of voluntary, devotional and forced labour – from the grinding labour of everyday subsistence in order to build these costly and numerous churches? Williams suggests that it is because 'the building of a house to God was an integral part of the mode of production itself', or perhaps a 'controlling element of the relations of production'.[24] But the crucial move in this case is to argue that it is only with capitalism that the economic rises to claim dominance, with the implication that in other periods – like the ones in which churches were built – other dimensions of society were determinant, such as religion itself. But, for Williams, this moment has passed. Taking their cue from Williams himself on the role of church building in the economic and cultural structure of feudalism, the *NLR* interviewers push hard on this issue, relating it to the Marxist problem of the relation between economics, culture and ideology. At this point, Williams engages in a rhetorical strategy that he would replicate elsewhere on the question of religion: he moves beyond the particular question of religion and focuses on the theoretical issue raised. The strategy itself functions as another register to his personal and historical location of religion in the past. The interviewers return to religion a couple of pages later by raising a crucial problem of the persistence of the material and cultural practices of the Church over a number of different socio-economic periods (slave-holding, feudal and capitalist) and civilisations, including Europe, the Middle East and Asia. And, again, Williams is terse, pointing out the internal transformations, the efforts at dealing with crises in long-running belief systems, the reinterpretation, redistribution of emphasis and certain denials as part of the reorganisation,

---

[24] Williams 1978a, p. 140.

before slipping all too rapidly to another point – human reproduction – on which he spends much more time.[25]

My other example of this historicising move comes again from his fiction. In the incomplete trilogy, *People of the Black Mountains*, Williams can allow himself a more sustained consideration of religion, but only because it belongs to a history well and truly removed from the present, however much it may be part of his beloved Wales. From the burial practices, hymns and worship at the longhouses – including a long description of 'The Long House at Midsummer'[26] – and the Druida of Volume One,[27] to the continual presence of the abbeys, monasteries, churches and the theologically saturated language of the medieval era in Volume Two,[28] religion is part of the fabric of what can best be described as a sprawling historical novel. However, the heroes with whom Williams's sympathies lie are those like John Oldcastle, whose 'heretical' faith leads him to criticise heavily the opulence and power of the pope.

The recourse to autobiography, then, has a double function in Williams's work. It allows him to relegate to his childhood a church that may be put away with the maturity of adulthood. The historicising tendency to speak of the Church in the past tense is another dimension of this relegation. Yet autobiography also enables him to draw out the values with which he identified – those of solidarity, commitment and so on that were so important for his politics. In the end, however, Williams finds the chapel a less than adequate location for such values, even though he recognises the importance of the chapel for his own people, the Welsh. My suggestion is that the more Williams downplays the role of the chapel in generating his favoured political and social values, the more do Welshness and the working class become their source. Or, even more strongly, Welshness and the working class become an alternative location for social and political values that were also those of the chapel.

---

[25] Williams 1978a.
[26] Williams 1989a, pp. 121–32.
[27] Williams 1989a.
[28] Williams 1992.

Welshness

Autobiography is, however, highly problematic, for not only does the preferred mode for Williams's own autobiographical material take the form of fiction, but autobiography always has the danger, especially in the work of a critic like Williams, of functioning as a recourse to an inviolable personal authenticity that is beyond reproach. This becomes clearer with Williams's re-found Welshness, which was his claim to authenticity. This was one of the reasons for the many revisions of *Border Country*, in which he gradually located his authenticity in Wales and which was published in the end with the assistance of the Welsh Arts Council. Further, as Williams began to identify himself as a 'Welsh European' and as his point of reference shifted from bourgeois England to Wales, it became increasingly important that his work was appreciated by Welsh intellectuals.

As far as the Welsh themselves are concerned, he locates, particularly in his novels, all that is politically good with the Welsh: they are naturally communist, especially in the pit valleys; they are aware of the necessity of ambiguity and contradiction in society and politics; trustworthiness, straight talking and honesty are Welsh traits, sought for in outsiders, who are rejected when they do not show the appropriate signs. Aware of divisions and differences among the Welsh, Williams always sought a path through them.[29] While always strong, communal solidarity comes to the fore in the General Strike of 1926, and then again in the miners' strike of 1984 that ended with the closure of most of the mines that set the Industrial Revolution and the British Empire running in the first place. When faced with a political problem, Williams often turned to mine a well-worked Welsh childhood for sources of a possible solution. There was something curiously postcolonial about his rediscovered Welshness, but it was often felt by others among the Left that Williams had turned to a fuzzy romanticism about the Welsh. His response was to locate the 'authentically differential communalism' of the Welsh in a particular history, rather than some racial or ethic essence.[30] What troubles me here is less the politics of such a move – in fact, politically, it was an excellent move, countering the dominating force of the English with a distinct cultural politics – than the claim to some deeper authenticity that would stand up against the most withering of

---

[29] See especially Smith 1989.
[30] Williams 1989b, pp. 73–4.

modernist winds. Part of this is due to the overlap with his autobiographical moves, but it is also because there is a third connection, the working class.

The working class

Williams made much of his status as a working-class intellectual, and his insistence that class remains a key category of analysis in the face of rapid social changes is a hallmark of his work.[31] Again, politically, this is a necessary move in the context of his academic work and writing, but there are some curious features of the way he evokes the working class. Obviously, it is very often autobiographical and Welsh, with the tendency to equate his kind of Welshness with working-class values. For instance, apart from *Border Country*, the connections run through his fiction: *The Fight for Manod* concerns the battle over the development of the valley of Manod in Wales,[32] whereas *Second Generation*, the successor to *Border Country*, tells the story of expatriate Welsh workers in a car factory. It can appear that the Welsh community in which he grew up, with its mix of railway workers, small farmers, and (on its fringes) the miners, as well as their wives and children in the background, functions as a definition and an image of the working class to which Williams devoted his work. I am not saying that he was not astutely aware of the issues of class identification and the cobbled way the designators of class in the English language – middle- and working- – came together in the first place.[33] But what does happen in his writing is a certain triangulation in which autobiography, Welshness and the working class function as a distinct source of energy and hope, as well as a defensive position behind which he retreats from time to time.

Williams also claimed that what might be called a vocabulary of socialism finds its source in this triangulated realm. As I have noted already, this vocabulary is not cynical or corrosively critical, nor does it engage in a wholesale debunking characteristic of certain types of ideological suspicion. The great range of his writing is mostly constructive, seeking out alternative, forgotten and buried traditions in the past in order to look differently at the future, to search out ways these traditions might be reshaped in a socialist society.

---

[31] See, for instance, Williams 1985, pp. 153–74.
[32] Williams 1979.
[33] Williams 1961, pp. 316–20.

And the terms that draw my eye as I read are ones of community, humanity, solidarity, belief, hope, and trust. For instance, in a review of a number of books about Wales, simply called 'Community', he remarks that, during the coal miners' strike of 1984, the three terms most commonly used were 'culture', 'community' and 'jobs', of which the first two were part of the language of working-class culture in Wales, which he then sets over against England. And this is, he states, the source of his own usage of culture and community that seemed so strange to many readers.[34] Indeed, in the last section of *Culture and Society*, the issue of community looms large in relation to communication and solidarity. He makes no overt reference to the experiential sources of such concepts in the text itself, preferring to characterise them as working-class traits. Yet, in the intense interaction of *Politics and Letters*, he argues that, in the closing discussion of the earlier book, he was, at the moment of his furthest intellectual distance from Wales, in fact describing Welsh social relations, assuming they were more widely available and not necessarily Welsh at the time.[35]

From a much wider range, I provide two examples. First, there is Williams's characteristic emphasis on the human dimensions of any political, cultural or economic policy. He castigates the Left for falling into the habit of using the terms of its opponents to describe the kind of society it wants: 'It has been one of the gravest errors of socialism, in revolt against class societies, to limit itself, so often, to the terms of its opponents: to propose a political and economic order, rather than a human order'.[36] Second, there is the claim that his own predilection for pacifism came from the 'constructive pacifism' of the Welsh and the ethos among working-class families that any strike must be orderly and disciplined so as not to give your opponents any excuse for violence.[37]

All of this – the values of a warm socialism that Williams locates in his own background, Wales and the working class – is part of a consistent politics, running through from the earliest to the latest texts, of resistance to bourgeois grasping and climbing, the individually shaped desires that the Right con-

---

[34] Williams 1989b, p. 60.
[35] Williams 1978a, p. 113.
[36] Williams 1961, p. 112.
[37] Williams 1978a, p. 409.

stantly seeks to put in place of 'the difficult practices of common and sharing provision'.[38]

Conclusion: the vanishing mediator of the Baptist chapel

How is all of this – the sources of the positive dimensions of socialism in Wales, the working class and Williams's own life – connected with the question of religion? The key lies with the chapel and its changing fortunes in Williams's thought. Let us return to the quotation from *Border Country* above, the conversation between the vicar Pugh and Matthew/Will. In particular, I am interested in the words of the vicar: 'God, you might say, is their formula for being neighbourly'. Or, to turn the whole thing around: 'Being neighbourly, you might say, is their formula for God'. Here is a recognition in Williams's work that subsequently slips away: the Welsh Baptist chapel was, in many respects, the centre for much of the community, solidarity, co-operation and neighbourliness that he so valued in the Welsh themselves and the working class.

However, within twenty years, he is not so keen on the chapel. The shift is in the end quite extensive: the passage in *Border Country* appeared finally in 1960, but by the 1979 interviews of *Politics and Letters*, the chapel has a distinctly negative register. A source of community to be sure, but for an in-group that Williams finds objectionable:

> I never trusted Aneurin Bevan, for the cynical reason that it takes one Welshman to know another. He came from only twenty miles away and I'd heard so much of that style of Welsh speaking since about the age of two that I was never as impressed by it as other socialists were. It is a marvellous form of public address which always assumes a faith in common. I think it comes out of the chapels where you didn't have to argue whether you should believe in God, everybody did that, so you could just be very witty about the ways of the world, or very indignant about its injustices. But it is not a style of serious argument, because your beliefs are presupposed from the start.[39]

---

[38] Williams 1989b, p. 34.
[39] Williams 1978a, pp. 268–9. Aneurin Bevan was part of Wilson's Labour Left, although he was subsequently expelled from Wilson's front bench.

In this important passage, we find all of the elements I have traced thus far: autobiography, Welshness, socialism – all in the context of a discussion about the Labour Left. The fourth item, the chapel, does not fare so well. In effect, it has been shown the door, taking its neighbourliness with it, at least in Williams's own thought.

It seems to me that Williams's dismissal of the chapel is actually a signal of its importance. I would suggest that the chapel acts a little like a vanishing mediator – to use Max Weber's famous description of Calvinism – for the positive values of socialism Williams sought to espouse. In other words, in his search for a source of these values he goes to his own autobiography, Wales and its working class, but these cannot be understood without a fourth factor, the Baptist chapel. In the narrative of the construction of the working class in Wales, the non-conformist chapel is a missing item in Williams's endless pages of writing about Wales. Or, to put it in Williams's own terms, the 'knowable community' of Wales very much includes the chapel. That the chapel should eventually vanish, like the forgotten Bible in his parents' home, does not diminish its importance.

The chapel, of course, is not merely a social institution but also a religious one. So it should come as no surprise that these key terms of Williams's work are also ones that are found in the tradition and practices of Christian theology. The ideal Christian community – which is nowhere to be found but always worked towards and hoped for – is one of co-operation, mutual aid and solidarity. And that community should be not so much a collection of individuals, but rather the individual gains his or her identity in the community and its inter-relations. Of course, no-one is ever able to live up to such a model, for invariably jealousy, bitterness, petty squabbling and divisiveness occur, but that is the nature of such communities. In the Welsh situation of the Baptist chapel, that theological and social community was not mainstream; it was an oppositional focus, a point of resistance to the imposition of the established Church of Wales. As a Dissenting church, it was frowned on and occasionally suppressed by the established church and English government. Inevitably it also formed an integral part of Welsh identity, so much so that it would often become the focus of community aid during strikes, providing a social focus for the strikers and their families. Here, too, we find the values that were so dear to Williams – community, neighbourliness, faith, trust and hope. Yet, after a moment of recognition, Williams soon enough closes the door on the chapel.

I have suggested that the chapel functions as a vanishing mediator for Williams. But now let me connect that term with my earlier comments on Agamben and Lukács regarding the passing moment, for the vanishing mediator is really another way of speaking about that passing moment. Williams leaves us with a series of questions. Is this vocabulary of the 'warm current' of socialism indebted to religious and theological categories in such a way that it is not possible to use such a vocabulary without considering this inescapable religious dimension? More than one apologist of religion (and I do not number myself among them), and Christianity in particular, has argued for the unavoidably theological underpinnings of most items of contemporary Western society and thought – its political structures, institutions, and disciplines of intellectual work. Or, is the religious nature of such a vocabulary merely one shape it may take among many? Rather than some inescapable source, does Williams's own approach to religion in fact show up another way of viewing the role of religion? His approach is to historicise religion or treat it, somewhat inadvertently, as a vanishing mediator. These are but specific ways in which one might relativise the absolute claims of religion. But, then, Williams himself is aware of such a need to relativise:

> Politics and art, together with science, religion, family life and the other categories we speak of as absolutes, belong in a whole world of active and interacting relationships, which is our common associative life. If we begin from the whole texture, we can go on to study particular activities and their bearings on other kinds.[40]

---

[40] Williams 1961, p. 39.

Conclusion

At the end of *Criticism of Heaven*, I indicated I was setting course for what may be called a materialist theology, although I hesitate to use the title since it is being bandied about quite a bit these days. What I am doing over what is now a five-volume series (collectively called *The Criticism of Heaven and Earth*) is gathering the various insights I draw from these sundry Marxist critics. It is a little like collecting various pieces of old timber and then pondering their size and shape in order to see what might be constructed from them. Or, to shift the metaphor: once I have collected these insights in my pack, I will sit down in a quiet spot, lay them out on the grass, rearrange them, explore the connections, and see if a reasonable system emerges from them, although 'system' may be a little pretentious. It is a way of thinking that takes place at the intersection between Marxism and theology, or, rather, it is a task that can happen after I have thoroughly immersed myself in the work of those Marxists who engage with theology.

I do not need to summarise the arguments of each chapter since there is a good summary of each in the introduction. So let us see what ideas I have gathered in my pack from the engagements in this book. Needless to say, they remain somewhat fragmentary and await the full exploration of the last book in this series. From Lucien Goldmann and his exploration of Jansenism and Pascal I drew two crucial ideas: a distinct insight into the opposition between the Elect and the Damned as well as that between rejecting the world and yet living within it. As a dialectic that is contained with any group or individual, I took this a step further and began exploring the tension between Marxism as both a secular and an anti-secular programme – perhaps the most important point Goldmann encouraged me to explore. Fredric Jameson has provided a dialectic of religion and utopia, especially in terms of the interaction between catastrophe and renewal from religious apocalyptic, as well as the revolutionary 'transcoding' of religion through Thomas More.

From those with an interest in matters biblical, I gathered various ideas. Rosa Luxemburg and Karl Kautsky gave me the political myth of Christian communism, although I did give it a twist towards myth and away from their assumption that it is historically verifiable. From Rosa Luxemburg, there also came the call for freedom of conscience. Kautsky's effort to reconstruct a longer history of communism that predates Marx and Engels is definitely reusable, although with a little less enthusiasm and more suspicion. Kautsky also enticed me to begin some Marxist-inspired reconstruction of the economics of ancient Israel, but, then, so did Julia Kristeva in her own way. If, in Kautsky's case, it was an incentive to continue what he has begun, for Kristeva it required an exercise in recovering a forgotten Marx. But Kristeva also has the intriguing argument that the success of the Christian myth (or fable as Badiou would call it), as well as the unstable collective of the 'Church', lay in its ability to respond to a whole range of pathologies. Alain Badiou gave me the necessarily fabulous nature of the Event and its truth, where the procedures of truth set in train by an Event have all the hallmarks of fable or myth. And Agamben, for all his flawed arguments, provided both the suggestion that revolutionary time may be understood as 'the time that is left' (although he calls it messianism) and, more importantly, the form of an approach in which the absolute claims of theology may be relativised.

This last theme for Agamben became the dominant feature of my treatments of both Georg Lukács and Raymond Williams. They opened up the possibility that religion may be a passing moment in the much longer trajectories of certain themes and categories. Since I have some problems with putting it in such a historicist way (not least because of an implicit classicism that seeks to bypass Christian theology by going to ancient Greece and Rome), I prefer to say that theology may be one of the uses to which these various themes are put. At this point, Kautsky's project of uncovering a pre-Marxist communist tradition may have something to say, although with a distinct twist to which I will return.

A real grab-bag of odds and ends, is it not? They are not quite as eclectic as they seem, especially when I reorganise them all as follows:

i) Marxist reconstruction of the economic and social conditions of religion, particularly those that endure and remain global forces.
ii) Necessary fables, especially in terms of the myth of Christian communism, the fable that provides a narrative for responding to psychological pathologies, and the very nature of apocalyptic scenarii.
iii) Revolutionary possibilities, where religion is a passing moment of longer revolutionary themes (so pointing to the futility of self-exorcism and relativising theology's claim to the absolute), and where religion itself may be 'transcoded' as a revolutionary impulse (the time that remains, unstable collectives, monasticism, Reformation etc.).
iv) Dialectics, particularly in terms of living in the world and yet not, which then becomes the dialectic of Marxism as both a secular and anti-secular project.

Now for some more detail. Marxist-inspired reconstructions of the economic, social and ideological histories of the major religions are unfinished projects. Since my expertise on this matter lies with ancient Israel and, to a lesser extent, with early Christianity, I restrict my comments to them. Luxemburg, Kautsky and Kristeva have all enticed me to continue my own efforts at reconstruction. And my proposal for a 'sacred economy', which I indicated briefly in the chapter on Kautsky, is part of that effort. The basic feature of such a sacred economy is a continued tension between what I call allocative and extractive economics. Within this tension we may identify a number of 'régimes' (a term I borrow from the regulation school of economic theory):[1] land, fertility, kinship, patron-client relations, the war machine, the judiciary, trade and tribute. The periods of economic collapse and rejuvenation throughout the history of the ancient Near East, of which ancient Israel was a part, are tied up with the jostling of the various régimes with each other. Above all, however, it is the fundamental tension between allocation and

---

[1] Boyer 1990.

extraction that characterises such periodic collapses, as well as the possibilities and limits of the sacred economy itself.

Of necessity, this is a broad picture and it is not one I need to pursue here in any further detail,[2] save to make the following points. To begin with, it provides the context for the writing and collection of the Hebrew Bible (Old Testament), as well as the distinct and often conflicting forms of religion expressed therein. Further, although it comes out of a tradition of Marxist reconstruction, both within biblical studies and in ancient Near-Eastern studies,[3] it really is a case of starting from scratch. It needs to do so in light of the new data that increasingly becomes available. The older Marxist economic models that have been used to describe the ancient Near East, such as the Asiatic mode of production, or even feudalism or the Ancient or slave-based mode of production, are not adequate any longer, at least for the ancient Near East. Nor, indeed, are the various modified modes of production suggested in other Marxist work, such as the tributary, domestic or clientelistic modes of production. Finally, as may already be evident, this is the topic for a whole project on its own, a project called the 'sacred economy' which is in its early stages. Needless to say, some of the questions Kautsky raises in particular are part of the project, questions such as the narrative of differentiation, the problem of transitions between modes of production (something I identify in the slow and brutal shift from the sacred economy to the slave system of the Roman Empire at the time of the New Testament), and the nature of the evidence available.

Under the idea of a necessary fable, I bring together the various contributions of Badiou, Luxemburg, Kautsky, Kristeva and Jameson. While that may seem an odd collection, my engagement with them has highlighted a number of connections. The glue that holds them together I have squeezed out of Badiou. It begins with his argument that Paul's letters in the New Testament provide an exemplary case of the procedures of truth. The way such procedures show up in Paul's texts – in terms of identifying and naming the 'Event' at the basis of the truth, the need for fidelity to and confidence in that truth and the militant organisation of which Paul then becomes the crucial enabler ('church') – links in with Badiou's identification of the nature of a Truth-Event.

---

[2] See further Boer 2007c.
[3] See Boer 2007e.

The catch is that the Event in question is a pure fable, or, as I prefer, a myth – the death and especially the resurrection of Jesus Christ. Now, this fable cannot be a pseudo-event, such as fascism, or even a mixed case of genuine and pseudo-event, as with the founding of the state of Israel,[4] for such pseudo-events show up in their fruits. Paul's Truth-Event, by contrast, is exemplary, for the procedures of truth are genuine. If so, then it opens up the possibility that the procedures of truth are also the procedures of the fable; or even that the Truth-Event is necessarily fabulous and mythical in some cases.

If this is the case, then Kristeva's argument that Paul's story of the death and resurrection of Jesus Christ actually provides a crucial narrative for dealing with and overcoming a whole series of psychological pathologies may have something to it. Thus, narcissism, masochism, fantasy, repression, death drive, oral sadism and the psychoses meet their match, as it were, in the fable of Christ's death and resurrection. In this sense, we may even be able to say that the ability to overcome such pathologies is another form of the truth procedures of a fabulous event. We can take this point a step further with Kristeva's interest in the new collective, the *ekklesia*. I am not interested in the image of a group of happy former psychotics or masochists or narcissists or whatever, but, rather, in the unstable and fragile collective that offers only a glimpse of something radically distinct. Paul's *ekklesia* replicates too many of the structures surrounding it – in terms of gender, hierarchy, relations of production (slaves and masters) and so on – to be an absolute break. And, yet, it does embody a glimpse into something else that Kristeva's more Marxist feminist side has seen, as indeed has Badiou's image of a militant group. But it is Luxemburg and Kautsky who provide far more, and that is Christian communism itself. In the picture of the early Church in the book of Acts in the New Testament, as well as various sayings attributed to Jesus, they find evidence of early Christian communism. I have already argued in my chapters on Luxemburg and Kautsky that early Christian communism is more fiction that fact, or as Badiou might put it, more like a fable than anything else. Yet, that is where the power of the story of Christian communism lies, if not the fable of primitive communism itself. What it embodies is the possibility of what might have been, or indeed, what *will have been* true (as Badiou's use of the future perfect would have it). In other words, as a fable or a myth, just like

---

[4] Badiou 2006c, pp. 208–9.

the one concerning the death and resurrection of Jesus Christ, Christian communism sets in train certain procedures of truth that still await their realisation. Communism, including Christian communism, is something that is still yet to be true.

That all of this is necessarily utopian hardly needs to be said. But it also allows me to bring in the last point concerning fabulous truths, namely Jameson's dabbling with (but ultimately avoiding) the nature of religious apocalyptic. I must admit that I am not very enamoured with apocalyptic, as both a genre of literature and as the ideology of some politico-religious movements. Too much fevered speculation about the end, it seems to me, too many religious crackpots leading small bands of followers to some ill-conceived and misguided end. And, yet, the basic feature of apocalyptic – the dialectical play between catastrophe and renewal – has all the hallmarks of yet another form of fable or myth. If one wishes to stress disruption as a basic feature of revolution, as Jameson among others wishes to do, then a discerning engagement with apocalyptic may not be a bad idea. Here, I would call on Ernst Bloch's very useful category of the discernment of myths, but I will not repeat my engagement with Bloch that I have already undertaken elsewhere.[5]

It is a small step to the third cluster of items I have picked up from my interlocutors – the revolutionary possibilities of religion, or, preferably, the way religion gives voice to revolutionary aspirations.[6] A good deal has been said on this theme, not least among them Slavoj Žižek,[7] as well as my own foray into this area.[8] The mention of names such as Thomas Müntzer, Gerrard Winstanley and the Diggers, or Camillo Torres, the guerrilla priest who was killed while fighting for the National Liberation Army of Columbia in 1966 are enough to point to a vibrant tradition of revolutionary Christianity. At this point, however, I would like to give the whole question a twist in light of my engagements with Lukács, Williams and indeed Kautsky. In short, it seems to me that the religious dimension is but one element in a much longer, more diverse and richer revolutionary tradition. That tradition is nothing less than the revolutionary-socialist effort to found a new society. In Kautsky's enthusiastic reconstruction of this stream, he was too ready to

---

[5] Boer 2007a, pp. 1–56.
[6] I develop this aspect more fully in the last three chapters of *Criticism of Earth*. See Boer in press-a.
[7] Žižek 2000.
[8] Boer 2007b.

ascribe its impetus to primitive communism, whether in the early Church, or the various heretical movements in the Middle Ages, or the radical Reformation, or, indeed, Thomas More. And he was too eager to attribute it to a distinct religious impulse that ran from early Christian communism through the monasteries and out into Thomas More's *Utopia*. In one respect, Kautsky was on the right track, as was Ernst Bloch in his effort to espy utopian elements within a whole range of religious movements. In another respect, they miss the mark. As I argued in my discussions of Lukács and Williams, it is not that the religious impulse is a primary one, a source of these revolutionary and communistic movements. Rather, it is but one form they can take, one manifestation of something that is far more than these religious movements. In short, this point effectively relativises theology's claim to the absolute. The implication is that, if the rebellious and insurrectionary element of religion is but one form that this tradition might take, then the same applies to Marxism. It is not that Marxism is the culmination and completion – as Luxemburg and Kautsky argued – of these earlier movements, but that it is one powerful form it has taken in our era. That is an implication we will have to face. Marxism then becomes one way of filling the terms of this revolutionary tradition, but so also is anarchism, the green Left, Christian communism, the rebellion of chaos against god and gods in the Bible and so on.

If religion is but one of the modes of this deeper revolutionary tradition may take, then the effort of Georg Lukács to exorcise the idealist and religious elements from his thought becomes unnecessary. Nor is it enough for Williams to seek sources other than religion for the various elements of his warm Marxism, elements such as neighbourliness, community, humanity, solidarity, trust and faith. A more viable approach would be to recognise these elements in some types of religion, but then also to recognise that religion is merely one – and by no means necessary – form they may take. The upshot is that religion is not an embarrassing source for the various revolutionary currents, a source that must be wiped out or bypassed. For example, the argument that Marx derives in part his revolutionary credentials from the prophets of the Hebrew Bible misses the point (and is simply not correct). The affinity between them lies in a much deeper common tradition to which both the Bible and Marx give expression, for all their missteps on the way.

This sense of religion (in some of its elements) being one mode of revolutionary and collective politics is how I would like to read Jameson's act of transcoding. His fascinating effort (following in Kautsky's footsteps) to interpret Thomas More's reforming passion as a revolutionary moment, even to the point that knowledge and use of Hebrew and Greek were seen as such in his time, is not so much an effort to avoid religion. Rather, it is a recognition that religion may with perfect legitimacy be read as embodying moments of revolutionary potential. I really should say that religion is one way in which the revolutionary tradition itself may be transcoded. The same applies to Jameson's identification of the collective appeal of monasticism for More, or Kautsky's argument that he drew on the primitive-communist elements of popular medieval Catholicism, or Kautsky's argument that monasticism carried on the impulse of Christian communism, or, indeed, Agamben's fascinating point that eschatology (I really prefer that term to his use of messianism for reasons that I have already spelled out in my chapter on Agamben) really means 'the time that is left' between the *kairos* and the end. At this point, many of the themes I have discussed earlier become various pieces of transcoding, from Christian communism to apocalyptic.

Finally, there is the dialectical point I drew from my discussion of Lucien Goldmann, namely Marxism as both a secular and an anti-secular project. I have, of course, derived this from Goldmann's analysis of the lived reality of Jansenism as a tension between living in the world and yet not being part of it. Here, we broach the whole question of secularism, so let me outline my own position. I suggest we define secularism as follows: it is a way of living, thinking and acting that draws its terms and points of reference from this world and this age (this is, after all, what *saeculum* and its adjective *saecularis* mean) rather than any world above (the gods) or in the future (utopia).

The upshot is that the other widely used senses of secularism become derivative or secondary: the perception that secularism is non-religious or even anti-religious; the separation of church and state; the distinction between scientific and faith-based disciplines; and, indeed, the distinction between science and religion. These derivatives have led to some curious and contradictory situations. As but one example, too often secularism is taken to be the opposite of religion, indeed that a secular project is by definition an anti-religious project. However, this anti-religious position is really a derivative of the basic sense of secularism as I have defined it above. It is also an aspect of secularism that faces deep contradictions, especially since secularism arose in part as an effort to deal with contradictions within religion and since we have the logical position of religious secularists, namely that secularism is another way to be religious.⁹ A similar point applies to the separation of Church and state, which arose in response to the contradictions of the Christian state, as Marx already pointed out.¹⁰ One has only to look at the current forms of the separation of Church and state to see that it is, in many respects, a legal fiction. In the United States, the strict separation of Church and state has led to a situation where they permeate one another to an excessive degree. Conversely, countries such as Denmark and Norway with their state churches are among the most non-religious countries in the world.¹¹

In light of the basic definition of secularism, what does it mean to say that Marxism is both a secular and an anti-secular programme? Marxism draws its terms of analysis and action from this world and this age, namely capitalism. It seeks to understand the deeper workings of capitalism, its forms of production and circulation, class and class conflict, institutions and ideologies, so as to espy its contradictions and bring about its collapse. In this sense, it is thoroughly secular. Yet, at the same time, Marxism is not committed to this age and this world. Far from it! It seeks the end of this capitalist age in the name of socialism or communism, whatever they may come to mean. In other words, it looks to a world to come, an age beyond this one which will, one hopes, be better in some way. One could say, therefore, that it also draws its terms of analysis and action from another world or age. In this sense, Marxism is thoroughly anti-secular as well.

---

⁹ See Taylor 2007.
¹⁰ Marx 1975b, pp. 156–8; 1976a, pp. 357–9.
¹¹ See further Boer 2007b.

References

Abraham, Richard 1989, *Rosa Luxemburg: A Life for the International*, Oxford: Berg.
Adorno, Theodor W. 1973, *The Jargon of Authenticity*, translated by Knut Tarnowski, and Frederic Will, Evanston: Northwestern University Press.
Adorno, Theodor W. 1989, *Kierkegaard: Construction of the Aesthetic*, translated by Robert Hullot-Kentor, Minneapolis: University of Minnesota Press.
Adorno, Theodor W. 2003a, *Gesammelte Schriften*, 23 vols., Frankfurt am Main: Suhrkamp.
Adorno, Theodor W. 2003b, *Jargon der Eigentlich: Zue deutschen Ideologie* in *Gesammelte Schriften*, Volume 6, Frankfurt am Main: Suhrkamp.
Agamben, Giorgio 1998, *Homo Sacer: Sovereign Power and Bare Life*, translated by Daniel Heller-Roazen, Stanford: Stanford University Press.
Agamben, Giorgio 1999, *Potentialities: Collected Essays in Philosophy*, translated by Daniel Heller-Roazen, edited by Daniel Heller-Roazen, Stanford: Stanford University Press.
Agamben, Giorgio 2000, *Il tempo che resta. Un commento alla Lettera ai Romani*, Turin: Bollati Boringhieri.
Agamben, Giorgio 2004, *The Open: Man and Animal*, translated by Kevin Attel, edited by Werner Hamacher, Stanford: Stanford University Press.
Agamben, Georgio 2005a, *The Time That Remains: A Commentary on the Epistle to the Romans*, translated by Patricia Dailey, Stanford: Stanford University Press.
Agamben, Giorgio 2005b, *State of Exception*, translated by Kevin Attell, Chicago: The University of Chicago Press.
Agamben, Giorgio 2005c, *The Time That Remains: A Commentary on the Letter to the Romans*, translated by Patricia Dailey, Stanford: Stanford University Press.
Alexander, Bryan N. 1998, 'Jameson's Adorno and the Problem of Utopia', *Utopian Studies*, 9, 2: 51–7.
Anderson, Perry 1974a, *Lineages of the Absolutist State*, London: New Left Books.
Anderson, Perry 1974b, *Passages from Antiquity to Feudalism*, London: New Left Books.
Arato, Andrew and Paul Breines 1979, *The Young Lukács and the Origins of Western Marxism*, New York: Seabury.
Badiou, Alain 1988, *L'Être et l'événement*, Paris: Éditions du Seuil.
Badiou, Alain 1997, *Saint-Paul: la fondation de l'universalisme*, Paris: Presses Universitaires de France.
Badiou, Alain 1999, *Manifesto for Philosophy*, translated by Norman Madarasz, Albany: SUNY Press.
Badiou, Alain 2000, *Deleuze: The Clamor of Being*, translated by Louise Burchill, Minneapolis: University of Minnesota Press.
Badiou, Alain 2003, *Saint Paul: The Foundation of Universalism*, translated by Ray Brassier, Stanford: Stanford University Press.
Badiou, Alain 2004a, 'Afterword: Some Replies to a Demanding Friend', in *Think Again: Alain Badiou and the Future of Philosophy*, edited by Peter Hallward, London: Continuum.
Badiou, Alain 2004b, *Theoretical Writings*, translated by Ray Brassier and Alberto Toscano, London: Continuum.

Badiou, Alain 2005a, *Handbook of Inaesthetics*, translated by Alberto Toscano, Stanford: Stanford University Press.
Badiou, Alain 2005b, *Metapolitics*, translated by Jason Barker, London: Verso.
Badiou, Alain 2006a, *Being and Event*, translated by Oliver Feltham, London: Continuum Press.
Badiou, Alain 2006b, *Logiques des mondes: L'Être et l'événement, 2*, Paris: Éditions du Seuil.
Badiou, Alain 2006c, *Polemics*, translated by Steve Corcoran, London: Verso.
Bailey, Anne M. and Josep R. Llobera 1981, 'The AMP: Sources of Information and the Concept', in *The Asiatic Mode of Production: Science and Politics*, edited by Anne M. Bailey and Josep R. Llobera, London: Routledge & Kegan Paul.
Barth, Karl 1985 [1919], *Der Römerbrief*, Zürich: Theologischer Verlag.
Be'er, Ilana 1994, 'Blood Discharge: On Female Im/Purity in the Priestly Code and in Biblical Literature', in *A Feminist Companion to Exodus to Deuteronomy*, edited by Athalya Brenner, Sheffield: Sheffield Academic Press.
Benjamin, Walter 1996, *Walter Benjamin: Selected Writings. Volume 1: 1913–1926*, Cambridge, MA.: Belknap.
Bishop, Kirsten 2003, *The Etched City*, Rockville: Prime Books.
Black, Fiona (ed.) 2006, *The Recycled Bible: Autobiography, Culture, And the Space Between, Semeia Studies, No. 51*, Atlanta: Society of Biblical Literature.
Bloch, Ernst 1972, *Atheism in Christianity: The Religion of the Exodus and the Kingdom*, translated by J.T. Swann, New York: Herder and Herder.
Bloch, Ernst 1985, *Werkausgabe*, Frankfurt am Main: Suhrkamp.
Boer, Roland 1996, *Jameson and Jeroboam*, Atlanta: Scholar's Press.
Boer, Roland 2003, *Marxist Criticism of the Bible*, London: Continuum.
Boer, Roland 2005a, 'A Level Playingfield? Metacommentary and Marxism', in *On Jameson: From Postmodernism to Globalism*, edited by Caren Irr and Ian Buchanan, Albany: State University of New York Press.
Boer, Roland 2005b, 'Terry Eagleton and the Vicissitudes of Christology', *Cultural Logic*, 8. Available at: <clogic.eserver.org>.
Boer, Roland 2005c, 'Women First? On the Legacy of Primitive Communism', *Journal for the Study of the Old Testament*, 30, 1: 3–28.
Boer, Roland 2006, 'On Fables and Truths', *Angelaki*, 11, 2: 329–38.
Boer, Roland 2007a, *Criticism of Heaven: On Marxism and Theology*, Historical Materialism Book Series, Leiden: Brill.
Boer, Roland 2007b, *Rescuing the Bible*, Oxford: Blackwell.
Boer, Roland 2007c, 'The Sacred Economy of Ancient "Israel"', *The Scandinavian Journal of the Old Testament*, 21, 1: 29–48.
Boer, Roland 2007d, 'The Search for Redemption: Julia Kristeva and Slavoj Žižek on Marx, Psychoanalysis and Religion', *Filozofija i Društvo [Philosophy and Society]*, 37, 1: 153–76.
Boer, Roland 2007e, 'Twenty Five Years of Marxist Biblical Criticism', *Currents in Biblical Research*, 5, 3: 1–25.
Boer, Roland 2008a, 'China Miéville's Imagination', *Arena Magazine*, 94: 48–50.
Boer, Roland 2008b, *Political Myth*, Durham, NC.: Duke University Press.
Boer, Roland 2009, *Political Myth: On the Use and Abuse of Biblical Themes*, Durham, NC.: Duke University Press.
Boer, Roland forthcoming, 'Jameson's Anomaly'.
Boer, Roland in press-a, *Criticism of Earth: On Marx, Engels and Theology*, Historical Materialism Book Series, Leiden: Brill.
Boer, Roland in press-b, *Political Grace: The Revolutionary Theology of John Calvin*, Louisville: Westminster John Knox.
Boyarin, Daniel 1994, *A Radical Jew: Paul and the Politics of Identity*, Berkeley: University of California Press.
Boyarin, Daniel 2004, 'Paul and Genealogy of Gender', in *A Feminist Companion to Paul*, edited by Amy-Jill Levine and Marianne Blickenstaff, London: T & T Clark International.

Boyer, Robert 1990, *The Regulation School: A Critical Introduction*, translated by C. Charney, New York: Columbia University Press.
Brenner, Athalya 1994, 'On Incest', in *A Feminist Companion to Exodus to Deuteronomy*, edited by Athalya Brenner, Sheffield: Sheffield Academic Press.
Briant, Pierre 2002, *Frm Cyrus to Alexander: A History of the Persian Empire*, translated by Peter T. Daniels, Winona Lake: Eisenbrauns.
Briggs, Sheila 2000, 'Paul on Bondage and Freedom in Imperial Roman Society', in *Paul and Politics: Ekklesia, Israel, Imperium, Interpretation. Essays in Honor of Krister Stendahl*, edited by Richard A. Horsley, Harrisburg: Trinity Press International.
Buchanan, Ian 1998, 'Metacommentary on Utopia, or Jameson's Dialectic of Hope', *Utopian Studies*, 9, 2: 18–30.
Bultmann, Rudolph 1948, *Theologie des neuen Testaments*, 2 vols., Tübingen: J.C.B. Mohr (Siebeck).
Caird, G.B. 1980, *The Language and Imagery of the Bible*, London: Duckworth.
Callahan, Allen Dwight 2000, 'Paul, Ekklesia, and Emancipation in Corinth: A Coda on Liberation Theology', in *Paul and Politics: Ekklesia, Israel, Imperium, Interpretation. Essays in Honor of Krister Stendahl*, edited by Richard A. Horsley, Harrisburg: Trinity Press International.
Carter, Warren 2006, *The Roman Empire and the New Testament: An Essential Guide*, Nashville: Abingdon.
Certeau, Michel de 1987, *La Faiblesse de croire*, Paris: Éditions du Seuil.
Certeau, Michel de 1988, *The Writing of History*, New York: Columbia University Press.
Cevasco, Maria Elisa 2005, 'Producing Criticism as Utopia: Fredric Jameson and Science Fiction', *Arena Journal*, New Series, 25–6: 52–62.
Clément, Catherine and Julia Kristeva 1998, *Le Féminin et le sacré*, Paris: Éditions Stock.
Clément, Catherine and Julia Kristeva 2001, *The Feminine and the Sacred*, New York: Columbia University Press.
Cliff, Tony 1980, *Rosa Luxemburg*, London: Bookmarks Publishing Co-operative.
Cohen, Mitchell 1994, *The Wager of Lucien Goldmann: Tragedy, Dialectics, and a Hidden God*, Princeton: Princeton University Press.
Corley, Kathleen E. 2004, 'Women's Inheritance Rights in Antiquity and Paul's Metaphor of Adoption', in *A Feminist Companion to Paul*, edited by Amy-Jill Levine and Marianne Blickenstaff, London: T & T Clark International.
Cunningham, Adrian, Terry Eagleton, Brian Wicker, Martin Redfern and Lawrence Bright (eds.) 1966, *'Slant Manifesto': Catholics and the Left*, London: Sheed and Ward.
D'iakonoff, Igor M. 1999, *The Paths of History*, Cambridge, England: Cambridge University Press.
D'iakonoff, Igor M. (ed.) 1969a, *Ancient Mesopotamia: Socio-Economic History. A Collection of Studies by Soviet Scholars*, Moscow: 'Nauka' Publishing House.
D'iakonoff, Igor M. (ed.) 1991, *Early Antiquity*, Chicago: Chicago University Press.
Davies, Philip 1995, *Whose Bible Is It Anyway?*, Sheffield: Sheffield Academic Press.
Davies, Philip 1998, *Scribes and Schools: The Canonization of the Hebrew Scriptures*, Louisville, KY: Westminster John Knox.
Day, John (ed.) 2004, *In Search of Pre-Exilic Israel*, Journal for the Study of the Old Testament Supplement Series, 406, London: T & T Clark International.
de Ste. Croix, Geoffrey E.M. 1981, *The Class Struggle in the Ancient Greek World from the Archaic Age to the Arab Conquests*, Ithaca: Cornell University Press.
de Vries, Hent 1999, *Philosophy and the Turn to Religion*, Baltimore: Johns Hopkins University Press.
Debray, Régis 1983, *Critique of Political Reason*, translated by David Macey, London: New Left Books.
Deissman, Adolf 1929, *The New Testament in the Light of Modern Research*, Garden City: Doubleday, Doran and Company.
Deissman, Adolf 1978 [1908], *Light From the Ancient East*, Grand Rapids: Baker Book House.

Delaney, Samuel R. 1983, *Nevèrÿona*, New York: Bantam Books.
Delaney, Samuel R. 1993, *Tales of Nevèrÿon*, Middletown: Wesleyan University Press.
Delaney, Samuel R. 1994a, *Flight from Nevèrÿon*, Middletown: Wesleyan University Press.
Delaney, Samuel R. 1994b, *Return to Nevèrÿon*, Middletown: Wesleyan University Press.
Desanti, Jean-Toussaint 2004, 'Some Remarks on the Intrinsic Ontology of Alain Badiou', in *Think Again: Alain Badiou and the Future of Philosophy*, edited by Peter Hallward, London: Continuum.
Dever, William G. 2001, *What Did the Biblical Writers Know and When Did They Know It? What Archaeology Can Tell Us about the Reality of Ancient Israel*, Grand Rapids: Eerdmans.
Douglas, Mary 1966, *Purity and Danger: An Analysis of Concepts of Pollution and Taboo*, London: Routledge and Kegan Paul.
Dunn, Stephen P. 1981, *The Fall and Rise of the Asiatic Mode of Production*, London: Routledge & Kegan Paul.
Durkheim, Emile 1995, *The Elementary Forms of Religious Life*, translated by Karen E. Fields, New York: The Free Press.
Eagleton, Terry 1966a, *The New Left Church*, London: Sheed and Ward.
Eagleton, Terry 1966b, 'The Roots of the Christian Crisis', in Cunningham, Eagleton, Wicker, Redfern and Bright (eds.) 1966.
Eagleton, Terry 1967a, 'The Slant Symposium', *Slant*, 3, 5: 8–9.
Eagleton, Terry 1967b, 'Why We Are Still in the Church', *Slant*, 3, 2: 25–8.
Eagleton, Terry 1968a, 'Anti-Medicine', *Slant*, 4, 4: 32.
Eagleton, Terry 1968b, 'Language, Reality and the Eucharist (1)', *Slant*, 4, 3: 18–23.
Eagleton, Terry 1968c, 'Language, Reality and the Eucharist (2)', *Slant*, 4, 4: 26–31.
Eagleton, Terry 1968d, 'Politics and the Sacred', *Slant*, 4, 2: 18–23.
Eagleton, Terry 1969, 'Priesthood and Leninism', *Slant*, 5, 4: 12–17.
Eagleton, Terry 1970, *The Body as Language: Outline of a 'New Left' Theology*, London: Sheed and Ward.
Eagleton, Terry and Adrian Cunningham 1966, 'Christians Against Capitalism', in Cunningham, Eagleton, Wicker, Redfern and Bright (eds.) 1966.
Eagleton, Terry and Brian Wicker (eds.) 1968, *From Culture to Revolution: The Slant Symposium 1967*, London: Sheed and Ward.
Eilberg-Schwartz, Howard 1990, *The Savage in Judaism: An Anthropology of Israelite Religion and Ancient Judaism*, Bloomington: Indiana University Press.
Elliott, Neil 1994, *Liberating Paul: The Justice of God and the Politics of the Apostle*, Maryknoll: Orbis.
Elliott, Neil 1997, 'Romans 13:1–7 in the Context of Imperial Propaganda', in *Paul and Empire: Religion and Power in Roman Imperial Society*, edited by Richard A. Horsley, Harrisburg: Trinity Press International.
Elliott, Neil 2000, 'Paul and the Politics of Empire: Problems and Prospects', in *Paul and Politics: Ekklesia, Israel, Imperium, Interpretation. Essays in Honor of Krister Stendahl*, edited by Richard A. Horsley, Harrisburg: Trinity Press International.
Elliott, Neil 2008, *The Arrogance of Nations: Reading Romans in the Shadow of Empire*, Minneapolis: Fortress.
Engberg-Pedersen, Troels 2000, *Paul and the Stoics*, Louisville: Westminster John Knox.
Engels, Frederick 1975 [1843], 'Progress of Social Reform on the Continent', in *Marx and Engels Collected Works*, Volume 3, Moscow: Progress Publishers.
Engels, Frederick 1978 [1850], *The Peasant War in Germany*, in *Marx and Engels Collected Works*, Volume 10, Moscow: Progress Publishers.
Engels, Frederick 1989 [1880], *Socialism: Utopian and Scientific*, in *Marx and Engels Collected Works*, Volume 24, Moscow: Progress Publishers.
Engels, Frederick 1990 [1894–5], *On the History of Early Christianity*, in *Marx and Engels Collected Works*, Volume 27, Moscow: Progress Publishers.

Ettinger, Elżbieta 1986, *Rosa Luxemburg: A Life*, Boston: Beacon Press.
Ettinger, Elżbieta (ed.) 1979, *Comrade and Lover: Rosa Luxemburg's Letters to Leo Jogiches*, Cambridge, MA.: MIT Press.
Evans, Mary 1981, *Lucien Goldmann: An Introduction*, Sussex: Harvester Press.
Exum, J. Cheryl 1993, *Fragmented Women: Feminist (Sub)versions of Biblical Narratives*, Sheffield: Sheffield Academic Press.
Fadini, Gabriele 2005, 'San Paolo e la Filosofia Contemporanea: Prospettive e Sviluppi', in *Instituto di Filossofia della Facolta di Lettere e Filosofia*, Padua: University of Padua.
Fatum, Lone 1995, 'Image of God and Glory of Man: Women in the Pauline Congregations', in *The Image of God: Gender Models in Judaeo-Christian Traditions*, edited by K.E. Børresen, Minneapolis: Fortress.
Feuerbach, Ludwig 1989, *The Essence of Christianity*, translated by George Eliot, Amherst: Prometheus Books.
Fitting, Peter 1998, 'The Concept of Utopia in the Work of Fredric Jameson', *Utopian Studies*, 9, 2: 8–17.
Fitting, Peter 2006, 'Fredric Jameson and Anti-Anti-Utopianism', *Arena Journal*, New Series, 25–6: 37–51.
Florence, Ronald 1975, *Marx's Daughters: Eleanor Marx, Rosa Luxemburg, Angelica Balabanoff*, New York: The Dial Press.
Foucault, Michel 1975, *The Birth of the Clinic: An Archeology of Medical Perception*, translated by A.M. Sheridan Smith, New York: Vintage.
Friedman, Milton 2002, *Capitalism and Freedom: Fortieth Anniversary Edition*, Chicago: University of Chicago Press.
Frölich, Paul 1969, *Rosa Luxemburg: Her Life and Work*, translated by Edward Fitzgerald, New York: Howard Fertig.
Gaventa, Beverly Roberts 2004, 'Our Mother St Paul: Toward the Recovery of a Neglected Theme', in *A Feminist Companion to Paul*, edited by Amy-Jill Levine and Marianne Blickenstaff, London: T & T Clark International.
Glancy, Jennifer A. 2006, *Slavery in Early Christianity*, Philadelphia: Fortress.
Goldmann, Lucien 1959, *Le Dieu caché: Études sur la vision tragiques dans les 'Pensées' de Pascal et dans le théâtre de Racine*, Paris: Éditions Gallimard.
Goldmann, Lucien 1964a, *The Hidden God: A Study of the Tragic Vision the Penséés of Pascal and the Tragedies of Racine*, translated by Philip Thody, New York: The Humanities Press.
Goldmann, Lucien 1964b, *Pour une sociologie du roman*, Paris: Gallimard.
Goldmann, Lucien 1975, *Towards a Sociology of the Novel*, translated by Alan Sheridan, London: Tavistock.
Goldmann, Lucien 1980, *Essays on Method in the Sociology of Literature*, translated by William Q. Boelhower, St. Louis: Telos Press.
Goldmann, Lucien 1981, *Racine*, translated by Alastair Hamilton, London: Writers and Readers.
Goldmann, Lucien (ed.) 1956, *Correspondance de Martin de Barcos, abbé de Saint-Cyran, avec les abbesses de Port-Royal et les principaux personnages du groupe janséniste*, Paris: Presses Universitaires de France.
Goldstein, Warren S. (ed.) 2006, *Marx, Critical Theory and Religion: A Critique of Rational Choice*, Studies in Critical Social Sciences, Leiden: Brill.
Gottwald, Norman K. 1999, *The Tribes of Yahweh: A Sociology of Liberated Israel 1250–1050 B.C.*, reprint with new preface, Sheffield: Sheffield Academic Press.
Gottwald, Norman K. 2001, *The Politics of Ancient Israel*, Louisville: Westminster John Knox.
Hardt, Michael and Antonio Negri 2004, *Multitude: War and Democracy in the Age of Empire*, New York: Penguin.
Harvey, David 1999, *The Limits to Capital*, Second Edition, London: Verso.
Hawkins, Faith Kirkham 2004, 'Does Paul Make a Difference?', in *A Feminist Companion to Paul*, edited by Amy-Jill Levine and Marianne Blickenstaff, London: T & T Clark International.

Hayek, Friedrich von 1960, *The Constitution of Liberty*, Chicago: University of Chicago Press.
Hegel, Georg W.F. 1961, *On Christianity: Early Theological Writings*, translated by T.M. Knox and Richard Kroner, New York: Harper and Brothers.
Heidegger, Martin 2004, *The Phenomenology of Religious Life*, translated by Matthias Fritsch and Jennifer Anna Gosetti-Ferencei, Bloomington: Indiana University Press.
Hindess, Barry and Paul Q. Hirst 1975, *Precapitalist Modes of Production*, London: Routledge and Kegan Paul.
Horkheimer, Max and Theodor W. Adorno 2002, *Dialectic of Enlightenment: Philosophical Fragments*, translated by Edmund Jephcott, Stanford: Stanford University Press.
Horkheimer, Max and Theodor W. Adorno 2003, *Dialektik der Aufklärung*, in *Gesammelte Schriften*, Volume 3, Frankfurt am Main: Suhrkamp.
Horsley, Richard A. 1989, *Sociology and the Jesus Movement*, New York: Crossroad Publishing Company.
Horsley, Richard A. 1992, *Jesus and the Spiral of Violence: Popular Jewish Resistance in Roman Palestine*, Philadelphia: Augsburg Fortress.
Horsley, Richard A. 1995, *Galilee: History, Politics, People*, Philadelphia: Trinity Press International.
Horsley, Richard A. 1996, *Archaeology, History and Society in Galilee*, Philadelphia: Trinity Press International.
Horsley, Richard A. 1998, *1 Corinthians, Abingdon NT Commentaries*, Nashville: Abingdon.
Horsley, Richard A. 2000, 'Rhetoric and Empire – and 1 Corinthians', in *Paul and Politics: Ekklesia, Israel, Imperium, Interpretation. Essays in Honor of Krister Stendahl*, edited by Richard A. Horsley, Harrisburg: Trinity Press International.
Horsley, Richard A. 2002, *Jesus and Empire: The Kingdom of God and the New World Order*, Minneapolis: Augsburg Fortress.
Horsley, Richard A. 2003, *Religion and Empire: People, Power, and the Life of the Spirit*, Minneapolis: Augsburg Fortress.
Horsley, Richard A. (ed.) 1997, *Paul and Empire: Religion and Power in Roman Imperial Society*, Harrisburg: Trinity Press International.
Horsley, Richard A. and John S. Hanson 1985, *Bandits, Prophets, and Messiahs: Popular Movements in the Time of Jesus*, Philadelphia: Trinity Press International.
Howard, Dick (ed.) 1971, *Selected Political Writings of Rosa Luxemburg*, New York: Monthly Review Press.
Hudis, Peter and Kevin B. Anderson (eds.) 2004, *The Rosa Luxemburg Reader*, New York: Monthly Review Press.
Hudson, Wayne 1982, *The Marxist Philosophy of Ernst Bloch*, London: Macmillan.
Jacob, Mathilde 2000, *Rosa Luxemburg: An Intimate Portrait*, translated by Hans Fernbach, London: Lawrence & Wishart.
Jameson, Fredric 1971a, *Marxism and Form: Twentieth-Century Dialectical Theories of Literature*, Princeton: Princeton University Press.
Jameson, Fredric 1975, 'World Reduction in LeGuin: The Emergence of Utopian Narrative', *Science Fiction Studies*, 2, 3: 221–30.
Jameson, Fredric 1981, *The Political Unconscious: Narrative as a Socially Symbolic Act*, Ithaca: Cornell University Press.
Jameson, Fredric 1983, 'Science Versus Ideology', *Humanities in Society*, 6, 2–3: 283–302.
Jameson, Fredric 1986, 'Religion and Ideology: A Political Reading of *Paradise Lost*', in *Literature, Politics and Theory: Papers from the Essex Conference 1976–84*, edited by Francis Barker, London: Methuen.
Jameson, Fredric 1991, *Postmodernism, or, the Cultural Logic of Late Capitalism*, Durham, NC.: Duke University Press.
Jameson, Fredric 1996, 'On the Sexual Production of Western Subjectivity, or, Saint Augustine as a Social Democrat', in *Gaze and Voice as Love Objects*, edited by Renata Salecl and Slavoj Žižek, Durham, NC.: Duke University Press.
Jameson, Fredric 1998a, 'Comments', *Utopian Studies*, 9, 2: 74–7.

Jameson, Fredric 1998b, *The Cultural Turn: Selected Writings on the Postmodern, 1983–1998*, London: Verso.
Jameson, Fredric 2002a, 'Radical Fantasy', *Historical Materialism*, 10, 4: 273–80.
Jameson, Fredric 2002b, *A Singular Modernity: Essay on the Ontology of the Present*, London: Verso.
Jameson, Fredric 2005a, 'The Antinomies of Utopia', *Arena Journal*, New Series, 25–6: 15–36.
Jameson, Fredric 2005b, *Archaeologies of the Future: The Desire Called Utopia and Other Science Fictions*, London: Verso.
Jobling, David 1991, 'Feminism and "Mode of Production" in Ancient Israel: Search for a Method', in *The Bible and the Politics of Exegesis: Essays in Honor of Norman K. Gottwald on His Sixty-Fifth Birthday*, edited by David Jobling, Peggy L. Day and Gerald T. Sheppard, Cleveland: Pilgrim Press.
Jobling, David 1998, *1 Samuel*, Collegeville: Liturgical Press.
Kadarky, Arpad 1991, *Georg Lukács: Life, Thought, and Politics*, Cambridge: Basil Blackwell.
Käsemann, Ernst 1980, *An die Römer*, Tübingen: J.C.B. Mohr (Paul Siebeck).
Kautsky, Karl 1899, *Die Agrarfrage. Eine Übersicht über die Tendenzen der modfernen Landwirtschaft und die Agrarpolitik*, Stuttgart: Dietz.
Kautsky, Karl 1908, *Der Ursprung des Christentums: Eine Historische Untersuchung*, Stuttgart: J.H.W. Dietz.
Kautsky, Karl 1947 [1888], *Thomas More und seine Utopie: mit einer Historischen Einleitung*, Third Edition, Berlin: J.W.H. Dietz.
Kautsky, Karl 1976 [1895–7], *Vorläufer des neueren Sozialismus*, 2 vols., Berlin: J.H.W. Dietz.
Kautsky, Karl 1988, *The Agrarian Question*, London: Unwin Hyman.
Kautsky, Karl 2001 [1953], *Foundations of Christianity*, translated by H.F. Mins, London: Russell and Russell. Available at: <www.marxists.org>.
Kautsky, Karl 2002 [1927], *Thomas More and His Utopia*, translated by Henry James Stenning, New York: International Publishers. Available at: <www.marxists.org>.
Kautsky, Karl 2002 [1897], *Communism in Central Europe in the Time of the Reformation*, translated by J.L. Mulliken and E.G. Mulliken, London: Fisher and Unwin. Available at: <www.marxists.org>.
Kautsky, Karl and Paul Lafargue 1977 [1922], *Vorläufer des neueren Sozialismus*, Stuttgart: J.H.W. Dietz.
Kittredge, Cynthia Briggs 2000, 'Corinthian Women Prophets and Paul's Argumentation in 1 Corinthians', in *Paul and Politics: Ekklesia, Israel, Imperium, Interpretation. Essays in Honor of Krister Stendahl*, edited by Richard A. Horsley, Harrisburg: Trinity Press International.
Koester, Helmut 1982, *Introduction to the New Testament. Volume 2: History and Literature of Early Christianity*, Philadelphia: Fortress.
Krader, Lawrence 1975, *The Asiatic Mode of Production: Sources, Development and Critique in the Writings of Karl Marx*, Assen: Van Gorcum.
Kristeva, Julia 1969, *Séméiôtiké: Recherches pour une sémanalyse*, Paris: Éditions du Seuil.
Kristeva, Julia 1974, *La révolution du langue poétique: L'avant garde à la fin du XIXe siècle, Lautréamont et Mallarmé*, Paris: Éditions du Seuil.
Kristeva, Julia 1977, *Polylogue*, Paris: Éditions du Seuil.
Kristeva, Julia 1980a, *Desire in Language: A Semiotic Approach to Literature and Art*, translated by Thomas Gora, Alice Jardine and Leon S. Roudiez, New York: Columbia University Press.
Kristeva, Julia 1980b, *Pouvoirs de l'horreur: Essai sur l'abjection*, Paris: Éditions du Seuil.
Kristeva, Julia 1981, *Le Langage, cet inconnu: Une initiation à linguistique*, Paris: Éditions du Seuil.
Kristeva, Julia 1982, *Powers of Horror: An Essay on Abjection*, translated by Leon S. Roudiez, New York: Columbia University Press.

Kristeva, Julia 1983, *Histoires d'amour*, Paris: Éditions Denoël.
Kristeva, Julia 1984, *Revolution in Poetic Language*, translated by Margaret Waller, New York: Columbia University Press.
Kristeva, Julia 1985, *Au commencement était l'amour: psychanalyse et foi*, Paris: Hachette.
Kristeva, Julia 1986, *The Kristeva Reader*, edited by Toril Moi, Oxford: Basil Blackwell.
Kristeva, Julia 1987a, *In the Beginning Was Love: Psychoanalysis and Faith*, New York: Columbia University Press.
Kristeva, Julia 1987b, *Soleil noir: dépression et mélancholie*, Paris: Gallimard.
Kristeva, Julia 1987c, *Tales of Love*, translated by Leon S. Roudiez, New York: Columbia University Press.
Kristeva, Julia 1988, *Étrangers à nous-mêmes*, Paris: Gallimard.
Kristeva, Julia 1989a, *Black Sun: Depression and Melancholia*, translated by Leon S. Roudiez, New York: Columbia University Press.
Kristeva, Julia 1989b, *Language the Unknown: An Initiation Into Linguistics*, translated by Anne M. Menke, New York: Columbia University Press.
Kristeva, Julia 1991, *Strangers to Ourselves*, translated by Leon S. Roudiez, New York: Columbia University Press.
Kristeva, Julia 1993, *Les Nouvelles maladies de l'âme*, Paris: Fayard.
Kristeva, Julia 1995, *New Maladies of the Soul*, translated by Ross Mitchell Guberman, New York: Columbia University Press.
Kristeva, Julia 1996a, *Julia Kristeva Interviews*, edited by Ross Mitchell Guberman, New York: Columbia University Press.
Kristeva, Julia 1996b, *Sens et non-sens de la révolte: Pouvoirs et limites de la psychanalyse I*, Paris: Fayard.
Kristeva, Julia 1998, *L'avenir d'une révolte*, Paris: Calmann-Lévy.
Kristeva, Julia 1999, *Le génie féminin: la vie, la folie, le mots: Hannah Arendt, Melanie Klein, Colette*, Paris: Fayard.
Kristeva, Julia 2000, *The Sense and Non-Sense of Revolt: The Powers and Limits of Psychoanalysis, Volume 1*, translated by Jeanine Herman, New York: Columbia University Press.
Kristeva, Julia 2001, *Hannah Arendt, Vol. 1, Female Genius: Life, Madness, Words – Hannah Arendt, Melanie Klein, Colette*, translated by Ross Guberman, New York: Columbia University Press.
Kristeva, Julia 2002, *Intimate Revolt: The Powers and Limits of Psychoanalysis, Volume 2*, translated by Jeanine Herman, New York: Columbia University Press.
Kristeva, Julia 2004a, *Colette, Vol. 3, Female Genius: Life, Madness, Words – Hannah Arendt, Melanie Klein, Colette*, translated by Jane Marie Todd, New York: Columbia University Press.
Kristeva, Julia 2004b, *Melanie Klein, Vol. 2, Female Genius: Life, Madness, Words – Hannah Arendt, Melanie Klein, Colette* translated by Ross Guberman, New York: Columbia University Press.
Kroeker, P.T. 2005, 'Whither Messianic Ethics? Paul as Political Theorist', *Journal of the Society of Christian Ethics*, 25, 2: 37–58.
Le Blanc, Paul (ed.) 1999, *Rosa Luxemburg: Reflections and Writings*, New York: Humanity Books.
LeGuin, Ursula K. 2001, *Earthsea Tetralogy*, Norwalk: Easton Press.
LeGuin, Ursula K. 2003a, *Tales of Earthsea*, New York: Penguin.
LeGuin, Ursula K. 2003b, *The Other Wind*, New York: Penguin.
Lemche, Niels Peter 1988, *Ancient Israel: A New History of Israelite Society*, Sheffield: Sheffield Academic Press.
Lemche, Niels Peter 1998a, *Prelude to Israel's Past: Background and Beginnings of Israelite History and Identity*, translated by E.F. Maniscalco, Peabody: Hendrickson.
Lemche, Niels Peter 1998b, *The Israelites in History and Tradition*, London: SPCK.
Lenin, Vladimir Ilyich 1972–6, *Collected Works*, Moscow: Progress.
Lévi-Strauss, Claude 1966, *The Savage Mind*, London: Weidenfeld and Nicolson.
Lichtheim, George 1990, 'Marx and the "Asiatic Mode of Production"', in *Marxian Economics*, Volume I, edited by J.E. King, Aldershot: Elgar.

Lindemann, Hugo and Morris Hillquit 1977 [1922], *Vorläufer des neueren Sozialismus*, Stuttgart: J.H.W. Dietz.
Looker, Robert (ed.) 1972, *Rosa Luxemburg: Selected Political Writings*, London: Jonathan Cape.
Löwy, Michael 1979, *Georg Lukács – From Romanticism to Bolshevism*, translated by Patrick Camiller, London: New Left Books.
Lukács, Georg 1962, *Die Zerstörung der Vernunft*, Neuwied: Hermann Luchterhand.
Lukács, Georg 1963, *Dier Eigenart des Ästhetischen*, in *Georg Lukács Werke*, Volumes 12–13, Neuwied: Luchterhand.
Lukács, Georg 1965, *Probleme des Realismus III: Der historische Roman*, in *Georg Lukács Werke*, Volume 6, Neuwied: Luchterhand.
Lukács, Georg 1967, *Der Junge Hegel: Über die Beziehungen von Dialektik und Ökonomie*, in *Georg Lukács Werke*, Volume 8, Third Edition, Neuwied und Berlin: Hermann Luchterhand.
Lukács, Georg 1968, *Geschichte und Klassenbewusstsein*, in *Georg Lukács Werke*, Volume 2, Neuwied und Berlin: Hermann Luchterhand.
Lukács, Georg 1970, *Writer and Critic, and Other Essays*, translated by Arthur D. Kahn, London: Merlin.
Lukács, Georg 1971a, *Die Seele und die Formen*, Neuwied: Luchterhand.
Lukács, Georg 1971b, *Theory of the Novel: A Historico-Philosophical Essay in the Forms of Great Epic Literature*, translated by Anna Bostock, Cambridge, MA.: MIT Press.
Lukács, Georg 1972a, *Political Writings, 1919–1929: The Question of Parliamentarianism and Other Essays*, translated by Michael McColgan, London: New Left Books.
Lukács, Georg 1972b, *Studies in European Realism: A Sociological Survey of the Writings of Balzac, Stendhal, Zola, Tolstoy, Gorki and Others*, translated by Edith Bone, London: Merlin.
Lukács, Georg 1973, *Marxism and Human Liberation*, New York: Delta.
Lukács, Georg 1974, *Soul and Form*, translated by Anna Bostock, London: Merlin.
Lukács, Georg 1975, *The Young Hegel: Studies in the Relations Between Dialectics and Economics*, translated by Rodney Livingstone, London: Merlin.
Lukács, Georg 1980, *The Destruction of Reason*, translated by Peter Palmer, London: Merlin.
Lukács, Georg 1983a, *The Historical Novel*, translated by Hannah Mitchell and Stanley Mitchell, Lincoln, NE.: University of Nebraska Press.
Lukács, Georg 1983b, *Record of a Life: An Autobiographical Sketch*, translated by Rodney Livingstone, London: Verso.
Lukács, Georg 1988, *History and Class Consciousness: Studies in Marxist Dialectics*, translated by Rodney Livingstone, Cambridge, MA.: MIT Press.
Lukács, Georg 1994, *Die Theorie des Romans: Ein geschichtsphilosophischer Versuch über die Formen der grossen Epik*, München: Deutscher Taschenbuch Verlag.
Lukács, Georg 1995, *The Lukács Reader*, edited by Arpad Kadarky, Oxford: Basil Blackwell.
Lukács, Georg 2000, *A Defence of History and Class Consciousness: Tailism and the Dialectic*, translated by Esther Leslie, London: Verso.
Luxemburg, Rosa 1903, 'Enquête sur l'anticléricalisme et le socialisme', *Le Mouvement Socialiste*, 9, 111: 28–37.
Luxemburg, Rosa 1970 [1913], *Die Akkumulation des Kapitals*, Fourth Edition, Frankfurt: Neue Kritik.
Luxemburg, Rosa 1976, *The National Question – Selected Writings by Rosa Luxemburg*, edited by Horace B. Davis, New York: Monthly Review Press.
Luxemburg, Rosa 1982 [1905], *Kirche und Sozialismus*, Frankfurt am Main: Stimme-Verlag.
Luxemburg, Rosa 2003, *Accumulation of Capital*, London: Routledge.
Luxemburg, Rosa 2004a [1903], 'An Anti-Clerical Policy of Socialism', *The Social Democrat*, August. Available at: <www.marxists.org>.
Luxemburg, Rosa 2004b [1972], *Socialism and the Churches*, translated by Juan Punto, Colombo: A Young Socialist Publication. Available at: <www.marxists.org>.

Maier, Joseph B. 1989, 'Georg Lukács and the Frankfurt School: A Case of Secular Messianism', in *Georg Lukács: Theory, Culture, and Politics*, edited by Judith Marcus and Zoltán Tarr, New Brunswick: Transaction.
Malina, Bruce J. and Jerome H. Neyrey 1996, *Portraits of Paul: An Archaeology of Ancient Personality*, Louisville: Westminster John Knox.
Mandel, Ernest 1968, *Marxist Economic Theory*, translated by Brian Pearce, London: Merlin.
Manuel, Frank and Fritzie Manuel 1979, *Utopian Thought in the Western World*, Cambridge, MA.: MIT Press.
Martin, Dale, B. 1995, *The Corinthian Body*, New Haven: Yale University Press.
Marx, Karl 1975a [1844], *Contribution to the Critique of Hegel's Philosophy of Law: Introduction*, in *Marx and Engels Collected Works*, Volume 3, Moscow: Progress Publishers.
Marx, Karl 1975b [1844], *On the Jewish Question*, in *Marx and Engels Collected Works*, Volume 3, Moscow: Progress Publishers.
Marx, Karl 1976a [1844], *Zur Judenfrage*, in *Karl Marx/Friedrich Engels – Werke*, Volume 1, Berlin: Dietz.
Marx, Karl 1976b [1888], 'Theses on Feuerbach (Edited by Engels)', in *Marx and Engels Collected Works*, Volume 4, Moscow: Progress Publishers.
Marx, Karl 1976c [1924], 'Theses on Feuerbach (Original Version)', in *Marx and Engels Collected Works*, Volume 4, Moscow: Progress Publishers.
Marx, Karl 1986 [1939–41], *Economic Manuscripts of 1857–58 (First Version of* Capital*): Bastiat and Carey*, in *Marx and Engels Collected Works*, Volume 28, Moscow: Progress Publishers.
Marx, Karl 1987 [1859], *A Contribution to the Critique of Political Economy*, in *Marx and Engels Collected Works*, Volume 29, Moscow: Progress Publishers.
Marx, Karl 1989 [1891], *Critique of the Gotha Programme*, in *Marx and Engels Collected Works*, Volume 24, Moscow: Progress Publishers.
Marx, Karl 1996 [1867], *Capital: A Critique of Political Economy, Volume I*, in *Marx and Engels Collected Works*, Volume 35, Moscow: Progress Publishers.
Marx, Karl 1998 [1894], *Capital: A Critique of Political Economy, Volume III*, in *Marx and Engels Collected Works*, Volume 37, Moscow: Progress Publishers.
Marx, Karl and Frederick Engels 1976a [1848], *The Manifesto of the Communist Party*, in *Marx and Engels Collected Works*, Volume 6, Moscow: Progress Publishers.
Marx, Karl and Frederick Engels 1976b [1932], *The German Ideology: Critique of Modern German Philosophy According to Its Representatives Feuerbach, B. Bauer and Stirner, and of German Socialism According to Its various Prophets*, in *Marx and Engels Collected Works*, Volume 5, Moscow: Progress Publishers.
McCaffrey, Anne 1968, *Dragonriders of Pern*, New York: Nelson Doubleday.
McKenzie, Steven L. 2000, *King David: A Biography*, Oxford: Oxford University Press.
McKinlay, Judith 2004, *Reframing Her: Biblical Women in Postcolonial Focus*, Sheffield: Sheffield Phoenix.
McNeill, Dougal 2005, 'Reading the Maps: Realism, Science Fiction and Utopian Struggles', *Arena Journal*, New Series, 25–6: 63–79.
McNutt, Paula M. 1999, *Reconstructing the Society of Ancient Israel*, London: SPCK.
Melotti, Umberto 1977, *Marx and the Third World*, translated by Pat Ransford, London: Macmillan.
Meyers, Carol 1988, *Discovering Eve: Ancient Israelite Women in Context*, Oxford: Oxford University Press.
Miéville, China 2004, *Iron Council*, London: Pan Macmillan.
Milbank, John 1990, *Theology and Social Theory: Beyond Secular Reason*, Oxford: Blackwell.
Mills, Catherine 2004, 'Agamben's Messianic Politics: Biopolitics, Abandonment and Happy Life', *Contretemps*, 5: 42–62.
More, Thomas 1989 [1516], *Utopia*, translated by Robert M. Adams, Cambridge: Cambridge University Press.
Negri, Antonio 2003, *Time for Revolution*, translated by Matteo Mandarini, London: Continuum.

Nettl, J.P. 1966, *Rosa Luxemburg*, 2 vols., Oxford: Oxford University Press.
Nettl, J.P. 1969, *Rosa Luxemburg*, Abridged Edition, New York: Schocken Books.
Nygren, A. 1953, *Agape and Eros*, translated by P.S. Watson, Philadelphia: Westminster Press.
Økland, Jorunn 2005, *Women in Their Place: Paul and the Corinthian Discourse of Gender and Sanctuary Space*, London: T & T Clark.
Pascal, Blaise 1950, *Pensées*, Paris: Hachette.
Pascal, Blaise 1954, *Oeuvres complètes*, edited by Jacques Chevalier, Paris: Éditions Gallimard.
Pascal, Blaise 1961, *The Pensées*, translated by J.M. Cohen, Harmondsworth: Penguin.
Pascal, Blaise 1967, *The Provincial Letters*, translated by A.J. Krailsheimer, Harmondsworth: Penguin.
Penner, Todd 2004, *In Praise of Christian Origins: Stephen and the Hellenists in Lukan Apologetic Historiography*, London: T. & T. Clark International.
Pryor, Frederic L. 1990, 'The Asian Mode of Production as an Economic System', in *Marxian Economics*, edited by J.E. King, Volume 1, Aldershot: Elgar.
Räisänen, Heikki 1983, *Paul and the Law*, Tubingen: J.C.B. Mohr.
Rashkow, Ilona 2000, *Taboo or Not Taboo: Sexuality and Family in the Hebrew Bible*, Minneapolis: Augsburg Fortress.
Rehmann, Luzia Sutter 2004, 'To Turn the Groaning into Labor: Romans 1.18-2.16', in *A Feminist Companion to Paul*, edited by Amy-Jill Levine and Marianne Blickenstaff, London: T & T Clark International.
Ricoeur, Paul 1970 [1965], *Freud and Philosophy: An Essay on Interpretation*, translated by Denis Savage, New Haven: Yale University Press.
Sanders, E.P. 1977, *Paul and Palestinian Judaism: A Comparison of Patterns of Religion*, Philadelphia: Fortress.
Schloen, J. David 2001, *The House of the Father as Fact and Symbol: Patrimonialism in Ugarit and the Ancient Near East*, Winona Lake: Eisenbrauns.
Schmitt, Carl 2005 [1922], *Political Theology: Four Chapters on the Concept of Sovereignty*, translated by George Schwab, Chicago: University of Chicago Press.
Schottroff, Luise 2004, '"Law-Free Gentile Christianity"' – What About the Women? Feminist Analyses and Alternatives', in *A Feminist Companion to Paul*, edited by Amy-Jill Levine and Marianne Blickenstaff, London: T & T Clark International.
Schwartz, Peter 1989, 'Imagining Socialism: Karl Kautsky and Thomas More', in *Karl Kautsky and the Social Science of Classical Marxism*, edited by John H. Kautsky, Leiden: Brill.
Shepardson, Donald E. 1996, *Rosa Luxemburg and the Noble Dream*, New York: Peter Lang.
Shiozawa, Kimio 1990, 'Marx's View of Asian Society and His "Asiatic Mode of Production"' in *Marxian Economics*, edited by J.E. King, Volume 1, Aldershot: Elgar.
Sichère, Bernard 2003, *Le jour est proche: la révolution selon Paul*, Paris: Desclée de Brouwer.
Silver, Morris 1983, *Prophets and Markets: The Political Economy of Ancient Israel*, Boston: Kluwer Nijhoff.
Simkins, Ronald 1999a, 'Patronage and the Political Economy of Ancient Israel', *Semeia*, 87: 123–44.
Simkins, Ronald 1999b, 'Class and Gender in Early Israel', in *Concepts of Class in Ancient Israel*, edited by Mark Sneed, Atlanta: Scholars Press.
Simkins, Ronald 2004, 'Family in the Political Economy of Monarchic Judah', *The Bible and Critical Theory*, 1, 1. Available at: <www.epress.monash.edu.au>.
Smith, Dai 1989, 'Relating to Wales', in *Raymond Williams*, edited by Terry Eagleton, Cambridge: Polity.
Smith, James A. 2005, *Marks of an Apostle: Deconstruction, Philippians, and Problematizing Pauline Theology*, Atlanta: Society of Biblical Literature.
Soler, Jean 1979, 'The Dietary Prohibitions of the Hebrews', *New York Review of Books*, 26: 24–30.

Stark, Rodney 1996, *The Rise of Christianity: How the Obscure, Marginal Jesus Movement Became the Dominant Religious Force in the Western World*, Princeton, New Jersey: Princeton University Press.

Steenson, Gary P. 1978, *Karl Kautsky 1854–1938: Marxism in the Classical Years*, Pittsburgh: University of Pittsburgh Press.

Stendahl, Krister 1976, *Paul Among Jews and Gentiles*, Philadelphia: Fortress.

Struve, V.V. 1969, 'The Problem of the Genesis, Development and Disintegration of the Slave Societies in the Ancient Orient', in *Ancient Mesopotamia: Socio-Economic History. A Collection of Studies by Soviet Scholars*, edited by Igor M. D'iakonoff, Moscow: 'Nauka' Publishing House.

Surin, Kenneth in press, *Freedom Not Yet: Liberation and the Next World Order*, Durham, NC.: Duke University Press.

Swancutt, Diana 2004, 'Sexy Stoics and the Reading of Romans 1.18–2.16', in *A Feminist Companion to Paul*, edited by Amy-Jill Levine and Marianne Blickenstaff, London: T & T Clark International.

Taubes, Jacob 2004, *The Political Theology of Paul*, translated by D. Hollander, Stanford: Stanford University Press.

Taylor, Charles 2007, *A Secular Age?*, Cambridge, MA.: Belknap.

Thompson, Edward P. 1966, *The Making of the English Working Class*, New York: Vintage.

Thompson, Edward P. 1993, *Witness Against the Beast: William Blake and the Moral Law*, Cambridge: Cambridge University Press.

Thompson, Thomas L. 1992, *Early History of the Israelite People: From the Written and Archaeological Sources*, Leiden: E.J. Brill.

Thompson, Thomas L. 1999, *The Mythic Past: Biblical Archaeology and the Myth of Israel*, New York: Basic Books.

Thompson, Thomas L. 2000, *Early History of the Israelite People from the Written and Archaeological Sources*, Leiden: Brill.

Thompson, Thomas L. 2005, *The Messiah Myth: The Near Eastern Roots of Jesus and David*, New York: Basic Books.

Trigano, Shmuel 2004, *L'E(xc)lu: Entre Juifs et chrétiens*, Paris: Denoël.

Troeltsch, Ernst 1992 [1911], *The Social Teaching of the Christian Churches*, 2 vols., Louisville: Westminster/John Knox.

Van De Mieroop, Marc 2007, *A History of the Ancient Near East ca. 3000–323 BC*, Second Edition, Oxford: Blackwell.

Vandermeer, Jeff 2003, *Veniss Underground*, London: Pan Macmillan.

Vandermeer, Jeff 2004, *City of Saints and Madmen*, London: Pan Macmillan.

Vandermeer, Jeff 2006, *Shriek: An Afterword*, London: Pan Macmillan.

von Boeckmann, Staci L. 1998, 'Marxism, Morality, and the Politics of Desire: Utopianism in Fredric Jameson's *The Political Unconscious*', *Utopian Studies*, 9, 2: 31–50.

Wan, Sze-kar 2000, 'Collection for the Saints as Anticolonial Act: Implications of Paul's Ethnic Reconstruction', in *Paul and Politics: Ekklesia, Israel, Imperium, Interpretation. Essays in Honor of Krister Stendahl*, edited by Richard A. Horsley, Harrisburg: Trinity Press International.

Waters, Mary-Alice (ed.) 1994, *Rosa Luxemburg Speaks*, New York: Pathfinder.

Wegner, Phillip E. 1998, 'Horizons, Figures, and Machines: The Dialectic of Utopia in the Work of Fredric Jameson', *Utopian Studies*, 9, 2: 58–73.

Weintraub, E. Roy 2002, *How Economics Became a Mathematical Science*, Durham, NC.: Duke University Press.

Williams, Raymond 1958, *Culture and Society 1780–1950*, London: Chatto and Windus.

Williams, Raymond 1960, *Border Country: A Novel*, London: Chatto and Windus.

Williams, Raymond 1961, *The Long Revolution*, London: Chatto and Windus.

Williams, Raymond 1968, 'Culture and Revolution: A Comment', in Eagleton and Wicker (eds.) 1968.

Williams, Raymond 1977, *Marxism and Literature*, Oxford: Oxford University Pres.

Williams, Raymond 1978a, *Politics and Letters: Interviews with 'New Left Review'*, London: New Left Books.

Williams, Raymond 1978b, *Second Generation*, London: Chatto and Windus.
Williams, Raymond 1979, *The Fight for Manod*, London: Chatto and Windus.
Williams, Raymond 1985, *Towards 2000*, Harmondsworth: Penguin.
Williams, Raymond 1989a, *People of the Black Mountains: The Beginning*, London: Chatto and Windus.
Williams, Raymond 1989b, *What I Came to Say*, edited by Neil Belton, Francis Mulhern and Jenny Taylor, London: Hutchinson Radius.
Williams, Raymond 1992, *People of the Black Mountains 2: Eggs of the Eagle*, London: Paladin.
Winstanley, Gerrard, William Everard, Richard Goodgroome, John Palmer, Thomas Starre, John South, William Hoggrill, John Courton, Robert Sawyer, William Taylor, Thomas Eder, Christopher Clifford, Henry Bickerstaffe, John Barker, John Taylor and John Coulton 1649, *The True Levellers Standard ADVANCED: OR, The State of Community Opened, and Presented to the Sons of Men*. Available at: <http://www.rogerlovejoy.co.uk/philosophy/diggers/diggers2.htm>.
Yassif, Eli 1999, *The Hebrew Folktale: History, Genre, Meaning*, translated by Jacqueline S. Teitelbaum, Bloomington: Indiana University Press.
Yee, Gale A. 2003, *Poor Banished Children of Eve: Woman as Evil in the Hebrew Bible*, Minneapolis: Fortress.
Žižek, Slavoj 1999, *The Ticklish Subject: The Absent Centre of Political Ontology*, London: Verso.
Žižek, Slavoj 2000, *The Fragile Absolute, or, Why is the Christian Legacy Worth Fighting For?*, London: Verso.
Žižek, Slavoj 2001, *On Belief*, London: Routledge.
Žižek, Slavoj 2003, *The Puppet and the Dwarf: The Perverse Core of Christianity*, Cambridge, MA.: MIT Press.

Index of Biblical References

Genesis
1   102
1:2   102 n. 26
2   102
2–3   201
3   67
12   135 n. 71
13: 2   96
15: 18   199
24–5   135 n. 72
29   135 n. 72
31: 44–54   199

Exodus
20: 4   65
23: 19   130 n. 46, 133 n. 68
24: 8   199
32   65
34: 26   130 n. 46, 133 n. 68

Leviticus   129, 133 n. 65, 134, 146 n. 111
11–14   xx, 123, 130, 133, 135, 136
11   131, 132
11: 3   131 n. 49
11: 9   131 n. 49
11: 13–19   131 n. 49
11: 21   131 n. 49
11: 29–31   131 n. 50
11: 41–43   131 n. 50
12   132, 133
12: 1–5   132 n. 61
12: 4   133 n. 62
12: 5   133 n. 62
12: 6–8   133 n. 63
13–14   132, 132 n. 59
13: 2   131 n. 52
13: 3–4   131 n. 53
13: 6–8   131 n. 55
13: 10   131 n. 54
13: 18   131 n. 52
13: 19–20   131 n. 53
13: 22–23   131 n. 55
13: 24   131 n. 52
13: 24–26   131 n. 53
13: 27–28   131 n. 55
13: 29   131 n. 52
13: 30–31   131 n. 53
13: 32–36   131 n. 55
13: 36–37   131 n. 53
13: 38–39   131 n. 52
13: 43   131 n. 53
13: 47–59   131 n. 56
14: 1–32   131 n. 57
14: 33–53   131 n. 56
15   132, 132 n. 60
19: 14   32

Deuteronomy   133
7: 9   199
14: 21   130 n. 46, 133 n. 68
26: 17–19   199

Joshua   97

Judges   97

Ruth   122

1 Kings
22   202 n. 78

Ezra   202

Nehemiah   202

Ecclesiastes   162
1: 10   162 n. 22

Song of Solomon (Songs)   122

Isaiah   34 n. 11
5: 8–9   97
11: 1–4   190 n. 36
42: 9   189

268 • Index of Biblical References

Ezekiel
  27: 17   96

Daniel   190

Amos
  4: 1–2   97

Matthew   71, 72
  19: 19   70
  19: 21   81 n. 44
  19: 24   70
  22: 7   70
  22: 39   70
  25   71, 72
  25: 34–36   71
  25: 35–36   113 n. 59
  25: 40   71
  26: 28   199

Mark
  10: 17   70
  10: 21   70, 81 n. 44
  10: 23   70
  10: 25   70, 113 n. 58
  12: 30   70
  12: 31   70

Luke   70
  10: 27   70
  18: 22   81 n. 44
  18: 25   70

Acts   66, 70, 75, 82,
                    84–6, 114–16,
                    187, 247
  2: 42–45   114 n. 60
  2: 44–45   81, 85
  4: 32–35   80, 85,
                    114 n. 60
  4: 35   84 n. 54

Romans   142, 151,
                    162, 182,
                    184 n. 13
  1: 2–6   145 n. 108,
                    175 n. 55
  1: 14   151 n. 129
  1: 16   151 n. 128
  1: 18–32   145 n. 107
  2: 1–11   145 n. 107
  3: 3   186 n. 20
  3: 19–20   186 n. 21,
                    195 n. 53
  3: 20–26   142 n. 97
  3: 21–24   194 n. 49
  3: 21–26   145 n. 108,
                    175 n. 55
  3: 24   195 n. 58
  3: 27   195 n. 56
  3: 28   195 n. 53
  3: 31   186 n. 20,
                    186 n. 21, 187,
                    195 n. 54
  4   199, 200
  4: 6   142 n. 96
  4: 14   186 n. 20
  4: 24–25   145 n. 108,
                    175 n. 55
  4: 25   142 n. 100
  5: 1–2   195 n. 58
  5: 15–21   195 n. 58
  5: 6–11   142 n. 96,
                    145 n. 108,
                    175 n. 55
  5: 15   142 n. 96
  5: 15–17   142 n. 100
  5: 20   142 n. 96
  6: 3–11   145 n. 108,
                    175 n. 55
  6: 3   142 n. 96
  6: 5   142 n. 96, 146
  6: 6   186 n. 20
  6: 14   142 n. 96,
                    142 n. 100,
                    144, 194 n. 49
  7: 12   186 n. 21,
                    195 n. 54
  7: 22–3   195 n. 57
  8: 11   145 n. 108,
                    175 n. 55
  8: 32   145 n. 108,
                    175 n. 55
  8: 22–23   137
  8: 29   4
  8: 31–37   142 n. 96
  10: 4   187
  10: 9   145 n. 108,
                    175 n. 55
  11: 5–6   195 n. 58
  11: 6   142 n. 99
  12: 4–5   149 n. 121
  13   138
  13: 8–10   148 n. 116
  13: 9   70
  14: 8–9   145 n. 108,
                    175 n. 55

1 Corinthians   150, 184 n. 13
  1: 23   32 n. 4
  1: 28   186 n. 20
  5: 9–13   150

6: 1–11	150	4: 22–26	194 n. 48
7	138	5: 14	70, 148 n. 116
7: 21–23	84 n. 57		
7: 39	84 n. 57	Ephesians	184 n. 13
10: 14–22	150	2: 12	199, 199 n. 70
11–14	150		
13	142	Philippians	139 n. 87, 184 n. 13
13: 8	186 n. 20		
13: 11	186 n. 20	Colossians	
14: 34–35	150 n. 126	1: 26	184 n. 13
15: 24	186 n. 20	1: 29	184 n. 13
2 Corinthians	184 n. 13		
3: 14	186 n. 20	1 Thessalonians	184 n. 13
		2 Thessalonians	184 n. 13
Galatians	184 n. 13	2: 3–9	187
2: 20	147 n. 112, 189, 192 n. 42	1 Timothy	
3	199, 200	4: 7–8	184 n. 13
3: 11–12	186 n. 21, 195 n. 53	Philemon	184 n. 13
3: 17	186 n. 20, 200 n. 72	James	
3: 23–24	200 n. 73	2: 8	70
3: 23–29	200		
4	200	Revelation	190

General Index

Aaron 65, 190
Abject 122, 126 n. 29, 130, 132, 133 n. 66
Abraham 96, 194 n. 48, 195, 199–200, 202
Absolutism 1, 20 n. 35
Adorno, Theodor W. xiii, 2, 178, 192, 204, 217
    On secularised theology 179, 189
Agamben, Giorgio x, xi, xiv, xv, xvii, xx, xxi–xxii, xxiii, 137, 140, 151, 153, 181–204, 206, 220, 241, 244, 250
    Homo Sacer 204
    State of Exception 204
    The Time That Remains: A Commentary on the Letter to the Romans xiv, 182
Agape 136–37, 141–42, 145, 148, 152–53 (see also: Love)
Albigensians 75
Allegory 9, 33 n. 5, 55, 220
Allocation 108, 135–36, 245
Althusser, Louis xiii, 36, 60, 205, 216
Anabaptists 37, 117
Ancient Near East xix, 92, 102, 103, 107, 110, 119, 245, 246
    Agriculture and 103
    Mode of production and xix, 104, 105–11, 135, 152, 246
    Soviet (Russian) scholarship on 105–06
    Village-commune and 105, 106, 108, 110
Anderson, Perry 102, 109 n. 48, 110, 226
Anti-clericalism 62, 76–80, 113
    Bourgeoisie and 77–79
    Socialists and 78–80
    Working class and 78–79
Anti-secular(ism) xvii, xxiv, 4, 29–30, 244, 245, 250, 251
Apocalyptic xviii, xxiii, 37, 48, 71, 75, 189, 190–91, 210, 245, 248, 250
    Utopia and xviii, 32, 49–53, 58, 208, 244

Apostasy 12, 207, 208, 222
Arendt, Hannah 127, 128
Arnauld, Antoine 15, 16
Arnold, Matthew 226, 227–28
Art 177, 220–21, 230, 241
    Truth and xxi, 156, 161, 162, 163, 164
Ascetic(ism) xviii, 13, 56, 116, 205, 219
Augustine 2, 12, 33, 122, 139
    Jansenism and 5, 166 n. 32
    Autobiography xxii, xxiii, 206, 215, 216, 219, 223, 224, 230, 232, 233, 235, 236, 237, 240
Avant-garde 57, 126, 166, 168, 170

Badiou, Alain x, xi, xiv, xv, xvii, xx–xxi, 17, 36, 137, 139–40, 144–45, 153, 155–79, 182, 183, 193, 194, 204, 244, 246, 247
    Being and Event xiv, 139, 156, 160, 163
    Logiques des Mondes xiv, 155, 170, 173
    Saint Paul: The Foundation of Universalism xiv, 139
    Theoretical Writings 156
Ballard, J.G. 51
Balzac, Honoré 209
(Baptist) Chapel xxiii, 231–33, 235
    as Vanishing mediator xxiii, 239–41
de Barcos, Martin 15, 16
Benjamin, Walter xiii, xxi, 52–53, 60, 185, 187, 216, 217
Benveniste, Emile 182, 197, 198
Bertken, Zuster 18
Bible xvi, xvii, xxii, 7, 8, 13, 32, 49–50, 53, 56, 66, 72, 97, 98, 116, 117, 119, 121, 122, 123, 136, 143, 168, 172, 190, 202, 217, 223–24, 226, 228, 229, 240, 249
    as Cultural product 93–94, 97–99
    Economic context of xix
    Hebrew Bible (Old Testament) xx, 95, 130, 136, 157, 183, 189, 190, 198, 199, 202, 246, 249
    Historical unreliability of 94, 95

New Testament xvi, xix, xx, xxi, 4, 57, 60, 63, 66, 70, 72, 83, 84, 86, 94, 112, 115, 123, 136, 137, 138, 147, 153, 182, 185, 190, 199, 203, 246, 247
  Social context of 92
  Use in historical reconstruction xix, 92, 95, 96, 97, 115
Biblical xiv, xvii, xx, 31, 52, 53, 58, 65, 66, 69, 70, 71, 95, 97, 122, 123, 134, 137, 152, 158, 168, 183, 184, 199, 244
  Criticism/scholarship/studies x, xvi, xix, 22 n. 39, 83, 84, 85, 92–3, 95 , 96, 101–02, 112, 121, 122, 130, 137, 138, 140, 141, 143, 168, 183, 193, 199, 202, 229, 246
  Interpretation xiv, 130
  Left 138
Bishop, Kirsten 45
Bloch, Ernst xiii, 2, 37, 40, 49–50, 88, 93, 117, 118, 154, 206, 217, 230, 248, 249
Boer, Roland
  Criticism of Heaven ix, xiii, xvi, 243
Bohemian Brethren 117
Bourgeoisie 9, 22, 25, 62, 67, 71, 72, 78–9, 85, 126
  Church and 62, 63, 67, 68, 75, 77, 78–79
British Empire 236
Buber, Martin 205
Bulgaria 122, 124, 129, 143, 158

Cabet, Étienne 85, 114
Calvin, John 5, 57, 194
Calvinism xvi, 6, 8, 9, 83, 174, 240
  Grace and 12, 19 (see also: Grace)
  Predestination and 9, 19, 29
  Tolerance and 9, 38 n. 22
Canaan 97, 100, 101
Cantor, Georg 156, 158, 160–61, 163, 164, 171
  Theology and 160
Capitalism 13, 15, 16, 17, 19, 25, 27, 29, 30, 35, 39, 45, 51, 67, 68, 72, 73, 77, 79, 83, 85, 88, 90, 103, 107, 108, 109, 117, 126, 129, 153, 181, 217, 226, 227, 231, 233, 234, 251
  Anti-capitalism 35, 52, 205, 216, 217, 220
Catastrophe 50, 51, 58, 196, 244, 248
  Catastrophism 19
Catholic/ism (Roman) xviii, 5, 32, 55, 58, 61, 75, 85, 89, 117, 143, 225, 250
  Left 55
  Workers xviii, 61
Charity 88, 101, 115, 164

China 13, 104
Christianity (Christian) xiii, xiv, xvi, xxii, 9, 15, 16, 28, 33, 35, 39, 43, 63, 66, 71, 73, 74, 75, 83, 84, 86, 87, 91, 92, 94, 95, 98, 99, 102, 112, 113, 119, 123, 138, 139, 141, 153, 155, 162, 163, 164, 165, 166, 167, 169, 170, 171, 172, 173, 174, 178, 189, 190, 191, 193, 206, 210, 211–13, 215, 224, 226, 227, 228–29, 230, 233–34, 241, 251
  Communism/socialism and xvi, xviii, xix, xxiii, 59–61, 63, 66, 70, 71, 77, 79, 80–82, 86–9, 93, 94, 99, 101, 113–17, 228, 244, 245, 247–50
  Early/primitive Christianity xviii, xix, 57, 60, 61, 63, 66, 69, 70, 72, 74, 75, 81, 83, 84–8, 93, 94, 97, 104, 110, 111, 113–17, 170, 245, 247, 249
  History of 85, 157, 190
  Historicity of 167–68
  Marxism and 28, 58
  Positivity of 206
  Theology 172, 183, 224, 240, 244
  (see also: Theology)
Christology xxi, 181, 182, 185, 189, 190, 191
  Church xix, xx, 16, 18, 36, 37, 60, 62, 63–9, 72–80, 81, 82, 85, 86, 88, 89, 90, 98, 101, 140, 143, 163, 164, 165, 168, 170, 184, 202, 203, 223, 227, 228, 229, 231, 233–34, 235, 240, 244, 246 (see also: Christianity; *Ekklesia*)
  Betrayal of: Christ(ianity) 69, 77, 80, 170; early Communism/socialism 61, 63, 77, 80; event 169
  Catholic xviii, 61, 75, 85
  Early xiv, xviii, xix, 66, 69, 72–3, 75, 82–6, 92, 98, 99, 104, 116, 119, 232, 247, 249
  History of 64, 72–73, 76, 83, 92, 94
  Of England xxiii, 232
  Of Wales 232, 240
  State and 29, 63, 65, 67, 79, 202, 250–51
Class 21, 22, 46, 73, 74, 75, 77, 78, 84, 88, 97, 99, 100, 101, 102, 103, 106, 107, 114, 201, 237, 238, 251
  Consciousness 34 n. 12
  Ruling xviii, 34 n. 12, 61–62, 73, 74, 78, 79
  Working/low(er) xxiii, 62, 63, 68, 72, 76–7, 78–9, 82–83, 117, 223, 227, 229, 230–32, 235, 237–38, 239, 240
Classicism (critique of) 158 n. 8, 204, 214, 222, 244

Clergy   63–7, 69, 71, 72, 74, 100, 202, 212
Cohen, Paul   159, 160, 171, 174, 178
Coleridge, Samuel Taylor   226, 227
Colette   127
Collective(s)   14, 17, 41, 47, 48, 56, 58, 73, 87, 90, 106, 118, 122, 137, 141, 146, 148–49, 151, 152, 153, 154, 247, 249, 250
    as Unstable   xx, xxiii, 244, 245
Commodity festishism   26
Communism   xix, xx, 56, 57, 64, 66, 67, 72, 74, 75, 85, 104, 115, 128, 129, 164, 169, 218, 219, 236, 251 (see also: Socialism)
    Christian   xvi, xviii, xxiii, 59–62, 70, 71, 77, 80, 82, 86–88, 93, 94, 99, 101, 113–15, 116, 117, 244, 245, 247–48
    Early/primitive   101, 102, 103, 114, 117, 201, 247, 249, 250
    Of consumption   xix, 61, 80, 86, 115
    Forerunners of   118
    History of   92, 244
    (Pre-)Marxist   xviii, 92, 93 , 118, 119
    Modern   117
    Of production   xix, 61, 80, 86, 115
Community   xxiii, 28, 50–51, 56, 73, 74, 84, 85, 86, 87, 105, 114, 115–16, 141, 146, 149, 212, 230, 231, 232, 237, 238, 239, 240, 249
Constantine   74, 115, 170
Constitutive exception   130, 134, 204
Counter-Reformation   5, 143
Covenant   183, 194 n. 48, 197, 198, 200
Cultural materialism   232

Davies, Philip   96, 102
Death drive   145, 146–47, 247
Debray, Régis   xv, n. 2
De Certeau, Michel   220, 221, 224
Delany, Samuel   45
Democracy/democrats   8, 9, 10, 16, 17, 61, 63, 65, 69, 71, 76, 82, 89, 128, 181, 212, 217, 219
Denmark   143, 251
Depravity   4, 5, 6, 19, 64
deus absconditus   27
Dialectic(s)   xvi, xxiv, 4, 8, 23, 24, 25–7, 28, 39, 40, 41, 50, 51, 55, 56, 90, 105, 154, 165–66, 178, 196, 209, 222, 244, 248, 250
    Hegel and   211, 213, 215
    Marxism/Marcxists   30, 31, 213, 245
    Of grace   xvii, 1, 3, 4, 12
    Of ideology/religion and utopia   xviii, 32, 33, 35, 53–54, 58, 244

Of the Elect and the Damned/Reprobate   xvi, xvii, 1, 25
Dick, Philip K.   51
Differentiation   196, 198
    Law, politics, religion and   197, 201–02
    Narrative of   xix, xxi, 74, 93, 99–104, 182, 201, 246
    Trigger of   102, 103, 201–02
    Slaves and   99–104
Diggers (True Levellers)   85, 114, 248
Disruption   24, 37, 53, 109, 112, 140, 173, 248
Dissent   225, 226
Dissenting churches   229, 240
Le divertissement   14
Dostoevsky   xxii, 206, 210
Doubt   11–3, 29
Douglas, Mary   130, 131
Durkheim, Emile   41

Eagleton, Terry   xiii, 55, 205, 225
    The Body as Language: Outline of a 'New Left' Theology   225
    From Culture to Revolution   225
    The New Left Church   225
    Slant   225
    Slant Manifesto   225
Ekklesia   141, 149, 150–53, 202
    Gendered   153, 247
    Psychic stress and   148
    Psychosis and   137, 148, 151, 247
    Unstable   152, 153
    (see also: Church)
Elect   xvi, xvii, 1, 5, 6, 7, 8, 12, 19, 29, 116
    Damned and   1, 3, 5, 6–10, 12, 23, 25, 29–30, 244
Eliot, T.S.   226, 227
    The Idea of a Christian Society   227
Engels, Friedrich xiv, xvi, xx, 2, 27, 33, 42, 69, 73, 83, 91, 92, 93, 104, 113, 117, 118, 244
    On the History of Early Christianity   xvi, 83
    The Peasant War in Germany   xvi
English Revolution   37
Enlightenment   38, 141, 149, 202, 212
Epic   207, 208, 210
Erasmus, Desiderius   57
Eschatology   37, 71, 149, 150, 189–91, 222, 250
Essenes   110, 113
Ethics   68, 142, 173, 216, 217, 236
    Good vs evil in   40, 54 n. 67, 55, 68–9

Event   xvii, xxi, 140, 155, 159, 160, 161–64, 167–72, 173, 174, 196
  Betrayal/fidelity of   161, 166–67, 168, 169, 171, 175, 176, 246
  Christianity and   165, 166
  Existentialism and   173
  Fiction/fable-event   175, 244, 247
  Jesus/Christ-event   94, 144, 164, 166, 167, 168, 169, 171, 172, 175, 179, 186, 188
  Miracle and   166
  Pseudo-event and   171, 247
  Truth-event   xxi, 162, 163, 166, 169, 171, 173, 174–79, 244, 24 (see also: Truth)
Evil   9, 23, 39–40, 46, 68, 146, 190 (see also: Ethics)
Existential(ism)   138, 164, 170, 173, 203
Extraction   101, 106–07, 108, 110, 125, 245–46

Fable   xxi, 48, 144, 156, 162, 174–79, 244, 247, 248
  as Necessary   xxi, xxiii, 175, 178, 245, 246
Faith   xxiii, 9, 11, 12–13, 24, 27, 28, 55, 69, 83, 89, 116, 141, 164, 170, 184, 188, 205, 208, 230, 231, 232, 233, 235, 239, 240, 249, 250
  Grace and   145, 193–94
  Law/pre-law and   xxi, 66, 182, 185, 187, 193–95, 196, 197–200, 202
  Marxist   28, 28 n. 56
  Paul and   188, 192
Fantasy (literature)   34, 40, 45, 46, 49, 58, 145, 146
  Magic and   xvii, 32, 37, 39, 41, 44, 46, 47
  Religion and   38–9, 41
  Science fiction and   xviii, 38, 40, 44, 49
  Utopia and   xvii, 40, 44
Fantasy (pathology)   145, 146, 147, 247
Feminism   126, 127, 137, 150
  Ideology and   129
  Kristeva and   127–28, 134, 148, 149, 247
  Liberal/individualist   127, 134
  Marxist/progressive/ communitarian 129, 152, 247
  Spirituality   123 n. 17
Fertility   75, 135–36, 152, 201, 245
Feuerbach(ian), Ludwig   xviii, 32, 39–44, 45, 47, 48–49, 53, 58
de Fiore, Joachim   49

Fraenkel, Abraham   156, 158, 159, 160
France   1, 9, 20, 22, 26, 75, 77, 122, 144, 211, 217
Franciscans   75, 85
Frankfurt School   34 n. 11
Freedom   44, 123, 128, 189, 209, 213
  Capitalism and   90
  Of conscience   xviii, xix, 61, 64, 88–90, 244
  Republican   xxii, 206, 211, 214
French Revolution   71, 77, 171
Freud, Sigmund   51, 68, 124, 127
Friedman, Milton   90

Genetic structuralism (see also: Homology)   xvii, 3, 21 n. 37, 26
God/god(s)   1, 5, 6, 9, 10, 12, 13, 14, 18, 23, 24, 25, 27, 28, 29, 39, 40, 43, 44, 47, 65, 66, 72, 83, 95, 105, 135, 138, 141, 145, 151, 153, 157, 158–59, 160, 164, 169, 171, 172, 173, 174, 178, 188, 190, 192, 195, 196, 198, 200, 214, 223, 228, 231, 232, 234, 239, 249, 250
  Abandoned by   xxii, 26, 27, 205 206, 207–10, 216, 217, 222
  as Inscrutable/unknowable   4, 5, 7, 10, 11, 12
  Kingdom of   70, 113, 116, 117, 164
  Omniscience of   6, 8
  Perfection of   5
Godless   76, 88
Golden Calf   65
Goldmann, Lucien   x, xiv, xv, xvi, xvii, 1–30, 31, 165, 243, 244, 250
  The Hidden God (Le Dieu Caché)   xiv, 2, 3, 27
  Towards a Sociology of the Novel   26
Good(ness)   5, 6, 9, 15, 16, 23, 39–40, 43, 46, 54 n. 66, 68, 70, 88, 122, 126, 137, 138, 146, 150, 152, 186, 190, 236 (see also: Ethics)
Gottwald, Norman   93, 102
Gödel, Kurt   156, 160
Grace   xxi, 6, 8, 9, 14, 16, 80, 140, 142, 152, 182, 196, 222
  Dialectic of   xvii, 1, 3, 4, 12
  Elect and Damned/Reprobate and 3, 9
  Faith and   145, 182, 193–94
  Inamissibility of   5
  Law/pre- law and   xxi, 142, 144, 151, 181, 182, 193–95, 197
  Paul and   142, 144–45
  Politics of   152
  Predestination and   4, 5, 14, 16, 19, 143

Undeserved/unexpected 5, 153, 195, 196
Works and 142, 151, 193–94
Gramsci, Antonio xii, 57–8, 60, 92
Greece/Greek(s) (ancient) xxii, 73, 100, 104, 112, 122, 151, 157, 158, 168, 198–99, 202, 204, 206, 210, 211, 214, 215, 229, 244
Greek (language) xvi, 32, 57, 83, 108, 172 n. 48, 178 n. 69, 183, 190, 191, 197, 250
Ground rent 108

Hasmoneans 96
Hayek, Friedrich von 90
Hebrew (language) 32, 57, 65, 122, 183, 191, 197, 198, 250
Hegel, G.W.F. xxii, 206, 211, 220
   Phenomenology of Spirit 215
   The Positivity of the Christian Religion 212
   The Spirit of Christianity and Its Fate 213
   Anti-/theological 211, 212, 213, 214
   Dialectic and 211, 215
   Economics and 211
   Idealism and 206, 213, 215
   Lukács on 211–15
Heresy/heretic 12, 37, 89, 116, 117, 129, 151, 169, 235, 249
Hermeneutics
   Of ideology and utopia 31, 32, 34, 35, 38, 40, 50, 54, 58
   Of suspicion and recovery 31, 33–4
Homer 97, 198–99, 208
Homology xvii, 3, 4, 19, 20, 21, 23, 26, 27 (see also: Genetic structuralism)
Humanism 56, 57
Humanity xxiii, 13, 40, 87, 230, 232, 238, 249
Hungary 210
Hutterites 75

Idealism xv, 129, 206, 213, 214, 215, 216, 117
Ideologiekritik 55
Ideology/ideologue xviii, 5, 14, 20, 22, 31, 32, 33, 34, 35, 36, 38, 40, 41, 50, 54, 56, 57, 58, 67, 82, 84, 89, 90, 98, 102, 121, 127, 128, 129, 135, 136, 138, 140, 152, 168, 226, 229, 233, 234, 237, 245, 248, 251
Immanent method xx, 124, 125
Incest 130, 134
Industrial Revolution 236

Infinity 158, 160, 170
Israel(ites) 131, 132, 247
   Ancient (early) xiv, xvi, xix, 66, 92, 94–95, 97, 99, 100, 101, 102, 103, 105, 107, 109, 119, 244, 245
   Economics and 118, 119
   Reconstruction of 92

Jameson, Fredric x, xiv, xv, xvi, xvii, xviii, 3, 24, 31–58, 244, 246, 248, 249, 250
   Archaeologies of the Future xiv, xvii, 31, 32, 35, 36, 49
   Political Unconscious 33
Jansenism xiv, xvi, xvii, 1, 2, 3, 4, 5, 6, 8, 9, 10, 12, 13, 14, 15, 17, 19, 20, 21, 22, 23, 24, 25, 26, 27, 29, 244, 250
Jansenius, Cornelius Otto 5, 20 n. 34
   Augustinus 5, 20 n. 34
Jesus Christ xvi, xxi, 66, 69–70, 80, 81, 83, 94, 95, 97, 113, 114, 141, 170, 184, 212, 213, 228
   Death/resurrection of 84, 142, 144, 145, 148, 175, 176, 188, 191, 195, 210, 247, 248
   as Messiah 185, 188–89, 191, 192
   as Rebel 113, 167, 169
   'Jesus Movement' 84, 111
Judaism (Jews) xv, n. 2, 9, 32 n. 4, 56, 85, 88, 89, 92, 96, 102, 137, 139, 142, 151, 157, 167, 193, 205
Judea 110, 111, 112, 113
Judiciary 108, 135, 136, 212, 245

Kant, Immanuel 2, 12, 26
Kautsky, Karl ix, x, xiv, xv, xvi, xix, 60, 74, 75, 91–119, 147, 201, 244, 245, 246, 247, 248, 249, 250
   Forerunners of Modern Socialism (Vorläufer des neueren Sozialismus) 116
   Foundations of Christianity xiv, xix, 91, 94, 118, 119
   Thomas More and His Utopia 93
Kierkegaard, Søren xvii, xxi, 26, 27, 155, 156, 173–74, 178, 179, 205, 214 n. 37, 217, 220
Klein, Melanie 127
Kristeva, Julia xiv, xv, xvi, xx, 99, 121–154, 183, 193, 244, 245, 246, 247
   Powers of Horror 122, 132
   'Semiotics: A Critical Science and/or a Critique of Science' xiv, xx, 124, 125, 126
   Strangers to Ourselves 122, 148–49
   Tales of Love 122, 148

Lacan, Jacques   127
Law   ix, 2, 66, 131, 133, 142, 151, 177, 181, 195, 197, 229
   Codification of   194, 202
   Deactivation of   185, 186, 187, 188, 191
   Differentiation of   197, 201, 202
   Faith and   xxi, 66, 182, 185, 193–95, 196, 197, 199, 200, 202
   Fulfilment of   196
   Grace and   xxi, 142, 144, 151, 181, 182, 193–95, 197
   Paul and   181, 186
   Pre-law and   xxi, xxii, 181, 182, 185, 194, 195, 196, 197–202, 203, 204
   Telos and   187, 195
Lefebvre, Henri   xiii, 205
LeGuin, Ursula   45
Lemche, Niels Peter   96, 101
Lenin, V.I.   105, 158, 163, 164, 219
Lévi-Strauss, Claude   46, 55
Lollards   116
Love   xiv, 9, 31, 37, 69, 70, 71, 113, 122, 141–42, 145, 147, 161, 163, 171, 174, 182, 192, 203, 213, 235
   as *Agape*   136, 148, 152
   Grace and   142
   Paul and   145, 193
   Truth and   xxi, 156, 161, 162, 163, 164, 171
Lukács, Georg   x, xv, xvii, xxii, xxiii, 2, 3, 4, 26–8, 118, 183, 203, 205–222, 241, 244, 248, 249
   History and Class Consciousness   xv, xxii, 206, 215, 218, 220, 222
   Soul and Form   3, 26, 27
   The Theory of the Novel   xv, xxii, 26, 27, 206–07, 211, 215, 216, 217, 218, 219, 220, 222
   The Young Hegel   xv, xxii, 206, 207, 211, 220, 222
   'Age of absolute sinfulness'   205, 206, 216–17, 220
   'Grand Hotel Abyss'   218
   'Messianic utopianism' and   xxii, 205, 207, 208, 216, 217, 218–19, 220, 222
   'Romantic anti-capitalism' and   205, 216, 217
Luther, Martin   5, 57, 117, 194
Lutheran   138, 143
Luxemburg, Rosa   ix, x, xiv, xv, xvi, xviii, xix, 59–90, 93, 114, 115, 244, 245, 246, 247, 249
   Accumulation of Capital   60
   'An Anti-Clerical Policy of Socialism'   xiv, xviii, 59, 77
   Socialism and the Churches   x, xiv, xviii, 59, 73, 80, 90
Machiavelli   57
Magic   38, 45, 46, 75
   Fantasy and   xviii, 32, 37, 38–41, 44, 45, 46, 47, 49, 58
   Law, politics and   201–02
   as Projection   40, 47, 53
   Religion and   38–39, 41, 44, 49, 201–02
Malraux, André   26
Mao(ist) Zedong   17
Maoist   144, 159
Marx, Karl   ix, xiv, xvii, xx, 2, 4, 14, 23, 24, 27, 28, 36, 39, 41, 42, 44, 62, 73, 91, 92, 93, 104, 105, 108, 110, 117, 118, 121, 123, 124, 125, 126, 129, 134, 136, 145, 152, 205, 212, 213, 216, 217, 244, 249, 251
   The Eighteenth Brumaire of Louis Bonaparte   62
   Hidden (within Kristeva)   xx, 121, 123, 124, 129, 130, 136, 137, 141, 147, 153, 247
   Immanent method in   125
Marxism/Marxist(s)   ix, xiii, xv, xvi, xvii, xviii, xx, 2, 3, 9, 12, 13, 14–15, 16, 17, 19, 21, 22, 25, 26, 27–28, 31, 33, 34, 35, 44, 47, 58, 60, 65, 68, 73, 74, 76, 83, 88, 91, 92, 93–94, 98, 99, 102, 103, 106, 108, 109, 110, 112, 118, 121, 122, 123, 125, 126, 127, 128, 129, 130, 134, 137, 139, 140, 141, 143, 148, 149, 150, 152, 153, 206, 207, 208, 211, 216, 217, 218, 219, 225, 226, 230, 232, 233, 234, 243, 245, 246, 249, 250, 251
   Historical reconstructions and   xiv, xix, xxiii, 104, 119, 201, 245, 246
   Secular and anti-secular   xvii, xxiv, 4, 15, 16, 29–30, 244, 245, 250, 251
   'Warm'   xxiii, 230, 249
Masochism   99, 145, 146, 147, 247
Materialist Theology   192, 243
Mathematics   155, 157, 158, 164, 165, 171, 177, 178
   God/theology and   158–59, 160
   as Ontology   155, 158, 177
May '68   128, 161, 175
McCaffrey, Anne   45
Mennonites   9
Messiah   52, 53, 171, 181, 185, 188, 189, 190, 191, 192, 203
   'Jesus Messiah'   185, 188–89, 191
   (see also: Messianic)
Messianic   53, 84, 187, 190, 194
   Christ(ianity) and the   88, 188, 189, 191, 196

Marxism and the 88, 206
Paul and the 140, 182, 187, 192
Time and xxi, 182, 185, 186, 188, 189, 192, 195, 196
Utopia(nism) and xxii, 205, 207, 208, 216, 217, 218–19, 220, 222
Miéville, China 32, 45, 46, 47, 49, 58
'Iron Council' (from *Iron Council*) 45, 46, 47–8
Mill, J.S. 227
Minimalists 95, 96
Miracle 98, 162, 165–66, 171–72, 173, 203, 204
Mode of production 73, 98, 109, 113, 226, 234
    Ancient/slave xix, xx, 85, 94, 99, 100, 101, 104, 105, 106, 110, 147, 152, 153, 246
    Asiatic 104, 105–06, 246
    Communal 110
    Sacred economy 112, 147
    Tributary 107
Molina, Luis de 6, 143 n. 102
    Concordia liberi arbitrii cum gratiae donis 6, 143 n. 102
Molinism 6, 143
Monasticism xxiii, 56, 58, 94, 228, 235, 245, 250
    Communism and 56, 56 n. 75, 99, 101, 115, 117, 249, 250
Monocausality 130
Morality/moralistic 67, 68, 110, 119, 133
More, Thomas xiv, xviii, 32, 36, 37, 56, 57, 58, 93, 103, 116 n. 66, 117, 244, 249, 250
    Utopia 32, 37, 51, 56, 58, 117, 249
Moses 65–66, 132, 190, 195, 199, 200, 202
Mother xx, 130–36, 137, 147, 152, 223, 233 (see also: Taboo)
Multiple, the 156–59, 160, 164, 169, 178
    'the One' and 156–58, 159, 160
    Trinity and 169
Müntzer, Thomas 33, 49, 64, 117, 175, 217, 248

Narcissism 68, 145, 147, 148, 247
Necessary fable xxi, xxiii, 175, 178, 245, 246
Negri, Antonio 53
Neighbourliness xxiii, 230, 232, 239, 240, 249
Netherlands, the 9, 15, 18, 20
New Testament xvi, xix, xx, xxi, 4, 57, 60, 63, 66, 70, 72, 83, 84, 86, 94, 112, 115, 123, 136, 137, 138, 147, 153, 182, 185, 190, 199, 203, 246, 247 (see also: Bible)
Nietzsche, Friedrich 71
noblesse de robe 1, 20, 23
Novel(ist) xv, xxii, xxiii, 26, 45, 46, 47, 48, 49, 51, 183, 206, 207–10, 211, 224, 230, 232, 235, 236
Nygren, Anders 141

Old Testament xx, 95, 130, 136, 157, 183, 189, 190, 198, 199, 202, 246, 249 (see also: Bible)
One, the 156–58, 159, 160, 161, 168
    The multiple and 156–58, 159, 160
    Trinity/God and 169, 171
Ontology 127, 155, 157–58, 159, 160, 163, 167, 169, 177
Opinion 21, 89
    vs. Truth 36
Order of being xxi, 161
Organisation Politique 17

Parables 71, 113
Pascal, Blaise xvii, xxi, 1, 2, 7, 8, 9, 10, 11, 18, 19, 22, 25, 155, 156, 167, 168, 169, 171, 172, 173, 174, 178
    Lettres Provinciales 17
    Pensées 10, 17, 24, 162, 165
    Conservative 2, 3
    Dialectic and 1, 8, 23, 28
    Jansenism and xvi, xvii, 3, 4, 6, 14, 17, 24, 27, 244
    Miracle and 162, 165, 166, 179
    Marx(ism) and xvii, 4, 12, 14, 24, 25, 28
    Truth and 165, 174, 176
    Wager 11, 12, 13, 169, 170
Pascal, Jacqueline 15 n. 26, 18, 20 n. 34
Passing moment (of religion/theology) xvi, xvii, xxii, xxiii, 183, 204, 206, 222, 241, 244, 245 (see also: Religion, Theology)
Pathologies xx, xxiii, 99, 132, 137, 141, 146, 148, 151, 152, 244, 245, 247
    Crucifixion of 145, 147, 152
Patron-client relations 107, 108, 111, 135, 136, 245
Paul xiv, xvi, xvii, xx, xxi, 4, 70, 84, 85, 111, 112, 122, 123, 129, 136, 137, 138, 139, 140, 141, 143, 146, 147, 148, 149, 150, 152, 155, 156, 162, 165, 166, 174, 176, 178, 179, 181, 182, 183, 184, 186, 187, 195, 199, 203
    Agape/love and 141, 145, 148
    Ekklesia/church and 148, 149, 150–51, 153, 164, 247

General Index • 277

Faith/*pistis* in   xxi, 188, 194, 198, 200
Grace in   xxi, 142, 144, 151, 193, 195, 196
Incoherence in   199, 201
Law/pre-law   xxi, 151, 181, 182, 186, 194, 197, 198, 199, 200, 202, 204
Messianic and   187, 189, 192
'New new perspective' on   138, 139, 143
'New perspective' on   139
Pathologies and   137, 146–47, 152
Political and   139, 140, 141, 143–45, 149, 152, 153, 173, 202
Scholarship   86, 137–43, 182, 183, 185, 193, 199
Truth(-Event) and   174, 175, 176, 246, 247
Peasant Revolt   117
pensée sauvage   46, 55
Personality cult   60, 192
Philosophy/philospher(s)   xxi, 12, 15, 16, 21, 55, 117, 137, 139, 140, 141, 142, 143, 144, 153, 155, 156, 157, 158, 159, 161, 162, 168, 169, 176, 177, 184, 185, 190, 193, 194, 195, 203, 204, 207, 208, 210, 215, 217, 229
Plato(nic)   35, 158, 177–78
Political myth   47, 49, 58, 96
   Christian communism as   xix, 60, 80, 85, 86, 88, 116, 244
Politics   ix, xviii, 13, 14, 17, 35, 45, 48, 57, 61, 66, 67, 71, 77, 78, 79–80, 99, 127, 143, 144, 150, 181, 197, 198, 201, 202, 203, 219, 225, 230, 232, 235, 236, 238, 241, 249
   Truth and   xxi, 156, 161, 162, 163, 164
Port-Royal   1, 10, 15, 18
Predestination   4, 5, 6, 7, 8, 9, 10, 14, 16, 19, 29, 33, 143
Pre-law   xxii, 203
   Differentiation and   xxi, 194, 196, 197, 201
   Faith, law and   185, 194, 197, 198, 200, 201
   Hellenism (and Hebrew)   182, 198, 202
   Law and   194, 195, 196, 204 (see also: Law)
   Moses and   200
   Magic, religion and   194, 196, 201
   Paul and   181, 182, 197–202, 204   194, 195, 196, 197–202, 203, 204
Pre-Socratics   204

Proletarian/proletariat   9, 82–3, 88, 101, 110–11, 113, 114
Prophet/prophecy   34 n. 11, 115, 145, 165, 166, 183, 189–90, 191, 249
Protestant(ism)   xviii, 32, 56, 57, 58, 64, 96, 143, 149, 226, 229
Pseudo-Pauline epistles/text   xxi, 184, 187, 200 (see also: Paul)
Psychoanalysis   34, 55, 230
   Kristeva and   xx, 121, 123–24, 130, 133, 136, 137, 143, 153
   Marx(ism) and   123, 124–25, 126, 127, 136, 137, 143, 153
   Paul and   137, 143
Psychosis/psychotics   99, 137, 148, 149, 151, 152, 247
Purification   10, 132, 133

Quixote, Don   209

Racine   xvii, 2, 14, 17
Reformation   xxiii, 57–8, 93, 116, 141, 143, 170, 229, 245, 249
   Counter-   5, 143
   Radical   9, 64, 117, 249
Reification   9, 26
Religion   xix, xxii, 9, 16, 59, 63, 66, 72, 74, 77, 80, 82, 83, 89, 90, 98, 110, 115, 116, 126, 130, 140, 150, 151, 152, 157, 163, 164, 169, 173, 174, 175, 179, 181, 190, 205, 206, 211, 213, 215, 216, 218, 220, 222, 223, 224, 225, 227, 228, 229, 230, 231, 232, 233, 234, 235, 239, 240, 246, 250 (see also: Passing moment [of religion/theology])
   Art/creativity and   40, 220–21
   Law/pre-law and   194, 196, 197, 198, 201, 202
   Magic/fantasy and   38, 39, 41–2, 44, 49, 201, 202
   Marxism/Marxists and   ix, xiii, xiv, xv, xvi, xvii, xviii, xxiii, 14, 28, 29, 31, 35, 44, 60, 61, 64, 68, 76, 92, 93, 117–18, 127, 128, 226, 230, 245, 249
   Medieval   39, 56, 75
   Politics and   197, 198, 201, 202, 248
   as Projection   41, 42, 43, 47
   Revolution and   37, 58, 118, 128, 225, 244, 245, 248, 249, 250
   Secularism and   29, 41, 250, 251
   Sidestepping of   35
   Supercession of   33–4, 35, 38, 54
   Theology and   ix, xv, xvi, xxii, 55, 56, 165, 214, 221, 241
   Utopia and   xviii, 31, 32, 33, 34, 35, 37, 38, 49, 50, 52, 53, 54, 56, 117, 214, 244, 249

Reprobate (Damned)   xvi, xvii, 1, 6–7, 10, 19, 68 (see also: Elect and Damned)
Revolt   46, 65, 85, 117, 238 (see also: Peasant Revolt)
Revolution/ary   xviii, xxiii, 37, 42, 45, 46, 48, 57, 61, 76, 93, 118, 126, 162, 164, 217, 219, 225, 244, 245, 248, 249, 250
   1848   62
   Chinese   175
   Christianity and   57–8, 64, 84, 141, 167, 169, 170, 173, 248, 249–50 (see also: Religion)
   French   71, 77, 171
   Industrial   236
   Russian   171, 222
Richelieu, Cardinal   20 n. 34
Ricoeur, Paul   33–34
Roman Empire   67, 73, 75, 82, 83, 84, 85, 94, 110, 111, 115, 138, 139, 143, 147, 152, 153, 167, 193, 246 (see also: Rome)
Romantic/ism   xv, xxii, 86, 205, 206, 216, 217, 218, 220, 222, 236 (see also: Lukács: 'romantic anti-capitalism)
Rome   xxii, 75, 82, 83, 84, 99, 100–01, 104, 139, 204, 206, 214, 215, 222, 244 (see also: Roman Empire)
Rupture   25, 53, 194, 204
   Utopia and   32, 52, 53
Russia   60 n. 8, 65 n. 19, 82, 89, 171, 222
Russian Revolution   171, 222

Sacred   13, 38, 89, 94, 118, 136, 149 n. 120, 178 n. 69, 190
Sacred economy   xx, 107, 112, 113, 135, 136, 147, 152, 245, 246
Sacrifice   131, 133, 145, 146, 164
Sadism (oral)   145, 147, 247
Saint-Cyran, Abbé de (Jean-Ambroise Duvergier)   15, 20 n. 34
Schmitt, Carl   184 n. 13, 187, 204
Science   xxi, 12, 34 n. 11, 36, 41 n. 30, 46, 55, 76 n. 36, 102, 103, 125–26, 159, 165, 203, 221, 241, 250
   Truth and   156, 161, 162, 163, 164
Science fiction   xiv, xviii, 31, 38, 39 n. 26, 40, 41, 44, 45, 46 n. 50, 49, 51, 183
Secular/secularism 41, 42, 52, 77, 78, 79, 162, 229, 250, 251 (see also: Secularised theology)
   Grace secularised   144
   Marxism as secular and anti-secular   xvii, xxiv, 4, 14, 16, 28, 29–30, 33, 244, 245, 250, 251
Secularised theology   179, 182, 185, 189, 192, 203, 216
Semiotic(s)   56, 124, 125, 126

Sin(ful/ness)   2, 4, 6, 10, 15 n. 26, 16, 19, 25, 32, 39, 66, 67, 85, 103, 133, 145, 146, 148, 151, 167, 195, 205, 206, 216, 217, 220, 222
Slave-based mode of production   99, 100, 101, 104, 105, 147, 153, 246
Slavery   82, 100, 107, 109–10, 115
Social Democrats   61, 63, 65, 69, 89
   Social-Democratic Party of Germany (SPD)   61 n. 10
   Social Democracy of the Kingdom of Poland and Lithuania (SDKPiL)   61, 76
Socialism/socialist   13, 82, 90, 116, 125, 128, 129, 219, 230, 232, 237, 238, 239–40, 241, 248, 251 (see also: Communism)
   Anti-clericalism and   62–3, 76, 77, 78, 79, 80
   Christianity/church/religion and   xiv, xviii–xix, xxiii, 28, 60 n. 8, 61, 64, 65, 66, 67, 69, 70, 71, 72, 77, 79, 83, 87–9, 93, 114 n. 63, 116, 117, 118, 167, 228
Solidarity   xxiii, 230, 232, 235, 236, 238, 239, 240, 249
Soviet(s)   17, 105, 106
Stalin(ism), Josef   128, 219, 220

Taboo   xx
   Boiling a kid in its mother's milk   130, 134
   Food/dietary   130, 132, 134
   Incest   130, 134
   Levitical   122, 123, 130, 132, 135, 136, 146 n. 111
   Menstrual   130
   of the Mother   xx, 130–01, 132, 134–36, 137, 152
   Skin diseases   130
Taborites   116
Theo-economics   135 (see also: Sacred economy)
Theology   ix, xv, xvi, xiv, xx, xxii, 2, 12, 13, 14, 19, 21, 33, 34, 37, 53, 54 n. 66, 55, 67, 68, 96, 121, 123 n. 18, 141, 143, 161, 162, 163, 165, 167, 168, 169, 171, 172, 173, 178, 181, 183, 193, 204, 206, 207, 208, 209, 212, 213, 214, 216, 217, 218, 220, 221, 222, 224, 227, 240, 241 (see also: Passing moment [of religion/theology])
   Anti/non-theological   211, 215
   Cantor/Zermelo/Fraenkel and   158, 160
   and the Event   161
   Grace   8, 152

Jansenist 13, 14, 15, 16, 20 n. 34, 27
Liberation 118 n. 59, 167
Marxism/Marxists and 2, 217, 243
Mathematics and 155, 159, 160
Medieval xviii, 32, 55–6, 58, 235
and 'the One' xxi, 155, 156, 157, 168, 169
Pascalian 8, 12, 24
Pauline 140, 142, 153, 184, 193, 197
Philosophy and 158, 159, 194, 204, 215, 217
Political 140, 153, 182, 203, 204, 215, 225
as Procedure of truth xxi, 163, 164, 174, 179
Relativisation of its absolute claims xvii, xxii, 181, 182, 203, 204, 221, 241, 244, 245, 249
Sciences an 29
Secularised/materialist 179, 182, 185, 189, 192, 203, 216, 243
Trinitarian 157
Thirty Years War (1618–48) 143
Thompson, E.P. 225
The Making of the English Working Class 225
Witness Against the Beast 225
Thompson, Thomas 96
Time (messianic/eschatological) xxi, xxiii, 71, 182, 185, 186, 188, 189, 190, 191, 194, 195, 196, 244, 245, 250
Tolerance 9, 37 n. 17
Tolkien, J.R.R. 39 n. 25
Torres, Camillo 248
Tragedy/tragic 2 n. 4, 15, 17 n. 32, 23 n. 43, 208, 210
Transcoding xviii, xxii, 54, 57, 58, 244, 245, 249, 250
Trust xxiii, 36, 198, 230, 232, 236, 238, 239, 240, 249
Truth 8, 15, 117, 164, 177, 178, 228
Art and xx, 156, 161, 162, 163, 164
Christ/ianity and xxi, 16, 95, 98, 165, 166, 168, 169, 171, 175, 179, 221, 246, 248
Fable and xxi, 156, 162, 175, 176, 177, 178, 179, 244, 247, 248
Love and xxi, 156, 161, 162, 163, 164
Miracle and 162, 165, 179
Pascal and 17 n. 32, 24, 162, 165, 166, 179
Paul and 174, 175, 176, 246, 247
Philosophy and 16, 28, 162
Politics and xxi, 16, 156, 161, 162, 163, 164

Procedures of xxi, 156, 161, 162, 163, 164, 174, 175, 176, 177, 178, 179
Science and xxi, 17 n. 32, 36, 156, 161, 162, 163, 164, 165
Theology as procedure of 156, 162, 163, 164, 171, 174, 179, 246, 247, 248
Truth-event xxi, 163, 166, 169, 171, 173, 174, 175, 176, 177, 178, 179, 244, 246, 247

Universal 8, 9, 12, 23, 32, 123, 133 n. 65, 138, 139 n. 87, 146, 151, 196
Utopia xiv, xvi, 31, 36, 40, 41, 44, 46, 47, 49, 50, 51, 54, 154, 214, 217
Apocalyptic and xviii, 49
Ideology and xviii, 31, 32, 33, 34, 35, 38, 40, 41, 50, 54, 58
'Messianic utopianism' xxii, 205, 207, 208, 216, 217, 218–19, 220, 222
Religion and xviii, 31, 32, 33, 34, 35, 36, 37–8, 39, 49, 52, 53, 54, 56, 58, 93, 117, 118, 244, 248, 249
Rupture and 32, 37, 52, 53

VanderMeer, Jeff 45
Vanishing mediator xxiii, 25, 239, 240, 241
Village commune 106, 108

Wager
Choice and 170–71
Marxist 13, 28
Pascal's xvii, 3, 7 n. 13, 9, 10, 11–2, 13, 23, 24 n. 46, 25, 166, 169, 170
Waldensians 116
Wales/Welsh xxii, xxiii, 230, 232, 235, 236, 237, 238, 239, 240
War/World War(s) 2, 51 n. 60, 62 n. 10, 77, 91, 108, 111, 112, 135, 136, 138, 143, 199, 217, 219, 245
'Warm Marxism' xxiii, 230, 249
Weber, Max 54 n. 67, 57, 240
Williams, Raymond xi, xv, xvii, xxii, xxiii, 118, 183, 223–41, 244, 248, 249
Beekeeper's Manual xxii, 223, 226
Border Country 230, 232–33, 236, 237, 239
Culture and Society xv, xxiii, 226–27, 238
The Fight for Manod 237
The Long Revolution xv, xxiii, 224 n. 3, 228, 229
People of the Black Mountains 235
Politics and Letters xv, xxii, 223, 226, 233, 234, 238, 239
Second Generation 237

Winstanley, Gerrard 85, 114, 248
Working class xxiii, 62, 63, 68, 72, 74 n. 33, 78–9, 117, 223, 224 n. 3, 225, 229, 230, 231, 232, 235, 237, 238, 239, 240
Works (vs. grace) 6, 142, 151, 164, 187, 193, 194, 195
World xix, xx, 6, 20, 25, 38, 39, 40, 41–2, 45–6, 47, 50, 51, 71, 89, 94, 98, 104, 105, 109, 110, 111, 129, 138, 144, 156, 158, 165, 166, 171, 176, 183, 185, 188, 191, 196, 211, 217, 221, 222, 224, 239, 241, 251
  'Abandoned by God' xxii, 26, 27, 205, 206, 207–10, 216, 217
  Living within and yet refusing it xvii, xxiv, 1, 2, 3, 6, 13–20, 27, 28, 29, 30, 165, 244, 245, 250
Wyndham, John 51

Zealots 111, 113
Zermelo, Ernst 156, 158, 159, 160
Žižek, Slavoj xiii, 123 n. 16, 139, 171 n. 44, 248

www.ingramcontent.com/pod-product-compliance
Lightning Source LLC
Chambersburg PA
CBHW071150070526
44584CB00019B/2739